The U.S. presidency is the most powerful office in the world, claiming a prerogative to exercise force in foreign affairs that, according to Harry S. Truman, would have made Caesar or Genghis Khan envious. This book offers a historical account of how presidents from George Washington to Bill Clinton have asserted their privilege as commander in chief, examining their penchant for using military might unilaterally and their reasons for doing so. It asks why a democracy allows presidents to exercise such immense power virtually as a personal right.

Taking in a wide range of sources in diplomatic history and presidential studies, Alexander DeConde shows how the expansion of executive authority began long before the United States became a world power. He explains how it has evolved that U.S. presidents exercise a greater authority and control over foreign affairs and military matters than is granted to most other heads of republican governments.

DeConde attributes much of this pugnacious behavior to "machismo"—the display of virility—on the part of men already attracted to power, concluding that even weak presidents act differently when flexing their military muscle. He reveals how presidential machismo has thrived as modern media and the American people celebrate executive accomplishments in foreign affairs, elevating those who wage successful wars to the status of heroes.

Presidential Machismo approaches this issue with an overdue irreverence that questions the bold use of executive authority and serves as a corrective to the cult of veneration fostered by scholars, journalists, and presidents themselves.

Presidential Machismo

Alexander DeConde

Presidential Machismo

Executive Authority, Military Intervention, and Foreign Relations

Northeastern University Press

BOSTON

NORTHEASTERN UNIVERSITY PRESS

LIBRARY OF CONGRESS CATALOGING-IN-PUBLICATION DATA

DeConde, Alexander.
Presidential machismo : executive authority, military intervention, and foreign relations / Alexander DeConde.
p. cm.
Includes bibliographical references and index.
ISBN 1-55553-403-1 (cl. : alk. paper)
1. Presidents—United States—History. 2. United States—Foreign relations. 3. Executive power—United States—History. 4. Intervention (International law)—History. 5. Presidents—United States—Psychology. 6. Machismo—United States—History.
I. Title.
E176.1.D42 2000
327.73—dc21 99-30588

Designed by Christopher Kuntze

Printed and bound by The Maple Press Company in York, Pennsylvania. The paper is Sebago Antique Cream, an acid-free sheet.

MANUFACTURED IN THE UNITED STATES OF AMERICA

03 02 01 00 99 5 4 3 2 1

To Glace

CONTENTS

Presidential Machismo

INTRODUCTION

Power is poison. Its effect on Presidents had been always tragic, chiefly as an almost insane excitement at first, and a worse reaction afterwards; but also because no mind is so well balanced as to bear the strain of seizing unlimited force without habit or knowledge of it.

Henry Adams, historian, 1918

AS that astute political theorist, Alexis de Tocqueville, noted, "It is generally in its relations with foreign powers that the executive power of a nation has a chance to display skill and strength." He also described the American president as possessing "almost royal prerogatives" and in 1835 predicted correctly that as the nation's foreign relations expanded the president's prestige would grow.[1] Indeed, the American presidency rose steadily to become the most powerful office in the world. Harry S. Truman claimed more, stating that in his time it had "become the greatest and most important office in the history of the world."[2] Its war power, he alleged, would have made a Caesar or Genghis Khan envious. Hyperbole aside, historians and political scientists who concern themselves with this phenomenon maintain that how and when the United States employs its massive military machine now rests mainly in the hands of the president, giving him "more power than any other human being has ever had."[3]

This book explores how presidents accumulated this power, focusing on their penchant for using military force unilaterally and their reasons for doing so. It asks why a democracy allows presidents to exercise this immense power in foreign relations virtually as personal prerogative. This account also departs from the historian's traditional practice of examining the causes of America's wars and police actions in impersonal terms such as clashing economic interests, nationalist rivalries, and maintenance of national security or honor.

Although numerous wars and other socially sanctioned violence frequently exploded out of impersonal forces, we know also that in many instances individuals made the crucial decisions that produced the bloodshed. Various close students of the presidency contend, therefore, that the office's "real potency does not show on the face of the Constitution" but in the personality of the individual in the White House.[4] Others maintain more, or that the impact of personality on how the presidency functions has grown beyond constitutional constraints.

In this work I argue that the expansion of personalized executive authority began early, long before presidents had behind them the resources of a world power. Although their constitutional authority never matched the puissance of monarchs and dictators such as Napoleon Bonaparte, Adolf Hitler, or Josef Stalin, American executives always possessed greater power in foreign than in domestic affairs and more control over military matters than did most other heads of republican governments. For this reason, except during Abraham Lincoln's administration, presidents could act on their own most often in relations with foreign peoples. Accordingly, as the nation grew, increasingly its executives behaved belligerently. As in the redundant phrase of George Bush, "Presidents [came to] define themselves through their exercise of Presidential power."[5]

Historians and others offer a bundle of reasons for this presidential pugnacity. Those with a psychological bent suggest, as had numerous other leaders, that American executives acted tough as though to validate their manhood. They manifested what the ancient Greeks termed hubris, what the Japanese viewed as the samurai spirit, what the British historian Lord John Acton perceived as the corrupting force of power, and what modern writers identify as chauvinism, autocratic conduct, imperial arrogance, or machismo.

Despite an extensive literature on these qualities and on the presidency itself, only a few scholars have probed the macho aspect of presidential behavior in foreign relations, and none, as far as I know, in a systematic historical assessment. Therefore, a few words on the definition of machismo as I employ it in this book may help the reader follow the theme.

Although a combative impulse in leaders appears often under various names, only in recent years in the United States have writers and others referred to it consistently as macho. This Spanish noun, meaning male, crept into the American language from Mexican usage around 1925 as an adjective. Soon after, North Americans employed the term macho randomly in its Latin American sense—a self-consciously tough individual who flaunts virility, disparages feminine behavior, and cherishes faith in manhood. By 1948, as the second edition of the *Oxford English Dictionary* states, this concept along with the noun machismo gained widespread expression while also connoting an exaggerated masculine pride, an admiration of physical aggressiveness, and an entitlement to dominate, associated often with military violence. Social scientists now recognize that the macho stimulus runs through much of American society.

Scholars agree, too, that macho behavior, or something similar to it, has long flourished because diverse peoples have admired "real men," have "had some idea about 'true' manhood," and as one analyst puts it, have made war "one of the most rigidly 'gendered' activities known to humankind."[6] Moreover, until recently most societies viewed the contest of arms as providing proof of male vigor. Their peoples linked virility and violence as well as masculinity and militarism while regarding the macho drive, or its equivalent, as valuable. They perceived chauvinist leaders as father figures who served others or as dragonslayers who "in manly fashion" fulfilled gallant ideals. Feminist writers in particular decry "the machismo of American foreign policy and our phallic approach to national security."[7]

In absolute terms, however, the American tradition of exalting toughness differs little from the approval of masculine behavior, and dominance, in other societies. The American practice varies notably in the unusual status it gives to a behavior in presidents that runs counter to aspects of democratic theory of governance.

Of course, numerous Americans criticize as well as praise chauvinist executive conduct and many engage in president bashing, especially in the heat of political campaigns. In all, though, presidential machismo could not thrive without the awe most Americans have for the presidency. Year after year Gallup and other polls indicate that Americans place the president, regardless of how competent or inept, at or near the top of the list of the nation's most admired men. At times, the more extreme president venerators treat the office as sacrosanct, as a "unique and noble institution" created out of "almost divine inspiration."[8] This reverence forms the basis of a cult that often elevates presidents, primarily those regarded as strong and who waged successful wars, to the status of heroes. After the Second World War membership in this cult mushroomed. Scholars and others built an industry out of the study of the presidency. They gave it fictitious qualities that defied reality.

Movies, television dramas, and documentaries celebrated presidents and their accomplishments, most often in foreign affairs. Universities launched courses on the study of the office, on its history, and on its role in the structure of the government. Books and articles about presidents proliferated. Former government officials published memoirs revolving around the presidency, scholars and journalists wrote multivolume biographies of presidents, and a university press launched an extensive American Presidency series covering every holder of the office. A special journal, *Presidential Studies Quarterly*, founded in 1978, dealt with all facets of executive activity. Later other periodicals, such as *Presidency Research* and *Congress and the Presidency*, took on similar tasks.

The federal government contributes to the growth of the cult with its presidential library system. The libraries provide fine research facilities but, like pharoahs' pyramids, they serve primarily as monuments for glorifying individual presidents. Furthermore, even though the ranks of scholars who use the libraries include critics of the presidents they study, most of these researchers write books and essays that contribute to the rites of deification.

Through memoirs and in other ways presidents themselves help shape the mythology surrounding their office. For instance, in urging all Americans to study the presidency Lyndon Johnson spoke of it as though mystical. He perceived the office as making "every man who occupied it, no matter how small, bigger than he was; and no matter how big, not big enough for its demands."[9] The intense popular interest in presidents provides a ready market for such exaggerated appraisals. Every day newspapers devote more front-page space, and television and radio broadcasts accord more coverage, to the doings of the president than to those of any other public figure. This attention exceeds what the worshipful in earlier societies showered on emperors.

Of course, attention does not always equal glorification. Of late, a number of writers and film producers have depicted presidents irreverently. For instance, *Absolute Power*, a 1997 movie produced by Clint Eastwood, portrayed a president as a macho villain who not only abused his power but also stooped to murder to retain it. Early in the next year another film, *Wag the Dog*, satirized a president whose aides tried to divert attention from his involvement in a sex scandal by concocting a phony war with Albania. Superpatriots perceive such portrayals as degrading to an institution that seemingly needs constant uplift. Others believe that the presidency should not be revered and that writers and artists who poke fun at it demonstrate the health of democracy.

Unlike the satirists, venerating cultists scorn presidents who out of constitutional or personal scruples eschewed reliance on force. Academics and biographers celebrate the activist, virile, strong leaders who magnified the powers of the executive office through military action. They view the "strong Presidency as a source of good works, as a force for betterment in domestic society and the world at large." Believing the executive should have more rather than less power, they argue that any effort to curb his authority would reduce him to little more than "an invaluable clerk." In their perspective, this would be a tragedy because the nation and "humankind need a strong Presidency."[10] Most historians agree. They usually rate toughness, decisiveness, and leadership in war, even if at times misdirected, as the most important qualities in appraising presidential performance.

Critics, usually a minority in presidential studies, view macho behavior as dangerous because not all presidents have been able to control it or use their power wisely and all have displayed the usual human frailties. Some have been men of limited intellectual background who could not make well-reasoned decisions and are undeserving of the approbation conventional literature showers on executive conduct. Most presidents, whether weak or strong, have been down-to-earth politicians at the apex of power who behaved as such, and not as exceptional beings.

In line with this outlook, I have long believed the country could benefit from "a little serious disrespect for the office of the Presidency,"[11] as the historian Arthur Schlesinger Jr. put it. When I began this study, therefore, I approached the foreign-policy and military behavior of presidents with what seemed to me a needed and overdue irreverence. Since then, the furor over the scandal surrounding William Clinton, his impeachment, trial, and acquittal, has made irreverence for the presidency more widespread—except when he used force on his own against foreigners.

CHAPTER I

Origins Of Activism

War is in fact the true nurse of executive aggrandizement. In war, a physical force is to be created; and it is the executive will which is to direct it. . . . In war the honors and emoluments of office are to be multiplied; and it is executive patronage under which they are to be enjoyed. Hence it has grown into an axiom that the executive is the department of power most distinguished by its propensity to war: hence it is the practice of all states, in proportion as they are free, to disarm this propensity of its influence. . . . It is in war, finally, that laurels are to be gathered, and it is the executive brow they are to encircle.

James Madison, "Helvidius" No. 4, Sept. 14, 1793

Two Constitutions

SCHOLARS debate the precise causes of the American Revolution but one prominent theory holds that "the dominance, through corruption, of the executive branch over the legislative branch" in the English government precipitated it.[1] Most rebel leaders, like their English forebears, however, distrusted executive authority more than that of the legislature. They blamed the Crown for the troubles that produced the revolt. This perspective influenced members of the rebel Congress and America's first constitution makers.

On July 12, 1776, ten days after the Second Continental Congress had voted for independence, a committee headed by John Dickinson of Pennsylvania presented a draft of America's first constitution, the Articles of Confederation and Perpetual Union, to the members for their consideration. For more than a year the delegates debated the powers they wished to entrust to a central government, until November 15 of the next year, when they formally adopted the articles and sent them to the states for ratification. Finally, on March 1, 1781, after all thirteen states had approved, the articles went into effect. In the words of Chevalier de la Luzerne, the French minister to the United States, they were "by everyone's consent an incomplete and irregular System of government."[2]

This criticism stemmed from the new government's lack of an executive office. Those who drafted the articles had omitted such a post deliberately because of the former colonists' experience with government under British rule, which had left them with a deep distrust of power concentrated in the hands of any one individual. Regarding the executive magistracy as the natural enemy of liberty, they associated executive authority with military tyranny as well as with the denial of individual rights. All of the state constitutions they framed, except that of New York, reduced the executive to a position of decided subordination to the legislature.

Reflecting this mistrust, the Articles of Confederation provided for a single legislature that would choose one of its members to preside over its sessions. This constitution also stipulated that no one could serve as president of the Congress for more than one year in any three-year congressional term. Furthermore, this floating executive had no special policymaking authority over foreign affairs, over their conduct, or over the waging of war. Only Congress could exercise those powers—but under constraint. It could not enter treaties and alliances or make war except with the consent of at least nine states.

In creating departments of foreign affairs and of war with secretaries who reported to Congress, the confederation government at least possessed the basis for a form of ministerial responsibility that might have developed into a parliamentary democracy. That government never had a chance to evolve in that direction. Critics abroad and elsewhere continued to exaggerate its weaknesses "as so many Anarchies, of which the people themselves are weary."[3]

The confederation appeared especially frail in dealing with foreign crises, as with the Barbary states—Morocco, Algiers, Tunis, and Tripoli—strung along the North African coast. Immediately following the new nation's independence, corsairs from these petty states preyed on its commerce and enslaved its seamen. In July 1785, encouraged by the British who wanted to frighten American traders out of the Mediterranean, Algiers even declared war on the United States.

John Jay, the secretary for foreign affairs and a former president of Congress, viewed the declaration as "made solely with Design to acquire Plunder" and hence favored responding with vigorous measures. As an astute observer noted, he had "acquired a particular ascendancy over the members of Congress." He handled the nation's important business, acting as a kind of de facto executive. His personal desire to make war with Algiers, therefore, carried considerable weight with Congress. "War alone can bring together the various States, and give a new importance to Congress," he asserted. "War, and war alone, will give us Citizens, patriotism, and soldiers" and "would serve as a bond to the confederation."[4] Despite his influence, Jay failed to persuade the necessary two-thirds of the Congress to accept his proposal.

Shortly thereafter, the disappointed Jay and other prominent political figures such as George Washington, Alexander Hamilton, and James Madison decided to do something about the perceived inadequacies of the articles, especially regarding the conduct of foreign relations. Hamilton maintained that "Congress is, properly, a deliberative corps, and it forgets itself when it attempts to play the executive." In the same vein, Madison contended "Our Executive is the worst part of a bad Constitution." He also averred that all members of Congress agreed "that the Federal government, in its existing shape, was inefficient and could not last long."[5]

Fearing disunion without a constitutional alteration, these leaders agitated for amendments to the articles that would establish a more powerful central government. In September 1786, a few of them tried to effect change through a convention held in Annapolis, Maryland, but failed. Nonetheless, they lobbied Congress to call for a second convention, which it did on February 21, 1787. Deputies appointed by the states were to meet for the sole purpose of revising the Articles of Confederation. That task began on May 25 in Philadelphia when delegates from seven states, sufficient to form a quorum, arrived. In the course of the proceedings, the members decided to dump the articles and frame a new constitution.

Unlike the earlier constitution makers, many of these delegates did not view an executive office as abhorrent. Realizing that other nations' legislatures did not conduct foreign policy, most of them regarded an energetic executive as necessary for a government that would involve itself in international affairs. Accordingly, they abandoned the old commitment to a supreme legislature. Even so, these founders recognized that regardless of what prevailed elsewhere, they had to take into account a still potent popular distrust of centralized authority. A Delaware Whig expressed this fear succinctly. "The executive power," he wrote, "is ever restless, ambitious and ever grasping at encrease of power."[6]

Others who opposed setting up a permanent presidential office contended that history, particularly of Europe, demonstrated the lust of rulers for wealth and other forms of power that brought about wars. The aged Benjamin Franklin, who favored plural leadership, warned that a single executive could be too ambitious and fond of war. Other delegates of this persuasion repeatedly denounced those in the convention who advocated a strong executive as adherents of monarchy. Elbridge Gerry of Massachusetts pointed out, for instance, that even if the convention were to recommend an executive in the form of a limited monarchy it might not work because "the genius of the people were decidedly averse to it." Charles Pinckney of South Carolina wanted "a vigorous Executive" but feared its powers "might extend to peace & war & which would render the Executive a Monarchy of the worst kind, to wit an elective one."[7]

As constitutional scholars point out, this discussion over the nature of the presidency consumed more of the convention's time than any other major problem. Throughout the course of the deliberations, the proexecutive framers attempted to create a head of nation who would possess authority without having overarching powers, notably in matters involving military action. How to attain this objective perplexed them more than anything else on their agenda. After spending twenty-one days debating the issue, the founders resolved the question by creating a presidential office that would operate under specified controls. They separated it from the legislative and judicial branches of government with a system of checks and balances that in theory would prevent the president from becoming a tyrant.

In keeping with this objective while fixing the extent of the executive authority, the framers placed more curbs on the president's power in domestic affairs than in matters of foreign policy. They also denied him the most vital of monarchical powers as practiced in eighteenth-century England and the paramount foreign-policy power, that of initiating war. They vested that authority in Congress. This restraint on the executive reflected the prevailing view that individual leaders had always been more prone to use the war power than had legislators or the people. In theory, the legislature's power to declare war—its "nearly complete authority over the commencement of war"—would check presidents' impulsive use of military force.[8]

As James Wilson of Pennsylvania, an accomplished legal scholar who favored strength in the executive, explained to his constituents, "This system will not hurry us into war; it is calculated to guard against it. It will not be in the power of a single man, or a single body of men, to involve us in such distress."[9] Once hostilities commenced, though, Wilson and the other framers placed the president in the restricted role of conducting the war as the civilian commander in chief of the armed forces. This assignment accorded with the practice of most other established countries where the executive commanded armies and navies.

The framers did not view the title of commander in chief as conferring control over the power to declare or instigate war. They perceived it as amounting to "nothing more than the supreme command and direction of the military and naval forces" so as to maintain civil authority over them. In later years, presidents, students of the office, and others would follow a far more expansive interpretation that would, in their judgment, make the Commander in Chief Clause "one of the most important in the Constitution." Even so, most constitutional scholars hold to the original view. It states essentially that the clause "vested in the president only the authority to repel sudden attacks on the United States and to direct war, 'when authorized or begun.'"[10]

Influenced by eighteenth-century political theory, the framers did leave an opening for possible discord by dividing authority over foreign relations between the executive and legislative branches. Constitutional experts point out, however, that the founders "did not intend the President to be an independent and dominating force, let alone the domineering one, in the making of foreign policy." When he might have need to use military force in carrying out policy, they envisaged him as the "agent of Congress." Under virtually all circumstances, the founders wished the legislature to control the armed forces and the "making and conduct of war."[11]

Even though the Constitution framers laid out the executive's role in this scheme with impressive clarity, future promoters of the strong president idea would question the limited authority allotted him. They would claim the founders had diluted their intent by allowing the executive a leeway in the use of military force that overlapped Congress's war power. Presidents, politicians, scholars, and others grasped this alleged blurring of responsibility to depict the executive power as indefinable or, at least, ambiguous.

Years later, a foremost constitutional analyst expanded this characterization by calling, in exaggerated rhetoric, the shared authority between legislature and executive "an invitation to struggle for the privilege of directing American foreign policy."[12] Devotees of the executive cult went further. They argued that the founders endowed the presidency with a considerable, even awesome, power in conducting foreign affairs and with the potential for acquiring more.

With noteworthy insight, critics of the presidency in the founding generation warned against such empowerment. Most of them argued the Constitution granted the president too much power, a vesting "dangerous to a free people."[13] Another dissenter predicted that once a man acquired the office "his greatest object will be to keep it . . . he will spare no artifice, no address, and no exertions to increase the powers and importance of it; the servile supporters of his wishes will be placed in all offices," constantly advance his views, and sound his praises.[14] In later years presidents, their political supporters, and their sycophants would act in this manner. Their lawyers and others would exploit constitutional ambiguities, whether real or imagined, to inflate executive authority.

For example, these counselors would latch on to philosopher John Locke's conception of inherent power, or what he called the executive prerogative. In England, he said, "that Prerogative was always *largest* in the hands of our wisest and best Princes." Being "satisfied with these princes, whenever they acted without or contrary to the Letter of the Law," the people acquiesced, letting "them inlarge their *Prerogative* as they pleased." From this thinking sprang the idea that the executive "must be granted great independence in the sphere of foreign relations" and over the related matters of war and peace.[15]

Analysts have shown, however, that the political thinkers of the founding generation seldom cited Locke. Indeed, investigators have found no evidence of intent by the framers to incorporate the godlike Lockean prerogative in the Constitution. Nor have they uncovered data that explains how the inherent-power idea leaped from their minds into the Constitution. In brief, the men at Philadelphia recognized no right to act against the basic written law. Later, though, upholders of the strong presidency would use Locke's doctrine of a natural executive power to justify presidential behavior whether or not for the public good, whether or not sanctioned by statute, and whether or not employed in defiance of the Constitution.

When the strong-executive advocates would seek to bolster their position with perspective from the founders, as in the employment of military force without a declaration of war, they would often take the framers' words out of context and bend their intended meaning. For further specific support, these believers in expansive presidential power often turned to Hamilton, a foremost defender of such authority. Writing for newspapers to persuade his fellow citizens to accept the Constitution, he attacked the prevailing wisdom "that a vigorous executive is inconsistent with the genius of republican government." He maintained, instead, that "energy in the executive is a leading character in the definition of good government."[16]

In the end, the framers and then the electorate agreed to what many of them had feared and had tried to prevent—an office that in some aspects, as in foreign affairs, through the reinventing of its powers had the potential to become a kind of elective kingship. The office moved in this direction because the force of presidents' personalities and their individual drives for power became more important than original intent.

George Washington

INITIALLY in the new government, the monarchical potential seemed to pose no real problem because the framers knew that Washington, who presided over the convention and already had become something of an icon, would be the first holder of the presidential office. They assumed he would not even attempt to abuse its authority. As John Paul Jones put it, "General Washington might be safely trusted with such tempting power as the Chief Command of the Fleet and Army," but in other hands it would endanger liberty. Jones and others who worried about the war power believed "the President should be only the first Civil Magistrate, let him command the Military with the Pen, but deprive him of the power to draw his sword."[17]

As anticipated, Washington did not betray Jones's trust but in comparison to the perspective of other founders he did take a broad view of presidential authority and worked to exalt the office. He perceived himself in his presidential capacity as having the power to enforce aspects of foreign policy even if his actions could lead to armed conflict. He first seized the initiative in the use of military force in dealing with security on the western frontier, where he perceived a foreign people—the Native Americans—as menacing the white inhabitants. While expressing a desire for peace, he wondered about the propriety of using force to protect the settlers. "In the exercise of the present indiscriminate hostilities," he wrote, "it is extremely difficult if not impossible to say that a war without further measures would be just on the part of the United States." Regardless of this doubt, he quickly decided that if the Indians "should continue their incursions, the United States will be constrain'd to punish them with severity."[18]

When the raiding continued, the president turned to Secretary of War Henry Knox, who recommended raising an army of five thousand troops. When the proposal went to Congress, Pennsylvania Senator William Maclay objected, asserting privately, "Give Knox his army, and he will soon have a war on hand; indeed, I am clearly of opinion that he is aiming at this even now . . . and will have a war in less than six months with the

Southern Indians." Regardless of such sentiment, Congress authorized a small army.

The president then raised a federal expedition, made up primarily of citizen-soldiers from the states, and placed Brigadier General Josiah Harmar in command. In October 1790 this army attacked an Indian village in the Northwest, failed, and suffered a rout. In December Washington informed Congress of the hostilities, prompting Maclay to comment, "War has actually been undertaken against the Wabash Indians without any authority of Congress, and what is worse . . . we have reason to believe it is unsuccessful."[19]

Again on his own, the president ordered a second, larger expedition under General Arthur St. Clair, governor of the Northwest Territory, to chastise the alleged aggressors for their "crimes." [20] In November 1791 the Indians butchered this army, too. These defeats prompted Congress to increase the size of the regular army more than sixfold, and contributed to an eroding of Washington's towering esteem. Enemies attacked his leadership with sufficient persistence to obtain a Congressional investigation of it. The president acquiesced in this accountability.

The frontier hostilities also led Congress in May 1792 to pass the Militia Act that authorized the states to enroll white males between ages eighteen and forty-five in military service. In a companion bill that became law at about the same time, and is often designated the Calling Forth Act, Congress delegated to the president its constitutional power to call out the militia to suppress insurrections and execute federal laws, but with restraints. He could resort to force only after a federal judge had certified that civil authority had been exhausted, and in the case of insurgents, only after they had been commanded to disperse and had refused. Several years later when the act expired Congress replaced it with legislation that removed the requirement for judicial certification.

Meanwhile, in May 1794, Congress had authorized the president to require the states to organize and equip thousands of militiamen to be ready to march at a moment's notice. With this power the president raised an army composed of regulars and disciplined militia under General "Mad" Anthony Wayne that in August crushed the Indian resistance on the Northwest frontier. A few months later, using the same authority and similar levies, Washington suppressed the Whiskey Rebellion in western Pennsylvania.

While expanding his power over the military, the president acted with greater independence in dealing with foreign-policy issues involving Europeans. This decisiveness became evident after Great Britain and France had gone to war in January 1793. On April 23, despite the nation's alliance with France, he unilaterally proclaimed the United States neutral. Political opponents and those friendly to France regarded his declaration as setting up a pro-British neutrality that would provoke France to hostilities they perceived as "a consequence naturally to be expected from the violation of solemn treaties."[21] Because the proclamation could place the nation in a state of de facto war, they denounced it as a usurpation of Congress's war power.

In a series of articles under the pseudonym Pacificus, Hamilton defended the president's neutrality decision as well as his right to make it on his own authority. Hamilton regarded it as an executive function that flowed logically from the conduct of foreign policy. Although he acknowledged Congress's power to initiate war, he maintained that the president had the authority to judge national obligations under treaties even if his action might affect that war power.

This assertion alarmed Thomas Jefferson, formerly Washington's secretary of state but now involved in building a political opposition to the emerging Federalist Party headed by Washington and Hamilton. Jefferson urged Madison to attack Hamilton's claim. Madison did so. Writing as Helvidius, he denied the president possessed the power to take actions that would precipitate war. "Those who are to *conduct a war*," he wrote, "cannot in the nature of things, be proper or safe judges, whether a *war ought* to be *commenced*, *continued*, or *concluded*."[22] He maintained that the president had no right to decide on his own the cause for war.

Madison distrusted presidential activism because "it is in war, finally, that laurels are to be gathered; and it is the executive brow they are to encircle. The strongest passions and most dangerous weaknesses of the human breast; ambition, avarice, vanity, the honourable or venial love of fame, are all in conspiracy against the desire and duty of peace."[23] Regardless of the validity of the Madison perspective on constitutional theory, Washington had indeed taken a bold step in setting a precedent for presidents to claim the right to determine foreign policy and, by extension, the power to initiate war.

Still, Washington reacted defensively to the criticism he had wrongly inflated presidential authority. "The powers of the Executive of the U. States," he wrote a short time later, "are more definite, and better understood perhaps than those of almost any other Country; and my aim has been and will continue to be, neither to stretch, nor relax from them in any instance whatever, unless imperious circumstances shd. render the measure indispensable." Two years later, when discussing the content of his farewell address, he wanted to make it clear to all he "could have *no* view in extending the Powers of the Executive beyond the limits prescribed by the Constitution." He thus tried to blunt the criticism of authoritarianism he expected to be leveled at him "with dexterity and keenness."[24]

Despite Washington's expressed devotion to a narrow constitutional perspective on the presidency, when he left the office critics still believed he had aggrandized executive authority in a manner that placed the country on the verge of war with France. The French attacked American shipping, mainly in the Caribbean, because they were convinced he had violated treaty obligations to them.

John Adams

LIKE Washington, John Adams, the vice president who succeeded him, held compelling views on the nature of the evolving presidency. Adams believed in a strong executive because "the unity, the secrecy, the dispatch of one man has no equal." He also felt "the executive power should be watched by all men" for abuses. He described the president as the head of "a monarchical republic" modeled on England's government who exercised power greater than did heads of government in Switzerland, Italy, the Netherlands, Poland, and even of "a king of Sparta." He viewed his prerogatives as "so transcendent that they must naturally and necessarily excite in the nation all the jealousy, envy, fears, apprehensions, and opposition that are so constantly observed in England against the crown." While he deplored limitations on the president's authority, as "in the cases of war," he still acknowledged that "the legislative power in our constitution is greater than the executive."[25]

Adams intended to exercise his executive prerogatives to resolve the crisis with France he had inherited. In July 1797 he sent a special three-man mission to Paris to work out an agreement that would avert expansion of the hostilities at sea. Hamilton and other hawks within the president's own Federalist Party suggested that if the negotiation failed, Congress should "declare that a state of war exists." In March 1798, the president learned that French officials had humiliated the emissaries by demanding a bribe merely for the privilege of negotiating. Appalled, he turned to his cabinet, asking in his message to Congress: should he recommend "an immediate declaration of war?"[26] The cabinet split, so he decided against seeking a formalized war at this time but sent copies of the envoys' dispatches to Congress. Out of concern for the safety of the commissioners, he substituted the letters W, X, Y, and Z for the names of the bribe seekers. He also asked Congress to authorize preparations for war with effectual measures of defense.

Adams had precedent from the confederation era and Washington's administration for using armed force to aid or rescue, when possible, endangered citizens in foreign lands. So he took steps to protect the lives and property of American citizens against French attacks as well as to convey an image of being a vigorous executive. He appeared to have proceeded astutely because the dispatches stunned the legislators, leading most of them to rally behind him.

Sensing in the situation an opportunity for additional political gain, ultra-Federalists persuaded Congress to publish the XYZ documents, an action that set off a ground swell for war. This sentiment affected Adams as though it were a narcotic. His defiance of an arrogant French regime gave him an instant and unaccustomed popularity. He gloried in the role of warrior monarch, delivering numerous combative speeches while sporting a military uniform and a sword. Rather than knuckle under to the French, he would typically tell approving crowds, "Let us have war," or "The finger of destiny writes on the wall the word: War."[27] Everywhere he gave the appearance of a leader eager for full-scale hostilities. Even Hamilton, who desired strong military measures, feared the president might become carried away with martial ardor.

Adams's bellicose posturing alarmed leaders of the opposition Democratic-Republican Party far more than it did Hamilton. "The management of foreign relations," Madison commented, "appears to be the most susceptible of abuse of all the trusts committed to a Government, because they can be concealed or disclosed, or disclosed in such parts and at such times as will best suit particular views; and because the body of the people are less capable of judging, and are more under the influence of prejudices, on that branch of their affairs, than of any other." George Logan, a prominent Quaker, summed up some of the reasoning behind the opposition to the president's policy, warning that "wars created by ambitious executives have been undertaken more for their own aggrandizement and power than for the protection of their country."[28]

Regardless of these views, Federalists in Congress voted to increase naval armaments, funded coastal fortifications, suspended commerce with

France, terminated the Alliance of 1778 with her, approved the seizure of armed French shipping, and authorized the raising of armies but did not fund them. Thus, for the first time under the Constitution, Congress empowered the president to deploy naval forces overseas on a scale larger than that of a policing action. Also, with the Alien and Sedition acts, Federalist legislators put into motion the first campaign of internal political repression. The Sedition law provided for the punishment of those who wrote critically of the government or the president of the United States with intent to defame.

Many in Congress regarded this flurry of legislation as defensive, or as recognizing a state of undeclared hostilities at sea, which later became known as the Quasi-War. Despite Adams's public bravado and belief in extensive executive power, he soon wavered in seeking to increase the hostilities but not because of an unwillingness to use force. He hesitated because he questioned his authority to wage war without Congressional consent. He believed also a declaration of war might not be forthcoming because the minority Democratic-Republicans, along with some moderate Federalists in Congress, viewed expanded hostilities as unwarranted and would vote against a declaration.

On the other hand, Adams's refusal to try to expand the Quasi-War led extreme Federalists, eager to add muscle to the presidency, to characterize him as lacking the virile qualities they regarded as necessary in the strong executive. They believed the president should demonstrate at least as much toughness as the legislative majority. In the House of Representatives, hawks even tried to obtain support for a declaration of war over his head. They failed. At this point, too, out of personal pique mixed with a sense of having been betrayed by many in his own party, Adams had changed his perspective on the war.

The president had good reason for suspecting ultra-Federalists of conspiring against him. They had forced him to place Hamilton, who had long dreamed of attaining military glory, in effective command of a provisional army of twenty thousand men to be employed against the French. Adams distrusted Hamilton and ultimately thwarted his plans by refusing to raise the troops for the new army. Furthermore, when the French offered a second round of peace negotiations, the president welcomed the overture, believing that the "great Body of Federalists, as well as the whole of the other Party" wanted to avoid full-scale war. He accepted also to foil Hamilton and the Ultras.

Accordingly, on February 18, 1799, the president sent to the Senate nominations for another mission to France, saying he did so in recognition of the ardent desire of the public for honorable terms. He also wished "the babyish and womanly blubbering for peace may not necessitate the conclusion" of a bad treaty. "There is not much sincerity in the cant about peace," he noted; "those who snivel for it now, were hot for war against Britain a few months ago, and would be now, if they saw a chance. In elective governments, peace or war are alike embraced by parties, when they think they can employ either for electioneering purposes."[29]

This observation applied as well to the Ultras, who adamantly opposed the peace mission. For months, therefore, Adams wavered in setting a date for its departure. When he became convinced beyond doubt that his cabinet was dancing to the tune of Hamilton and other political opponents, he asserted he had no alternative but to be president in fact as well as in name. In October these fundamentally personal reasons persuaded Adams to take the last step in sending off the commissioners, and he did so without even informing his official family. As though the president had committed a crime, Secretary of State Timothy Pickering informed fellow Ultras that "the great question of the mission to France has been finally decided by the *President alone*." Pickering denounced this action as of a "magnitude surpassing . . . every other since the formation of the federal government."[30]

Those who, like Pickering, had castigated Adams for lacking energy now denounced him for passion, vanity, petulance, and failure to uphold national honor. These ultra-Federalists decided surreptitiously, therefore, to replace him as the party's candidate in the forthcoming presidential election. The expansion of the war then became an issue throughout the campaign in 1800, with the Democratic-Republicans portraying themselves and their candidate, Thomas Jefferson, as the friends of peace and Federalists as the partisans of war.

Who would benefit from that issue depended on the negotiations in France. They culminated on October 1 when the three American commissioners signed the Convention of Mortefontaine, which averted the full-scale war the president had come to oppose. Thirteen days later, without knowledge of the negotiated peace, the citizens in the various states voted for the electors who would choose the president. Ultimately, electors decided on Jefferson. Usually, historians regard Hamilton's plans for a presidential war and imperial expansion as a more potent danger to the nation than Adams's action. Adams believed that the intemperate attacks of extreme Federalists on merely his effort to seek peace had alienated voters.

He had hoped, though, the terms of the negotiated peace would help re-elect him but news of it reached the United States too late to benefit him.

Adams's unilateral decision for peace set a noble example for posterity. We should not forget, though, that before his conversion to peacemaker he had tried but had not been able to parlay his presidential prerogatives into authority to wage all-out war on his own. Furthermore, his circumscribed use of naval force served as a less admirable precedent for presidents who would follow him. They would invoke it to support the concept of implied constitutional powers when they employed the military unilaterally in limited hostilities, but usually against less potent foes than France. As at the start of the Quasi-War, Congress would go along with their bellicosity, on the assumption that in meeting minor crises in the conduct of foreign relations, the president should have flexibility.

To his credit, Adams later came to regard his decision for peace as the "most disinterested and meritorious action of my life." He asked that his gravestone bear the inscription, "Here lies John Adams, who took upon himself the responsibility of peace with France in the year 1800."[31] In claiming to have sought peace out of an irresistible sense of duty, he conveniently put aside memory of his eagerness for extended war, his truculent posturing, and his truckling to the war hawks. Posterity, perhaps properly, has usually paid less attention to Adams's macho behavior than to his peacemaking.

Thomas Jefferson

WHEN Jefferson, polished politician, writer of the Declaration of Independence, and ambiguous slave-owner took over the presidency, he, too, regarded himself a man of peace, one who had spoken frequently of his hatred for war. He did not, however, flinch from the idea of bashing weak foreign foes, an ambivalence he would show throughout his life. While minister to France during the initial clashes with the small states of the Barbary shore, for instance, he had asserted "it would be best to effect a peace thro' the medium of war." When the government purchased peace he acquiesced but commented, "I should prefer the obtaining it by war."[32] During a quarrel with Spain over navigation rights on the lower Mississippi River when he was secretary of state, he again favored the use of force if he could not attain his objective through diplomacy. He foresaw no difficulty in defeating Spain's weak garrison in Louisiana.

As president, Jefferson believed he headed the strongest government on earth while holding to a strict constructionist interpretation of the Constitution. In seeming contradiction with this outlook but in accord with a desire to keep the nation strong, he selectively favored a large construction of presidential authority. For instance, he claimed without basic substantiation that the transaction of business with foreign nations is executive altogether. This tilt toward the powerful, activist executive became evident quickly in his behavior in renewed clashes with the Barbary states.

The trouble had begun in October 1800 when Yusuf Qaramanli, the pasha of Tripoli, demanded an increase in the tribute the Adams administration had been paying him. Jefferson regarded the levy as money thrown away. So, two weeks after his inauguration, he decided to send a squadron of four warships to North Africa to protect American shipping and lives. Six weeks later he discussed the situation with his cabinet, asking, Should we go to Congress for a declaration of war?

Secretary of the Treasury Albert Gallatin dismissed a formal declaration as unnecessary. "The Executive cannot put us in a state of war," he contended, "but if we be put into that state either by the decree of Congress *or the other nation*, the command and direction of the public force then belongs to the Executive." Jefferson agreed, commenting that "a body [Congress] containing 100 lawyers in it, should direct the measures of a war is, I fear, impossible." So, on his own and without consulting Congress, he decided on war against what he perceived to be an easy foe. When the punitive squadron he authorized sailed out of Norfolk, Virginia, in June 1801 its commander, Richard Dale, carried orders to protect commerce and punish the Muslim powers for their insolence "by sinking, burning or destroying their ships & Vessels wherever you shall find them." The president's officials noted that Algiers had some naval strength but the "forces of Tunis & Tripoli are contemptible."[33]

In this confident manner, as a prominent historian of this venture wrote, began a commitment "with ever increasing forces to a police action fought in the interests of commerce, in distant waters, and without the sanction of a Congressional declaration of war."[34] When Dale anchored his squadron at Gibraltar a month later, he learned that Yusuf, angry because Algiers received a larger tribute than he did, had declared war. The fighting that followed fell within Jefferson's conception of what an activist president could and should do. He saw himself as an enemy of all bribes, tributes, and humiliations in the dealings with the Barbary states.

After learning of Yusuf's declaration, Jefferson authorized more force against the pasha. "I know that nothing will stop the eternal increase of demand from these pirates," he said, "but the presence of an armed force." In several engagements the Americans defeated the Tripolitan corsairs, allowing the president in December to report that "our squadron dispelled the danger" to American shipping. He also admitted to having acted in a manner "unauthorized by the Constitution, without the sanction of Congress to go out beyond the line of defence" but did not claim any special power to continue to act on his own against the North African raiders. He did retain some of his credibility as a strict constructionist by asking Congress to consider authorizing "measures of offence also" against Yusuf. The president thus deferred, publicly at least, to the power of Congress in this "important function."[35]

This deference angered Hamilton. Under the pseudonym Lucius Crassus he argued that "when a foreign nation declares, or openly and avowedly makes war upon the United States, they are then by the very fact *already at war*, and any declaration on the part of Congress is nugatory; it is at least unnecessary."[36] He again made the case for the strong executive, more powerful even than in Jefferson's conception and markedly so in the use of military force.

As for dealing with the Barbary privateers, Congress in February agreed to the president's request, authorizing him to employ the navy at his discretion. During the next three years, despite the loss of one warship—the *Philadelphia* in October 1803 with its crew of three hundred taken prisoner—American naval units steadily destroyed Tripolitan shipping. In April 1805, a motley army of American marines, local Greeks, and Arabs, under the leadership of William Eaton, former American consul in Tunis but now in the naval service, captured Derna, Tripoli's second city.

On June 4, Yusuf made peace on terms generally favorable to the United States. Jefferson hated to pay tribute, but out of fear that Yusuf might execute the crew of the *Philadelphia* and other Americans he had imprisoned, the president paid a ransom of sixty thousand dollars. The majority in Congress accepted the settlement without much comment because it assumed force had ended the Tripolitan navy's raids on American shipping and that the president had protected national honor. Federalist critics, however, denounced the "stupid manner in which we have carried on a four years' war."[37]

Meanwhile, Jefferson's strict constructionist views had clashed again with his belief that decisions on foreign policy belonged solely to the president, notably after learning in May 1801 that France had reacquired Louisiana from Spain. He opposed physical consummation of that acquisition but initially followed the principle of negotiating with France rather than confronting her with possible force, because unlike the Barbary states she was powerful. Soon, his attitude changed. In memorable words, he asserted that when France took possession of New Orleans she would become "our natural and habitual enemy," and "from that moment we must marry ourselves to the British fleet and nation."[38]

The president did not, however, abandon negotiation. In January 1803 he sent his friend James Monroe on a special mission to France. There Monroe presented Napoleon Bonaparte—who with the title of first consul ruled virtually as a dictator—with a proposal to buy New Orleans and territory at the mouth of the Mississippi River. "If we cannot by a purchase of the country insure to ourselves a course of perpetual peace and friendship with all nations," the president explained, "then as war cannot be distant, it behooves us immediately to be preparing for that course."[39] Thus, despite his avowal that "peace is our passion," to achieve his expansionist goal he stood willing to use force even against a strong foe if he could have the backing of a powerful ally such as Great Britain. He resorted to bellicosity because it had popular support, because he perceived it as proper tool of statecraft, and because it fitted his own conception of virile leadership.

The belligerent posturing proved unnecessary because in June, for a price, Bonaparte offered Jefferson all of Louisiana, from the Mississippi to the Rocky Mountains. Once more, though, the president hesitated to act on his own. He thought he needed a constitutional amendment to take over this immense territory inhabited by a foreign population and to incorporate it into the Union. Soon, as Gallatin suggested, he pushed aside these qualms and negotiated the purchase. The president assumed that both friends and foes would recognize it as a fait accompli.

Jefferson admitted seizing the "fugitive occurrence" with "an act beyond the Constitution" but justified it as advancing the good of the country. He hoped that like himself the legislators would cast "behind them metaphysical subtleties," ratify what he had done, and provide the funding necessary to take over Louisiana. Again Jefferson had set aside his strict constructionist principles. Later he warned Secretary of State Madison, "the less we say about constitutional difficulties respecting Louisiana the better, and that what is necessary for surmounting them must be done sub silentio."[40]

In this transcending of the Constitution, Jefferson gave the appearance of acting on principle rather than out of expedience. Conveniently, he perceived himself as the people's trustee who had acted in their best interest whether or not they realized it. As he had hoped, he succeeded easily in converting this perception into substance because the involved public, his own Republican stalwarts, and many Federalists in Congress and out approved of the purchase. More directly than had Adams in the Quasi-War, Jefferson thereby helped set precedent on how to expand presidential power.

Jefferson also used this extended authority in claiming, on questionable grounds, West Florida as part of the Louisiana purchase. He encouraged the House of Representatives in February 1804 to pass the Mobile Act, which permitted him to establish a customs district in Mobile Bay. If implemented, this legislation, which assumed American dominion over West Florida to the Perdido River, could have provoked war with Spain.

No compelling danger to the national interest required Jefferson to pursue this goal, but he did so persistently and with passion. To Congress he justified his bellicosity by stating that Spanish authorities would continue "to advance on our possessions until they shall be repressed by an opposing force." He favored breaking relations with Spain and seizing the Floridas as well as Texas.

As in the Louisiana matter, in August 1805 the president considered an alliance with England that would take effect when "a war shall take place with Spain or France." Two weeks later he wrote, "I do not view peace as within our choice." When he consulted Gallatin on this matter the secretary advised against war on the basis of flimsy boundary claims. He pointed out "that a resort to arms for that cause will, I think, appear unjustifiable in the opinion of mankind and even of America." Even though the president considered it a "dangerous error that we are a people whom no injuries can provoke to war," he kept the peace.[41]

In his annual message to Congress on December 3, however, Jefferson again breathed indignation against the Spaniards for various reasons but markedly because they refused to pay spoliation claims while still resisting his territorial demands. He implied that further diplomatic efforts to achieve satisfaction would be useless because some injuries to national honor "could be met by force only." A few Americans regarded his words as the equivalent of a declaration of war against Spain but most approved of his stance, seeing it as proof of presidential manliness. Even Federalists praised the message, calling it, for example, "more energetic and warlike than any he ever sent to Congress."[42]

Despite such support and Jefferson's broad view of the president's authority to exercise military force on his own, he decided against precipitating hostilities. He refrained, he said, out of respect for Congress's constitutional authority over "changing our condition from peace to war." He also explained that the crisis in Europe provided an opportunity, for which "not a moment should be lost," to coerce Spain. "Formal war is not necessary," he told Congress, "but the protection of our citizens, the spirit and honor of our country require that force should be interposed to a certain degree." Despite his expressed deference to Congress, he thus asserted a right to employ force with what would become conventional presidential reasoning in such instances.[43]

On the larger issue of assaulting Spanish territory, constitutional qualms had little to do with the president's hesitation. He balked because of the moral and practical weakness of his position and the deteriorating relations with Britain and France. Without support from the British navy, he did not dare seize West Florida.

The confrontation with Britain revolved around the Royal Navy's seizure of American shipping and the impressment of American seamen. The most serious crisis occurred on June 22, 1807, when the British warship *Leopard* attacked the American naval frigate *Chesapeake* off Norfolk, Virginia, killing three and wounding eighteen sailors. The many Americans who denounced this bloody outrage demanded forceful retaliation. "There appeared but one opinion—War," a senator from Maryland concluded, "in case that satisfaction is not given."[44] The president, too, seemed eager for a contest of arms. Throughout the summer he called for increases in the regular army and in volunteer regiments and made other preparations for war.

Soon, when Jefferson realized that public sentiment for war had dwindled, he backed away from direct hostilities with the powerful state. He tried instead, through a policy of economic pressure he called peaceable coercion, to compel the British to give up impressment and to respect American maritime rights as he perceived them. He put the most important part of this strategy into effect on December 22 with an embargo, or self-blockade, that prohibited American ships from sailing to foreign ports. Although Congress approved and granted Jefferson extensive authority in applying the embargo, he expected popular support "based on faith in him as President."[45] That did not happen. The embargo met with considerable resistance, leading him to characterize as traitors those who defied the measure. In addition, he employed strong-arm tactics at executive discretion to enforce conformity. He regarded the embargo, should it fail, as the last measure before war. Much to his surprise, on March 4, 1809, his last day in office, Congress repealed the embargo but did not seek war. He left the presidency shaken, expressing relief in shaking off the shackles of power. Despite these feelings and the public resistance to his coercive use of authority, he still retained wide popularity.

Although disappointed in the failure of his essentially personal embargo policy, Jefferson still maintained faith in what he regarded as the need for a strong, activist executive willing to exploit military force on his own. Despite his constitutional concerns and moments of unhappiness while in office, he loved power. In exercising it, he had long resorted to truculence when he deemed it advantageous and had assumed the electorate desired militant behavior. "In time of peace," he stated a year later, "the people look to their representatives; but in war, to the executive solely."[46]

James Madison

WHEN Jefferson's close friend Madison took over the White House, he brought with him the experience of having helped create the presidency and, as secretary of state, of having administered foreign affairs for eight years. Even so, Madison had less confidence in executive authority than did Jefferson. As we have seen, Madison expressed in different words at various times the view that the president, "being a single individual, with nothing to balance his faults and deficiencies, was as likely to go wrong as the average citizen."[47]

This cautious approach to executive power led Federalist critics to describe Madison, inaccurately, as "little better than a man of straw" who showed not "half the independence of an old clucking hen." In other words, to them his rhetoric and behavior gave the appearance of weakness. Yet at this juncture of his public life he believed "in the large construction of the Executive authority," particularly in the conduct of foreign affairs.[48] These and Madison's other commentaries on the presidency, on the conduct of foreign affairs, and on the waging of war reveal that he lacked consistency. His views fluctuated over time and even changed dramatically. Where previously he had warned against a propensity in the executive for abuse of authority, he now contended the president must be lean, decisive, unencumbered by ordinary domestic restraints, and must demonstrate energy.

Consistently, though, Madison professed abhorrence of violence. In his inaugural he praised the cultivation of peace as "the true glory of the United States." He promised to "cherish peace and friendly intercourse with all nations having corresponding dispositions" and announced in all cases he preferred peace, amicable discussion, and reasonable accommodation of differences "to a decision of them by an appeal to arms." As president, he belied these words by continuing Jefferson's menacing policy toward West Florida, taking on the role of a saber rattler and flexer of "the nation's military muscle."[49]

On his own initiative, Madison covertly backed American settlers who in July 1810 seized West Florida by force from its Spanish authorities, declared it independent, and sought annexation to the United States. As planned, he wanted to move ahead and take over the territory, believing such action as "within the Executive competency." Yet for a time he hesitated, fearing such openly unilateral action would raise "serious questions as to the authority of the Executive" and that Congress might charge him with "being premature and disrespectful, if not of being illegal."[50]

This concern did not last long. Citing the Louisiana treaty as the basis for annexation, the president on October 27 secretly proclaimed West Florida, stretching from the Mississippi eastward to the Perdido, part of the national domain. He ordered William C. C. Claiborne, the governor of the Louisiana territory, to occupy West Florida. Unaware of the proclamation, anxious expansionists perceived vacillation. They demanded coercive action, commenting wishfully but accurately "that Mr. Madison has the nerve to do whatever is expedient, we have no doubt."[51]

In his message to Congress in December, the president presented the acquisition as a fait accompli, declaring, "I did not delay the interposition required for the occupancy of the territory west of the river Perdido, to which the title of the United States extends." Even so, antiexpansion and antiadministration Federalist legislators denounced the invasion by American troops as an act of war, "an unwarrantable assumption of power and a violation of the Constitution." Outsiders, such as the British, protested the annexation as taken under the cover of "a title which is manifestly doubtful." In contrast, many Americans, among them Senator Henry Clay of Kentucky, applauded what they now praised as presidential strength. Another senator asserted that if Madison had not taken West Florida, "he would have been charged with imbecility."[52]

In January 1811, Congress in effect rewarded this aggressive conduct by secretly giving the president a free hand to seize East Florida from Spain. Madison orally authorized General George Mathews and Colonel John

McKee, American agents, to foment an insurrection there that would lead to the colony's annexation. In March 1812 American patriot forces under Mathews's command seized Amelia Island, off the coast at the Georgia-Florida border, and St. Augustine, the capital of East Florida. In the following month, Madison disavowed Mathews's activities, but not because he lacked the will to use force. The president backed off in part because Congressional critics denounced the overt military venture as contrived, petty, and an unconstitutional plunge into undeclared war. He retreated also because he faced possibly heavier hostilities with Britain or France. Nonetheless, the American occupiers remained in East Florida until May 1813.

All the while Madison had been pondering the possibility of hostilities with Britain or France. Just prior to taking office he had promised to call Congress into special session to address this problem "with an understanding that War will then be the proper course, if no immediate change abroad shall render it unnecessary." For almost three years he continued Jefferson's policy of economic coercion, which he'd had a hand in shaping, while keeping at bay the hawks and political foes who demanded stronger measures. In the autumn of 1811, as the economic policy appeared to fail, even staunch constituents joined this mounting body of opposition to condemn Madison as "whiffling Jemmy," who acted as Jefferson's "political pimp." These hawks asserted that in dealing with England "war or submission are now the only alternatives" and that "*the voice of every American is* FOR WAR."[53]

Confronted with this pressure, Madison felt he could no longer procrastinate. He must do something to demonstrate presidential virility, even against a formidable foe. He called the Twelfth Congress into session one month early, telling it on November 5 that the English had trampled "on rights which no independent nation can relinquish." The time had arrived, he declared, "to put the United States into an armor, an attitude demanded by the crisis, and corresponding with the national spirit and expectations." He asked the legislators to expand the military forces to prepare for an invasion of Canada. On June 1, 1812, he requested that Congress declare war because of four major grievances against Britain. He cited her violations of American neutrality authorized by executive decrees called orders-in-council, impressments, inciting of Indians on the frontier against American settlers, and illegal naval blockades of American shipping. Britain's actions, he said, amounted to a state of war against the United States.

At this point the president consciously made himself the principal instrument for bringing the nation to the threshold of hostilities. Nonetheless, in keeping with his earlier view that the executive could not on his own commence war, he reserved the final decision, that "solemn question which the Constitution wisely confides to the legislative department of the government," for Congress.[54] In the House of Representatives the war hawks quickly gathered 79 votes in favor of hostilities while 49 Congressmen cast ballots against. The Senate debated the issue for two weeks before reluctantly voting, 19 to 13, on June 18 for the nation's first declaration of war.

Ironically, two days earlier the London government had moved to eliminate one of the basic causes Madison cited for the war—the orders-in-council—and repealed them a week later. News of that action reached Washington in August, too late to prevent hostilities. Even though considerable information indicated the people were divided over war or obviously did not want it, Madison did not seek to revoke the declaration.

Why did Madison, allegedly a man of peace and books, lead a divided country into hostilities when Britain posed no physical threat to the United States? Did he have a personal agenda that outweighed theoretical scruples? Analysts who hold he did not condemn his alleged weakness, saying he gave in too readily to the hawks and that war came not out of his initiative but despite him.

Those who argue Madison had a personal war agenda portray him "as the author of his own policy," a leader who shared the views of the hawks, and who mixed "violence with individual interest and ambition."[55] They aver that in keeping with his theory of the energetic executive, he wanted to appear strong to counter his popular image as a vacillator. In their opinion, he called for war out of a compulsion to demonstrate a manly courage that would make points with the vocal, aggressive elements of the electorate and thus assure his reelection in November. As historian Henry Adams noted, "Proverbially wars are popular at their beginning; commonly in representative governments, they are declared by aid of some part of the opposition."[56] But in this instance the party in power quickly lost strength.

The composition of the Congress that had come to power in the previous year also influenced the president. Its bellicosity helped bolster his perception of hostilities as preferable to a disgraceful, or at least uncomfortable, peace and conveyed the impression that he now had a mandate for war. Furthermore, the decision for war would silence arguments on public policy and rally the whole nation, not just those of his own party, around him.

The president's calculations proved inaccurate. Although many republicans had demanded war, their convictions did not reflect a truly broad national sentiment—one that cut across lines of party, class, ethnicity, and sectional allegiance. In brief, as opponents believed, those who favored hostilities constituted an insufficiently significant portion of the public to justify Madison's decision for war.

Noting the flaws in the president's reasons for hostilities, Federalists and the New Englanders who opposed the war as wrong and unnecessary asked, "Where is the real cause to be found?" Many of them had little difficulty in personalizing the conflict by blaming the president for it. John Lowell, a prominent Massachusetts Federalist, epitomized this sentiment in "two of the most powerful anti-administration pamphlets—*Mr. Madison's War* and *Perpetual War, the Policy of Mr. Madison*."[57] These contemporary critics, as well as some later analysts, perceived the conflict as emanating from a tangible act—Madison's request to Congress. Since that decision catalyzed wavering legislators to support him, it stands as a crucial determinant for war and as a significant exercise of presidential power in foreign relations.

Madison could not, however, exploit this power without considerable public defiance, which began immediately. Upon receiving the declaration of war, Governor Caleb Strong of Massachusetts proclaimed a day of fasting to mourn fighting "against the nation from which we are descended."[58] Many gave comfort to the enemy or worked to cripple the war effort. When, as commander in chief, Madison attempted to call state militias into federal service, Strong and other New England governors flouted him by refusing to release their militias for war duty. The high courts in the resisting states upheld the governors. The Supreme Court then overruled the state courts, holding that the power over the armed forces belonged exclusively to the president.

As for the conflict itself, as is well known, the British inflicted heavy losses on American forces along the Canadian frontier, practically wiped out the American merchant marine, and in August 1814 torched Washington. So many New Englanders opposed the war that the Federalist leaders among them met secretly on December 15 in Hartford, Connecticut, with the aim of revising the Constitution. One resolution they adopted called for a two-thirds majority of both houses of Congress for a declaration of war. Nothing came of it because on December 24, after protracted negotiations in Ghent, the British and American adversaries accepted a peace treaty. When the news reached Washington, the talk of secession and even of possible civil war accompanying the Hartford Convention dissipated.

As contemporaries such as Daniel Webster, then a young Congressman from New Hampshire, noted, the "professed objects" of crushing impressment and seizing Canada also disintegrated, and the war itself "bereft us of our commerce, the great source of our wealth." They disparaged Madison for these failures. Many of them perceived him as insufficiently aggressive, too benevolent—hence as "unfit for executive leadership" or "the storms of war"—and as being "perhaps 'too good' a man for the responsible office he holds." Scholars later characterized Madison as a failed war executive or dismissed him as "one of the weakest war leaders in the nation's history."[59] In dealing with Spain over the fate of the Floridas, however, Madison had been as tough as any of his predecessors. Consequently, a number of historians rate him an effective leader though not a dynamic one.

In addition, for its failed objectives rather than for its flawed causes, many historians regard the War of 1812 as futile. Most of them, however, grope to find some virtue in it. In defending the war, and by implication Madison's role, they and contemporary justifiers such as Gallatin and Clay maintain it preserved "national honor," the republic's existence, and the "prestige of republicanism," or that it promoted "national self-confidence," revitalized liberal republicanism, created a new "sense of nationhood," consolidated national character, earned the nation "a respected place in the world community," "demonstrated the special place of the United States in the eyes of God," and brought other amorphous benefits.[60] These assumptions, based on intangibles, are as difficult to prove as to disprove.

Meanwhile, the difficulties with the Barbary corsairs had cropped up again. The problem started again largely because during the Napoleonic Wars Jefferson had withdrawn most of the nation's fleet from the Mediterranean. Much of the trouble came from Hajj 'Ali Pacha, the dey of Algiers, who during Madison's hostilities with Britain had plundered American commerce, imprisoned Americans for ransom, and in 1814 had declared war on the United States. Early in the next year, therefore, Madison asked Congress to declare war on Algiers. Instead, in March, it authorized him to use force against the dey without voting a declaration. In May the president dispatched a flotilla, commanded by Captain Stephen Decatur, to Algiers. It captured two of the dey's warships. Then in June Decatur forced him to release his American captives and renounce his demand for annual tribute—terms embodied in a peace treaty. In the next two months, with threats of force Decatur concluded similar agreements with Tunis and Tripoli. Taken together with the earlier fighting in the Mediterranean, Jefferson and Madison had set a compelling precedent for presidential policing of troublesome weak states.

James Monroe

TWO years later James Monroe, a Revolutionary War hero who had served in Congress, had been governor of Virginia, and Madison's secretary of war and state, succeeded Madison in the White House. Despite this wide experience in public service, Monroe had the reputation of being slow in comprehension. "Nature has given him a mind neither rapid nor rich," his attorney general William Wirt wrote of him, "and therefore he cannot shine on a subject which is entirely new to him." Historians often characterize Monroe as a pragmatic politician committed "to listen and interpret [rather] than to lead." He did shine though as a hands-on president who "held tightly to the final executive authority," who "gave closest attention to matters of foreign affairs," and who acted as an uncompromising advocate of military preparedness. His inaugural address reflected this affinity for a tough national posture. He self-consciously attempted to justify the recent unpopular conflict with Britain, praised war, and stressed patriotism. To "support our rights" and liberties, he warned, we "may be again involved in war." He called national honor a "property of highest value" that should be cherished, and urged strengthening of the military "in time of peace to be better prepared for war." [61]

Although Monroe did not involve the nation in war or plunge it into warlike situations, he quickly belied his reputed passivity toward leadership by initiating executive agreements that enhanced the president's power in matters touching on war and peace. Without Congressional participation or approval, in the Rush-Bagot Agreement of April 29, 1817, he arranged with Britain to limit naval armaments on the Great Lakes. A year later, to assure continuation of the arrangement, the president sent this kind of a treaty to the Senate. Since it served an obviously good cause the legislators unanimously endorsed the fait accompli. Slowly this practice would become the president's most effective means of bypassing constitutional limitations on the making of treaties, a prelude at times to a commitment of troops to combat.

In December 1817, when Monroe ordered General Andrew Jackson into Spain's East Florida to chase Seminole Indians who had raided white American settlements, he again bypassed Congress. The president claimed the right to pursue an enemy across an international border on the principle of self-defense. This conviction corresponded to Jackson's own views except that he perceived the concept of defensive action as well as his orders more broadly than had the president. In the course of his pursuit, Jackson attacked Spanish fortifications, seized them, occupied the colony of a country at peace with the United States, and in April 1818 executed Seminole leaders and two Englishmen who had cooperated with the Indians. Although Monroe denied he had authorized Jackson's offensive assault on East Florida, his equivocal instructions and his attitude toward the unilateral use of military force indicated that at least he had encouraged it. Talk of war with Spain and England followed but neither reacted with force. Later, Robert S. Castlereagh, the British foreign secretary, claimed he could have had war by "holding up a finger."[62]

In July when the president and his cabinet discussed the affair, they decided Jackson had indeed warred on Spain. Secretary of War John C. Calhoun wanted to court-martial the general for exceeding his authority but Secretary of State John Quincy Adams, reputedly "the staunchest advocate of his time of a strong executive branch, particularly for the conduct of foreign policy" and "the use of force," defended Jackson. Adams pointed out that the general's actions also involved "the Executive power to authorize war without a declaration of war by Congress." The secretary argued that regardless of the ambiguity in this affair, "it is better to err on the side of vigor than of weakness—on the side of our own officer, who has rendered the most eminent services to the nation." A few days later he confided in his diary that "the disclaimer of power in the executive is a dangerous example; and of evil consequences."[63]

By this time, largely as a reaction to popular sentiment that hailed Jackson as a hero for his macho conduct, Monroe had shed any such disclaimer. The president now openly embraced Jackson's and his secretary's view on the war-making power and also the general's determination to acquire East Florida. So, while reprimanding Jackson, Monroe also excused his conduct, saying the general had taken the initiative "as an act of patriotism, essential to the honor and interests of our country."[64] This transformation of the armed invasion of a neighbor's territory—a neighbor who posed no tangible threat to the nation—into an expression of self-defense represented, for an allegedly modest and unassuming executive, a kind of hubris divorced from reality.

Legislative critics could not swallow the president's action or its tortured self-defense argument. They denounced the Florida invasion as an act of war without sanction from Congress. "If it be not war," one of them asserted, "and we must give it some other name, let it be called a man-killing expedition which the President has a right to direct whenever he pleases."[65]

Monroe reluctantly returned the captured forts to the Spaniards but despite the Congressional and other criticism of his policy, he continued to take an expansive view of his military power. Determined to acquire East Florida, he threatened on his own authority to seize it again with military force. A weak Spain gave in to this coercion by agreeing in the Adams-Onís Treaty of June 22, 1819, to cede East Florida to the United States, to renounce claims to West Florida, and to surrender its right to territory stretching to the Pacific coast north of California. In turn, the United States gave up its claim to Texas and agreed to assume Spain's payments, up to five million dollars, to Americans to whom she owed money.

Four years later, Monroe faced another international crisis, this one involving the Latin American wars of independence. Militant activists wanted him to defend Spain's rebelling colonies from reconquest. In response to the pressure, he consulted his cabinet as to the constitutional propriety of intervention. Secretary Adams advised he did not need legislative approval because "the act of the Executive could not, after all, commit the nation to a pledge of war." So, once again Monroe decided to act unilaterally but without force. On December 2, 1823, he warned the European powers not to interfere in the New World struggles or attempt to recolonize South America. Senators and others regarded this statement, which became known as the Monroe Doctrine, not as a pledge for "this nation to go to war" but as a statement designed "to produce a moral effect abroad."[66]

This doctrine is the highlight of Monroe's foreign policy. In all, his term in office signaled the end of the revolutionary generation's domination of the presidency. Historians and others note that the executives of this era professed respect for legislative and constitutional authority and hence did not claim an inherent war-making power freeing them from control by Congress. As we have seen, however, the presidents' actions did not always match their words. Sometimes secretly, presidents initiated the use of armed force to coerce weaker countries in limited, undeclared hostilities and against a formidable adversary—Britain—in a declared war. In all, their behavior set precedents for presidents to use force aggressively to acquire territory and to expand their power to make war.

These presidents placed faith in aggressive leadership against outsiders because, in part, Americans admired the strong, manly, activist executive who placed his mark on foreign policy. Already, as scholars tell us, "Americans from all walks of life" viewed the president, rather than Congress, as the proper maker of "policy that was best for the country as a whole."[67] All of these executives, even mild-mannered Madison, favored force when they could use it advantageously. They formulated the essentials of what would become the macho style.

CHAPTER 2

Commander in Chief Enhanced

The war power—the power to make war—is, as a grant to Congress, a mere illusion—a form without substance [because]... the real power of making the war resides elsewhere—resides in the Executive Government alone—which, in its power to conduct our foreign relations, has power to make a quarrel with any nation that it pleases; and when the quarrel is got up, our people will fight.

Thomas Hart Benton, senator from Missouri, June 1854

John Quincy Adams

JOHN Quincy Adams's preparations for high office began as a youth in Russia and Great Britain where he observed the working of diplomacy firsthand. Then followed education in Europe and at Harvard University; service as minister to the Netherlands, Prussia, and Russia; a stint in the Senate; chairmanship of the commission that negotiated the peace ending the War of 1812; and eight years as James Monroe's secretary of state. Each step in his career took him closer to the presidency. Moreover, he grew accustomed to looking upon the "office as a family inheritance." Shunning feigned modesty, he told himself, "A man must fulfill his destiny."[1]

Adams achieved that destiny but under inauspicious circumstances. The election of 1824 fractured his Republican Party and threw selection of the president into the House of Representatives, which chose him even though he received fewer popular and electoral votes than Andrew Jackson. Adams thus entered the White House as a minority president who opponents charged had gained office through a corrupt bargain with Henry Clay of Kentucky, the Speaker of the House.

As president, John Quincy held a more expansive view than had his father, John Adams, of the president's authority to commit the nation's military forces to combat. The younger Adams spoke of devotion to peace, but as had Monroe, he alleged that "the finest security of peace is the preparation during peace of the defense of war."[2] Assuming that his destiny included vigorous leadership, a mode of conduct he had long favored, he was determined to become a strong president with an activist foreign policy. These goals eluded him. Dogged for four years by the corruption charge, he did not lead adequately, demonstrated no executive flair, and showed no special competence in conducting foreign affairs on his own. He left office embittered, saying that throughout his tenure he had suffered, as no one knows, a severe agony of mind. Why, we may ask, did intelligence, careful preparation for executive office, and extensive experience in government service, especially as a diplomatist, fail him?

Adams proved inadequate in the presidency for a variety of reasons but notably because of unbending personal traits, hubris, a disdain for popular politicking when such activity was on the rise, and an unvarnished nationalism at a time of intensified sectionalism. In relations with foreign countries, he had no war to wage or crisis to manage that afforded opportunity for triumphant, bellicose behavior. He chafed under Congressional restraints that he viewed as efforts to dictate to the president "how he *may* perform his duty."[3] He thus lacked even the leeway to manufacture a foreign confrontation that could possibly have brought plaudits and popularity.

Andrew Jackson

IN the election of 1828, with the reemerging of a two-party system and with it dirty personal politicking, Andrew Jackson won in a landslide. He came to the presidency as a military hero who had fought in the Revolutionary War, the War of 1812, and Indian wars and police actions. He was also a seasoned politician who had served in both houses of Congress. He possessed a striking personality, an imperious temperament, and a reputation as a vigorous, no-nonsense leader—characteristics that an expanded white-male electorate admired and rewarded. Critical contemporaries described him as energetic, "prone by nature and habit to the use of force, covetous of power, and a despot by nature."[4]

In his inaugural, Jackson promised to "keep steadily in view the limitations as well as the extent of Executive power" and to function in the presidency "without transcending its authority."[5] Initially, in the conduct of foreign relations, he appeared to act accordingly through his secretaries of state to whom he usually left the details in the execution of policy.

Jackson's expansive view of presidential power in dealing with foreigners did not surface until almost three years later in a dispute over the Falkland Islands—las Islas Malvinas as the South Americans called them—

situated 380 nautical miles off the southern tip of Argentina. Both Argentines and Britons claimed the islands, but in June 1820 the government at Buenos Aires backed its asserted ownership over them, as well as over Tierra del Fuego and other islands near Cape Horn, with colonization. In August 1831, agents of the Malvinas's Argentine governor, Louis Vernet, seized three American seal-hunting schooners. They imprisoned their crews on charges of violating the local fishing regulations the governor had imposed. One vessel escaped, another continued its operations with a license from Vernet, and the third remained in detention. George W. Slacum, the American consul in Buenos Aires, protested the seizures as illegal but the Argentine authorities brushed him aside.

When Jackson learned of the incident, he denounced it as a gross violation of American rights, even though he had slim evidence for the accusation. On December 6, he explained to Congress he had ordered "an armed vessel to join our squadron in those seas" to aid allegedly endangered Americans. He also requested "authority and means" for "a force adequate to the complete protection of American fishing and trading in those seas."[6] Soon thereafter he sent Francis Baylies, a Massachusetts politician, to Buenos Aires as chargé to seek amends for what his instructions, without evidence, designated as lawless and piratical acts.

Slacum, meanwhile, had conferred with Silas Duncan, the commander of the USS *Lexington*, a sloop of war. They decided, in seeming accord with presidential policy, to retaliate against Vernet. On January 1, 1832, marines under Duncan's command scrambled ashore on East Falkland, dispersed the captors, freed the American ship and crew, arrested most of the island's inhabitants (or forty people), and deported six of them. Authorities in Buenos Aires protested this violence. When Baylies arrived, he tried for three months to negotiate a settlement based on his characterization of Vernet as a pirate and his demand for reparations for captured American property. Neither side budged.

Before sailing for home in September, Baylies advised Washington that these "petulant fools . . . *must be taught a lesson*, or the United States would be viewed with contempt throughout South America." Hostilities seemed possible. That threat passed in part because in January 1833 the British seized control of the Falklands, deported the Argentines, and promised not to hinder American fishing vessels. As for Jackson, despite demonstrating an aggressiveness that some analysts construe as bringing "the United States to the brink of war with Argentina," he never resorted to the naval action he had threatened.[7]

On his own initiative Jackson did authorize naval force in another incident in a distant land. The trouble began on February 7, 1831, when marauders from the town of Kuala Batu on the north coast of Sumatra assaulted an American ship engaged in the pepper trade. While plundering the vessel, the Sumatrans killed three and wounded three of the crew. When news of the attack reached Washington, it infuriated the president. He immediately ordered retaliation for "this outrage," instructing John Downes, the commander of the frigate *Potomac*, to inflict on the pirates "such a chastisement as would deter them and others from like aggressions."[8] On the morning of February 6, 1832, an assault force of 262 heavily armed marines and sailors from the *Potomac* attacked Kuala Batu. In two and a half hours of combat the Americans slaughtered more than one hundred Sumatrans, some of them women, and torched the town.

At home Jackson's opponents held him personally responsible for this sanguinary affair, charging him with committing an act of war without Congressional consent. They wondered, "If the President can direct expeditions with fire and sword against the Malays . . . why may he not have the power to do the same in reference to any other people. Under this construction, it appears to us, what has been considered a very important provision of the Constitution may in time become a mere nullity." Another critic reacted more bluntly, declaring, "Neither the President of the United States nor the Captain of the Frigate has power to make or proclaim war."

Defenders, however, praised Jackson for his executive energy. Privately, the president was appalled by Downes's violence. Publicly, though, Jackson commended him for avenging "an act of atrocious piracy" that has brought "an increased respect for our flag in those distant seas and additional security for our commerce."[9]

At the same time, in domestic quarrels, political opponents such as those who had attacked Jackson in the Sumatra affair accused him of seeking to establish an executive tyranny. His first confrontation with such dissidents began in November 1832 when South Carolina adopted an ordinance nullifying two federal tariff laws and threatened to secede from the Union. On January 16, 1833, after he had been reelected, the president asked Congress for authority to use military force, if necessary, against the nullifiers. This crisis faded when the legislators adopted a compromise tariff.

A second confrontation erupted in September when Jackson, in his determination to close down the Bank of the United States, removed federal deposits from it. This action shocked opponents because it could set a precedent for the executive's full control over the currency with the power to dominate elections. On December 26, Henry Clay asked the Senate to censure Jackson for misusing presidential authority. Anti-Jackson legislators voted to curb "executive usurpation" but Democrats loyal to the president later reversed the censure. Nonetheless, the concern over the use of presidential power became a significant reason for Jackson's foes to form the opposition Whig Party.

Early in 1834, for instance, James Kent, the legal scholar and jurist, wrote, "I look upon Jackson as a detestable, ignorant, reckless, vain and malignant tyrant. . . . This American elective monarchy frightens me." Justice Joseph Story concurred, saying "though we live under the form of a republic we are in fact under the absolute rule of a single man."[10]

Jackson did not govern as a tyrant but his imperious style carried over into another foreign dispute, this time with France over its refusal to pay debts it owed to American citizens. In December, he asked Congress to authorize "reprisals upon French property," even if they led to "hostilities." Despite denying any overt intent to menace France, he sought contingent authority to wage limited war. Congressional opponents denounced the request as "nothing more or less than a declaration of *war* against France."[11] It hardly amounted to that. Supporters, too, resorted to hyperbole. Even John Quincy Adams argued the Constitution placed no limit on the president's exercise of the war power.

Regardless of the bellicose talk and pressure from the president, Congress refused in this instance to delegate its war-making power. Moreover, resenting his tough rhetoric, the French refused to concede anything. Privately, Jackson believed "it is high time that this arrogance of France should be put down and the whole European world taught to know that we will not permit France or any, or *all* the European Governments to interfere with our domestic policy, or dictate to the President what language he should use."[12] Ultimately he backed away from actual hostilities, leaving to British mediators the task of settling the dispute. Even though the quarrel ended peacefully, the whole affair illustrates the crucial influence a president's personality could have on foreign policy. Jackson's attitude had magnified a minor issue into a crisis that aroused many Americans to the point of favoring war against a friendly nation.

This episode, along with other aggressive conduct, led critics to view Jackson as a most determined expander of presidential power. Even so, he did not exercise authority irresponsibly. In major foreign policy matters, despite his harsh rhetoric, he frequently acted with caution. We can see his mix of boldness and practicality in his reaction to the rebellion in June

1835 of American settlers in Texas, the Mexican province he had tried to acquire through purchase. He proclaimed neutrality, but the rebels sought and expected help from their brethren across the border and they received it. Sympathizers in the United States formed volunteer companies that rushed to Texas and fought alongside the rebels. Other Americans supplied the Anglo-Texans with funds for arms, medicines, and other supplies, aiding them so openly that the nation's laws prohibiting the raising of hostile forces for service in a friendly state appeared meaningless.

When Mexico protested these violations of neutrality, Jackson responded he had tried to stop them but could not do so effectively because public sentiment overwhelmingly favored the Texans. In reality, he made only feeble efforts to enforce a fair policy toward the belligerents. He further ignored neutrality by authorizing General Edmund P. Gaines to send troops across the Texas border at the Sabine River to occupy Mexican territory, ostensibly to protect Louisiana from Indian raiders. Jackson perceived this unilateral deployment, and hence possible hostilities, as within his legal powers as president.

John Quincy Adams, who by this time had abandoned his earlier advocacy of an expansive presidential war authority, questioned this "most extraordinary power." It implied, he asserted, that the president "could authorize a commanding general to march into a foreign country; to commit an act of war; to make war; without the consent of Congress." Pressure within Congress to support Jackson and the popularity of aiding the Texas rebels blunted this concern. Gaines's troops occupied the disputed land and the majority in Congress acquiesced. As for Adams, he now had to admit that the startling "idea that the Executive Chief Magistrate has the power of involving the nation in war, even without consulting Congress," had taken root. It had come about, Adams maintained, through the "experience of fifty years" because "in numberless cases" the president had de facto "exercised that power."[13]

In April 1836, largely with American assistance, the Texans, led by Jackson's friend Sam Houston, won independence, proclaimed a republic, and then sought annexation to the United States. The president personally desired it. However, he reacted with practical caution, noting that recognition of new states could be "equivalent under some circumstances to a declaration of war." At this point, therefore, he did not recognize Texan independence or move to annex the province because either action could trigger war and upset the delicate balance in the Union between slave and free states. Finally, on March 3, 1837, the day before he left office, he abandoned caution to recognize Texas as independent.

Citing the Texas confrontation, as well as those with Argentina, France, and Indian tribes, as evidence, historians generally characterize Jackson as a strong executive, a two-fisted leader who reshaped the presidency. Much more than had his predecessors, he stressed that only he, among all elected officials, represented all the people. On this basis, he claimed that he rather than Congress embodied the true will of the nation. He used this argument to defy the Supreme Court over the fate of Indian lands in Georgia. His style in dealing with this problem, other internal crises, and minor conflicts with foreign powers made him an exemplar of the virile executive.

At the same time, Jackson ordinarily accepted the Constitution's limitations on his authority and recognized the primacy of Congress over the war-making power. Even in his brutal uprooting of some forty-six thousand Choctaws, Cherokees, and other Indians from their homelands and moving them across the Mississippi, he had Congressional consent.[14] His reputation for aggrandizing presidential power and setting precedents for its further expansion rests more on his domestic than on his foreign policy. His tough words and macho strutting did not lead to war or to the use of extended military force on his own authority to meet real or feigned foreign crises.

Martin Van Buren and William Henry Harrison

STILL popular when he left office, Jackson exploited his position as well as his personal influence to select the man to succeed him. He tapped Martin Van Buren, an accomplished politician from New York who had served him as secretary of state and as vice president. With this support, the New Yorker won the presidency. In demeanor and personality, Van Buren represented a striking contrast to Jackson. Even the new president's best friends considered him a man of prudence rather than of bold and decisive action in the macho manner.

When Van Buren took office, he stated what constitutionalists would regard as proper presidential demeanor in foreign relations and what advocates of activism would view as the principles of the weak executive. He pledged "strict adherence to the letter and spirit of the constitution as it was designed." In addition, he praised the standards of the nation's foreign policy as so satisfactory "as to constitute a rule of Executive conduct which leaves little to my discretion."[15] In foreign affairs, consequently, he followed his mentor's caution rather than his bluster, as in dealing with the Texas issue and relations with Mexico.

Van Buren had opposed Jackson's recognition of Texas but could not stop it. However, from the start of his administration, in a determined effort to keep the peace with Mexico, Van Buren refused to go beyond recognition. When the Anglo-Texans, on August 4, 1837, formally requested annexation of their newly proclaimed nation, he still stood firm. He declined to consider the proposal, contending its acceptance would violate the nation's neutrality as well as the Constitution, because that basic document did not provide for taking over an independent foreign state. Moreover, as had Jackson initially, Van Buren feared that annexing Texas would upset the balance between the free and slave states. So, even though many Americans favored the acquisition, he bucked their considerable pressure. This stance and domestic problems, notably the panic of 1837, eroded his popularity and made him a one-term president.

The next chief executive, William Henry Harrison, an experienced politician, Indian-fighter, and war hero, reputedly had a thirst for lucrative office regardless of how he obtained it. He won the presidency as a Whig and in a rambling inaugural on March 4, 1841, outlined that party's view of the office as one of precisely limited powers and subordination to the legislature. "It is preposterous to suppose that the President," he declared, "could better understand the wants and wishes of the people than their own immediate representatives."[16] He viewed the concentration of power in the executive a prelude to despotism and was determined to stop it. Harrison could do little to place this perspective into practice or to deal with the Texas question because within a month he died of pneumonia.

John Tyler

JOHN Tyler, the vice president and anti-Jackson Democrat turned Whig who assumed the office on April 4, took a different stance on executive authority. Although some contemporaries characterized him as a man "with talents not above mediocrity," he immediately demonstrated a tough independence.[17] Staunch Whigs who distrusted him maintained he could hold office only as acting president. Believing the Constitution made his succession automatic, he defied them by insisting on exercising full executive power, thus breaking with the Whig Party. Already alienated from the Democratic Party, he had to rule with virtually no political base of consequence.

This awkward situation affected Tyler's policy toward Texas and toward the Whig theory of executive power, which in its extreme expression limited the president to approving cabinet decisions and executing legislation. Although a believer in states' rights as opposed to federal power, he wanted to bring Texas into the Union in part for personal reasons. To achieve this goal, he felt no qualms about overriding principle to employ federal force. Moreover, that kind of expansionism against a demonized but weak neighbor fitted his need for a national issue that would demonstrate his strength and virility and help him gain election to the presidency on his own. Accordingly, he instructed Secretary of State Abel P. Upshur to negotiate a treaty of annexation with the Texans but to proceed secretly so as not to arouse opposition from antislavery Americans. Through Upshur, the president promised the Texans that during the negotiations he would order a large naval squadron to their coast and troops to their claimed border to deter a possible Mexican vengeance.

On January 28, 1844, before Usher could complete the negotiations, he died. Several days later, the American chargé in Austin, imprudently and in writing, promised the Texans more—that the president would not permit Mexico or "any other power" to "invade Texas, on account of any negotiation which may take place." Although this sentiment coincided with his own views, Tyler disavowed the chargé's pledge as exceeding the executive's constitutional power. The president also placed John C. Calhoun, South Carolina's proslavery intellectual, in the vacated secretaryship of state. Now in the twilight of his career, Calhoun accepted the post with the intent of acquiring Texas as a kind of triumph for the nation's slavocracy. He promptly assured the Texans that the president, despite his previous disavowal of any resort to force, had ordered "a strong naval force to concentrate in the gulf of Mexico to meet any emergency" and that he would "protect Texas from all foreign invasion."[18]

On the following day, April 12, Calhoun concluded the treaty of annexation. On May 15, Tyler, acting as commander in chief, informed the Senate of his deployment of the armed forces. Henceforth, he announced, he would "regard any attempt by a foreign power to invade Texas as an act of hostility to the United States and one which he would be justified in resisting by the employment of the military forces at his disposal."[19] Tyler thus stretched the war power to new limits.

Calhoun's linking of annexation with the expansion of slavery and Tyler's bellicose actions aroused bitter opposition, leading the Senate on June 8 to reject the treaty. Shortly thereafter, its foreign relations committee lectured the president on his powers as Whigs saw them. Committee spokesmen explained the president's role as "to follow, not to lead, to fulfill, not to ordain the law; to carry into effect, by negotiation and compact with Foreign governments, the legislative will, . . . not to interpose with controlling influence, not to go forward with too ambitious enterprises."[20]

Despite this admonition, Tyler remained determined to acquire Texas, even after he lost his bid for retaining the presidency. He persisted in his expansionist hopes because of the campaign of the Democratic winner, James K. Polk, a protégé of Jackson. Polk, who had served fourteen years in the House of Representatives and a term as governor of Tennessee, had entered the presidential race as the nation's first dark-horse candidate and as an apostle of Manifest Destiny. He ran on an expansionist platform calling for the reoccupation of Oregon and the reannexation of Texas. Believers in manifest expansionism based this slogan on the dubious assumption that Texas belonged to the United States as part of the Louisiana Purchase until 1819 when in the Florida treaty Monroe erroneously had accepted Spain's claim to the province.

Even though in November Polk won narrowly, Tyler chose to view his victory as a mandate for expansion. The lame-duck president asked Congress to annex Texas through a joint resolution that required a mere majority vote. Critics, such as Albert Gallatin, denounced this maneuver as an effort to circumvent the Constitution's rule that two-thirds of the Senate had to approve a treaty, bashed him for abusing the powers of his office, and even urged impeachment. Regardless, both houses voted for the resolution and, on March 1, 1845, three days before leaving office, Tyler signed it. Despite his weakness as a president, he had come up with a method for placing more power in the hands of the executive at the expense of Congress, a procedure other presidents would adopt. As critics pointed out, his strategy validated the manipulations of a president who knowingly set the nation on the path to war in good measure to satisfy his own agenda. As Tyler explained later, he was able to do so because in "his role as chief executive in the field of foreign affairs . . . he had been freer of the furies of factional politics than he had been in domestic affairs."[21]

James K. Polk

AS for Polk, despite the popularity of Manifest Destiny, he prepared to take office with much of the public viewing him as a mediocrity who lacked presidential stature. This reputation bothered him because, as his foremost biographer notes, his "whole life had been an unremitting effort to prove himself." Now at the peak of his career—

because the belittling continued—as a proud, stubborn man Polk vowed to overcome this popular perception of him by asserting vigorous leadership. He hoped for harmonious cabinet counselors but "in any event," he confided to a friend, "I intend to be *myself* President of the U.S." In his inaugural, however, he promised "to assume no powers not expressly granted or implied in the Constitution." He also advanced a peculiar version of peace linked to expansionist goals designed to please aggressive-minded constituents. He maintained awkwardly that "to enlarge the nation's limits is to extend the dominions of peace over additional territories." In contradiction he also announced, "the world has nothing to fear from military ambition in our Government" because it "can not be otherwise than pacific."[22]

At the same time, despite the potential for war in his predecessor's commitment to take over Texas, Polk defended the annexation and rejoiced in it. He also informed cabinet officials and others around him that he would personally control the making of foreign policy. This take-charge toughness, modeled on Jackson's behavior, enhanced Polk's stature even among skeptics in a public ready, if not eager, for a call to arms.

In addition, the president quickly brought to a head the quarrel over the Oregon territory to which Britain had a stronger title than the United States. In keeping with his campaign slogan, he demanded the whole of Oregon, asserting that the American title to it was clear and unquestionable. When told his truculence might lead to war, he responded that "the only way to treat John Bull was to look him straight in the eye." Furthermore, he considered such "a bold and firm course" pacific. He also confessed privately, "If we must have war with Great Britain, we may as well have it now as leave it to our successors."[23] Finally, to concentrate his energy on the anticipated war with Mexico, in the spring of 1846 he negotiated a peaceful compromise with Britain, embodied in a treaty in June, that settled the Oregon dispute to the advantage of the United States.

Meanwhile, in June 1845, after Texans meeting in a special convention had consented to annexation, Polk ordered a large concentration of troops under Brigadier General Zachary Taylor into Texas at the extreme of its extravagantly claimed boundaries. The army occupied disputed land between Texas and Mexico with the implicit, if not explicit, purpose of precipitating war. Polk's defenders maintain, however, that he was not trying at this time "to provoke a Mexican attack" or war.[24]

The troops remained there for eight months. To this extended provocation, Polk added efforts to wrest other territory, notably California and

New Mexico, from Mexico. He professed to accomplish this without war. First he tried purchase. When that failed he offered to assume debts Mexico owed American citizens if in exchange it would cede California and accept an ignominious settlement of the Texas boundary. In November he sent a special emissary, John Slidell, a former House member from Louisiana, on a secret mission to Mexico City to negotiate these terms. The Mexican government rejected Slidell, in part because he showed "the same feelings of contempt for Mexico and Mexicans that governed the whole policy of the Polk administration."[25]

Using the failure of the Slidell mission as an excuse, Polk now decided on war without waiting for a precipitating act of hostility by Mexico even though that nation did not meaningfully threaten the United States or have the capacity to do it significant harm. At this point, critics noted a marked inconsistency in the president's martial ardor. With Britain he willingly negotiated the fate of the Oregon territory with some give and take but refused to discuss the status of Texas with Mexico with comparable openness. This discrepancy led at least one skeptic to ask, "Why should we not compromise our difficulties with Mexico as well as with Great Britain?" He went on, "If it is wicked to go to war with England for disputed territory, it is not only wicked but cowardly to go to war with Mexico for the same reason."[26] Another answer to the question, simply put, was that Polk followed the classic policy of aggressive but realistic leaders—compromise with the strong but bash the weak.

As was usual with such rulers, the president contrived to justify his truculence. On April 28, 1846, he brought the matter of dealing with Mexico before the cabinet. Dutifully, its members urged a message to Congress recommending we "take redress into our own hands for the aggravated wrongs done to our citizens in their persons and property by Mexico." Fortified with this support for bellicosity from his own appointees, Polk directed Secretary of State James Buchanan to search the archives and prepare "a succinct history of those wrongs as a basis of a message to Congress, at his earliest convenience."[27] Unknown to both men, three days earlier, Mexican units had attacked the American occupiers in the no-man's-land north of the Rio Grande, killing sixteen and capturing others.

When the president learned of the clash, he realized he now had the desired hostile act. He revised his war message, telling Congress on May 11 of accumulated grievances against Mexico spanning twenty years. These reasons included Mexico being too feeble to govern her provinces, her inability to keep European powers from taking California, her unpaid debts to American claimants, her insult to Slidell, and her unwillingness to back down in the disputes over boundaries.

Those offenses, Polk said, had already exhausted the "cup of forbearance." He added, "After reiterated menaces, Mexico has passed the boundary of the United States, has invaded our territory, and shed American blood upon the American soil. She has proclaimed that hostilities have commenced, and that the two nations are now at war." Since, he went on, "war exists . . . by the act of Mexico herself," I ask "Congress to recognize the existence of the war." Later, Abraham Lincoln, a critical Whig representative from Illinois, asked the president, in what became known as the Spot Resolutions, whether or not the spot where Americans bled was Mexican soil and whether or not "our citizens, whose blood was shed," were "*armed* officers, and *soldiers*, sent into that [Mexican] settlement by the military order of the President."[28]

Congress accepted Polk's deception, rather than Lincoln's perspective, in good measure because popular opinion appeared enthusiastic for a war of conquest, and ostensibly Polk followed what had become established practice sanctioned loosely by the Constitution—that the president could use force to repel a sudden attack. In this case, however, the president had initiated the hostilities by maneuvering troops in a manner to incite Mexicans to retaliate. Thus, by giving precedent a new twist, Polk persuaded a hardly peace-minded majority in the legislature to resolve on May 13 that by the act of Mexico a state of war existed. Congress thereby did not on its own declare war; it ratified what the president had wrought.

The dissenters, most of them Whigs in and out of Congress, reacted harshly, charging that "a secretive, evasive, and high-handed president himself had provoked Mexico into firing the first shots." They attributed the war to his own aggressive impulses and regarded it as "impolitic, illegal, and immoral." Calhoun, now a senator from South Carolina who had turned against Polk's policy, asked, How could the president assert that war existed by act of Mexico "when he had no evidence on which to affirm it?" He called Polk's request "monstrous" and as proposing "a hasty and thoughtless course" because "it stripped Congress of the power of making war." The senator argued that the passage of the war bill did "great mischief." It "sets the example," he warned, "which will enable all future Presidents to bring about a state of things, in which Congress shall be forced, without deliberation, or reflection, to declare war, however opposed to its convictions of justice or expediency."[29]

Other opponents, among them John Quincy Adams, attacked Polk's war message "as a direct and notorious violation of the truth," alleging he had usurped Congress's war-making power. "It is now established as an irreversible precedent," Adams claimed, "that the President of the United States has but to declare that War exists, with any Nation upon Earth, by the act of that Nation's Government, and the War is essentially declared." Another senator, John Middleton Clayton, asserted, "I do not see on what principle it can be shown that the President, without consulting Congress and obtaining its sanction for the procedure, has a right to send an army to take up a position, where, as it must have been foreseen, the inevitable consequence would be war."[30]

Furthermore, others noted that countries such as England, France, Spain, Holland, Naples, and Denmark had committed offenses against the United States without triggering war. These critics denounced "the outrageous war waged by the Executive, upon an unoffending people."[31] They deplored a key device Polk used and that other presidents would employ repeatedly in controlling the war power regardless of constitutional restraints—the manipulation of Congress into backing hostilities the executive had commenced unilaterally.

Earlier, while still talking about the peaceful acquisition of California but lurching toward war, Polk had ordered well-armed troops under Captain John Charles Frémont to that virtually undefended province to foment a rebellion by American settlers against the Mexican authorities. In October 1845, the president had also ordered Commodore James D. Sloat, in anticipation of actual hostilities, to occupy California. Frémont committed acts of war such as raising the American flag over a neighbor's territory because, as he said later, the president "wanted and intended to push the war with Mexico." Hostilities followed on June 10, 1846, a month after the outbreak of war, when the American settlers launched what came to be known as the Bear Flag revolt. Frémont, who began designating himself the military commander of United States forces in California, took over a leadership role in the brief uprising.[32] Within six months, other more powerful American military forces, such as those under Sloat, brought the province into the Union through conquest, thereby completing a prime part of the president's bold program.

This agenda and Polk's inability, despite battlefield victories, to bring the war to a swift conclusion emboldened his opponents. They continued to characterize him as the chief architect of both the expansionist goals and the war. Hence they termed the conflict an "Executive war" or "Mr. Polk's War, " launched by his "imprudence, indiscretion, and mismanagement." Northern Whigs and abolitionists tended to view the conflict in these terms but also as part of a slave-holders' conspiracy abetted by the president. They clung to this interpretation even as the war was about to end. One of Polk's opponents, Representative George Ashmun of Massachusetts, tacked on to a resolution honoring General Zachary Taylor a censure saying the war had been "unnecessarily and unconstitutionally begun by the President of the United States."[33] The measure passed by a vote of 85 to 81 but the Senate would not go along with it.

Among those who voted for the censure, Lincoln expressed notable concern over the nature of the war power. "Allow the President to invade a neighboring nation, whenever *he* shall deem it necessary to repel an invasion, and you allow him to do so, *whenever he may choose to say* he deems it necessary for such purpose—and you allow him to make war at pleasure," he wrote. "Kings had always been involving and impoverishing their people in wars," he added, "pretending generally, if not always, that the good of the people was the object." Here, though, "*no one man* should hold the power of bringing this oppression upon us."[34]

Despite this intense minority opposition, the determined Polk held to his course and in the Treaty of Guadalupe Hidalgo of February 2, 1848, ended the war in triumph. He deprived Mexico of half of her national domain while bringing into the Union what he properly called a great empire comprising Texas, California, Nevada, Utah, New Mexico, Arizona, and parts of Wyoming and Colorado. He accomplished all of this by stretching the president's power as commander in chief more than had any of his predecessors.

Why did the Whigs and others fail to stop this aggrandizing of presidential power? They proved ineffective because Polk had fused his own agenda and hubris with patriotism, because he had acted in harmony with a majority sentiment that craved an expansion it justified as divinely destined, because loyal Democrats in Congress had readily approved his conduct, and because it paid off with reasonably prompt and impressive results at low cost. In subsequent years, Polk's macho style earned him the enduring admiration of the strong-presidency cult.

Zachary Taylor and Millard Fillmore

POLK'S successors, the Whig military hero Zachary Taylor, known as "Old Rough and Ready," who died suddenly in July 1850, and Millard Fillmore, the New York politician who succeeded Taylor from the vice presidency, faced no foreign crises that offered opportunity for truculence involving hostilities. Taylor, who had no experience in foreign affairs, promised to accept constitutional limitations in conducting them and in crises "to exhaust every resort of honorable diplomacy before appealing to arms."[35] Fillmore, too, functioned primarily as a constitutional executive who accepted the limitations that role implied. For these and other reasons, historians usually regard these men as weak leaders.

Both presidents opposed territorial expansion, such as at the expense of Cuba, but Fillmore did not conduct foreign policy so timidly as to shy away from the possible use of military force when he thought it appropriate. He employed it to coerce Japan, a country that for 250 years had largely secluded itself from the rest of the world. Early in the nineteenth century, Europeans seeking trade, food, and water had occasionally intruded on Japanese shores but did not linger. When storms wrecked their ships and stranded survivors on Japanese soil, xenophobic authorities frequently treated them harshly. As the United States expanded its trade in the Pacific, its seamen encountered similar treatment. Traders and others, therefore, urged the American government to establish formal relations with the Japanese.

In June 1845, the Polk administration responded by sending a commissioner to Japan with the authority to negotiate a commercial treaty, but he fell ill. Commodore James Biddle took over the mission, arriving at the port of Uraga on July 20 with a ninety-gun warship. He remained ten days but encountered so much hostility that he could not venture ashore without exerting force. He departed empty-handed. In the next several years, more American seamen returned home with stories, sometimes exaggerated, of Japanese brutality. A segment of the public alarmed by these reports, traders eager for profit, missionaries desiring converts, and nationalists anxious to show the flag all urged the government to pressure the Japanese into opening their ports and to do something to protect the lives of American mariners.

These concerns led Fillmore in his annual message to Congress in December 1851 to suggest, in a surge of "virile determination," some muscle flexing.[36] In the spring he announced he would send a substantial naval expedition to Japan, justifying it primarily as needed to alleviate the plight of the stranded sailors. Nothing in the Constitution gave the president authority to offer such protection, but he had precedent. By this time on a number of occasions, as we have noted, executives had sent military forces abroad to safeguard American lives. They had not necessarily acted with legislative backing or out of militarist motivation but usually on what they perceived as inherent or implied executive authority in the Lockean sense.

They did so because the line between employing force to save lives and military posturing was hazy. That fuzziness marked the encounter with Japan.

Expansionists hailed the expedition while critics saw in it mainly the danger of confrontation. One opponent of the plan protested what he perceived as a presidential effort "to establish commercial relations with Japan *at all hazards*," even at the risk of hostilities.[37] In the election campaign of 1852, Democrats denounced the expedition while, ironically, constitutionalist Whigs defended it. Regardless of these differences, on November 24, 1852, on his own authority, Fillmore sent an armada to Japan of ten ships, four of them warships, with more than two thousand men and commanded by Commodore Matthew C. Perry, to force an arrangement.

Perry's instructions, prepared by the acting secretary of state, cautioned him not to "resort to force unless in self defense." They also directed him to "do everything" to impress the Japanese with the power of the United States. Since Perry regarded the Japanese as "a weak and barbarous people" and had a reputation for the impulsive use of force, the secretary of the navy reminded him that "Congress alone has the power to declare war" and hence to exercise prudence "in the great work in which you are engaged."[38]

Despite the admonitions, on reaching Okinawa in May 1853 the commodore went ashore with a troop of marines armed with two field pieces, marched on Naha, the capital, and with the threat of force compelled the Okinawans to accept his authority. He wanted to annex the Ryukyus as well as the Bonin Islands. S. Wells Williams, the missionary who accompanied the expedition as interpreter, commented in his journal, "A more high-handed piece of aggression has not been committed by anyone."[39]

Perry continued his brazen conduct when on July 8 he appeared in the harbor before Edo, Japan's capital city, with four warships, decks cleared for action. He landed with an armed escort of four hundred men, left a letter from the president demanding treaty arrangements for the protection of Americans who might enter Japan, and announced he would come back in the spring with a larger force for the answer. Perry returned to Edo on February 12 of the next year with a more menacing armada of ten ships and two thousand men. He warned the Japanese, "If your country becomes an enemy, we will exhaust our resources if necessary to wage war, we are fully prepared to engage in a struggle for victory." He backed this threat with the example of Mexico's recent fate, saying "circumstances may lead your country also into a similar plight."[40]

After six weeks of negotiation mixed with such menace, the Japanese on March 31 agreed to a treaty that gave Americans access to two small ports, provided for a consul, and contained protection for shipwrecked sailors. Perry had exceeded his instructions, so the new Democratic president, Franklin Pierce, rejected the proposed annexation of the Ryukyus and Bonins. Like other executives in such circumstances, however, Pierce accepted the commodore's other aggressive actions because he deemed them beneficial to his own objectives.

In all, even though the intimidation that opened Japan to foreigners had come in the person of Perry, it had emanated essentially from the president. After Perry's departure, American presidents continued their pressure through force because the initial coercion had not overcome Japanese xenophobia. Beginning in 1859, with disturbing regularity they attacked Europeans in their midst. In January 1861 antiforeign Japanese murdered an interpreter for the American legation.[41] In May, even though civil conflict had already erupted at home, Secretary of State William H. Steward proposed a naval force to suppress the anti-Western violence.

President Lincoln took no action until Choshu clan leaders, with guns emplaced on the narrow strait of Shimonoseki, fired on European shipping and, in June 1863, poured shot on the *Pembroke*, an American merchant ship. A six-gun naval sloop retaliated, sinking two Choshu ships while losing six men. In December, Lincoln reported to Congress that "in common with other western powers, our relations with Japan have been brought into serious jeopardy."[42] To curb the Japanese assaults, the Western powers in September of the following year assembled an international force composed of one American vessel and British, French, and Dutch warships that twice bombarded Japanese towns along the strait, landed troops, crippled the attackers, and later obtained an indemnity.

American participation in this international police action, even though minor, marked a first. Previously, presidents had employed force to protect Americans abroad in isolated incidents, mainly against weak foes such as the Barbary states. Against the Japanese, however, a president for the first time authorized a ship carrying the American flag to join a foreign armada in an effort to force another nation to live up to treaty obligations, to punish it for harming American nationals and other foreigners, and to bring its behavior in line with European and American standards. American ships remained engaged in this kind of policing for a decade solely on presidential initiative. The Senate did, however, approve the treaties that executive emissaries negotiated with Japanese authorities.

Franklin Pierce

MEANWHILE Pierce, the proslavery New Hampshire politician who in 1853 had come to the presidency as a leader of the Young America movement, which demanded a vigorous, expansionist foreign policy, tried to carry out that commitment. He announced immediately that "the policy of my administration will not be controlled by any timid forebodings of evil from expansion." Most of all, he wanted to seize Cuba. Referring to it indirectly, he alleged that "the acquisition of certain possessions not within our jurisdiction are eminently important for our protection."[43]

In the first year of his administration, Pierce expected a filibustering expedition led by John A. Quitman, a former governor of Mississippi with extreme proslavery views, to wrest Cuba from Spain to prevent its "Africanization." That plan collapsed, but before it did the president had at hand the incident he could use as an excuse for war and seizing Cuba by force. The crisis began on February 28, 1854, when Spanish authorities in Cuba confiscated the cargo of an American steamship, the *Black Warrior*, for a technical violation of port regulations.

In the United States, among concerned nationalists this affair produced a wave of anti-Spanish sentiment along with a demand for action. On March 15 Pierce asked Congress for authority "to obtain redress for injuries received, and to vindicate the honor of our flag."[44] Secretary of State William L. Marcy instructed Pierre Soulé, the American minister in Madrid, to demand an apology from Spain and an indemnity for damage to the ship. The minister delivered the note as a forty-eight-hour ultimatum. Spain ignored the ultimatum but resolved the dispute through negotiation with the ship's owners. Pierce reluctantly accepted the settlement in part because he knew that at this time Congress would not back a war to conquer Cuba. He remained determined, though, to carry out his own plan to obtain the island.

A short time later, in keeping with this desire, the president tried to buy Cuba. When that effort failed, he again turned to coercion. For nine days in October, three of his diplomats met in Ostend, Belgium, and in Aix-la-Chapelle (or Aachen, Germany) to discuss how best to take the island. If all else failed, they wrote in a secret document that later became known as the Ostend Manifesto, "by every law, human and Divine, we shall be justified in wresting it from Spain, if we possess the power."[45] The president could not follow that advice. Indeed, he had to repudiate the document because news of the meeting leaked, causing an international furor, and because his domestic opponents made political capital out of his efforts to steal Cuba. Moreover, now he did not dare to launch a war on his own that would bring the island into the Union as slave territory. To do so would risk the catalyzing of civil strife at home.

Several months earlier, a lesser foreign problem had aroused the president's ire. The managers of the American-owned Accessory Transit Company in Greytown (presently San Juan del Norte), a free city under British protection in Nicaragua, stumbled into a fracas with local residents. A mob damaged company property and assaulted the American minister to Central America, slightly injuring him. Viewing this attack as an insult to the nation, Pierce ordered a sloop of war, the SS *Cyane,* to Greytown with instructions to the skipper to teach the people there that the United States will not tolerate such outrages. When the authorities did not meet the demand for apology and reparation, the warship bombarded the city for two hours and then marines burned it.

British authorities denounced this violence as an outrage and the New York *Tribune* condemned it as "a needless, unjustifiable, inhuman exercise of force." Other critics assailed the president for violating Congress's war-making power. Pierce finally defended the destruction by characterizing Greytown as "a pretended community, a heterogeneous assemblage gathered from various countries." It did not stand "before the world in the attitude of an organized political society." He also dismissed the city as "a piratical resort of outlaws or a camp of savages," whose status justified the violence against it. A Congressman questioned the president's right to sanction such conduct, asking, "What is the limit to his power? What but his own will shall prevent him involving the country in war at any time?"[46]

Despite such concern over presidential aggrandizement, this minor episode became significant to historians primarily because a Greytown resident sued the United States for the destruction of his property. Six years later a federal circuit court upheld Pierce's position. In validating the president's discretion in the use of force, the court ruled he had a duty to protect American citizens and property abroad. But Pierce had used force to avenge a slight offense and not to save lives because none were endangered. Against a powerful country, such intervention would have been an act of war, but against a weak community even a president considered lacking in leadership qualities could exercise his macho impulse with little risk of rebuff.

James Buchanan

PIERCE'S successor, the Pennsylvania Democrat James Buchanan, had served in both houses of Congress, had held important diplomatic posts, had been secretary of state under Polk, and had won the presidency in 1856 on a platform calling for the annexation of Cuba. He tried immediately to ingratiate himself with popular expansionist sentiment by adopting an aggressive foreign policy, especially against weak Latin American countries. In rhetoric, at least, as a biographer points out, "he was prepared to annex everything from the Rio Grande to Colombia at the risk of war if necessary."[47]

Mostly, however, Buchanan's recorded views on presidential activism, particularly in the unilateral use of the war power, exuded caution. "The executive government of this country, in its intercourse with foreign nations," he averred, "is limited to the employment of diplomacy alone. When this fails it can proceed no further. It cannot legitimately resort to force without the direct authority of Congress, except in resisting and repelling hostile attacks." This attitude governed his approach to the great internal crisis over slavery. Historians consequently characterize him as timid and weak. He failed as president, they contend, because he "left all decisions" on the secession of southern states to Congress and "bowed meekly" to its refusal to use military force.[48]

Abraham Lincoln

WHEN Lincoln, who had switched from the Whig to the newly established Republican Party, won the election to succeed Buchanan he, too, indicated a distaste for war, even in the massive crisis facing the nation. Shortly before entering the White House, he told an audience that had expressed apprehension over the nation's future, "The man does not live who is more devoted to peace than I am. None who would do more to preserve it. But it may be necessary to put the foot down firmly." In another speech to concerned citizens, he said he saw "no need of bloodshed and war" and that "there will be no blood shed unless it be forced upon the Government."[49]

On this issue of war and peace, as on others, biographers maintain that by temperament Lincoln had an aversion to making bold moves. Soon, though, as president he put these feelings aside. He dealt with the secession crisis with unprecedented boldness. That emergency, not any foreign peril, led him to reverse his earlier condemnation, as in Polk's case, of the executive's unilateral exercise of the war power. Lincoln chose to view the South Carolinians' firing on Fort Sumter in Charleston Harbor on April 12, 1861, as a sudden attack, an insurrection, that as head of the nation he had the authority to repel. Between that date and the convening on July 4 of a special session of Congress, he professed devotion to peace while taking measures that "irrevocably committed the country to a definite war policy." He seemed impelled by the notion that if he were to save the divided Union he must do so with authority beyond the Constitution. In these weeks in his use of executive power, he "set the pattern for his whole administration."[50]

The president could have called Congress into session had he desired. Instead, without legislative authority he converted state militias into a volunteer army of thirty thousand, added 23,000 men to the regular army and 18,000 to the navy, and paid two million dollars from unappropriated funds in the Treasury to persons unauthorized to receive it. He also closed the postal service to what could be construed as treasonable correspondence, proclaimed a blockade of Confederate ports in violation of international law, suspended the law of habeas corpus in several places, and took other war measures on his own initiative without statutory authority. In all, his government arrested without charge at least fifteen thousand civilians, and military courts convicted hundreds of others.[51] Lincoln thus became the first president to assume such power on his own to wage a major war.

In one case in May, involving the suspension of habeas corpus in southern Maryland, Chief Justice Roger B. Taney denied the right of the executive to take such action on his own. Taney maintained that only Congress had the authority to put aside the writ and pointed out that the Constitution did not permit indefinite imprisonment of a citizen without trial. Democrats sided with the chief justice while Republican lawyers rushed to Lincoln's defense, arguing he had exercised an emergency authority in line with the old Lockean theory of inherent power, proper in time of rebellion. Regardless of the merits of the case, scholars note, "Taney commanded no troops and could not enforce his opinion, while Lincoln did and could."[52]

The president expressed regret for these questionable tactics while also excusing them. "The duty of employing the war-power in defense of the government," he asserted, was forced upon him. "These measures, whether strictly legal or not," he told Congress, "were ventured upon, under what appeared to be a popular demand, and a public necessity: trusting then, as now, that Congress would readily ratify them." He countered criticism of his use of illegal imprisonment, for example, with a question that later became famous. He asked, "Are all the laws *but one* [habeas corpus] to go unexecuted, and the government itself to go to pieces lest that one be violated?"[53] He thus implied that in an emergency, which the president himself defined, he could on his own authority partially suspend the Constitution. As had Jefferson with the Louisiana Purchase, Lincoln also claimed the right to manipulate the powers of his office and impinge on those of Congress for the good of the people as he perceived it.

Opponents spoke of "Dictator Lincoln," compared him to Nero or Caligula, and friends, too, expressed alarm over his exercise of "despotic power." Nonetheless, on August 6 Congress accepted all of Lincoln's emergency military measures "as though they had been taken with prior approval," even though it possessed no constitutional authority to forgive presidential illegalities "after the fact."[54] It did nothing about the other actions of dubious legality, thereby permitting them to remain in force. Congress recognized the president's fait accompli as necessary, just as he thought it would. Throughout the war, consequently, he continued to act independently of the other two branches of government. Even though Congress had the constitutional power to declare war, he asserted the right to use military force on his own because the executive had the power to suppress rebellion.

Lincoln justified this high-handed behavior as falling within his authority as commander in chief. He saw that title as enabling him to take any measure needed to subdue the enemy. With acts that were imaginative as well as bold, he used his military role to direct the war against the Confederacy and to further the reach of presidential power. He exercised this expansive policing power not against a foreign foe but against those of his own people who wished for independence but in a slave-holding society.

Despite the debatable legal aspects of Lincoln's conduct, he stretched executive authority for a noble cause. He did so notably when he issued his Emancipation Proclamation, the preliminary version on September 22, 1862, and the final form on the following January 1. It declared freedom for slaves in areas of the country in rebellion. At one point, he called it an act of justice allowed by the Constitution. At another time he defended it, as he had other questionable deeds, by declaring, "I think the Constitution invests its commander-in-chief, with the law of war, in time of war."[55]

Later, though, he said the proclamation had no "constitutional or legal justification, except as a military measure." Although he freed no slaves in territory where he had the ability to unshackle them, with the proclamation he took an irreversible move toward the abolition of slavery throughout the nation.

Even admirers point out that with the proclamation and other unilateral measures, such as authorizing military trials for disaffected citizens where civil courts functioned, Lincoln hurdled constitutional restraints on his authority. Critics portray him as acting at times virtually as a dictator who established a military despotism.[56]

The Supreme Court did not defend constitutional rights against executive use of the war power until after Lincoln's death. It expressed its view in the case of *Ex parte Milligan* in December 1866, involving Lambdin P. Milligan of Indiana, a foe of the Union who a military commission had sentenced to death. The court ruled presidentially decreed military commissions for civilians illegal and freed Milligan. Justice David Davis, a man troubled that his close friendship with Lincoln conflicted with his respect for the Constitution and who spoke for the Court, went further in an attempt to uphold the rule of law even during war. He declared that "wicked men, ambitious of power, with hatred of liberty and contempt of law, may fill the place once occupied by Washington and Lincoln; and if this right is conceded . . . the dangers of human liberty are frightful to contemplate."[57] While often quoted by those who wished to restrain unilateral executive use of the war power, future presidents would ignore the Court's ruling as Davis expressed it.

Numerous other contemporaries, most members of Congress, the courts, and scores of scholars since have defended Lincoln's arbitrary rule as commander in chief, usually with arguments similar to those he had used to justify it. They maintain he respected the legal limitations on his power, but to keep the imperiled Union intact at given instances he had no choice other than to circumvent them. As historian Bruce Catton put it, "If there had not been a strong Presidency and a strong President in 1861, the country unquestionably would have broken apart. . . . There simply is no question about it."[58] In this perspective, national salvation and the emancipating of four million slaves were worth the cost of essentially minor civil rights violations.

In appraising Lincoln, these Americans and others often overlook contradictions in the man. They portray him as a vigorous wartime leader, but he was often indecisive. They praise him as a humble, compassionate man of the people but in using power ruthlessly to subvert civil rights, he showed little mercy for victims of this behavior. Americans acclaim him as the Great Emancipator, but he long resisted the abolition of slavery. They glorify him as the savior who reunified the nation, which indeed he was, but seemingly they forget he had promised to do so without war. Even so, historians, the public, and others generally celebrate him as the nation's greatest president and in the process virtually deify him.

Adulation aside, Lincoln gave substance to the idea that in a crisis the president would or should dominate the government and that the people, Congress, and the courts would defer to him. With disarming modesty rather than with macho swagger, he enhanced the role of commander in chief and swelled the war power beyond what the framers of the Constitution or what previous presidents had done or perhaps even contemplated. Time and again macho successors would exploit this precedent, especially in the conduct of foreign affairs. They would cite it effectively to deflect criticism because a beloved president had linked it with benevolent causes—the freeing of human beings from bondage and the preserving of the Union.

Conventional wisdom holds that with Lincoln's passing, Congress reasserted much of the authority it had surrendered to him. This backlash supposedly ushered in three decades of decline in the exercise of presidential power. This interpretation characterizes the chief executives of this era—of booming industry, plutocracy, governmental scandal, political corruption, and a massive immigration—often called the Gilded Age—as mediocrities who readily accepted the sway of Congress as well as Whig principles of conduct. Actually, the idea of the activist executive willing to use military force in foreign affairs remained attractive to most men who entered the White House in this period, even though a number of them did not fit that model well.

Andrew Johnson

ANDREW Johnson, the self-educated Tennessee Democrat who had served as Lincoln's vice president, was one of these executives. Driven by ambition, he wanted to be a strong president who would make a mark nationally and internationally but, because of conflict with Congress over Reconstruction policy, he never achieved that goal. He felt so hard pressed by his political enemies that he delegated much of his foreign policy authority to his secretary of state, William H. Seward. As always, though, the president retained control over the final decisions. Only once did Johnson show "signs of taking matters in his own hands" for a more aggressive stance than that adopted by Seward.[59] It occurred in October 1865 when other advisers, Civil War generals, and public sentiment demanded that he resort to military force to expel the French troops that had invaded Mexico.

Johnson wanted to use the power he had inherited from the martyred Lincoln against the French. "We should regard it as a great calamity to ourselves . . . and to the peace of the world," he announced in December, "should any European Power challenge the American people" in their "defence of republicanism against foreign interference." Less than two months later, after American and French troops had clashed in a brief skirmish along the Rio Grande, he again expressed dissatisfaction with the French presence in Mexico. He told Napoleon III he could promote peace with "an early withdrawal of your troops."[60]

Johnson did not act as daringly as his rhetoric indicated because Seward persuaded him to rely on coercive diplomacy rather than force to achieve his goal and because Congress passed a series of laws restricting presidential initiative. Johnson protested these constraints. "Whilst I hold the chief executive authority of the United States, whilst the obligation rests upon me to see that all the laws are faithfully executed," he announced while under attack, "I can never willingly surrender that trust or the powers given for its execution."[61]

When Johnson defied the restraints in the matter of Reconstruction policy and misused some of his powers, the House of Representatives in January 1868 impeached him. He escaped dismissal from office by one vote. In all, because of his stubbornness, his troubles with Congress, his curtailed powers, and the lack of a foreign war, he had no readily available chance to demonstrate macho qualities in dealing with other countries.

Ulysses S. Grant

THE next president, Ulysses S. Grant, the nation's foremost military hero, came to the office without experience in, or even sound knowledge of, local, national, or international politics. Unlike other office-seekers, he did not hunger for power for its own sake or because he had an individual goal to attain. As a friend noted, "he enjoyed the possession of power as evidence of the public confidence."[62] Another contemporary, historian Henry Adams, wrote that Grant viewed the presidency from the perspective "of the commander of an army in time of peace" and believed "it was the duty of the President to follow without hesitation the wishes of the people as expressed by Congress."[63] Grant also expressed admiration for strong presidents and, in one instance, in an attempt to carry out an old plan to acquire the Dominican Republic, he tried to act like one.

Grant's effort began after real-estate speculators and other parties who would benefit from a takeover had informed him the Dominican people yearned for annexation to the United States. On his own initiative, therefore, in July 1869 the president sent his personal secretary, General Orville E. Babcock, as his special agent to explore means of carrying out this transaction. Babcock signed documents with Dominican leaders in which, for the sum of $1.5 million, they agreed to annexation. Shortly after, Grant presented this arrangement to his cabinet. "Babcock has returned as you see," he explained, "and has brought a treaty of annexation. I suppose it is not formal, as he had no diplomatic powers; but we can easily cure that."[64]

The president then vested Babcock with proper diplomatic credentials and sent him back to Santo Domingo along with a warship to lend "the moral support of its guns" to the acquisition scheme. On November 29 Babcock concluded a treaty of annexation and a convention for the lease of the Bay of Samaná. Grant believed "San Domingo is weak and must go some where for protection," so why not to him?[65] Therefore, in the president's name, Babcock promised protection to the Dominican regime, then beset by rebels and neighboring Haitian forces, until ratification of the agreements.

Eager to consummate the annexation, Grant tried to accelerate the approval process by lobbying senators. On January 2, 1870, he even visited the home of Charles Sumner, the chairman of the Senate Committee on Foreign Relations, whom he heartily disliked, to enlist his assistance for approval of the treaties. After an awkward conversation, the president departed believing he had obtained the support he desired. On January 10, he submitted the treaties to the Senate. He also deployed naval vessels in the Bay of Samaná. When the head of the beleaguered regime, Buenaventura Baez, appealed for additional help, Grant sent more warships until by the end of February seven of them were cruising in Dominican or Haitian waters. He made clear that any attack on the Dominican government would be "considered an act of hostility to the flag of the United States" and would "provoke hostility in return."[66] Baez then proceeded with a rigged plebiscite to demonstrate that the people of the island country were burning with desire for the annexation.

Believing the scheme to be corrupt, President Grant ignorant in international matters, and his action impulsive, Sumner's committee voted five to two against approval of the treaties and, on March 15, reported this recommendation to the full Senate. In the debate that followed, within a period of two days Sumner spoke for more than five hours, denouncing the treaty of annexation. Proponents then secured a recess on the debate. Sumner's opposition infuriated Grant. He regarded it as a personal betrayal as well as an injury to a possible key accomplishment of his administration.

With his pugnacity aroused, the president intensified his pressure on the legislators, advancing a number of incongruous reasons why he felt "an unusual anxiety for the ratification of this treaty." He contended that the people of Santo Domingo thirsted for the protection of America's free institutions, that the acquisition "will redound greatly to the glory of the two countries," and would be "an adherence to the Monroe Doctrine."[67] He failed to convince. On June 30 the Senate voted down the treaty.

Nonetheless, the president kept the warships in place and in his annual message in December again brought up the question of the annexation, asking for the Dominican people, "Shall we refuse them?" Sumner in turn renewed his attack on the proposal. In a discursive address on December 21, known as his "Naboth's Vineyard" speech, he condemned the proposed acquisition as an attempt to commit Congress to a "dance of blood" in a scheme "upheld by violence." In sum, he insulted the president. In retaliation, in March 1871, through political arm-twisting Grant forced Sumner from his committee chairmanship. On the day of the ouster, the president told some senators it had been "necessary to make an example of Sumner in order to teach these men that they cannot assail an administration with impunity."[68]

On March 27 Sumner struck back with a speech to the Senate on "Violations of International Law, and Usurpations of War Powers." He assailed the president's use of the navy against Haiti, "a friendly nation," to advance his own whim and for seizing "the war powers . . . without the authority of Congress." He called this seizure of "the war powers" a usurping of authority prohibited by the Constitution.[69]

Grant's defenders argued he had not employed violence because the naval force he had deployed fired no guns. Sumner's true purpose, they charged, was "to fix a crime upon the President of the United States." The critics countered that war could exist without battles. Finally, in April, Grant gave up the Dominican project, saying he still "believed that our institutions were broad enough to extend over the entire continent."[70]

Since he did not have his way, this effort to play the part of a strong foreign policy leader with a misguided project failed. No one, of course, could or did censure his macho behavior. Even Grant's friends and fellow Republicans, however, denounced what they perceived as an imperious exercise of presidential power replete with the intent to employ force if he deemed it necessary.

Traditionally, in polls and histories, Americans rank Grant as one of the least capable of presidents, even as something of a buffoon—which he was not—who diminished executive prestige. They often cite the scandals of his administration, his bullying tactics in the Dominican affair, and his humiliating feud with Sumner as reasons for the negative judgment. For the presidency, his clash with Congress in the Dominican fiasco has a deeper significance. It demonstrates how even a wrong-headed and so-called weak executive can use power, as though a proverbial bull in a china shop, to attempt to crush legitimate legislative opposition and almost prevail in advancing a pet foreign policy project.

CHAPTER 3

To The Stewardship Theory

My view was that every executive officer . . . was a steward of the people. . . . Under this interpretation of executive power I did and caused to be done many things not previously done by the President and the heads of the departments. I did not usurp power, but I did greatly broaden the use of executive power.

Theodore Roosevelt, *Autobiography*, 1913

Rutherford B. Hayes and Chester A. Arthur

CONVENTIONAL perspective tells us the presidents who immediately followed Ulysses S. Grant functioned, like him, in an ambiance of congressional ascendancy and executive weakness. To Americans who admire the makers and shakers—the virile leaders who do not hesitate to use military force—this appraisal appears logical. In the matter of force, however, the interpretation requires modification. No matter how weak or strong presidents may have been, as commanders in chief they controlled troops they could employ in warfare against Indian tribes and in the protection of American citizens abroad. Occasionally, they also resorted to military coercion in foreign affairs, usually with congressional approval but at times with mere acquiescence.

In several instances, allegedly passive executives behaved with a pugnacity similar to that displayed by acknowledged strong leaders. Presidents tagged by tradition as weak thus made evident that with the rising wealth and power of the nation, hardly any chief executive, regardless of his philosophical views on constitutional authority, could resist employing the increasingly potent military resources at his disposal.

This readily available power tempted even Rutherford B. Hayes, the Ohio Republican whose Whig background, a biographer notes, had "conditioned him to consider the Presidential office as subservient to the Congressional power." In his inaugural in March 1877, shadowed by a cloud over his election, he promised "a government which submits loyally and heartily to the Constitution and laws." In now standard vocabulary, he also pledged peace and no interference in the affairs of foreign nations.

Immediately, though, he had to deal with the problem of Mexican marauders who frequently slipped across the southern border to raid American settlements. In May he expressed a "determination to put an end to the invasion of our territory by lawless bands intent upon the plunder of our peaceful citizens" by ordering federal troops to pursue the "outlaws" into Mexico.[1]

The Mexican government protested Hayes's hot-pursuit directive. In addition, it stationed troops on the frontier with instructions to repel any invasion of its territory. These preparations, despite their potential for bloodletting, had little impact on popular sentiment in the border areas and elsewhere in the United States. The attentive public applauded the president's policy. Minority critics concerned with constitutional niceties, however, denounced it. They accused him of invading—without the consent of Congress—the territory of a peaceful neighbor. They argued also that he wished to provoke war with Mexico to divert attention from domestic problems stemming from the ending of southern Reconstruction and to annex more Mexican territory. "There is nothing secret or underhand in the Mexican policy," Hayes responded angrily in denying the accusations.[2] He explained his employment of military force as merely a proper means to protect American citizens against brigands.

The president followed the hot-pursuit policy for nearly three years, defying skeptics who accused him of lying, his congressional opponents, and the Mexican threats. In February 1880, after the Mexican government policed its own frontier effectively enough for the raids on American towns to cease, he ended the armed cross-border incursions. Hayes viewed this hard-line course as one of his tangible successes. Therefore, he defended the executive's unilateral right to use force with a verve that would fit the macho model. He faced no other foreign problem that elicited such toughness. Along with some other aspects of his administration, this episode demonstrates that while in word he embraced the Whig theory of the presidency, "his practice was almost the opposite."[3]

James A. Garfield, another Republican from Ohio, had little interest in foreign affairs and no time to develop a concern in them. Six months after taking office in March 1881, an assassin's bullet cut him down. His successor, Chester A. Arthur, a New York Republican tainted by scandal, has the reputation of a nonentity who should never have gained entrance to the White House. To deal with foreign affairs, he retained his predecessor's secretary of state, James G. Blaine, giving him for a time virtually a free hand in their management.

Blaine tampered with the War of the Pacific involving Chile, Peru, and Bolivia. Even though he favored Peru, he offered his good offices to seek an end to the fighting. He could not, however, shake off his partiality. In the president's name, he threatened to break off diplomatic relations with Chile if it did not accept his offer and even implied forceful American intervention.

The next secretary of state, Frederick Frelinghuysen, smelled corruption in a deal that allegedly linked Blaine, the State Department, and American financiers to the pressure on Chile. The new secretary believed "we were on the highway to war for the benefit of about as nasty a set of people as ever gathered about a Washington Department."[4] Arthur had no intention of facing either more scandal or war. So, as Frelinghuysen advised, he reversed Blaine's vigorous policy toward Chile. This change mollified Chile, which won the war. As for Arthur, he governed in the Whig pattern, did not himself cope with any significant foreign policy crisis, and hence as president exhibited no overt macho arrogance against foreigners.

Grover Cleveland

GROVER Cleveland, a Democrat and former governor of New York, came to the presidency with limited intellectual concerns, no discernible interest in foreign affairs, and no desire to become a warrior chieftain. His foremost biographer claims he possessed a deep sense of pride in himself, a drive for personal power, and "a virility or energy which enabled him to impose his qualities upon others in any crisis." Cleveland believed in a strict interpretation of the Constitution. He promised to take "a cautious appreciation of those functions" that the Constitution and the laws had "especially assigned to the executive branch." Despite his limited conception of the presidency, he regarded it as superior to any executive office in the world, implying "it had divine sanction." In office, he bridled at legislative restraints, claiming at times an executive independence similar to that of Andrew Jackson. Like him, Cleveland perceived the president as responsible directly to the electorate, a kind of "people's tribune."[5]

In his first term, Cleveland had to deal with a number of complex foreign policy issues such as treaty rights for a transisthmian canal, fishing privileges in the North Atlantic, and seal hunting in the Bering Sea. Only the canal problem prompted him to use military force.

The difficulties in Colombia's province of Panama began in April 1885 when rebels damaged United States property and temporarily interrupted operation of the railroad that traversed the isthmus. Cleveland reacted with surprising toughness. On the basis of his own interpretation of a treaty with Nueva Granada (Colombia's former name), which gave the United States transit rights across the isthmus, he landed more than twelve hundred marines backed with artillery to assure the unencumbered use of the transit and to enforce civilization on the people of Panama. Thus, even though he had intervened in "a purely domestic broil" that did not menace the United States, he consciously conveyed the impression that the rebels threatened a vital American interest.

Jingoes, such as journalist Irving King, hailed the operation, reporting "that the eagle screams from Colón to Panama, and the United States has asserted itself with a vigor that has not been equaled since the Stars and Stripes flaunted in the halls of Montezuma." King exaggerated but the American occupiers joined Colombian officials in crushing the uprising. Cleveland then withdrew the marines from Panama. The chauvinists who had commended him and wanted him to seize the isthmus now felt betrayed. Their praise turned to scorn. A leading Republican senator remarked that there had "never been a weaker or more puerile act."[6] As for Panama's residents and even Colombian officials, they hated the marines, condemned the brief occupation as an invasion, and regarded Cleveland as a bullying imperialist.

Despite the furor Cleveland's armed intervention had bred, he thrust himself also into a messy situation in Samoa. Earlier, Germany, the United States, and Great Britain, in treaties with Samoan monarchs, had each obtained the right to construct a naval base in the archipelago. Beginning in 1887 Germany, the country with the most extensive interests in Samoa, launched a campaign to obtain dominance, if not exclusive control, of the islands. The effort ran into trouble because indigenous Samoans put up a stiff resistance and the United States and Britain opposed the German plan. American journalists and others who followed developments in the archipelago demanded vigorous action against the Germans, even alluding at times to war.

Believing that by treaty the United States had an obligation to safeguard Samoa's independence, Cleveland responded positively to the anti-German agitation. "I have insisted," he explained in requesting congressional authority to police the situation, "that the autonomy and independence of Samoa should be scrupulously preserved."[7] When the legislators appropriated funds for the protection of American lives and property, he sent three warships to the islands. In the harbor of Apia, as though poised for war, they faced German and British naval units. When Otto von Bismarck, the German chancellor, gave up the challenge to Samoan independence, the immediate crisis passed. Cleveland cooled off but the confrontation at Apia continued.

In 1886 the president had also urged the Senate to approve the renewal of a nine-year-old reciprocity treaty with the Hawaiian monarchy that Secretary of State Thomas F. Bayard had negotiated. Its key amendment permitted the United States to establish a naval base at Pearl Harbor. On January 20, 1887, the Senate approved it. Two years later, Hawaii's white ruling elite offered to convert the kingdom to a United States protectorate. Cleveland did not bite, because he opposed anything closer than a commercial connection unless the Hawaiian people desired more. Hence, the question of annexation carried over into the administration of Benjamin Harrison, a successful Indiana lawyer and the grandson of former president William Henry Harrison.

Benjamin Harrison

ACCORDING to reputation, Benjamin Harrison was one of the few men who came to the presidency undriven by ambition or a compulsion to amass power. He believed that circumstances had thrust the responsibilities of high office upon him. He appeared willing, therefore, to accept congressional preeminence in many policy areas. He also had no preconceptions about foreign affairs but stated in his inaugural he would promote peace, protect the personal and commercial rights of Americans domiciled abroad, and promote a deeper patriotism.

Harrison's first encounter in international politics began with the situation in Samoa where he demonstrated both firmness and restraint. On March 16, 1889, less than two weeks after he assumed office, a tidal wave struck the islands, destroying the American and German ships stationed there and taking one hundred lives. This disaster had a sobering effect on the warlike attitudes of the Western rivals. On April 29 their diplomats met in Berlin with the intent of avoiding possible hostilities over the distant islands. Before departing in June, they established a three-power protectorate over the Samoans, the first such international venture for the United States. It did not work well. So, throughout the remainder of his term, Harrison himself, rather than his secretary of state, James G. Blaine, resisted German and British efforts to obtain control of the archipelago.

In the year following the Samoa confrontation, Harrison's reputed disdain for the exercise of power changed (or contemporaries had misperceived his true feelings on the matter). Biographers indicate that having tasted executive power, he became entranced with it. As with others who came to the presidency with modest ambition and changed, he discovered he could exercise that power most decisively in dealing with foreign affairs. Accordingly, he adopted an "aggressive foreign policy" and implemented it with macho conduct. A few analysts argue that he chose to act tough largely out of "political considerations," meaning he wanted to appear strong to delegates in the approaching 1890 Republican convention and later to voters in the presidential election.[8] Other writers maintain that in carrying out policies he considered important, he acted with militancy out of personal conviction.

Regardless of the reason for Harrison's cocksure attitude toward foreign problems, his bellicosity first became apparent in a minor crisis with Italy. The trouble flared up when a jury in New Orleans on March 13, 1891, acquitted or refused to convict nine Italians accused of murdering a well-liked superintendent of police. The next morning, out of a feeling that justice had miscarried and with inflamed ethnic emotion, a mob of some seven thousand people descended on the parish jail. While the authorities stood by and did nothing, the vigilantes lynched eleven of the Italians and Italian Americans housed there.

Most people condoned the bloodletting, but it enraged Italians and their American kin. Under widespread pressure to do something, the Italian government protested, demanded punishment of the killers, and asked compensation for the victims' families. When Harrison and Blaine reacted haughtily, Italy severed full diplomatic relations. Many Americans believed that the modern Italian fleet might attack coastal cities. The more emotional nationalists welcomed the possibility of war. The White House even received an offer from one of them to raise a company of soldiers "to invade Rome, disperse the Mafia, and plant the stars and stripes on the dome of St. Peter's."[9]

For a time Harrison took a hard line in the dispute, stating in September, for instance, that he would not negotiate while Italy had no minister in Washington. Then after talk of war subsided and tempers cooled, the two governments worked out an amicable solution. In December the president characterized the slaughter "as a most deplorable and discreditable incident" and offered an apology and an indemnity. A mollified Italian government restored normal diplomatic relations. Militant legislators, however, resented the indemnity. So, on his own, Harrison bypassed Congress and paid the indemnity out of the State Department's emergency fund. Since legislators were already rankled by his behavior, they perceived this act as usurping their prerogative. It jolted many of them into realizing that even in an era of presumed legislative ascendance, the struggle between Congress and strong-willed presidents for control of foreign policy remained unresolved.

Harrison showed firmer will and less restraint in a concurrent crisis with Chile. The confrontation followed the visit of the USS *Baltimore*, a warship commanded by Captain Winfield Scott Schley, to Valparaíso on October 16, 1891, a time of strained relations with Chile. When sailors on shore leave got into a saloon brawl with Chilean seamen and civilians over women, a mob killed two of the Americans and wounded others. Accepting fully Schley's interpretation of the incident, which placed the blame on Chilean authorities, Harrison demanded an apology and reparations.

When Blaine, who now wished to "make a friend of Chile—if that is possible," tried in a cabinet meeting to downplay the incident, he angered the president. Gesticulating emphatically, Harrison said pointedly, "Mr. Secretary, that insult was to the uniform of the United States sailors." As the Chilean government moved slowly to make amends, Harrison impatiently took direct command of the negotiations, substituting his own harsher words for those of the State Department. Close observers reported "there is not an official in the government who doesn't regard war as imminent and not a few who believe it inevitable." A British diplomat in Washington perceived Blaine as preventing "war with Chile so far" but noted also that "the President and the Navy are bent on it."[10]

Two days later, on January 21, 1892, Harrison served Chile with an ultimatum threatening to terminate diplomatic relations and implying the use of force. After waiting several days for a reply, he spent a whole day on a war message sent to Congress. Stating that "our sailors were assaulted, beaten, stabbed, and killed" because of Chilean hostility to the United States, he urged the legislators to help enforce his demands. "If the dignity as well as the prestige and influence of the United States are not to be wholly satisfied," he warned, "we must protect those who in foreign ports display the flag or wear the colors of this Government."[11]

Even though earlier Harrison had been willing apparently to defer to the legislature on most matters, in this instance he presented the ultimatum in a manner that preempted Congress's authority to choose between war or peace. It had to react to "events already shaped for war." Thus, in the view of later critical analysts, he curtailed the legislative branch's war power, "as decisively as if he had unilaterally committed troops in the field." He behaved in this manner, another writer maintains, out of "patriotism," an "excessive national chauvinism, ethnocentrism, and a romantic, gallant, sporting view of war."[12]

Staggered by Harrison's browbeating, Chile, with far less power than the United States, had no choice. It accepted every one of his demands and later paid an indemnity. Critics of the administration claim that the Chileans had apologized before the dispatch of the ultimatum, whereas its defenders insist the note of surrender and apology did not come until the following day. Chileans regarded the American stance as reprehensible, and London's *Spectator* remarked that "Anglo-Saxon bullying is apt to lack grace and finesse, as has been shown 100 times over in our own history."[13] In any case, Harrison received widespread approval for his macho behavior toward a weak potential foe. Still, the approbation he received on this issue, and for his general toughness in foreign confrontations, did not, as he had hoped, remain strong enough to carry him through the election of 1892. Domestic issues, such as the free coinage of silver, determined the outcome.

The loss of the election did not abate Harrison's willingness to use military force aggressively even as he prepared to leave the White House, this time to determine the fate of Hawaii. Earlier, after Cleveland turned down the Anglo-Hawaiians' proposal for a protectorate, native Hawaiians and others of color who wanted "Hawaii for Hawaiians" reacted with anti-American riots. In turn, in July 1889 Harrison landed seventy marines from a warship to restore order in Honolulu and then stationed a naval vessel in Hawaiian waters.

Open anti-Americanism subsided, but beneath the surface of everyday life it simmered until January 1891 when the king, Kalakaua, died and his strong-willed sister, Liliu Kamakaeha Liliuokalani, came to the throne. She sought to curb the power of the whites in the government and expressed hostility to the United States. Taking note of the situation, Harrison contended that "the necessity of maintaining and increasing our hold and influence in the Sandwich Islands is very apparent and very pressing."[14] Less than three months later, in his annual message to Congress he recommended the actual equipping of Pearl Harbor as a naval station. Concurrently Hawaii's white political leaders, mostly of American origin, formed an annexation club. They plotted revolution, really a coup, with

John L. Stevens, Harrison's expansionist minister in Honolulu, who assured them of American assistance in their endeavor.

As planned, on January 16, 1893, when the whites revolted, the commander of the cruiser USS *Boston*, stationed in Honolulu's harbor as per Harrison's order, landed 165 marines, ostensibly to protect American lives and property. The marines prevented the queen's government from quelling the uprising. This action permitted the rebels to force the queen to surrender power, to proclaim a new government of their own, and to send commissioners to Washington to negotiate annexation.

Lame-duck Harrison, whose policy had abetted the uprising, greeted them with open arms. On February 14 his new secretary of state, John W. Foster, signed a treaty of annexation. The next day the president submitted it to the Senate. He ignored the collusion between Stevens and the rebels and the role of the American marines, asserting disingenuously that "the overthrow of the monarchy was not in any way promoted by this Government." Even though he professed to being "not much of an annexationist," he also insisted "the influence and interest of the United States in the islands must be increased, not diminished."[15]

Despite the president's plea and his government's involvement in the use of force in Hawaii, on this matter he did not have his way. The Democrats in the Senate took advantage of his weak bargaining position because he had only two weeks remaining in his term. They blocked action on the treaty until he vacated the presidency. Even so, Harrison departed with a sense of pride in his virile conduct. In later years, though, he again modified his perspective, especially as it pertained to the presidential use of force abroad. He told a journalist, "We have no commission from God to police the world."[16] In all, the macho aspects of Harrison's foreign policy had fit the times.

In this last decade of the century when British, French, and other colonialists dominated much of the globe with victories in numerous small wars, many Americans embraced a rejuvenated sense of mission that led them to believe that their government, too, should colonize with the sword. Popular fascination with military power increased. Intellectuals, publicists, politicians, and others who had access to presidents and their advisers praised war and the policing of lesser peoples as a positive good. "War," Admiral Stephen B. Luce wrote, "is one of the great agencies by which human progress is effected." In another instance, Admiral Alfred Thayer Mahan maintained that Americans could thwart foreign dangers by honing their "masculine combative virtues."[17]

Grover Cleveland Again

CLEVELAND took over the presidency again in this ambiance of bellicosity. On March 9, 1893, five days after his second inaugural, he recalled the Hawaiian treaty from the Senate. Nine months later, after sending a special commissioner to Honolulu to investigate the sources of the revolution, for personal and moral reasons he refused to carry out the annexation. He concluded that the only "honorable course . . . was to undo the wrong that had been done by those representing us and to restore as far as practicable the status existing at the time of our forcible intervention." He also wanted "the *people* of the islands instead of the *Provisional Government*" to determine policy but he did not attempt to bring this about by restoring the queen to power.[18] A restoration would require military force that he would not attempt "without the authority of Congress." Moreover, neither Congress nor the public would countenance use of the military against the now well-established government of white men that on July 4, 1894, declared Hawaii a republic.

In contrast, in a dispute involving the boundary between British Guiana and Venezuela, Cleveland took unilateral actions with a potential for war. He stewed over this distant quarrel for almost two years, largely because of domestic pressures to do something about it. Much of the press denounced Britain for supposedly violating the Monroe Doctrine, an attitude that influenced Congress. In January 1895 it passed a resolution urging Britain and Venezuela to arbitrate. Having become convinced that the British, under the guise of boundary claims, sought unjustifiably to expand their colony's territory with the aim of obtaining control of the mouth of the Orinoco River, Cleveland signed it. He maintained duty compelled him to defend the doctrine and, by inference, to assume the role of an international policeman.

Therefore, at the president's behest and with his crucial participation, Secretary of State Richard Olney warned the British on July 20 that their quarrel with Venezuela involved both the honor and interests of the United States and warranted its intervention. "Today," he wrote, "the United States is practically sovereign on this continent, and its fiat is law upon the subjects to which it confines its interposition." He demanded that Britain submit the boundary question to arbitration. The president, who later dubbed the note Olney's "twenty-inch gun," regarded it as "the best thing of the kind I ever read."[19]

Understandably, the British took offense at the note, denied the Monroe

Doctrine had any standing in international law or relevance to the boundary dispute, and refused arbitration. Infuriated, the president on December 17 told Congress he would appoint a commission to run the boundary even at the risk of hostilities with the British and asked funds for the undertaking. Indicating the possible use of force, he declared he would not submit supinely "to wrong and injustice and the consequent loss of national self-respect and honor." Twelve days later, he professed, "We do not threaten nor invite war because [Britain] refuses" but he did not retreat from his position.[20]

The Senate responded to the message with "the most spontaneous demonstration" in the memory of living members while the House, much of the press, and the public cheered Cleveland's virile stance, or "call to arms," with similar enthusiasm.[21] Critics, however, condemned him for joining the jingoes. Fortunately, the British backed down. Faced with troubles with Boers in South Africa and a hostile Germany, they wanted no war with the United States over far less vital issues in South America. When tempers cooled, the adversaries turned to negotiations that allowed Britain to retain dignity and Cleveland to attain his goal of settling the boundary dispute through arbitration.

Historians explain Cleveland's saber rattling, which risked war over a foreign quarrel posing no threat to the United States or to its vital interests, with various interpretations. Some contend the "crisis existed independently of the action of the President," that he wished to appease "a new spirit of manifest destiny," or that he sought to advance the nation's economic interests and strengthen its strategic position in the hemisphere. Others maintain he wanted to enhance his political stature by shifting public attention away from domestic troubles, or that he acted tough because he had his eye on "the approaching Presidential election."[22]

These appraisals slight the personal equation. Politicians, journalists, and other influential groups had long attacked him for being timorous in not standing up to the British. In part to overcome this image as well as the charge of being pro-British, he rashly hovered on the brink of war. With this behavior he identified his judgment with righteousness and national honor while portraying the stance of his opponent as immoral, a common ethnocentrism in macho conduct.

Cleveland demonstrated similar characteristics minus bellicosity in dealing with an anticolonial insurrection in Cuba. It arose out of the discontent of Cubans who in February 1895, in an effort to overthrow Spanish rule, began destroying sugar plantations, mills, and tobacco farms, many of them owned by American investors. Public sentiment in the United States, fueled by propaganda, Anglo-Saxon racism, and economic and other concerns, favored the rebels. So did most of the Congress.

On the other hand, the president wanted to see the struggle end in a compromise that would retain Spain's presence in Cuba without involving the United States. He viewed those who clamored for the recognition of Cuban independence as warmongers eager to exploit a popular though wrongheaded cause for political gain at his expense. As in the Venezuela crisis, his political opponents tried to push him into a corner. They persuaded the Senate in February 1896 to resolve that he should use his friendly offices to secure Cuban independence. Two months later both houses repeated the request. Cleveland offered to mediate the conflict but Spain rejected the intervention. When the American consul general in Havana asked him to flaunt force by sending a warship to the city, he refused. "I do not want *now*," the president said, "anything of that kind made a convenient excuse for trouble with Spain."[23]

Still, many in Congress stepped up the pressure on Cleveland, demanding aggressive action to force Spain to relinquish her colony. "We have about decided to declare war against Spain over the Cuban question," legislators informed him. Cleveland responded, "There will be no war with Spain over Cuba while I am President." When one of them retorted angrily that Congress had the authority to declare war, he countered that the Constitution also made him commander in chief. As such, he said, "I will not mobilize the army." We could purchase Cuba for $100 million, he added, while "a war will cost vastly more. . . . It would be an outrage to declare war."[24] Nonetheless, in his last annual message he warned Spain if she did not "end the contest" in Cuba the United States could intervene in the role of sheriff. In this instance, Cleveland's individualistic perception of presidential authority produced a standoff with Congress that lasted until he left office.

As in his other foreign confrontations, Cleveland based his Cuban policy on his own temperament, judgment, psychology, and view of morality. In all, he perceived himself as the fearless executive armed to meet any crisis. Republican cartoonists frequently displayed him in the toga of a Roman emperor, suggesting he had gone too far in his use of presidential power. Admirers of strong leadership, however, counter with praise. They argue he belies the perception of Gilded Age executives as weak. He demonstrated strength, they contend, by expanding "the presidential role," primarily through "extracting it from close congressional control."[25]

William McKinley

AS with Cleveland, the reputation of William McKinley, in the matter of his strength or weakness in the conduct of foreign affairs, has fluctuated. Historians depict him as both passive and dominant. For years, most who wrote about him agreed with the assessment of his contemporaries. They pictured him as an amiable, church-going Republican, known often as the Christian Statesman, who had evolved into a skilled politician with a focus always on domestic issues. He retained that outlook when he became president. The conventional assessors point out he also brought with him a respect for congressional authority and a view of the office circumscribed more by its limitations than its power.

In the inaugural, as had become a kind of ritual on this occasion, McKinley professed love for peace along with a commitment to "a firm and dignified foreign policy." He declared also, "We want no wars of conquest; we must avoid the temptation of territorial aggression. War should never be entered upon until every agency of peace has failed; peace is preferable to war in almost every contingency."[26] Soon, though, these questions of war and peace pressed upon him and came to dominate his presidency.

Although McKinley opposed intervention in Cuba, pressure from the hawks in his own party compelled him promptly to take up the problem of strained relations with Spain. At the end of the year he told Congress that his most important foreign relations problem was the Cuban insurrection. He urged Spain to declare Cuba free. She resisted but in January 1898 conceded some autonomy. Still, the tension remained and then intensified because of several incidents.

On February 9 the New York *Journal* published a filched personal letter of Enrique Dupuy de Lôme, the Spanish minister in Washington. It painted McKinley as "weak and a bidder for the admiration of the crowd, besides being a would-be politician who tries to leave a door open behind himself while keeping on good terms with the jingoes of his party."[27] Six days later the American battleship *Maine*, ostensibly on a goodwill mission to Havana, blew up in the harbor, killing 266 of the crew.

The president stated that an investigation of the incident indicated an exterior explosion had caused the destruction. He thus implied the Spaniards had done it. Even though lacking proof, much of the public, whose anti-Hispanic sentiment had been fanned by yellow journalism, took the cue and immediately blamed Spain. Later inquiry, however, indicated the blast came from an internal source, a discovery that exonerated the Spaniards but was unknown to the Americans at that time. Many of them demanded military action. McKinley refused to rush into hostilities, explaining, "I am doing everything possible to prevent war." Jingoes and much of the vocal public, which demanded executive bellicosity, questioned his manhood and fitness for the presidency. Editorialists claimed "The people need a man at the helm" or that they wanted a "declaration of American virility." In theaters crowds hissed McKinley's name and in city streets they burned his effigy. Reflecting a similar impatience, Theodore Roosevelt, the bellicose vice president, referred to his chief as "that white livered cur."[28]

Within the next few weeks, McKinley accepted what he had come to regard as the inevitability of war unless Spain gave up Cuba. He feared that with the report of the investigating committee on the *Maine* explosion, he could not prevent Congress from opting for war over his head. On March 20 Secretary of State William R. Day demanded that Spain make peace in Cuba and offer a full reparation for the *Maine*. Seven days later the president served Spain with an ultimatum calling for an immediate armistice. On April 9 Spain suspended hostilities and the American minister in Madrid, Stewart L. Woodford, wrote, "I hope that nothing will now be done to humiliate Spain as I am satisfied that the present Government is going and is loyally ready to go as fast and as far as it can. With your power of action sufficiently free, you will win the fight on your own terms."[29]

Having already asked Congress for discretionary power to use the armed forces, McKinley rejected this advice. Two days later, in what many have called his war message, he told Congress that the situation in Cuba was intolerable. He declared "the forcible intervention of the United States as a neutral" justifiable on rational grounds. "In the name of humanity, in the name of civilization, in behalf of endangered American interests, which give us the right . . . to act," he proclaimed, "the war in Cuba must stop." Then he requested authority to "use the military and naval forces" to terminate it.[30]

Republicans eager for war criticized him for being evasive because he did not insist on immediate armed intervention. On the other hand, Democrats protested that he sought too much power. Senator Edmund W. Pettus of Alabama summarized the Democratic attitude by questioning why Congress should "give the President power to intervene and make war, if he sees fit, without declaring war at all."[31]

Regardless of this minority opposition, Congress in the next week debated not the why for war but the how. On April 19 it responded to the president with a joint resolution demanding that Spain withdraw from Cuba and grant it independence. That legislation also empowered the president to use the nation's entire land and naval forces to achieve that end. On the following day McKinley signed the resolution along with another ultimatum to Spain. She immediately severed diplomatic relations. The president ordered Cuban ports blockaded, thereby initiating hostilities. Spain declared war on April 24. The next day, Congress voted that a state of war had existed since the 21st, the date of the blockade.

Students of the decision for war and of the presidency divide sharply on McKinley's role. Those skeptical of his behavior, and others too, contend the United States could have achieved its goal of a free Cuba through diplomacy. Possibly, a senator explained, "the President could have worked out the business without war, but the current was too strong, the demagogues too numerous, and the fall elections too near." A later critic assessed McKinley's part in the war making as more decisive. In view of Spain's yielding to most of his demands, this writer asserts, the president asked for hostilities "when a cause for war no longer existed."[32] Revisionists go further. They ascribe to McKinley the critical role in the decision making. They portray him as a "strong man" who cut "through a muddle of inefficiency and divided counsels" to lead the nation through its self-created crisis and ensuing war.[33]

In contrast, those who characterize McKinley as a feeble executive argue that at first he "used all his talent, tact, and charm, to prevent war." Then he succumbed to pressure from jingoes, a rabid pro-war press, hysterical public sentiment, and a Congress that threatened to declare war over his head. So, unwillingly he headed the nation into "a war he did not want for a cause in which he did not believe" and that involved no vital American interest. A variation of this thesis states that this was a "popular war . . . forced upon a reluctant leadership by the people."[34]

The claim for presidential impotence presents a problem. Among contemporaries, McKinley had a reputation for having more influence with Congress than any previous president. Initially he also regarded presidential power as limited. If during the war crisis, as has often been maintained, he converted to a belief in the strong executive with a commitment to guarding its powers, why could he not persuade Congress to accept his concern over the war power? Why did he fear the possible humiliation of Congress exercising it independently? In later reflections McKinley provides at least a partial answer. He explains that the drive for war had a momentum of its own. Neither Congress nor the president could control it. He also characterized the "declaration of war against Spain" as "an act which has been and will always be the greatest grief of my life. I never wanted to go to war with Spain."[35] Some historians take these words at face value because they believe, as he did, that he could not have prevented war.

This kind of thinking hardly fits the model of a strong executive. It suggests McKinley accepted war in the passive mode. While he went along with popular and congressional sentiment, he also convinced himself of the propriety to use force because peaceful coercion had failed. In the revisionist perspective, therefore, "his decision for war followed logically from his own policies rather than from public or congressional pressure."[36] Thus, regardless of the depth of his reluctance to shed blood, he became part of the initiative that brought on war.

Thereafter, cloaking himself in ambiguous morality, the president shed his alleged passivity. He adopted the qualities of aggressive virility and personally participated in the military and diplomatic decisions of the war, which lasted slightly more than three months. Through executive action, he willingly took on the responsibility of policing another country's possession.

All the while, a hardly passive McKinley had moved decisively in using the power of his office to acquire Hawaii. A confrontation between the Hawaiian government and Japan gave urgency to this agenda. After the start of the Spanish-American War, the president picked up support for annexation by envisioning the Hawaiian Islands as an essential base for the Pacific fleet aimed at the Philippines. Still, he could not command a two-thirds majority in the Senate for approval of the acquisition. He slipped by this obstacle by pressing ahead to achieve incorporation with a joint congressional resolution. On June 16 he submitted a treaty of annexation to the Senate, stating, "annexation is not a change, it is consummation."[37] Regardless, approval bogged down in a bruising debate over imperialism.

The specter of Japan hovered over the deliberations because it protested the proposed acquisition on the grounds that the rights of its subjects in the islands, who made up a quarter of the population, must be protected. To back up its position, Tokyo sent a cruiser to Honolulu. Newspapers then came alive with anti-Japanese editorials, warning for instance, "It is Japan that will seize the islands if we do not."[38] The president ordered the navy to take Hawaii by force if the Japanese made threatening moves. Finally, on July 7, after House approval, the Senate passed the resolution of annexation by a simple majority vote. McKinley then governed Hawaii through a presidential commission.

Shortly after, on August 12, a beaten Spain agreed to an armistice to be followed by a peace treaty negotiated in Paris. McKinley now had to decide the terms, including further overseas acquisitions. Although he desired Hawaii, he did not at first want to annex the Philippines. Soon, though, he discovered reasons for changing his mind. In doing so, he discounted pressure from anti-imperialist leaders who decried territorial expansion as "uncalled for, totally foreign to our system of government, not within our duty," and as probably calamitous for the nation. In September the *Literary Digest* published a nationwide poll of 192 newspaper editors. A solid majority favored taking the islands.

Sensitive to what he perceived as popular sentiment, McKinley told a friend, "You and I don't want the Philippines, but it is no use disguising the fact that an overwhelming majority of the people do." His secretary of war, Elihu Root, believed "the whole country would have risen in indignant protest against any President who dared not do it."[39] So, even though Filipinos had made clear their determination to fight for independence, on October 25, two weeks before election day, McKinley officially announced his decision to take over all of the Philippine archipelago.

On December 10 the peacemakers in Paris concluded their work. They granted Cuba independence and allotted the Philippines, Puerto Rico, and Guam to the United States. The president now spoke of the Filipinos as unfit for self-government and as prone to anarchy and misrule. Accordingly, on December 21 he prepared instructions for a formal announcement in Manila of the annexation and for extending military government throughout the islands. He also proclaimed he would educate, uplift, civilize, and Christianize Filipinos through a program of benevolent assimilation. When Filipino nationalists who had expected independence learned of McKinley's mailed-fist attitude, combined with pious condescension, their leader, Emilio Aguinaldo, protested. They proclaimed an independent Philippine republic. Skirmishing followed, with war beginning on February 4, 1899, two days before the Senate approved the peace treaty with Spain.

McKinley declared "the first blow was struck by the inhabitants" and there would be "no useless parley" with them. In substance, though, his determination that "we must keep all we get; when the war is over we must keep what we want," initiated the conflict.[40] As for the Filipinos' demand to rule themselves in their own land, he dismissed it outright. He insisted the liberator would not submit important questions concerning liberty and government to the liberated while they were shooting down their rescuers. With this attitude, he deployed on his own more troops, directed the hostilities, and defended the American role.

Congress declared no war in the Philippines but it backed the president in the hostilities that escalated into protracted conflict marked by atrocities on both sides. At this time the president exercised full authority over the military and the governance of the islands. Anti-imperialists and others attacked his hypocrisy in trying to justify this war as legitimate police action. Some of them asked, "How can a president of the great republic be blind to the truth that freedom is the same, that liberty is as dear and that self-government is as much a right in the Philippines as in the United States?" At his will, others pointed out, "we are laying waste the country with fire and sword, burning villages and slaughtering the inhabitants, because they will not submit to our rule."[41]

In June 1900, while this war still raged, McKinley again exerted his will in another military venture. Under his own interpretation of the war power, he sent five thousand troops to China on the now well-established principle of protecting American lives and property—in this instance, against assaults by Boxer rebels. He intervened also for political purposes, essentially to demonstrate virile leadership in foreign relations in an election year. American troops joined an international expeditionary force made up of troops from Britain, Russia, Germany, France, and Japan. They battled for more than two months, besieged Peking, captured it on August 16, and sacked it. The Chinese signed a treaty of surrender and paid huge indemnities.

The president argued he had acted purely defensively and had not engaged in war against the Chinese nation even though its government had declared war against the United States. Both critics and supporters of this intervention viewed it as warfare. The newspaper mogul William Randolph Hearst, a supporter, saw it as a "war—bloody, desperate war—that confronts us in China," a "death struggle with innumerable murderous fanatics." The critical Philadelphia *Times* termed the intervention itself "an absolute declaration of war by the executive without the authority or knowledge of Congress, and it is without excuse because it is not necessary." The vice president, however, maintained that the administration had simply done its part in "a bit of international police duty."[42]

A year later a federal court held that in China a condition of war existed. Even though McKinley had not consulted Congress in this armed venture, it did not object. This intervention had as a precedent Lincoln's collaboration in the international policing of Japan but the scale of McKinley's armed force—one warship—and the cooperation with other powers were much greater. This expedition also initiated a shift in the way presidents deployed troops overseas. Previously they had committed policing forces mainly against nongovernment groups and minor political entities. Following McKinley's example, they had precedent for sending them also against established sovereign states.

In the meantime, in the campaign for the presidency in November 1900, Democrats tried to make imperialism the paramount issue. They failed. McKinley won the election with the largest popular plurality any candidate had yet polled. Many supporters, and historians too, claimed therefore that imperialism had received a ringing endorsement. Actually, the election did not pivot on imperialism or any other single issue, but McKinley's military activism did contribute to his victory. As he surmised from his own limited soundings of public sentiment, Americans as a whole approved his use of force whether in Cuba, the Philippines, or China. Overlooking his earlier perceived passive attitude, many identified his virile posturing with patriotism and responded positively to the campaign slogan "Stand by the President."[43]

All the while the reputedly take-charge Congress, which had regarded McKinley as weak in dealing with Spain, approved of his toughness against the Japanese, Filipinos, and Chinese. Members seemed to consider such behavior proper in a president, or they simply did not want to resist his policing activities. In any case, regardless of precisely why, in matters of war and peace Congress allowed McKinley to broaden executive power.

Ironically, for years few historians paid attention to McKinley's unilateral employment of force or to his belligerent qualities. They focused instead on his passive period, on his repeated professions of hating war, and lumped him with the alleged weakling executives of the Gilded Age. Recent biographers, usually as admirers of the strong presidency, view him differently. They play up what they perceive as his in-command, virile qualities.

These revisionists claim that, as had Polk and Lincoln, McKinley stretched executive reach by leaving Congress with little room to counter his actions. They perceive his military activism as a creative use of authority as commander in chief and as a major virtue of his presidency. They paint him as a decisive, "courageous, and principled" executive who expertly maneuvered the public and Congress into accepting the "primacy of the President in foreign affairs." In particular, they praise him for asserting executive power in external affairs during a time of purported congressional ascendancy. This they regard as a major accomplishment of his presidency.

Although the revisionist appraisal exaggerates the quality of McKinley's leadership, certainly, after he took the plunge into war with Spain the passive image ceased to fit him. Thereafter, as though intoxicated by the military power at his disposal, he proved himself tough and energetic, if not thoroughly macho.

Theodore Roosevelt

FOLLOWING McKinley's assassination on September 6, 1901, Theodore Roosevelt, who took over the White House, immediately promised to continue his predecessor's policies and did so. Scholars as well as popular writers credit him also with transforming the presidency by bringing to it remarkable popularity, pugnacity, dynamic leadership, and empowerment. As we have seen, in the conduct of foreign relations the growth in executive power, especially as evident through the combative impulse, had never really ceased. In matters touching on military force and foreign policy, therefore, Roosevelt's coming marked a significant incremental change rather than an abrupt transition from impotence to strength.

Roosevelt's assertive personality, his words, his love of the international spotlight, his appetite for power, and his infatuation with war—all contributed to his reputation as a strong executive. Biographers usually play down his compulsive activism, contending he seldom acted without deliberation. A contemporary, though, recalled him as "the most impulsive human being I ever knew." Others remember that "he craved the excitements of war," that he gushed "over war as the ideal condition of human society." He perceived it, especially when against alleged savages and lesser peoples, as a true test of virility. Like most presidents, he also often expressed a desire for peace. In all, his rhetoric, which often accented the need for "manful behavior" even for nations, along with his faith in "stern and virile virtues which move men of stout heart and strong hand," smacked of the macho impulse. Frequently, so did his deeds.[44]

These characteristics can be seen in Roosevelt's decision to continue the war in the Philippines while evading the nettlesome question of the morality of employing massive force against a weak people who sought mainly to be free of alien overlords. In his first annual message to Congress he cautioned that departure from the islands would be followed by "murderous anarchy" because, like McKinley, he regarded Filipinos "unfit" for independence, demeaned their struggle as "an affair of local banditti and marauders," and promised "the sternest measures with the Filipinos who follow the path of the insurrecto and the ladrone." A year later the president justified this military campaign as part of a mission to keep "barbarous and semi-barbarous peoples" in line, "a necessary international police duty which must be performed for the sake of the welfare of mankind."[45] Knowledgeable Filipinos correctly disputed this unwarranted assumption of their being unfit to govern themselves, pointing out they had long lived on their own in civilized societies.

Roosevelt also had to deal with a challenge from Nelson A. Miles, the commanding general of the army. Miles, who revealed that American troops had inflicted "cruelties and barbarities" on Filipinos, announced he would terminate these acts, and offered to end the warfare through personal negotiations with Filipino nationalists. In March 1902, when the president rejected the proposal, the general leaked it to the press. Roosevelt wanted to sack him for this challenge to executive authority but held back because of political considerations. Miles had a following among potent veteran groups the president did not wish to antagonize.

Roosevelt did, however, go out of his way to praise the American soldiers in the Philippines who, in his purple rhetoric, fought for "the triumph of civilization over forces which stand for the black chaos of savagery and barbarism." He also defended the soldiers' conduct, declaring that "every guilty act committed by one of our troops" was matched by "a hundred acts of far greater atrocity" perpetrated by "the hostile natives upon our troops."[46] On July 4, when he hastily declared the conflict over, he again exaggerated in the macho manner, calling it the most glorious war in the nation's history. A short time later a close friend would admit privately that it "has cost us a great a deal of money; and any benefits which have resulted from it to this country, are as yet, imperceptible to the naked eye." Such views had little impact on the president. In the following month he reiterated old misconceptions, stating that "wars with uncivilized powers are largely mere matters of international police duty" as well as his praise for the "courage," the "kind-heartedness, and humanity of our troops."[47]

Despite Roosevelt's assurance at this time that the war had entirely ceased, the problems and costs of police duty did not stop. American forces had reduced Filipinos to a sporadic guerrilla resistance but many of them—especially Moros or Muslims in the south—continued the fight for several more years. The casualties in these hostilities were lopsided—4,200 Americans dead and 2,800 wounded, more than 18,000 Filipino military and well over 100,000 civilians dead.[48] These were the results of an essentially presidential war Roosevelt viewed as a triumph.

Roosevelt also claimed success for unilateral bellicosity in dealing with an international crisis revolving around Venezuela. In 1902 Cipriano Castro, the country's dictator, defaulted on debts owed to major European powers. As usual in such cases at the time, on December 9 Germany, Britain, and later Italy resorted to force to collect the debts. Their warships sank part of Venezuela's navy and blockaded her major ports. In January 1903 German warships alone bombarded two Venezuelan cities.

Roosevelt and others assumed Germany intended to seize Venezuelan territory in defiance of the Monroe Doctrine. He contended he resolved the crisis with a personal threat of force. He claimed to have told the German government he had ordered the Caribbean fleet under Admiral George Dewey to move against its naval units in Venezuelan waters unless it accepted a solution to the confrontation through arbitration. Faced with this ultimatum, Germany backed down. No documentary evidence supports Roosevelt's assertion. Regardless, in later years, he pointed to this alleged macho conduct as an example of how he produced foreign policy achievements.

We can see a better documented example of Roosevelt's macho impulse in his dealing with Colombia when its senate on August 12, 1903, refused to ratify a treaty giving the United States a right of way for a canal through the Isthmus of Panama. Enraged by the rebuff, he dismissed the Colombians as a "lot of jack rabbits," "inefficient bandits," and "would-be blackmailers" who he would not allow to obstruct a "future highway of civilization." In the draft of a message to Congress, he recommended taking possession of the isthmus without further palaver with Colombia and regardless of possible bloodshed. He hesitated, apparently, because "as yet the people of the United States are not willing to take the ground of building a canal by force."[49] Soon, other tactics made the sending of his request to Congress for a direct assault unnecessary.

The president also considered the possibility of destabilizing the Colombian government but claimed to cast aside such underhanded means to foment a revolt against Bogotá. Privately, he encouraged revolution and said he would "be delighted if Panama were an independent State."[50] On November 3, three weeks later, a bizarre group of Panamanians rebelled against the connection with Colombia. As though in concert with this uprising, Roosevelt on his own authority had already ordered warships to Panama. On the day of the insurrection their marines landed to block Colombian efforts to suppress it. Three days later he recognized Panama as de facto independent. As had Cleveland in his policing eighteen years earlier, Roosevelt justified this intervention by force with a slanted interpretation of the 1846 treaty with Colombia to keep the transit open. On November 18 he concluded a treaty with Panama that gave the United States a perpetual grant to a canal zone ten miles wide and made the new country essentially Washington's protectorate.

Critics called this hardly disguised use of force sordid and a shameful usurpation of constitutional authority. "You have no right to take Colombia's land in the interest of civilization," Colorado Senator Henry M. Teller lectured. "That . . . is the robber's claim of might makes right."[51] Roosevelt defended his forceful tactics, declaring, for instance, that more than a half-century's experience demonstrated Colombia's utter inability to keep order on the isthmus. Only his intervention enabled her to preserve even a semblance of sovereignty. By this logic, he had to violate another country's sovereignty in order to protect it.

Nothing in international law justified Roosevelt's action. Admirers who overlook this aspect of his behavior praise him. They perceive "his Panama diplomacy as a symbol of presidential strength and a new American internationalism." Roosevelt himself repeatedly put a positive spin on the question of "whether or not I acted properly in getting the canal, but while the debate goes on the canal does too."[52] Throughout the rest of his life he remained unrepentant for his high-handed conduct.

Roosevelt employed similar big-stick tactics to keep other small countries of South America and the Caribbean in line. He acted "solely on the theory," he explained, "that it is our duty, when it becomes absolutely inevitable, to police these countries in the interest of order and civilization."[53] He alone defined the duty and the circumstance, as in Venezuela, Panama, and then in the Dominican Republic.

In November 1903, shortly after Roosevelt wrapped up the Panama affair, revolutionary violence rocked the island republic. In February insurgents fired on an American warship offshore from the city of Santo Domingo. The president ordered the commanding officer to protect American lives and property. The officer shelled rebel forces, landed marines, and patrolled the town's waterfront area. Roosevelt explained this unilateral intervention as the reluctant action of a policeman trying to bring order to a chaotic situation.

That summer, as the revolutionary violence continued, the Dominican government verged on default of its international debts. The more powerful debtors, among them Italy and Germany, threatened force to obtain payment. Roosevelt regarded this kind of debt collecting as a facade for an eventual takeover of the country. As he had stated several times in slightly different phraseology, he announced that among weaker nations "chronic wrong-doing, or an impotence which results in a general loosening of the ties of civilized society," may require "intervention by some civilized nation." In the Western Hemisphere it would be the United States because its Monroe Doctrine may force it "to the exercise of an international police power."[54] Thereafter, this concept, known as the Roosevelt Corollary to that doctrine, became the basis for a number of presidential interventions in the Caribbean area.

The turmoil in the Dominican Republic quickly led Roosevelt, as he saw fit, to become the first president to put teeth into the corollary. In February 1905 the Dominican government accepted a protocol that essentially allowed Americans to manage the debt situation. Congress objected. "The President has no more right and no more authority to bind the people of the United States by such an agreement," a senator maintained, "than I have as a member of this body."[55] Nonetheless, when the Senate rejected the agreement Roosevelt sent troops into the republic anyway, turning it into a protectorate. Finally, in February 1907, after he had negotiated a new treaty with the Dominicans, the Senate approved the intervention.

Earlier, in May 1902, Roosevelt had terminated an American occupation of Cuba. In the next few years bitter civil strife rocked the island nation. He expressed loathing for the thought of intervening but asserted, "We cannot permanently see Cuba a prey to misrule and anarchy." Then he fumed. "I am so angry with that infernal little Cuban republic," he wrote, "that I would like to wipe its people off the face of the earth."[56] He felt this way mainly because they had, in his judgment, misbehaved. In September 1906, therefore, at the request of the republic's president and under the authority of the Platt Amendment, he landed marines. With their bayonets he imposed a regime on the protectorate that exercised authority for three years.

As elsewhere in the Caribbean, Roosevelt had exercised force unilaterally to occupy a weak country that posed no fundamental threat to the United States. He justified this bypassing of Congress with the argument "that it is for the enormous interest of this Government to strengthen and give independence to the Executive in dealing with foreign powers."[57]

The president also employed threat to inject himself into the diplomacy of the Russo-Japanese War, ostensibly because he wanted to prevent possible European intervention. When the conflict broke out in 1904, he notified Germany and France that if they should intervene in support of Russia he would "promptly side with Japan and proceed to whatever length was necessary on her behalf."[58] At the same time, on his own word through Secretary of War William Howard Taft, he committed the country to an unofficial partnership in the Anglo-Japanese alliance. He assured the Japanese confidentially that in case of trouble they could expect help as though the United States were under treaty obligation. This attitude had an impact on the peacemaking in the following month in Portsmouth, New Hampshire, which he mediated and for which he received the Nobel Peace Prize.

Two years later, when relations with Japan had soured and American journalists, foreign leaders, and others spread rumors of war, Roosevelt alerted troops in the Philippines to prepare for a possible Japanese assault. In July 1907 he also ordered the entire battleship fleet to San Francisco. From there he sent it on a world cruise that would take it to Japan. He acted out of mixed motivation. First of all he wanted to impress the Japanese with his own toughness and with American power, asserting later that the time had come "for a show down." He remarked also that the fleet's cruise "was the best example that I know of, 'of speaking softly and carrying a big stick.'"[59] In addition, he wished to stimulate popular enthusiasm for maintaining an expensive navy as well to help his party in forthcoming elections. He slighted the potential of this muscle-flexing for provoking war.

This conduct accorded with Roosevelt's personal conception of executive power. With variation on a theme expressed by John Adams and other earlier thinkers on American government, he believed "there inheres in the Presidency more power than in any office in any great republic or constitutional monarchy in modern times." He saw no harm "from the concentration of powers in one man's hands." He boasted he had "*been* President most emphatically," had "used every ounce of power there was in the office," and cared not a rap for critics who spoke of his usurpation of power. In addition, he admitted to having acted consciously to "establish a precedent for strength in the executive," notably in "external affairs," because, he stated, "I believe in a strong executive; I believe in power."[60]

A month or so before leaving the White House, while deflating some of former secretary of state John Hay's pretensions, Roosevelt again summed up his own macho outlook. "The biggest matters . . . , such as the Portsmouth peace, the acquisition of Panama, and sending the fleet around the world," he asserted, "I managed without consultation with anyone; for when a matter is of capital importance, it is well to have it handled by one man only."[61]

This attitude fit comfortably within the concept derived from Lincoln's extraordinary use of executive power that Roosevelt adopted as his own—the stewardship theory of the presidency. It claimed "that the executive power was limited only by specific restrictions and prohibitions appearing in the Constitution or imposed by Congress under its constitutional powers." Acting on this expansive view, he "did and caused to be done many things not previously done by the President."[62] As constitutional scholars point out, this theory made every executive officer accountable, in effect, to an elective monarch.

While Roosevelt gloried in the macho impulse as much and probably more than most presidents, it did not in his case contribute to bringing the nation into a major war. It expressed itself mainly in small conflicts or police actions in the Philippines and the Caribbean that the interested public applauded. Critics maintain, though, that he had a grander design, the "conception of America as a global policeman."[63]

William Howard Taft

ROOSEVELT decided upon and virtually drafted his successor, his secretary of war and friend William Howard Taft, in what political scientists have deemed a forced succession to the presidency. Although Taft, a jurist from Ohio, disliked involvement in elective politics and had virtually no experience in them, he accepted the honor and ran for the office. He became the only elected executive up to this time who never really wanted to be president. In love with the law, he preferred a seat on the Supreme Court and was never happy in the White House. "The Presidency," he wrote in later years, "is not a place to be enjoyed by a sensitive man."[64]

Unlike Roosevelt and other presidents, Taft reputedly lacked a passion for power, macho pride, or visceral bellicosity. Students of his presidency portray him as governing in the Whig tradition as a constitutional executive or as an engineer concerned mainly with making government run smoothly. Some even dismiss him, wrongly, as a glorified clerk who lacked creativity in the exercise of executive authority. As had most other presidents upon assuming office, he spoke of peace becoming the driving force of his administration. He promised to make every effort to "avoid a resort to arms" but also to assert national "rights with a strong hand."[65] True enough, he settled various foreign policy disputes, such as over fishing rights in the Bering Sea, by pacific means and backed a campaign for world peace through arbitration treaties.

Despite his passive qualities, Taft, too, could not readily resist the blandishments of power, especially when dealing with foreign affairs. He acted in Asia and the Caribbean in support of dollar diplomacy, an interventionist policy he characterized in moral terms as substituting dollars for bullets. But he did use bullets, taking upon himself the role of an international policeman who did not hesitate to employ force as he deemed necessary. He directed his policing primarily against allegedly inferior peoples in Central America that his secretary of state Philander C. Knox and others in the administration denigrated as "dagos." In 1909, for instance, Taft ordered marines into Nicaragua to undermine the government of dictator José Santos Zelaya, which had executed two Americans fighting with antiadministration insurgents. The president wanted "to have the right to knock [the Central Americans'] heads together until they should maintain peace between them."[66] By August 1910 the pro-American rebels controlled the country.

Two years later, Taft again used muscle in Nicaragua. This time he sent several warships and landed more than twenty-five hundred marines and bluejackets. They fought to crush a liberal rebellion against the regime he had in effect installed earlier. In the process they occupied Léon and several interior cities and imposed political and economic control over the country. To secure what had become a de facto protectorate, the president stationed a legation guard of one hundred marines in Managua. They remained for the next two decades.

In July 1911, Taft also intervened militarily in Honduras. Furthermore, in anticipation of a revolt in Cuba in 1912, he massed four companies of marines at Guantánamo Bay. Throughout these interventions he claimed to employ force to protect American lives and property but not everywhere. He coerced only small, weak states that had no real means of resistance. In China, where his dollar diplomacy met determined opposition from great powers, he intervened primarily for economic reasons in support of the Open Door policy as he perceived it but did not resort to force.

In the case of Mexico, where in 1910 revolution erupted against the long-time dictator Porfirio Díaz, Taft at first reacted impulsively and then prudently. When revolutionaries raided American border communities for horses and other supplies, he quickly ordered, in his capacity as commander in chief and without consulting even his own State Department, twenty thousand troops to the Mexican border and naval vessels to San Diego and Guantánamo Bay. He did so, he maintained, to protect Americans should the need arise. As for Mexico, even though the reformer Francisco I. Madero in May 1911 overthrew Díaz, the turmoil continued. Altogether between 1910 and 1912, forty-seven Americans lost their lives in the fighting, mainly along the border.

Despite these losses, anti-American riots in Guadalajara, Mexico City, and elsewhere, and the urging from military advisers eager for combat to intervene, Taft in this instance refused to call out the military. When the press reported he would use force "on Mexican soil to protect American lives or property," he denied it. "I seriously doubt whether I have such authority under any circumstances," he explained as though oblivious to his previous interventions, "and if I had, I would not exercise it without express Congressional approval."[67]

In the following year, after more provocations from Mexicans and increased domestic goading to exercise force, the president still refused to violate Mexico's borders. "You know I am not going to cross that line," he told the State Department. "That is something for which congress will have to take responsibility. But I suppose it will do no harm to threaten them a little."[68] A bit later when leaders of his own party prompted him to take drastic action against Mexico to boost Republican fortunes in the elections of November 1912, he still refused, a stand he maintained "regardless of personal or party fortunes."[69]

Even when president Madero's chief general, Victoriano Huerta, deposed him and on February 22, 1913, as widely believed, murdered him, Taft would not intervene. In addition, despite pressure from the State Department and elsewhere, he refused to recognize Huerta's provisional government as legitimate. In opting for restraint, Taft demonstrated in this situation that a constitutional president could act as decisively as a conventionally strong executive—for peace, not war. He left the question of dealing with Huerta to his successor.

Although, as we have seen, Congress had invariably acquiesced when presidents deployed military forces in foreign lands, as had Taft in the Caribbean, some members objected to the practice. At this time, therefore, Senator Augustus O. Bacon of Georgia proposed that Congress deny appropriations for overseas policing without its consent except in emergencies. Elihu Root, who now held a seat in the Senate for New York, opposed the measure. "Congress could by law," he conceded, "forbid the troops' being sent out of the country." He contended, though, any Congress that blocked the commander in chief from aiding Americans abroad would hear from the people. He insisted "there is no law" and that there will never "be a law to prevent the Commander-in-Chief" from protecting citizens.[70] The Senate rejected the Bacon measure, thereby reinforcing, even during an administration of presumed passivity, the executive's assumed international police power.

As for Taft, in later years he defended his presidential style, mainly in response to Roosevelt's assertions in his *Autobiography*, especially the pretensions expressed in the stewardship theory. The two men had destroyed their friendship over their differences in the use of presidential power. Unlike Roosevelt, Taft perceived "the true view of the Executive functions" narrowly, or "that the President can exercise no power" unless granted by the Constitution or by an act of Congress. He has, Taft asserted, "no residium of power which he can exercise because it seems to him to be in the public interest."[71] Notwithstanding his espousal of this limited legal theory of the presidency and his announced distaste for the office, Taft did not regard himself as a passive executive. Although he lacked the hubris of Harrison or Roosevelt, for example, in his own way, on the international stage, he strove to be a vigorous leader. In doing so, he employed force frequently in the macho manner but without its usual accompanying fanfare.

CHAPTER 4

Iron-Fisted Morality

The President is at liberty, both in law and conscience, to be as big a man as he can.

Woodrow Wilson, 1907

Woodrow Wilson

NO one since John Quincy Adams had come to the presidency as well prepared for its duties through intellect, study, and administrative experience as the Virginian Woodrow Wilson. He had practiced law, taught history and government at the college level, served as president of Princeton University, and been governor of New Jersey.

Early in his career Wilson came to hold strong views on presidential power. In his first book, written at age twenty-eight, he asked, "Has the President any very great authority in matters of vital policy?" He answered no because at this time he regarded Congress as the predominant wielder of federal power. As did many of his contemporaries, he viewed the executive as the servant of Congress and hence even in foreign relations as "feeble and irresolute" or virtually insignificant. Nonetheless, Wilson "never doubted that for good government there must be a strong Executive," one who would initiate foreign policy and control its conduct.[1]

Later, in a book written four years before he ran for president, Wilson still saw the need for a muscular executive but reversed himself on how much power he could command in competition with Congress. At this time he declared that once the president won the admiration of the country, "no single force can withstand him, no combination of forces will easily overpower him." He "is at liberty, both in law and conscience, to be as big a man as he can. His capacity will set the limit." Wilson believed the president could exercise his greatest power in foreign affairs. The president's capacity to initiate policy, he contended, gives him "virtually the power to control them absolutely." In sum, Wilson maintained that the executive "office will be as big and as influential as the man who occupies it."[2]

Wilson brought this latter perspective, as well as a "conviction that his decisions were guided by God," to the White House. He told a supporter, for instance, that God ordained he should be president. Accordingly, in the great issues of war and peace, he perceived himself as among the select few statesmen of superior mind and will who could understand these matters better and judge them with greater wisdom than could the masses.

Views such as these, as well as close observation, led friends and associates to describe Wilson as steeped in self-esteem, intolerant of advice, addicted to dominating behavior, and as viewing "all opposition to be merely irritation." Also, in the words of a prominent biographer, he possessed a "tendency to feud" that supposedly "ran strongly in his blood."[3] While these assessments include exaggeration, as with most executives, Wilson did have a hunger for power that drove his presidency.

Despite this drive and Wilson's scholarly reflections on foreign policy, as with many of his predecessors, neither he nor his secretary of state, William Jennings Bryan, had practical or other significant experience in international relations. "It would be the irony of fate if my administration had to deal chiefly with foreign affairs," Wilson told a friend just before his inaugural.[4] In keeping with this attitude, in his address on that day he ignored foreign affairs. Immediately, however, he had to cope with a foreign question, whether or not to recognize the regime of Victoriano Huerta in Mexico. That problem brought out his pugnacity wrapped in moral sentiment. Biographers differ in describing this mixed quality. Some view it as part of a missionary impulse to do good while others perceive it as a compulsion to dominate. In any case, Wilson was convinced he could police lesser peoples for their own benefit and could "teach the South American republics to elect good men." If their rulers resisted his tutoring, he believed in good conscience he could apply force to uplift their peoples.[5]

In dealing with Huerta, the president initially took the morally correct position. "I will not recognize a government of butchers," he explained privately. He decided Huerta must go but for a while resisted demands from constituents to exercise vigorous force against the Mexican general. Instead, Wilson tried to undermine him indirectly by lifting an arms embargo against Mexico's quarreling factions so that Huerta's opponents could receive American guns. Later, Wilson threw his support behind another revolutionary leader, Venustiano Carranza, the governor of the northern state of Coahuila, whom he considered a good man but who spurned his backing. Carranza and his followers aimed to replace Huerta's regime on their own with a constitutional government, hence they called themselves constitutionalists. Huerta, however, clung to power, leading an impatient Wilson to reverse his stand on force and to consider instead a war that would topple the Mexican chieftain quickly. Wilson's personal adviser noted his determination to attain his goal, commenting also that "the President seems alert and unafraid."[6]

Several months later, on April 9, 1914, a minor incident gave the president his excuse for direct military intervention. At Tampico, where federal forces and constitutionalists were locked in battle, Huertistas arrested an American naval officer and seven sailors who had gone ashore to obtain supplies but in doing so penetrated federal lines without permission. After Huerta's troops had seized them, the local commander quickly released them and apologized. Huerta, too, expressed regret. This did not satisfy the admiral in command of United States forces. He demanded a formal twenty-one-gun salute to the American flag, which Wilson backed with an ultimatum threatening the gravest consequences if the Mexican leader declined.

When Huerta refused to yield, Wilson insisted "the salute will be fired." The president told Congress he hoped "in no circumstances to be forced into war with the people of Mexico." Then, in contradiction, he asked it to sanction the use of military force to uphold impugned national honor. He claimed constitutional authority to act on his own "without recourse to the Congress" but said also that in this grave matter he preferred to have its approval. Some members of the House of Representatives believed the alleged provocation did not justify a violent reaction. The Republican leader noted that if the reported incident had involved England, Germany, France, "or any other great power," few would demand military action. Since Mexico "is weak," he added, "we think we have the moral right to declare practical war against her."[7] Nonetheless, that same day the House overwhelmingly voted the authorization the president had requested.

The following day, while the Senate hesitated, the activity in Mexico switched to Vera Cruz to prevent a German ship from bringing arms to Huerta. Without waiting for the Senate to act, Wilson on his own authority as commander in chief quickly ordered naval personnel to occupy the city. Warships bombarded Vera Cruz; then some seven thousand marines stormed ashore, slaughtering 126 resisters, many of them young naval cadets, while suffering nineteen deaths. The next day, as the violence raged, Congress voted a joint resolution in support of military force. As had Wilson, the legislators disclaimed hostility to the Mexican people or any desire to make war on Mexico. Essentially, "by a straight party vote," they had "consented to a *fait accompli*."[8]

Wilson asked Enoch C. Crowder, his judge advocate general, where this seizure of a foreign country's city stood in international law and in particular if it constituted an act of war. Crowder then posed the question to Felix Frankfurter, at the time a young attorney in government service. Frankfurter responded, "It would be an act of war against a great nation; it isn't against a small nation." Crowder countered, "I can't give him that." Frankfurter shot back, "I know you can't but that's the answer." Another legalist, former president William Taft, perceived Wilson as pursuing a personal agenda or "playing to the gallery." Wilson implicitly denied such intention. Subsequently, in a memorial address for the dead, he gave another version of his rationale for the intervention. "We have gone down to Mexico to serve mankind if we can find a way," he stated, and added that "a war of service is a thing in which it is a proud thing to die."[9]

Few outside the president's coterie found such reasoning plausible. Most observers could see no intellectually satisfying justification for the military violence against Mexico. Many perceived it as a capricious use of power against a feeble opponent. Some commented that "the President appeared ridiculous, a person willing to make war over an obscure point of honor." London's *Economist* declared, "If war is to be made on points of punctilio raised by admirals and generals, and if the Government of the United States is to set the example for this return to mediaeval conditions it will be a bad day for civilization."[10] Regardless of such disapproval, while the marines occupied Vera Cruz Wilson continued to speak virtually as a pacifist, professing his love of peace and hatred of war.

Later, in another defense of his invasion, Wilson tried to explain to Mexicans the contradiction between his words and actions. On the one hand he had espoused in abstract the principle that the internal "affairs of Mexico was none of our business" and we had "no right" to interfere with them while on the other he had used force against them. "When we sent troops to Mexico," he elucidated, "our sincere desire was nothing else than to assist you to get rid of the man who was making the settlement of our affairs for the time being impossible."[11] He hoped that Mexicans, as with other peoples bullied by powerful nations, would understand his motivation of doing them a disinterested service for their own good.

Comparable logic also led Wilson to employ force unilaterally in Haiti. As had happened often in that island republic, a revolt broke out in January 1914, forcing the current ruler from power. American sailors briefly intervened, ostensibly to maintain order until a new regime could take control. A year later when more turmoil followed, the president contemplated another armed intervention but held off until the moment when he might have a credible pretext. It came after Haiti's president, Vilbrun G. Sam, executed 160 political prisoners.

On July 27, 1915, in Port-au-Prince, angry mobs surged through the streets, chased Sam and his henchmen to the French legation where they sought refuge, pulled them out, and tore them to pieces. The next day, four hundred American marines and sailors landed, seized the city, and restored a measure of order. Wilson and his new secretary of state, Robert Lansing, wanted to expand the police action to an occupation that would discipline the Haitians. Lansing pointed out, however, that international law could not justify such intervention though humane reasons might. Responding that he, too, feared "we have not the legal authority to do what we apparently ought to do," the president decided anyway "to take the bull by the horns and restore order."[12]

As the occupation spread to other parts of the country, Haitian *cacos*, or guerrillas, fled to the mountains and fought the invaders. The American government called the hostilities pacification while critical observers characterized them as a racial war of extermination. Wilson thus employed armed force against another weak nation, using once more as justification his personal conviction of being compelled to act in support of a righteous cause. Although he reported his action to Congress only after he had taken control, it acquiesced as it usually did when a president deployed the military forces on his own.

Wilson also resorted to force in dealing with a revolution in the neighboring Dominican Republic where American agents had been supervising that nation's finances. Interpreting a civil war there as anarchy, he dispatched a commission that warned Dominicans if they did not behave properly he would occupy the country. For a time the fighting subsided but then flared up again. On May 15, 1916, therefore, the president on his own authority sent in six hundred marines who quickly occupied the capital city, placed warships before every major port, and policed the country with troops commanded by a naval officer.

Administration officials advanced various reasons for this military venture. They alleged that by increasing their public debt without American permission as required by treaty, "the Dominicans had caused the intervention." The apologists said also the troops invaded "to reestablish domestic peace" and protect American strategic interests, such as its "southern coast and the Panama Canal."[13] The president's conviction that he knew what would be best for a benighted people, his determination to dominate the Caribbean, and his compulsion to flex muscle offer a more basic explanation. Dominican nationalists, who protested the destruction of their sovereignty as illegal under international law, mounted a peasant guerrilla resistance of harassment and sniping that lasted more than five years.

Meanwhile, because ascertainable American and world opinion had recoiled against Wilson's use of force in Vera Cruz, he turned to a diplomacy that helped avoid what such sentiment indicated would be an unpopular war with Mexico. The new confrontation began after the American occupiers left Vera Cruz and Mexico's constitutionalists in July 1914 had driven Huerta from office. This victory did not end the civil war because Carranza's most dynamic general, Francisco "Pancho" Villa, tried to wrest control of the revolution from him. In August Wilson switched his support to Villa. Beginning in January 1915, Carranza's forces inflicted heavy losses on the Villistas, forcing them to retreat northward to Pancho's stronghold in Chihuahua. Finally, in October the constitutionalist victories persuaded Wilson to abandon his pro-Villa policy and recognize Carranza's regime as Mexico's de facto government.

An enraged Villa then attacked Americans in northern Mexico, murdering sixteen of them on January 11, 1916, in Santa Ysabel. Many in Congress demanded prompt punishment of Mexico or full-scale war. Privately, however, as his secretary reported his words, Wilson vowed, "'*there won't be any war with Mexico if I can prevent it*,' no matter how loud the gentlemen on the hill yell for it and demand it. It is not a difficult thing for a president to declare war, especially against a weak and defenceless nation like Mexico." He held back also because he dreaded the aftermath of war "with all its tears and tragedies."[14]

On March 9 Villa's guerrillas raided Columbus, New Mexico, killing nineteen Americans and burning this border town. Still, Wilson announced, "there is no intention of entering Mexico in force." Quickly, as congressional and public pressure for intervention mounted, his reluctance to risk hostilities changed. He stated that "an adequate force will be sent at once in pursuit of Villa with the single object of capturing him and putting a stop to his forays."[15] Other considerations also motivated the president's decision to move on his own, as the military suggested, with a swift strike to catch Villa. For one, he wished to forestall possible passage of a congressional resolution calling for an intervention that could hamper his freedom of action. He also felt compelled to appear tough to an electorate that in seven months would vote on his bid for a second term. In addition, he assumed that without acting decisively he would hand Republicans an opportunity to attack him for lacking manly vigor in the conduct of foreign policy.

This strategy, based considerably on Wilson's personal anxieties, did not take into account Carranza's attitude. He refused to allow American forces to enter Mexico without obtaining reciprocal border rights for Mexicans. Wilson attempted to finesse this condition by insisting he had in mind a mere expedition, not an invasion as Carranza feared. So, on March 15 a punitive expedition of nearly six thousand men commanded by Brigadier General John J. Pershing crossed into Mexico, a sovereign nation, without the consent of either Congress or the Carranza government. Two days later Congress approved the incursion.

Carranza perceived Wilson's actions as indicating a willingness to initiate hostilities if he should attempt to block Pershing's expedition. Grudgingly therefore after the fact the Mexican leader yielded to superior force by granting a vague permission, within narrow limitations, to the intervention. Soon, he reversed himself, deciding to oppose the invasion.

As for Pershing's troops, they penetrated 350 miles into Mexico, took on the coloring of an army of occupation, clashed twice with government troops, suffered casualties, and failed to catch their man. Ultranationalists, in Congress and out, urged expanded hostilities. The Hearst press, for example, asked in bold headlines, "Shall We Play the Fool or Play the Man in Mexico?" It asked that "the Government of the United States shall manfully and righteously employ the full naval and military strength of the nation in effective and irresistible intervention TO PUT AN END TO THE TROUBLES IN MEXICO."[16]

In May, when Villa struck again, this time at the settlement of Glen Springs, Texas, fifteen miles north of the Rio Grande boundary, killing several United States soldiers, the pressure on Wilson to deploy more troops increased. He then nearly doubled the expedition to more than eleven thousand men. Carranza demanded its withdrawal, threatening to attack if it moved in any direction but northward. Counterthreats followed. On June 21 near Carrizal, American and Mexican government troops clashed, with each side suffering casualties. The two nations teetered on the brink of war. Wilson resisted demands for expanded hostilities, saying "the easiest thing is to strike." In a speech in New York, for instance, he asked, "Do you think the glory of America would be enhanced by a war of conquest in Mexico?" At this point, as though one man, the audience of some six hundred shouted, "No!"[17]

Shortly thereafter Wilson and Carranza agreed on conditions for withdrawal of the American troops that allowed Wilson to campaign for reelection with the Mexican confrontation neutralized. In January 1917, however, the negotiations broke down. He proceeded to evacuate the troops anyway but not necessarily because he disagreed with the manful use of force in what he regarded as a righteous cause. He retreated because he perceived a need to deal with a larger crisis—that of possible hostilities with Germany, battling in the Great War that had broken out in Europe in August 1914.

At first the possibility of involvement in that distant conflict had seemed remote because the president, his advisers, and most Americans believed they had no vital stake in its outcome. Various minority groups, because of ancestral and other connections to the belligerents, thought otherwise. Sensitive to this factionalism, Wilson had promptly spoken out against ethnic divisiveness, saying it "would be fatal" to the nation's peace. He pleaded with his fellow countrymen to "be impartial in thought as well as action," and proclaimed neutrality. His appeal quickly lost meaning because he, as well as the majority of Americans, favored the Allied side. In his own way, however, despite his feelings of "kinship with England" and "deep reverence for Anglo-Saxon institutions," Wilson tried to maintain a balanced stance.[18] Soon, even though both sides violated American neutrality, his personal preference affected policy toward the belligerents.

The president began taking a stronger stand against the Central Powers than against the Allies when Germany on February 4, 1915, declared the waters around the British Isles a war zone where submarines would attack Allied merchant vessels and even neutral shipping without warning. Six days later, he cautioned the German government he would hold it "to a strict accountability" for any destruction of "American lives and property" or denial of their "acknowledged rights on the high seas."[19] Shortly thereafter, German submarine attacks took the lives of several Americans. Then when a U-boat on May 7 torpedoed the British passenger liner *Lusitania*, bringing death to 128 Americans, the president took a tougher stand. He demanded that submarines refrain from warring on Allied ships carrying American passengers.

Secretary of State William Jennings Bryan objected to this denunciation of German tactics without comparable condemnation of what he regarded as equally harsh Allied measures, such as the food blockade of Germany. He viewed the president's policy as influenced by partiality for the Allies.

Moreover, he believed it "would be likely to cause a rupture of diplomatic relations [with Germany] and this might rush us into war in spite of anything we could do."[20] Convinced his objections carried no weight with the president, on June 8 he resigned.

Wilson replaced Bryan with Robert Lansing, who, like the president, favored a hard line. Through Lansing the president warned Germany he would regard more sinkings, "when they affect American citizens," as "deliberately unfriendly" and possibly as cause for war.[21] Essentially, Wilson wanted to police Germany because he deemed her a lawbreaker who violated the rules of cruiser warfare and also because he viewed himself as a defender of international law. Under this pressure, Germany partially leashed her submarines.

Despite the rising tension with the Central Powers, Wilson in seeking reelection in 1916 campaigned against the presumed bellicosity of Charles Evans Hughes, the seemingly unbeatable Republican candidate. Wherever possible, the president tried to capitalize on popular peace sentiment, embracing the slogan inserted in the Democratic platform, "He Kept Us Out of War." While he did not pledge, if reelected, to insulate the country from future involvement in the European conflict, he implied it. On one occasion he cautioned citizens, "If you elect my opponent, you elect a war." Several times he declared, "I am not expecting this country to get into war."[22]

While the peace issue alone did not bring about Wilson's narrow victory, it proved a key factor. Anti-interventionists perceived it as crucial. Senator Robert M. La Follette of Wisconsin declared the president "must accept the outcome of this election as a clear mandate from the American people to hold steadfastly to his course against war." As did others, Bryan maintained "the election showed the country is against war. It is opposed to intervention in Mexico, and it protests against being drawn into the war in Europe."[23]

Two months later, on January 9, 1917, Germany, which had come to view the United States as an Allied arsenal, decided as of February 1 to resume unrestricted submarine warfare. Within two days, the president severed diplomatic relations. He also refused to stop Americans from placing themselves in harm's way by traveling on armed ships, stating he could not consent to any abridgment of citizens' rights in any respect. To strengthen this stand, he requested legislation allowing him to arm merchant ships, claiming "no doubt I already possess that authority without special warrant of law." He asked because he wanted "to feel that the authority and the power of Congress are behind me in whatever may become necessary for me to do."[24] When senators whom he dismissed unjustifiably as a "little group of willful men, representing no opinion but their own," blocked his proposal, he proceeded anyway on his own authority with the arming. He ordered gun crews on merchant vessels to fire on submarines but withheld further measures against the Germans until they backed their announcement with overt acts.

On March 5 the president told the nation, "We have been deeply wronged upon the seas, but we have not wished to wrong or injure in return." We have been obliged, however, to arm ourselves to maintain a minimum freedom of action and thus to "stand firm in armed neutrality." At the same time he warned, circumstances may still draw us into "the great struggle itself." Five days later his son-in-law and secretary of the treasury, William G. McAdoo, said "war was inevitable, & would unite people & bring blessings in its wake."[25] As he, the president, and other advisers anticipated, on March 18 Germany proceeded with overt acts. Its submarines sank three American merchant vessels with heavy loss of life.

The president then summoned Congress to a special session. On April 2 he appeared before it in person to condemn "German submarine warfare against commerce" as "a warfare against mankind." He dismissed armed neutrality as impractical and ineffectual without having given it a real try. Recognizing that the people apparently preferred to abandon rights on the seas, rights that had little tangible meaning for most of them, rather than defend them with arms, he did not ask Congress to declare war. Instead, he requested it to "declare the recent course of the Imperial German Government to be in fact nothing less than a war against the Government and people of the United States." He did not, however, make it evident that Germany directly threatened the nation's well-being. Nevertheless, he asserted the "status of belligerent" has been "thrust upon" us.[26] With this tactic he hoped to avoid acrimonious debate. Instead of asking for war on the broad principle of imperiled national security, he requested it on the narrow issue of submarine attacks, in effect to police on a grand scale the conduct of another nation he considered menacing.

During the next few days people from "all walks of life" begged the legislators "to vote against a war resolution."[27] These pleas had little effect on the debate that followed in Congress because most members supported the intervention. The Senate approved it by a vote of 82 to 6 and the House by 373 to 50. On April 6 the president signed the resolution and American participation in another war began.

As Wilson's foremost biographer and others point out, he "played the dominant role in the conduct of foreign policies, wrote much of the important diplomatic correspondence, and made all the vital decisions, often contrary to the advice of" those in his entourage.[28] His will rather than any overwhelming popular demand stands out as "the greatest force" that took the nation from neutrality to armed neutrality and then to war. "His position, his opinions, his decisions, and his actions were decisive," outweighing the economic, psychological, ideological, strategic, balance of power, or propaganda reasons usually advanced as the causes for the intervention."[29]

Immediately, as commander in chief, the president requested and Congress granted vast authority to mobilize the nation's resources for waging war. A frustrated opponent asserted Wilson commanded power "greater than has ever been exercised by any king or potentate on earth," and more than that "exercised by the Kaiser of the Germans. It is a power such as no Caesar ever employed over a conquered province."[30] Regardless of such hyperbole, Wilson did assume dictatorial authority in the belief he needed it to win the war. His decisions consequently added to the already set precedents for expanding executive power.

For example, when the Bolshevik Revolution erupted in Russia in November 1917 followed within two months by a great civil war, British and French leaders pressured the president to intercede. Presumably, the intervention would aid the Allied cause by reopening the eastern front the revolutionaries had abandoned and bolster the will of pro-Allied Russians to fight. On this matter, an increasingly self-centered Wilson held the key to action. As an assistant secretary of state noted, "Everything great and small must be referred to the President, who receives no one, listens to no one, seems to take no one's advice." Because the use of military force for this purpose amounted to taking sides in a swirling internal struggle—even if the president meant to help the Russian people, as he indicated he might, for their own good—a number of his advisers opposed any armed interference. As one minor official pointed out, "No child can ever be convinced that it is spanked for its own benefit."[31]

So, out of pragmatic considerations, on July 6, 1918, the president refused to undertake this particular intervention. Soon, though, he cast aside advice to remain fully aloof by agreeing to send an armed expedition to support British forces at Archangel and Murmansk. He also took the lead in a joint intervention with Japanese troops at Vladivostok. He explained his latter decision to his secretary of war in terms of a need "to fall in with" the wishes of the Allies. "I have, however," Wilson added, "stipulated that the American contingent in both cases is to be small." He wished also to assist Russian "efforts at self-government or self-defense" but ironically refused to have "any dealing with the Bolsheviki" who figured prominently among those contending for power.[32]

Students of Wilson's decision to embroil the military in a situation that involved no vital American interest offer a number of reasons for it beyond those he stated. They contend he intervened to counter German influence in northern Russia, to rescue a Czech legion fighting its way across Siberia, "to prevent the Japanese from occupying large parts of Siberia," and "to combat bolshevism."[33] Regardless of his precise incentive, he did provide secret financial and military assistance to anti-Bolsheviks, thereby angering the Soviets, who controlled much of the intervention areas. Soviet leaders made clear their intention to oppose any imperialist invasion, be it German or Allied. Ultimately, the president thrust fourteen thousand troops into what contemporary critics dubbed "Mr. Wilson's little war with Russia."

Virtually from the start, the troops ordered to the north battled Bolshevik forces in various offensive operations. At Archangel, as though aligned with the most reactionary elements, the American occupiers meddled in Russian internal affairs by trying to protect a fragile anti-Bolshevik government. On November 11, 1918, when the armistice quieted the guns on the western front, American troops, alongside Allied contingents, were locked in a savage battle with Red Army forces on the Northern Dvina River.

The fighting continued for months. All the while, Wilson enjoined his aides at the peace conference at Paris to make it "very plain" to the British "that we are not at war with Russia and will in no circumstances," presently foreseen, "take part in military operations there."[34] Being a hands-on president, Wilson could not have been unaware of the depth of the involvement he had initiated. Furthermore, at this time the Russian intervention, which he now characterized as a humanitarian rescue mission, had become the most delicate issue in domestic politics in the eyes of concerned president-watchers and others. Political opponents denounced the intervention as lacking proper authority and a usurpation of power belonging to Congress.

The Chicago *Tribune* reflected this sentiment by editorializing that "our men are dying for a cause, the purpose of which they are no more certain than we in America. America has not declared war on Russia, but

Americans are killing Russians or are being killed by them." From a similar perspective, an aide told the president, "Our people are not prepared for us to undertake the military policing of Europe while it boils out its social wrongs."[35] Such anxiety even led the Senate to pass a resolution calling for withdrawal of the troops. In response to this pressure, Wilson on July 23, 1919, terminated the intervention in northern Russia. In Siberia, however, American forces remained until April 1920, or a month after he left the White House.

Wilson's unilateral commitment of military force to Russia followed the pattern evident earlier in the Mexican and Haitian ventures. First came his protestations of intervention as urged by others, then his commitment to military force, and finally his justification stating he proceeded for the benefit of the victims of his action. All this rationalizing became entangled in "his own *amour propre*."[36]

While still involved in the peace negotiations in Paris, Wilson had tried in a sense to elaborate on his personal role in ordering men to fight and die as in Russia, France, and elsewhere. In an address before the graves of American soldiers, he explained his reasoning. "By the Constitution of our great country," he pointed out, "I was the Commander in Chief of these men. I advised the Congress to declare that a state of war existed. I sent these lads over here to die."[37] They died not just for this reason but also in service to a cause that he, as president, saw as just and right.

This claimed righteousness applied also to the squelching of antiwar and other dissenters at home. Under Wilson, the executive branch had proceeded against them more fiercely than had Lincoln against dissidents during the Civil War. Critics maintain Wilson "established the precedents for presidential dictatorship in time of war or of grave international crisis."[38] As we know, dictatorship did not take root. Furthermore, his infraction of civil rights during the war and immediately after caused much less harm than did the violation of such rights in the enemy and Allied nations. Nonetheless, the Wilson abuses not only existed but also contributed to a rising alarm over the extent of executive authority.

Unlike the critics, friendly biographers who view "Wilson's strengthening and extension of the presidential powers" as virtuous see no reason for concern. They contend he did his job extraordinarily well and that his inflating of executive authority "constituted perhaps his most lasting contribution to American political practice." This interpretation overlooks the hubris of one man who exploited this extended executive power to resort to extensive force more often than any other president before or since his time. Regardless of scholarly or popular views on his proper use or abuse of power, successors would often cite his actions in foreign and domestic matters when claiming the right to curb civil liberties in the guise of national emergencies, to safeguard national security with questionable means, or to defend macho behavior.

Wilson employed force on his own with impunity because, for one reason, up to this time the Supreme Court consistently had refused to pass on the right of presidents to assume emergency authority as part of their constitutional war power. In December 1919, in a reaction against Wilson's practices, the Court began applying judicial review even to war measures but it "still refused to examine the motives behind a purported war law."[39]

The Court's actions did not still the clamor of those who believed Wilson had assumed powers belonging to Congress. For instance, John Bassett Moore, the distinguished student of international law, identified in Wilson an arrogance that later would be called machismo. Moore contended that the framers of the Constitution "never imagined that they were leaving it to the executive to use the military and naval forces of the United States all over the world for the purpose of actually coercing other nations, occupying their territory, and killing their soldiers and citizens, all according to his own notion of the fitness of things, so long as he refrained from calling his action war or persisted in calling it peace."[40]

Warren G. Harding

IN 1920 the election campaign became in part a referendum on Wilson's conduct of foreign policy, his use of the war power, and his stubborn stance on membership in the League of Nations he had largely created. In good measure to take advantage of the public backlash against presidential arrogance and wartime activism as exhibited by Wilson, the Republicans chose as their candidate Warren G. Harding, an affable, handsome former newspaperman and senator from Ohio. He had no hunger for accumulating power and, "at least initially," like William Howard Taft, had no interest "in running for the presidency."[41] Harding entered the race mainly to boost his senatorial reelection effort. His geniality, modest intellectuality, and indeed his whole personality contrasted sharply with Wilson's sharp mentality and haughty aloofness.

As a senator Harding had abhorred Wilson's treatment of Congress while stretching executive power at its expense. During the campaign he opposed membership in the League of Nations and attacked Wilson's military ventures against "helpless neighbors in the West Indies" such as the forcing on one of them, Haiti, a constitution "at the point of bayonets borne by the United States marines." Harding promised that if elected he would not "misuse the power of the executive to cover with a veil of secrecy repeated acts of unwarranted interference in the domestic affairs of the little republics of the western hemisphere." This pledge of a retreat from pugnacious foreign interventionism, along with the public's wrath against Wilson, helped Harding swamp his Democratic opponent, Governor James M. Cox of Ohio, with 60.2 percent of the vote—the largest popular majority for a president up to that time.[42]

In his inaugural Harding devoted considerable attention to foreign affairs, expressing in particular opposition to international entanglements, such as with the League of Nations. "A world super-government," he announced, "is contrary to everything we cherish and can have no sanction by our Republic." In line with tradition, he spoke of cherishing peace, adding, "we shall give no people just cause to make war upon us; . . . we dream of no conquest, nor boast of armed prowess."[43] As president, he retained his faith in the separation of powers and respect for congressional prerogatives. He viewed the concept of the strong executive with suspicion because, in line with the seemingly moribund Whig tradition, he believed presidents should exercise power within narrow constitutional limits. If they acted beyond such bounds, abuse of power and trouble with Congress would follow. While he approved of the president presenting legislation to Congress, he opposed coercive efforts to prevail over the legislature.

Accordingly, the brief Harding administration engaged in no military ventures abroad. It quickly terminated the formal hostilities with the enemy countries of the First World War with separate treaties. It also initiated the diplomacy that would end the American military commitment in the Caribbean, notably the occupation of the Dominican Republic where, as biographers contend, Harding "personally played a central role." Despite its peacefulness, this presidency, in the view of most scholars, ranks as perhaps the worst in the nation's history, as "an American tragedy." They portray Harding as a notoriously ineffective executive, one who surrendered major responsibility for the definition of American foreign policy to Charles Evans Hughes, his secretary of state. Ironically, they also claim Harding's "blunted thinking colored the foreign policy of his administration."[44]

In addition, historians condemn Harding for his lack of leadership; his isolationism, or failure to understand the nation's role in world affairs; his flawed character; extramarital affairs; and most of all for his presiding over a government wracked by scandal and corruption. For example, his secretary, Judson Welliver, commented, "You see, he doesn't understand it: he just doesn't know a thousand things he ought to know. And he realizes his ignorance." As though confirming this assessment, the president told a newspaper editor, "My God, but this is a hell of a place for a man like me to be!" Similarly, at another time he sighed to his secretary of state, "Hughes, this is the damnedest job."[45] Yet when this passive president died in office on August 2, 1923, from a stroke, he was so immensely popular that reelection had seemed assured.

Calvin Coolidge

As have most men who succeeded to the presidency by accident, Calvin Coolidge promised to continue his predecessor's foreign policy. Having risen high politically with a concern for domestic matters, he had even less experience in foreign affairs than Harding. Furthermore, Coolidge had no real interest in them. He had never been abroad and lacked knowledge in dealing with foreign peoples but seemed happy in his provincialism. Like Harding, although retaining his power of final decision, he left the handling of international problems largely to his secretaries of state. As Coolidge himself explained, he led the nation by referring "technical matters . . . to the proper department of government which has information about them." This fitted his principle of "never doing anything that some one else can do for you."[46]

Coolidge revealed at least something of his thinking on matters of war and peace when on December 6 he broke an air of mystery and silence to deliver his first message to Congress. "For us peace reigns everywhere," he said. "We desire to perpetuate it always." He concluded by stating, "The world has had enough of the curse of hatred and selfishness, of destruction and war. It has had enough of the wrong use of material power. . . . The time has come for a more practical use of moral power," rather than reliance on force. Eight months later, on accepting his party's nomination for the presidency in his own right, he expressed a bit more of his outlook on leadership. "It is not in brilliant conceptions and strokes of genius that we shall find the chief reliance of our country," he claimed, but in simple things like home, country, and religion.[47]

The country appeared quite willing to accept Coolidge's placid approach to his office as long as he emphasized peace. Indeed, so many

Americans felt concern over involvement in foreign problems, especially in consequence of presidential initiatives in the use of military force, that they embraced efforts to curb executive power. For this reason, at this time both the Democratic and Progressive Party platforms in 1924 endorsed the idea of a popular referendum on war. This issue did not harm Coolidge because he had made clear his own antiwar convictions. He won the presidential election overwhelmingly.

On matters of war and peace Coolidge indicated he would not venture knowingly beyond the Constitution, which he interpreted "almost literally as far as the Chief Executive's powers were concerned." He believed that "for all ordinary occasions the specific powers assigned to the President will be found sufficient to provide for the welfare of the country. That is all he needs."[48] Analysts point out that in line with this narrow view of executive authority under the Constitution, he rarely took the initiative in foreign affairs, deferring usually to the will of Congress as he understood it.

Coolidge also declared he had no wish "to interfere in the political conditions of any other countries." Despite these words and his allegedly passive approach to the conduct of foreign policy, in two instances he succumbed to aggressive impulses and to special-interest pressure to employ force in police actions.[49] In doing so, he followed precedent set by his predecessors, who in the latter decades of the nineteenth century had stationed naval squadrons in foreign seas to protect American lives and property—a policy usually called gunboat diplomacy. In Asian waters, this practice continued into Coolidge's time and became entangled with a nationalist movement in China. Students and workers determined to save their country from Western imperialism, extraterritoriality, unequal treaties, and warlordism formed the backbone of the movement. Their demonstrations and attacks against foreigners produced stepped-up armed Western intervention in China.

The circumstances that prompted Coolidge to become a part of such intrusion began in Shanghai on May 30, 1925, in a clash between students and a police establishment headed by Europeans. From that city the antiforeign movement spread across the nation. Angry demonstrators attacked Westerners and their property, as in an assault on January 3, 1927, on the British concession at Hankow. In Foochow rioters overran and looted an American Methodist church, a hospital, and missionary residences.

Even though upset by the violence, Coolidge refused to withdraw

Americans from the danger zones, saying in the case of those in Shanghai that they lived there under right of law and deserved protection. Critics, such as Senator William E. Borah of Idaho, thought differently. They favored bringing Americans "out of danger until the danger is passed." Up to this time, eight hundred marines stationed in nearby gunboats had provided limited security. The president now augmented this force with some fifteen hundred more marines and three cruisers carrying additional troops. However, he resisted pressure to send a large force of regular soldiers because it would "involve us probably in making war" and would meet with public and congressional opposition.[50]

The president realized, nonetheless, that China's civil war would likely continue to "do injury to American nationals." For this reason, he explained, the naval forces must remain in Chinese waters. As anticipated, on March 24 more xenophobic violence erupted, this time in Nanking where it led to the death of an American missionary. To protect other endangered Americans, armed bluejackets rushed ashore but proved inadequate against the more numerous Chinese. An American and a British gunboat then laid a barrage of gunfire that drove off the attacking nationalist soldiers. At home public sentiment, as expressed in the press, approved of the president's limited use of force. It also opposed a larger military intervention, as in cooperation with other powers, against Chinese nationalism.

As had other presidents in comparable situations, Coolidge did not regard his deployment of armed forces in China as warfare but as a police action, a distinction hazy at best. The civil turmoil, he said, had "compelled" him "to send naval and marine forces to China to protect the lives and property of our citizens." Fortunately, as he put it, "their simple presence there has been sufficient to prevent any material loss of life," but not of property.[51] In all, he did not hesitate to use force, though on a lesser scale than some constituents demanded, as he thought proper and as long as he had what he perceived as popular support.

Coolidge intervened less judiciously and on a larger scale in much smaller Nicaragua. From his viewpoint, the problem there arose in August 1925 after he had withdrawn the marines who had been on guard duty in that country since the Taft years. They left behind a shaky military dictatorship that quickly became embroiled in civil war. In that contest, Coolidge and his secretary of state, Frank B. Kellogg, chose to side with Adolfo Díaz, a conservative, pro-American general. On January 10, 1927, in a special message, the president told Congress that developments in

Nicaragua jeopardized canal rights, endangered American lives and investments, and had been "connived at by Mexico."[52] Kellogg went further. He claimed Bolsheviks had fomented the trouble. Coolidge then renewed the interrupted intervention by restoring the legation guard in Managua. On February 20 he stepped up this tampering with an invasion mounted by warships that landed two thousand troops on the Nicaragua shore.

At home and abroad critics condemned the assault as demonstrating a continuing commitment to dollar diplomacy and to more irrational muscle-flexing against a weak neighbor. Few domestic opponents, however, disputed the president's authority to deploy military force. Rather, they questioned his wisdom in doing so. A number of them, mainly congressional Democrats, called the incursion Coolidge's "private war." He bristled. "We are not making war on Nicaragua," he asserted, "any more than a policeman is making war on passersby."

In April the president sent Henry L. Stimson, formerly Taft's secretary of war, to Nicaragua to "see a way to clean up that mess." In the following month at Tipitapa, threatening forcible pacification, Stimson arranged a peace between the contending forces that included elections the American troops would supervise. One revolutionary group led by Augusto C. Sandino, however, refused to accept the truce, launched a guerrilla campaign, and in July fought a bloody battle with American marines and the local constabulary they had trained. When this clash prompted more criticism, Coolidge dismissed the Sandinistas as bandits. He repeated his earlier reasons for imposing the marines on Nicaragua but added he had responded to the "earnest and repeated entreaties" of a government that needed help to counter Mexico's assistance to the revolutionaries.[53]

In the following year, from early March until November, a beefed-up force of 5,480 marines and their constabulary allies tried without success to capture Sandino.[54] John James Blaine, a Republican senator from Wisconsin, proposed cutting off funds for this military venture and hence to curb presidential power. He failed but Congress nonetheless viewed this policing venture, now directed obsessively against the Sandinistas, with increasing distrust. This mild disapproval bothered thin-skinned Coolidge because he perceived it as directed at him personally. He believed he had acted selflessly for the national interest.

Later, using arguments similar to those of his activist predecessors and to those he employed to support the China intervention, Coolidge defended his use of force. The United States, he wrote, had a duty "to protect its citizens in Nicaragua or any foreign country." Nicaragua's government, he added, "should deal with bandits. We have not set up a protectorate but in a neighborly way tried to help Nicaragua provide her own law and order."[55] He still missed the main point of his strong-arm tactics. By what right, other than by his own impulse and the power at his command, could a president order the policing of the streets of a sovereign country?

In the main, though, Coolidge claimed to understand a president's impulsive behavior. He attributed it to "some power outside and beyond him" that somehow "became manifest through him." He also took a humble view of the polluting influence of power. "It is a great advantage to a President, and a major source of safety to the country, for him to know that he is not a great man," he wrote. "When a man begins to feel that he is the only one who can lead this republic, he is guilty of treason to the spirit of our institutions."[56]

Herbert Clark Hoover

HERBERT Hoover favored a similar view of the constitutional basis of presidential power, particularly as applied to foreign affairs. "I had felt deeply that no President should undermine the independence of the legislative and judicial branches by seeking to discredit them," he explained in his memoirs. "The constitutional division of powers is the bastion of our liberties and was not designed as a battleground to display the prowess of Presidents."[57]

Unlike most of his predecessors, Hoover seemed to possess attributes that would contribute to an outstanding presidency. His work as a mining engineer took him over much of the world while permitting him to compile an impressive record of public service. During the First World War he served as Wilson's food administrator and was a member of his war council. Hoover retained national prominence by holding an appointment in Harding and Coolidge's cabinets. A contemporary quipped he was "Secretary of Commerce and Under-Secretary of all other departments."[58] Hoover enjoyed his bureaucratic experience and wide exposure to international affairs but they left him with a major deficiency that would cloud his presidency. He had no practical political experience. Prior to being chosen president, he had never held an elective office.

Hoover's upbringing as a Quaker, an orphan, and his rise as a self-made man colored his thinking on political matters but his seasoning in business and government shaped it. He touted "rugged individualism," or a muddled concept of self-reliance that would somehow stimulate "each individual to achievement," to a "sense of responsibility," and to attain freedom from "coercive institutions." He also desired efficiency in government as well as in business. On the matter of presidential power, he believed the "increasing ascendancy of the Executive over the Legislative arm . . . has run to great excesses" and that the legislature's authority "must be respected and strengthened."[59]

This conviction did not prevent Hoover from wanting to shape foreign policy in his own way. From the start he laid out his goal, stating, "we have no desire for territorial expansion, for economic or other domination of other peoples." As he would repeat often, he perceived his task in dealing with other nations as leading "the United States in full cooperation with world moral forces to preserve peace." While not a pacifist, as were many Quakers, out of personal experience with the miseries conflict spawned he hated war. This practical knowledge helped shape a philosophy of international affairs that buttressed his determination as president to participate directly in all issues relating to war and peace. Thus, when in this area a policy problem came up, he usually took command of the procedure designed to address it.

A number of Hoover's predecessors had expressed a similar desire to uphold peace but he stuck to his antiwar convictions with the zeal of religious commitment. He insisted the president should abate war, not stimulate it, and should as a primary task "insure freedom from war to the American people." As with many who had faith in the Kellogg peace pact, he believed the power of public opinion would suffice to check military violence. Hence, he opposed the buildup of armaments and the intervention "*by force*" in the affairs of other nations "except actually to save American lives."[60]

Hoover's effort to de-emphasize the military aspects of foreign policy began immediately after his election but before his inauguration in a trip to Latin American countries he called "the friendly visit of one *good neighbor* to another." About a month after entering the White House, he repudiated his own party's identification with dollar diplomacy, announcing he "would not intervene by force to secure or maintain contracts between our citizens and foreign States or their citizens."[61]

In his first annual message to Congress ten months later, the president pointed out, "We still have marines on foreign soil—in Nicaragua, Haiti, and China. In the large sense we do not wish to be represented abroad in such a manner." We have, he added, "already reduced these forces materially and we are anxious to withdraw them further." For various reasons,

State Department and other officials urged holding back on the removals in Nicaragua where some sixteen hundred marines remained. Hoover persisted, telling his secretary of state, Henry L. Stimson, that regardless of consequences and other aspects of foreign policy "we should get out anyway."[62]

In keeping with this stance, the president, as had Wilson, refused to exercise recognition as a club for toppling governments in Latin America that did not adhere to American standards of legitimacy. A wave of revolutions that swept over much of Latin America in the latter part of 1930 in the wake of a worldwide economic depression tested the recognition policy repeatedly, as in upheavals in Argentina, Brazil, and Peru. Still, he did not employ that policy as an instrument for intervening in the affairs of the affected countries.

Earlier that year, the president permitted publication as a public document a memorandum J. Reuben Clark, undersecretary of state in the previous administration, had prepared but that Coolidge disliked and had put aside. It declared the Roosevelt corollary as not "justified by the terms of the Monroe Doctrine."[63] Although the memorandum's content concurred with Hoover's views on nonintervention, his handling of the document has puzzled historians. Some maintain he readily accepted it and "published it to the world." Others point out that many in the State Department did not like it, that he himself felt uncertain about it and, unlike Stimson, refused to embrace it publicly because of a conflict with Congress over presidential independence.[64] In content, the Clark memorandum accorded more with his views on intervention than with those of Stimson. Hoover later claimed its substance as having always been a part of his foreign policy, a policy that stood opposed to the practice of stretching executive authority to cover policing operations abroad.

We can see aspects of this policy in Hoover's response to Japan's conquest, beginning in September 1931, of China's province of Manchuria. He was determined to avoid involvement in this warfare between Japan and China that would in any way require the commitment of American armed forces. Although personal, this attitude coincided with widespread public sentiment as indicated in December in a *Literary Digest* poll of newspaper editors. They, as well as many of their papers' readers, opposed measures that could lead possibly to involvement in the hostilities. Nonetheless, in this instance, in contrast to his policy in Latin America, Hoover did become involved diplomatically. He used the withholding of recognition of Japan's conquest as a form of moral pressure on aggressors. On January 7, 1932, through Stimson, he announced a doctrine stating the United

States would not recognize as legal the fruits of conquest in defiance of the Kellogg-Briand peace treaty and of world opinion.

Despite initial agreement on nonrecognition as a principle, the president and his secretary differed over the practical application of the doctrine. As Hoover put it, they did not have "one and the same policy in mind." The president saw the nonrecognition doctrine as carrying no threat of economic or military coercion. He viewed it primarily as placing "some moral teeth in the Kellogg Pact." Stimson perceived it as a prelude to imposing economic sanctions on aggressor nations. This construction not only alarmed Hoover, it also led him to conclude that his secretary "was at times more of a warrior than a diplomat." On the other hand, Stimson characterized Hoover as "so much a man of peace that he did not like the notion of even unspoken threats of war." The president, he said, made it "perfectly clear that no economic or warlike measures would be taken by his administration against Japan."[65]

Hoover refused to go beyond moral sanctions because he was convinced that anything stronger could trigger war. He believed that "one who brandishes a pistol must be prepared to shoot." Furthermore, he perceived the use of force or the imposition of economic sanctions as smacking of a program to police the world, a task he refused to undertake. As for Stimson, even though he regarded Hoover's view of the doctrine as "wholly inadequate" because it did not go beyond "moral condemnation," he still claimed his own version of it as "the greatest constructive achievement of his public life." He viewed his interpretation of the document, which he and others of his persuasion called the Stimson Doctrine, as securing "a united front against approval of conquest by military power."[66]

In contrast, Hoover stood firm for moral standards because, as he told Stimson, "if I recommended the use of force it would be a recommendation that Congress should declare war; and that was wholly unjustified." He believed, as he wrote later, that if Stimson had his way, "he would have had us in a war with Japan."[67] The two men never reconciled these differences. Given the president's initiative in expounding the nonrecognition principle and his power to make his view prevail, he insisted that what he had in mind was the true version of what he called the Hoover Doctrine. Journalists and others who did not distinguish between the two versions of the principle spoke of it, as expounded by the administration, as the Hoover-Stimson Doctrine. Ironically, even though the secretary of state considered Hoover's definition of the nonrecognition principle as inadequate, the whole concept became best known as the Stimson Doctrine.

Meanwhile, three weeks after the enunciation of the moralistic nonrecognition policy, the Japanese bombarded and seized Shanghai. This assault led the president to modify his attitude toward the policing of foreign peoples. He demonstrated a willingness, as had most predecessors, to employ armed force "to protect the lives of Americans" when they seemed to be, rather than only when they actually were, endangered. In this circumstance he thought a display of force perhaps could be effective in deterring harm. He dispatched naval vessels stationed in Asia as well as hundreds of troops to the Shanghai area. As he did so, Japan in February 1932 completed its conquest of Manchuria and proclaimed the puppet state of Manchukuo. In March the assembly of the League of Nations accepted the nonrecognition principle as an instrument of its own diplomacy but did not attempt to enforce it with either military or economic sanctions.

Whereas Stimson saw the league's action as creating international support for his version of nonrecognition, Hoover and those of similar persuasion viewed the league's position as a vindication of his moral policy toward Japan and China. In any case, later in the year, in accepting his second presidential nomination, Hoover expressed pride in his foreign policies, which he described as "devoted to strengthening the foundations of world peace." He reiterated, "We shall enter into no agreements committing us to any future course of action or which call for use of force in order to preserve peace."[68]

The president clung to this commitment even when he had a legal basis for intervention, as in Cuba through the Platt Amendment to a treaty of 1903. Beginning in August 1931 and through the rest of his presidency revolutionary violence rocked the island, with most of it directed against the tyranny of dictator Gerardo Machado y Morales. Varied constituents urged Hoover to deploy troops out of the Guantanamo naval base because only then, they claimed, could Cubans expect meaningful reform. He refused, maintaining he would not exercise tutelage over the island. Even early in 1933 as he prepared to leave office, he held firmly to his noninterventionism in dealing with Cuba, in removing all the marines from Nicaragua, and in preparing for their impending withdrawal from Haiti.

In these instances, as in others, Hoover hardly behaved as a weak executive. He acted within the limits of his conception of proper leadership to meet pressing crises. Contemporaries, and later historians, however, usually regarded him a one-term failure. They did so in good measure because he refused to take an expansive view of his powers to combat the Great Depression and to use them forcefully against the Japanese, Cubans, and others. Friends and critics also fault him for his cold personality, his political obtuseness, and what many viewed as his zero charisma. "He lacked a certain spark . . . the spark of leadership," the hero Charles A. Lindbergh maintained, "that intangible quality that makes men willing to follow a great leader even to death itself."[69]

Hoover also puzzled pundits with his paradoxical thought and behavior. He considered himself an internationalist but acted as an isolationist. For instance, even though while working for Wilson he had supported entry into the League of Nations, as president, as had his Republican predecessors, he backed away from endorsing the league. He also frequently expressed racist attitudes common among his contemporaries. For instance, he voiced contempt for Japanese and other Asians, implying they belonged to "lower races."[70] At the same time he spoke against the holding of colonial possessions and the bullying of lesser peoples.

On this score, in his earlier public career, Hoover had upheld imperialism but as president he opposed it and favored freedom for the Philippines. On January 13, 1933, however, ostensibly for strategic reasons among those his advisers had given him, he vetoed the Hare-Hawes-Cutting bill that called for independence in ten years. Congress promptly overrode the veto. Usually, though, he demonstrated courageous leadership in insisting upon peaceful diplomacy in the face of pressure for combativeness.

In addition, Hoover acted with a seeming disdain for the grandeur of his office as well as for the accoutrements of worldly power common among chief executives. He spilled no blood in ideological crusades or presidential warfare. In the words of a careful biographer, he governed as the "President closest to being a pacifist." He turned down "more opportunities for intervention than any President since Benjamin Harrison, always figuring the sensible, decent, self-interested moral way to stay out of war."[71] Furthermore, he resisted the impulse to use armed force to offset the shortcomings of his internal policies. Regardless of his reputation for ineptness in domestic affairs and for what many considered a deplorable isolationism, on big international issues he wielded power effectively. Whether rightly or wrongly for his time, unlike other presidents who claimed to be strong, he used his power to place peace ahead of military machismo, not just in rhetoric, but also in practice.

CHAPTER 5

Presidential War as Prerogative

There is a lure in power. It can get into a man's blood just as gambling and lust for money have been known to do.

Harry S. Truman, April 16, 1950

Franklin Delano Roosevelt

IN common with his predecessor, Franklin D. Roosevelt brought to the presidency considerable knowledge of national government and familiarity with international affairs, having served as assistant secretary of the navy under Woodrow Wilson and having worked with various foreign statesmen. He differed from Herbert Hoover in his experience with the uses of power in domestic as well as bureaucratic politics, having won election to the state senate in New York, made a run for vice president, and earned two terms as governor of New York. This hands-on involvement in several levels of government served Roosevelt well because the problem of the Great Depression, not foreign affairs, demanded his immediate attention.

Most of the public, political leaders, and influential pundits perceived the depression as requiring an unprecedented exertion of executive authority. Journalist Walter Lippmann, who desired strong presidential leadership, urged the president-elect to be forceful in meeting the crisis. "The situation is critical, Franklin," he wrote. "You may have no alternative but to assume dictatorial powers." The Republican governor of Kansas, Alfred M. Landon, offered similar advice. "Why not," he asked, "give the President the same powers in this bitter peacetime battle as we would give to him in time of war?" Regarding dictatorship as "a system for sheep," Roosevelt resisted such advice but not necessarily out of established principle. Whereas he had adopted no consistent philosophy of government, he did have, as we shall see, "an overall coherent view of foreign policy" and a "set of assumptions, principles, and values" that guided his presidency.[1] They included his own conception of executive power and a willingness to use it boldly to achieve what he perceived as desirable goals.

Roosevelt came to this view of power through service in government, experience as governor, observing the conduct of the presidents he knew, and the reading of American history. He believed the executive should not hesitate to show strength but he should take care not to dictate. From his politicking, when his physical condition had become an issue, he knew the public admired the bold, virile leader. At the cost of pain and emotional drain, he tried therefore to hide signs even of physical weakness, especially his legs, which in August 1921 had been crippled with polio. For instance, he never allowed newspaper or film people to photograph him in a wheelchair or in his steel braces. He carefully released many pictures of his earlier years showing him as a "man of action—running, jumping, doing things." Indeed, up to the time of his death "he conspired with the public to present the image of the President as vigorous and physically fit."[2]

As with his handicap, in shaping foreign policy Roosevelt relied on help from many individuals and used it to his advantage. Nonetheless, he guarded his constitutional prerogatives jealously and, as those close to him noted, "he personally considered all matters of importance and made all major decisions."[3] Virtually always he had the last word. This domination of policymaking, as well as his actions being based on the assumption that laudable ends at times justified high-handed means, led critics to ascribe to him dictatorial qualities he denied possessing.

Roosevelt made his concern with executive power evident in his inaugural, where he pronounced the economic crisis his primary concern. If necessary, he told the nation, "I shall ask Congress for . . . broad Executive power to wage a war against the emergency, as great as the power that would be given me if we were in fact invaded by a foreign foe." The audience responded to this war metaphor with its loudest cheer. In his brief reference to foreign affairs, he promised dedication "to the policy of the good neighbor."[4]

Quickly, the turmoil in Cuba put his words to a test. With the aim of helping to replace a repressive regime headed by dictator Gerardo Machado y Morales with a democratic government, Roosevelt sent his friend Sumner Welles to that republic as ambassador. In August, an army coup ousted Machado and brought to power, as president, Carlos Manuel de Céspedes, a man acceptable to Washington. An insurrection followed. Then on three occasions, Welles asked Roosevelt to land troops for a "limited intervention." He wanted to assist the "legitimate government" with "an armed force lent by the United States as the policing power."[5]

Roosevelt responded that armed intervention "is absolutely the last thing we have in mind. We don't want to do it." He refused to send ground troops but did resort to the threat of force by ordering thirty naval vessels of varying sizes to Cuba to cope with "potential threats against American lives."[6] He intervened further by manipulating recognition policy to influence the outcome of the internal struggle that produced four regimes in ten months. In the following year, as part of his Good Neighbor Policy, he tried to overcome the distrust this patronizing behavior had generated by abrogating the Platt Amendment and by completing the withdrawal of the marine occupiers from Haiti.

From the outset, too, Roosevelt had to contend with a public influenced by the theory of revisionist historians and publicists that intervention in the First World War had risen out of a malign presidential discretion in foreign affairs. Americans of this persuasion favored circumscribing executive authority in matters of war and peace. He and much of the nation's intellectual community did not. Indeed, the liberal establishment as a whole deemed it proper for presidential power in foreign affairs to expand at the expense of Congress. So did the courts, which ironically acted conservatively in decisions affecting Roosevelt's domestic New Deal program. At this point, the judiciary played a more significant role than the liberals in amplifying executive authority on matters of foreign policy, most strikingly in the *United States v. Curtiss-Wright Export Corporation*.

This case arose out of the war between Bolivia and Paraguay over jungle terrain known as the Chaco Boreal. In May 1934 Congress in a joint resolution authorized the president, at his discretion, to clamp an embargo on the sale of arms to these belligerents if he thought it might contribute to peace. By executive proclamation he promptly imposed such a ban. In January 1936, federal officials indicted Curtiss-Wright for selling aircraft machine guns to Bolivia in violation of the prohibition. The corporation argued that the proclamation did not have the status of a law whose violation the judiciary could punish because Congress could not legally delegate its embargo authority to the president. In a rare ruling against executive aggrandizement in international affairs, a federal district court decided in favor of the corporation.

The government appealed to the Supreme Court, which reversed the lower court's decision. The high court ruled that the constitutional restriction on the federal government in domestic matters, where it could exercise only enumerated powers, did not apply to foreign affairs. By upholding the idea that power in foreign affairs came not only from the Constitution but also from the law of nations, this ruling supported the president's right to accrue power.

Justice George Sutherland of Utah, who wrote the new ruling, earlier had served on the Senate Foreign Affairs Committee where he advocated "a vigorous diplomacy which strongly, and even belligerently, called always for an assertion of American rights." He incorrectly described the president as "the sole organ of the federal government in the field of international relations." Sutherland thus reinvigorated the old pre-Revolutionary theory of inherent power, stating that in foreign relations the executive had an authority "independent of constitutional limitations."[7] As though having fallen under the spell of rediscovered gospel, presidents, government lawyers, the Supreme Court, and others henceforth would cite Sutherland's flawed opinion to support the executive's unilateral exercise of force. His decision would confer a kind of judicial legitimacy on presidents who would handle matters of war and peace virtually on their own as they thought proper.[8]

In assessing the Curtiss-Wright judgment, constitutional scholars often shrugged, characterizing it as just another example of the courts' partiality for supporting "the power of the president in matters involving foreign affairs." Legalists do point out though that "Sutherland uncovered no new constitutional ground for upholding a broad, inherent, and independent presidential power in foreign relations." Moreover, the courts did not need his decision to sustain extensive presidential power. With or without *Curtiss-Wright*, the judiciary regularly refused to rule on claims of presidential usurpation of legislative power in foreign affairs. Consequently, numerous historians, lawyers, and others view the courts as abdicating "their function of preserving constitutionalism as well as our dual democracy."[9]

During the course of these legal proceedings a widespread antiwar sentiment, based on disillusion with the experience in the First World War and associated usually with isolationism, led numerous Americans to view executive power from a different perspective. They feared that fascist dictators Benito Mussolini and Adolf Hitler, who had risen to power in Italy and Germany, as well as the militarists in Japan, would pull the United States into war. The president, who shared this concern, asked the State Department to draft legislation to prevent such involvement from possibly happening. The department proposed a law which, while keeping the United States technically neutral, would allow the president considerable discretion in penalizing, as with a discriminatory arms embargo, the belligerents he deemed aggressors in any war.

Reflecting the nation's isolationist mood, distrust of the executive, and a suspicion that through the device of flexible neutrality the president would or could manipulate the nation into war, the Senate rejected the proposal. In its place Congress passed the first of a series of bills, known as neutrality acts, designed to impose a "rigid neutrality to prevent American entanglement in the war that was coming" and to rein in the president's power of possibly initiating war. Secretary of State Cordell Hull condemned the legislators' bill because he viewed its requirement of an impartial arms embargo an invasion of the executive's "traditional power." Roosevelt, however, believed the legislation took "away little Executive authority" and by accepting it he might quiet the "fear in the country of excessive presidential control." On August 31 he signed it into law while disparaging its "inflexible provisions" as more likely to "drag us into war instead of keeping us out."[10]

Four days later, Italian fascists invaded Ethiopia, putting the statute to a test. The results of the embargo dissatisfied Congress. In the course of the Italo-Ethiopian war, therefore, the legislators decided to place another curb on executive discretion. As for Roosevelt, even though favoring aggrieved Ethiopia, he reiterated that "the primary purpose of the United States is to avoid being drawn into war."[11] He also disliked the new legislation under consideration but did not react strongly against it because of his bid for reelection.

From the start of the campaign, Roosevelt tended to avoid discussion of foreign-policy issues because he did not wish to alienate isolationist sentiment among his New Deal supporters. Accordingly, on February 29, 1936, he reluctantly signed a second neutrality act that placed additional limitations on his presumed power to involve the nation in possible hostilities.

In November, Roosevelt won reelection with a huge popular endorsement. Soon his concern with presidential prerogative reemerged in an effort to reconstruct the Supreme Court because of its opposition to his domestic program. In his first term, the Court had struck down a number of key laws in his New Deal designed to overcome the depression. On February 5, 1937, he submitted his reorganization plan to Congress, touching off a furor. Critics denounced it as a scheme to circumvent the checks and balances of the Constitution, primarily by his seeking to pack the Court with his own appointees. In one of his Fireside Chats to the nation, he met these charges headon, claiming, "The Court has been acting not as a judicial body but as a policy making body." As such, it had crippled the functioning of government by the three theoretically cooperating branches. He would remedy this problem by providing courts that "would enforce the Constitution as written."[12] His defense proved unconvincing. By July he had lost the battle, leaving many Americans with the impression he had wished mainly to aggrandize his own authority.

Roosevelt elicited a similar reaction when he moved circumspectly to make the exercise of executive power more efficient. He desired reform because he wished additional time to deal with matters of war and peace and other big issues but felt hampered by the need to attend to lesser problems subordinates could handle. He had placed his plan in motion in March 1936 with the appointment of a committee on administrative management, known also as the Brownlow Committee. The committee's report in January 1937 recommended an expansion of the White House staff.

When Roosevelt transmitted the report to Congress, he wrote, "what I am placing before you is not a request for more power, but for the tools of management." Opponents attacked it as the "dictator bill," a wedge for creating one-man rule in the style of fascist leaders in Europe. Even though the president forcefully defended the plan, announcing publicly, "I have no inclination to be a dictator," he could not overcome the still prevalent distrust of the executive.[13] On April 8, 1938, more than a year later, after much debate Congress defeated the bill.

During this time, the president had persisted in attempting a bolder initiative in international affairs by switching publicly from a commitment to noninvolvement in foreign conflicts to a plea for collective action. His determination to speak out emanated from his view of militarists and dictators as gangsters who should be caged. He also wished to demonstrate his opposition to the neutrality laws. In Chicago, on October 5, 1937, he called for a quarantine against aggressors he regarded as the principal threats to world peace, namely Japan, Italy, and Germany. Without declaring war and without warning or justification, he pointed out that nations were killing civilians and taking sides in civil wars against peoples who have done them no harm. "If those things come to pass in other parts of the world," he warned, "let no one imagine that America will escape, . . . that this Western Hemisphere will not be attacked." He castigated isolationism and urged peace-loving nations to cooperate in stemming the growing international anarchy. Then he contradicted this approach by stating his determination "to pursue a policy of peace" and "to adopt every practicable measure to avoid involvement in war."[14]

Various polls indicated that Congress and the public had reacted with mixed feelings. While many Americans expressed immediate approval, most others denounced the speech as warmongering, causing the president to feel he was "fighting against a public psychology of long standing—a psychology which comes very close to saying 'Peace at any price.'" Sadly, he acknowledged, "It's a terrible thing to look over your shoulder when you are trying to lead and to find no one there."[15] Essentially, the public still distrusted presidential latitude in policies that could entangle the nation in another war. At this time, the most potent manifestation of that attitude came out of an old war referendum movement that clashed with Roosevelt's determination to lead boldly.

The referendum idea had been popular in 1916 when many Americans feared that through the actions of the executive the nation could become involved in the First World War. The Wisconsin progressive, Senator Robert La Follette, led the most notable of the peace efforts of this nature. In April he sponsored legislation calling for an advisory ballot on war that would follow any break in diplomatic relations with a European country. The bill died in committee but the referendum idea lived. For ten years beginning in 1925 advocates brought before Congress seventeen resolutions calling for an amendment to the Constitution that would require public consent through a vote of the citizenry before the government could declare war.

In 1935 Louis Ludlow, a journalist who had become a Democratic congressional representative from Indiana, took over leadership of the movement. In the possible use of the ballot box to ascertain the public will, he perceived a means of "reducing executive force in diplomacy" as well as a way of preserving peace. He proposed a constitutional amendment that, except in the event of attack or invasion, would require voter approval in a nationwide referendum before a declaration of war could become effective. The proposal quickly gained widespread public support but failed to make its way out of the House Judiciary Committee. This tactic did not diminish the Ludlow bill's popularity. A 1937 Gallup poll indicated that 80 percent of the population liked it, with many believing it would "advance the cause of popular rule" and even banish war in the United States.[16]

The administration, scores of academics, and others committed to the concept of the strong presidency thought differently. They opposed the bill for a variety of reasons but mainly because they saw it properly as a spear aimed at the heart of executive power in foreign affairs.

On December 12, while Ludlow's proposal lay moribund in committee, Japanese warplanes deliberately bombed, strafed, and sank the American gunboat *Panay*, bedecked with huge red, white, and blue flags, while it was on assignment on the Yangtze River above Nanking. The attackers killed two of the crew and wounded thirty. Like fire carried by a windstorm, talk of war swept over the country and with it fear. Within twenty-four hours, dread of possible hostilities stimulated an antiwar sentiment that benefited Ludlow. He had circulated a petition to discharge his bill from committee and bring it before the full membership of the House as a motion. Now he obtained enough additional votes from fellow legislators to achieve his objective.

Immediately Roosevelt moved to defeat the measure without allowing it publicity. He argued it "would cripple any President in his conduct of our foreign relations" and instead of "keeping the United States out of war, it would have the opposite effect." Citing the Spanish-American War as an example, he claimed that at times the executive could avoid war better than could an excited public. "Under a Ludlow proposition," he maintained, "we would have gone to war anyway." Then alluding disdainfully to William McKinley's alleged weakness, he added, "If we [had] happened to have a strong President, he would have averted war."[17]

Despite Roosevelt's direct opposition and a powerful campaign against the Ludlow measure that condemned it as isolationist, when the motion to discharge came to a vote on January 10, 1938, it barely lost. To many observers this narrow victory suggested caution in the expansion of executive authority but not to the president. He perceived the referendum campaign as a danger primarily because it appealed "to people, who, frankly, have no conception of what modern war, with or without declaration of war, involves," implying that as the nation's steward he knew better than the people.[18] A significant number of Americans, particularly those who still distrusted presidential discretion in the exercise of the war power, thought differently. With such sentiment as a base, Ludlow continued to press for a constitutional referendum but Congress virtually ignored him. As for the *Panay* incident, the president made clear his desire to avoid war, and the Japanese apologized, paid an indemnity, and the popular fear of hostilities subsided.

All the while as war loomed in Europe, especially after the Munich crisis in September and despite earlier setbacks to his views on executive authority, Roosevelt became increasingly assertive about his prerogatives. He told the Senate in January 1939 that "as Chief of the Army and Navy and Head of the Executive Department" he would provide arms to Britain and France for defense against a menacing Germany and do everything he possibly could "to prevent any munitions from going to Germany, Italy or Japan. Why? Because self-protection is part of the American policy," he asserted, and "that is the foreign policy of the United States."[19]

Two months later the president again focused on how war might affect the United States. He explained the difficulty of defining war, making his point with allusions to the Quasi-War with France. He referred to it as "actual warfare," hence as illustrating properly but in simplified terms that "this business of carrying on war without declaring a war" was something "not new." This example fit with his conviction that if "a nation were to attack the United States . . . it is undoubtedly the Constitutional duty of the President to defend it without the declaring of war."[20]

This belief, the validity of which hinged on what constituted an attack, guided Roosevelt's thinking when on September 1 Hitler's army invaded Poland, thereby launching the Second World War. The president formally declared neutrality but did not, as had Woodrow Wilson, ask Americans to remain neutral in thought as well as deed. Within the scope of his power, Roosevelt promised "there will be no black-out of peace in the United States." As usual in times of international crises, the president's standing in the polls shot up. With both confidence and an awareness of prevalent peace sentiment, he initiated measures to oppose Nazi Germany.

At the same time, Congress had enacted into law its own diluted version of Roosevelt's bill for reorganizing the executive branch. Promptly, he imaginatively used the limited powers granted him in implementing the reorganization. On September 8, the same day he proclaimed a "limited national emergency" for "enforcing" neutrality and "strengthening our national defense," he created the executive office of the president. It began as an advisory body and a kind of personal intelligence service with a few assistants and budget analysts. In later years, it would grow into a huge bureaucracy dedicated to advancing the president's legislative agenda and his independent policymaking.

As for Roosevelt, he proceeded with emergency authority and increasing independence of the isolationist Congress to expand executive power, most aggressively after June 1940 when Germany defeated France. He moved in this direction initially with two significant measures. The first came with his decision to break precedent and run for a third term and the second followed when on his own authority he decided to step up aid provided to Great Britain, then facing invasion and pummeling by air.

As the nominating season approached and the question of whether or not the United States would become involved in the war became the foremost issue facing the electorate, Roosevelt denied any desire to remain in office. He claimed, nonetheless, that in view of the war crisis many people insisted he must run. As his intimate adviser, Harry L. Hopkins, put it, "The only thing that matters is to take care of the war situation. Nothing else. . . . The only man who understands the situation is Roosevelt and he has got to run." Others, too, flattered the president, saying he was the only "man big enough to handle the world situation," that "it was his duty to run," or told him, "You must not let us down." He speculated that "he could win in November, unless the war should stop."[21] With a keen awareness of his crisis-based popularity and with the sense of indispensability it inspired, he indicated that for the welfare of the country he would accept a draft. In July the Democratic Party drafted him and he ran.

As noted above, Roosevelt's move toward a decisive, larger public commitment to Britain had begun earlier. Just before France fell, Britain's prime minister, Winston Churchill, had pressed him to do more. He asked Roosevelt to abandon neutrality by proclaiming nonbelligerency, a status in international affairs that technically would allow the president to help Britain with everything short of actually engaging armed forces. In addition, the prime minister requested the loan of forty or fifty destroyers the United States had been holding in storage since the First World War. The president had sympathized but on the next day responded he could not act without the specific authorization of Congress.

As a battered Britain prepared defenses against the Nazi onslaught, Churchill and even King George VI pleaded for the war vessels, calling their transfer a matter of life and death. In July Roosevelt told the British ambassador he thought it probable the United States would enter the war. In August, after the British offered to swap bases in the Western Hemisphere for the warships, Roosevelt changed tack. He persuaded himself "that the survival of the British Isles . . . might very possibly depend on their getting these destroyers."[22] So, even though he had doubts about the deal's legality and thought it might imperil his reelection, he decided to go ahead.

The president then asked Attorney General Robert H. Jackson to substantiate the legality of the swap and to find a way of transferring the destroyers without going through Congress. Jackson, the hired counsel for the administration, admitted he would give his client "the benefit of a reasonable doubt as to the law." He did that and more. Using Sutherland's flawed precedent as a guide, he played with the wording of the legislation prohibiting such a transaction in a way allowing him to assure Roosevelt that as commander in chief he had the authority to dispose of the destroyers as he saw proper for "the total defense of the United States." In summary, Jackson advised, "It is not necessary for the Senate to ratify an opportunity that entails no obligation" and hence the president could meet the British request with an executive agreement.[23]

On September 3, Roosevelt put aside concerns over possible impeachment and gave fifty overage destroyers to Britain in exchange for the use of naval bases in the western Atlantic. In defending the exchange, he mutilated both history and precedent by lauding it "as the most important action" taken for national defense "since the Louisiana purchase."[24]

Opponents whom the president disparaged as legalists, viewed the transaction differently. In an advertisement placed in leading newspapers, the St. Louis *Post-Despatch* announced: "Mr. Roosevelt today committed an act of war. He also became America's first dictator." Wendell Willkie, the Republican candidate for president who had approved Roosevelt's aim but objected to the circumventing of Congress, soon denounced the transaction as "the most dictatorial and arbitrary act of any President in the history of the United States." Academic critics attacked Jackson's assumptions, asserting the transfer of the vessels to a "belligerent is a violation of our neutral status, a violation of our national law, and a violation of international law." They also pointed out that the transaction breached at least two statutes and "represented an assertion by the President of a power which by the Constitution is specifically assigned to Congress, essentially the authority to initiate war."[25]

These dissenters represented a distinct minority. Much of the public, hawks, and backers of the strong presidency applauded Roosevelt's initiative, seemingly without regard for its basic intent. He and Churchill publicly exaggerated the military importance of the transaction but privately they underscored its true significance as political rather than nautical. It fitted Churchill's resolve "to involve the United States inextricably in the Allied cause." Years later, he characterized the transfer of the destroyers as "a decidedly unneutral act" that would have justified a declaration of war from Hitler on the United States. Later writers perceived in the deal notable long-term significance for presidents bent on accruing power. For example, critics called it "a watershed in the use and abuse of presidential power, foreshadowing a series of dangerous and often disastrous adventures abroad."[26]

Willkie, meanwhile, sought to benefit from the widespread peace sentiment by accusing the president of warmongering. He proclaimed that if elected he would "do all that is humanly possible to avoid war." He also promised that American boys "will never go to a foreign war under my direction." Placed on the defensive, Roosevelt made peace the foremost issue in his campaigning but insisted that aid to Britain would keep the nation at peace. In Philadelphia, he confronted the repeated charge that he wished to lead the country into war, denouncing it as false and insisting we "are following the road to peace." Seven days later in Boston he told American mothers and fathers, "I have said this before, but I shall say it again and again and again: Your boys are not going to be sent into any foreign wars." He later rationalized this commitment, to himself as to others, by saying "If we're attacked it's no longer a foreign war."[27]

Roosevelt's peace strategy paid off. He won the election by a narrow margin but nonetheless viewed it as a mandate to give Britain all aid short of war. Soon after, in a Fireside Chat via radio, he explained why he had decided to oppose the Axis powers. The "United States has no right or reason to talk of peace," he declared, until the aggressors "abandon all thought of dominating or conquering the world." Recent experience proves "beyond doubt that no nation can appease the Nazis." Then he described his policy as not "directed toward war" but "to keep war away from our country and our people." To do this, "We must be the great arsenal of democracy."[28] Congress gave at least tacit approval to this program by appropriating funds to build the bases on the sites acquired from Britain.

The president also hardened his position against Japan's conquering spree but not to the point of war. For instance, in June when the Japanese had demanded that France surrender control over parts of its Indochina colony, the French authorities appealed to him for help. He responded he could not draw the nation into hostilities but did warn the Japanese if they used force in Indochina he would retaliate with other means. Undeterred, Japan on September 24 invaded northern Indochina. Two days later, unlike Hoover in the case of Manchuria, Roosevelt applied limited economic sanctions against Japan in the form of an embargo on scrap metal. The next day, Japan concluded an alliance with Germany and Italy aimed at the United States.

This arrangement did not change Roosevelt's perception of Hitler as the foremost menace to American and European democracy. The president now recognized that hostilities with Nazi Germany would probably trigger an attack from Japan. He chose, therefore, to limit the sanctions so as to stave off Japan "as long as possible . . . and to avoid at all costs a military commitment in the Pacific."[29]

In his next move, Roosevelt deepened the commitment to beleaguered Britain by providing her with masses of war matériel at little or no cost, or in his words, by eliminating "the silly, foolish old dollar sign." As with the destroyer deal, he presented this lend-lease proposal not as another step toward hostilities but as one that would lead away from war. Again Congress went along, this time by passing on March 11, 1941, the Lend Lease Act, which empowered the president whenever he deemed it "in the interest of national defense," to sell, lease, or lend arms and other equipment of war to belligerents he favored. "In brief," Edward S. Corwin, a foremost constitutional critic, wrote, "the act delegated to the President the power to fight wars by deputy; to all intents and purposes, it was a qualified declaration of war." This academician also saw it as the most "sweeping delegation of legislative power" ever made "to an American President."[30] Other analysts offered similar criticism, but the president's numerous admirers, and those eager to battle Hitler, rejoiced.

Roosevelt took other measures that pointed to a shooting war in the Atlantic. He garrisoned bases in British possessions ranging from Newfoundland to Guiana; provided escorts for British convoys, which he called patrols to evade legal restrictions on this armed assistance to a belligerent; and, in April, with Denmark's permission, occupied Greenland. He did all this with unilateral executive action, proceeding as though he had decided the country should enter the war. On May 17 he told a cabinet officer he was waiting to be pushed into this situation. Four days later, for the first time and contrary to Hitler's orders, a German submarine deliberately torpedoed and shelled a freighter, the *Robin Moor*, flying the American flag and carrying contraband.

Aides perceived this sinking as providing the provocation the president desired for a counterattack but he did not view it as such. Two days later, when the cabinet urged him to make it a cause for war, he responded, "I am not willing to fire the first shot." He seemed still to be waiting for the Germans to provide him with a galvanizing incident that Hitler took care to avoid.[31] Roosevelt did exploit the freighter episode by enlarging his powers with the proclamation on May 27 of an unlimited national emergency. He also ordered naval units to sink on sight any foreign submarine found in waters he designated as defensive.

Several weeks later, on June 22, the Nazis invaded Russia. Roosevelt promptly promised and shortly delivered material aid to the Soviets. On July 7, he informed Congress that American warships were dropping depth charges in self-defense against Axis submarines. On his own on that day, he also ordered troops to occupy Iceland, in theory to preempt a German seizure of the island. A prominent defender of this deed, Senator Tom Connally, a Democrat from Texas, claimed that as commander in chief the president could deploy armed forces wherever he wished. The senator supported this contention with a list of eighty-five instances when presidents had committed troops abroad. None of them, however, carried sufficient legal weight to uphold his broad reinterpretation of presidential authority. While the nation remained at peace, the alleged precedents also could not justify the hostile actions taken for the first time by a president under his vague authority as commander in chief against belligerents in a major war.

Regardless, on July 26, two days after the Japanese occupied southern Indochina, Roosevelt exercised similar authority against Japan. Although he still considered it "terribly important for the control of the Atlantic for us to help keep peace in the Pacific" and hence did not impose a full embargo on oil, he froze Japanese assets in the United States and added to his banned list such items as high-test aviation gasoline.[32]

The president also reinforced the partnership with Britain. On August 14, for the first time, he met with Churchill at Placentia Bay in Newfoundland for four days of secret talks. They discussed war aims as though the United States had already become a belligerent. Roosevelt promised to support Britain in the naval battle of the Atlantic even "at the risk of war, tipping from most benevolent neutrality to active belligerency."[33] Then, in the form of a press release, the two leaders issued the Atlantic Charter to announce their common objectives.

Less than a month after, a U-boat fired at the USS *Greer*, a destroyer that had been tracking it for more than three hours as a service to the British. On September 5, a few days later, Roosevelt spoke to the nation about the incident in another Fireside Chat. Ignoring the provocation, he denounced the attack as piracy and announced that henceforth American warships would strike first at Axis raiders and submarines. "We sought no shooting war with Hitler," he said. "We do not seek it now." He characterized his order as defensive. In passionate rhetoric he called German submarines "the rattlesnakes of the Atlantic," asserting that "their very presence in waters which America deems vital to its defense constitutes an attack."[34] He used the snake analogy as though justifying a resort to force, saying that when you see a rattlesnake poised to strike you should crush it before it attacks.

On that same day, again citing his authority as commander in chief, the president dispatched armed forces to Iceland, which recently had declared itself independent of Denmark. He explained his action as preemptive, designed to prevent the Germans from getting there first and gravely threatening the flow of munitions to Britain. Senator Robert A. Taft, a Republican from Ohio, protested that the president had no legal or constitutional right to send the troops without congressional authorization. Other Roosevelt opponents argued he had no legitimate authority to take upon himself the role of international policeman to stop aggression or resist governments because he found their philosophies repugnant.

This opposition bothered the president because, even though no nation had attacked or threatened to attack the United States, he was convinced that "entry into the war was almost unavoidable." He realized, however, if he asked Congress for a declaration of war he would not get it; he would suffer a "certain and disastrous [political] defeat"; and "opinion would swing against him." So he dismissed declarations of war as out of fashion and stood firm in his determination continually to step up the aid to Britain.[35]

More incidents followed. On October 17, in a pitched battle, a German submarine torpedoed the destroyer USS *Kearny*, killing eleven Americans. Ten days later, the president announced the "shooting war has started." On October 30, a German torpedo sank the destroyer *Reuben James* with the loss of one hundred lives. As the nation edged closer to full-scale war, he took note of critics who questioned the legality of his actions. "In spite of what some people say," he announced, "I seek always to be a constitutional President."[36]

All the while, Roosevelt had continued babying the Japanese, as he put it, while trying to deter them from further conquests with the threat of more sanctions. In August, however, he warned that if they continued in their violence, he would take stronger measures. In September he restricted the flow of more strategic goods, such as oil, to Japan. On his own, without announcing his decision, he had critically expanded the sanctions. With the end of the stalling strategy, the squeeze on trade slowly strangled Japan.

This toughness, signaled also by the repeal on November 13 of the neutrality legislation and with it an increase in presidential discretion in the use of the war power, brought the Pacific crisis to a head. On November 26, Secretary of State Cordell Hull, who believed in "practically no possibility of an agreement being achieved with Japan," sent a ten-point proposal, often called an ultimatum, to the Japanese. It reiterated the administration's most stringent position, insisting they must withdraw from "China and Indo-China completely and immediately," a step they would not take. Since cryptographers had broken Japan's principal secret code and, four days earlier, had learned that soon "things are automatically going to happen," the president and his advisers realized that the Japanese rejection of Roosevelt's proposal meant war. Early in December, as he waited for the Japanese to act, he gave Churchill what he had long desired but previously had promised only indirectly; "a commitment of armed support in the case of a Japanese attack on British or Dutch territory or on Thailand."[37]

The blow Roosevelt and his aides expected fell on December 7 when Japanese naval aviators attacked Pearl Harbor. As Secretary of War Henry L. Stimson noted, news of that assault brought relief "that a crisis had come in a way which would unite all our people." In line with this feeling, the president told his advisers, as though what he desired at last had happened, "We are in it."[38] The next day, after informing Congress that as commander in chief he had taken full measures of defense, he asked it to recognize that a state of war with the Japanese empire already existed. The legislators backed him with only one dissenting vote. On December 11, Germany and Italy declared war on the United States. It immediately declared war on both.

Isolationists, conservative political opponents, and some unfriendly academics, then and since, charged Roosevelt with leading the country into war through deception. They, as well as intellectuals who admired his domestic policies, portrayed him as trying to goad Hitler into hostilities because he could not persuade Congress to declare war. When that tactic failed, they as well as revisionist historians argued that Roosevelt, through back-door diplomacy, had maneuvered the Japanese into firing the first shot. From an opposite position, liberal and internationalist critics, and some from the Left, denounced him as an "appeaser" who "waited for Hitler to force America into the European war" and who had moved too slowly in becoming a warrior.[39]

Roosevelt's defenders point out correctly that no one has provided proof for these theories. Supporters also cite data, usually the president's own words, showing that up to the last minute he wanted no war with Japan. Roosevelt did say later, however, "that if the Japanese had not attacked the United States he doubted very much if it would have been possible to send any troops to Europe." His boosters see nothing sinister in such a comment while cynics discount his claimed desire for peace. The latter argue he never sought a genuine accommodation with Japan. Nonetheless, most scholars, even many who perceive him as pushing for war, praise him for seeing "more clearly than the isolationist voters" the peril the Axis powers posed to the nation. They acclaim his foresight in helping to rid the world of a great menace.[40]

Regardless of the bitter contention over the propriety of Roosevelt's motivation, most students of his policy recognize that step by step, he had moved the nation toward belligerency. They also believe he did so wisely in the interest of national security. Regardless of precise motivation, or whether intervention would have come anyway under other leadership, once more presidential initiative stood out as a noteworthy ingredient in the causes that brought the United States into a war.

Roosevelt quickly embraced his enhanced wartime role which, as head of the armed forces, freed him from the usual peacetime restraints on the presidency. Hull and others observed, "he loved the military side of events, and liked to hold them in his own hand." Biographers, too, noted that "he wanted to be a soldier, a professional."[41] Now Roosevelt preferred being addressed as "Commander-in-Chief rather than President." He did not transform himself into a militarist but he eagerly grasped the opportunity to demonstrate virility as a warrior. He led the nation's military forces on a global scale, conducting the war with virtually dictatorial authority. He rarely referred to Congress and made clear to all, as had Abraham Lincoln, that to achieve victory he would use any power at his command.

On February 19, 1942, in his capacity as commander in chief, Roosevelt exercised his augmented power to sign Executive Order 9066 for the incarceration of more than 120,000 Japanese residents on the West Coast. Nearly two-thirds of them were American citizens. The following month, a congressional resolution supplemented his order. Here, as had Wilson, the president exhibited a disregard for civil rights and abused the vast authority he had appropriated. This detour from the altruism of his war aims seems explainable in his private characterization of himself. Roosevelt described himself as a juggler who never let his right hand know what his left hand did. "I may be entirely inconsistent," he confessed, "and furthermore I am perfectly willing to mislead and tell untruths if it will help win the war."[42]

Seven months later, in seeking authority to institute price controls, the president publicly acknowledged the extraordinary scope of his authority and explained why he used it as he did. He told Congress if it refused his request he would act on his own, averring he had the legal right "to take measures to avert a disaster which would interfere with winning the war."

He described his responsibilities as very grave. "This total war, with our fighting fronts all over the world," he emphasized, "makes the use of executive power far more essential than in any previous war." He could not foretell what powers he might have to exercise but declared, "I shall not hesitate to use every power vested in me" to win the war. "When the war is over," he added, "the powers under which I act automatically revert to the people—to whom they belong."[43]

Roosevelt implied he possessed a special, almost intuitive, relationship with the people that at times seemingly placed him above the law, but regardless of how he used his power, he perceived his position as legal. As the nation's steward, he viewed his role as personal and institutional. He staged his Fireside Chats, press conferences, and well-publicized summit conferences with world leaders in order to maintain his populist image. Since he knew this strategy worked and most people supported his wartime leadership, he rarely allowed anything to brake his exercise of power. Not even the courts attempted to restrain him. They upheld the constitutionality of every war statute that came before them in his favor. Nonetheless, Roosevelt's use of the war power continued to alarm the enemies of executive aggrandizement.

Through much of Roosevelt's third term these dissenters could not buck his popularity. He enjoyed the adulation, still cherished being president, and relished power so much he played with the idea of running for a fourth term. First, though, he again performed the rituals of denial. "God knows I don't want to," he told an adviser early in 1944, "but I may find it necessary." Later he said, "all that is within me cries out to go back to my home on the Hudson River." He added that "as a good soldier" he would continue to serve if "so ordered by the Commander-in-Chief of us all, the sovereign people of the United States."[44] He assumed they would see the need for him, above anyone else, to wrap up the war and shape the peace, and that they would keep him in power. He decided to run and, as expected, in November the people again chose him—but by a narrower margin than in his previous elections.

With a political victory in hand and a military victory in sight, Roosevelt could now give more attention to planning for the postwar world. He thought in terms of linking peace with the concept of a policing power similar to that of his cousin Theodore but now often expressed as collective security. "Peace, like war," the president had stated shortly before his reelection, can succeed only where there is a will to enforce it. For this reason, he explained, the council of the new world organization he sponsored, the United Nations, "must have the power . . . to keep the peace by force if necessary."[45] As he desired, the United Nations charter placed this power in the hands of what he called the four policemen—the United States, the Soviet Union, Britain, and China. To enforce peace, these victors would "wield police powers." Thus, to the end of his life on April 12, 1945, Roosevelt exercised executive power with few restraints but used it also in an effort to reform the international politics of the postwar world.

In all, in his thirteen years in the White House, mostly while directing a war of unprecedented global dimensions, Roosevelt raised presidential power in foreign affairs to a level higher than that reached by any of his predecessors. Some scholars claim he transformed the office. Certainly, in this longest presidency in the nation's history, he wrought changes that endured, not the least being the reshaping of the model for what many would regard as presidential machismo. This model flourished, in part, because it grew in tandem with the rise of the United States to a superpower; won the admiration of scholars, journalists, and much of the public; and benefited from Roosevelt's status as a savior. Like Jefferson, Lincoln, Polk, and others, he took decisive action to expand the presidential war power because he believed he had to do so to rescue the nation from great peril.

Numerous critics, such as the well-known historian Charles A. Beard, perceived Roosevelt more as a devil than a savior, charging him with nullifying the Constitution, practicing deception, and acting on "the theory of limitless power in the Executive" in matters of war power and peace. Close friends and aides in the White House also expressed alarm over the president's exercise of authority. They hoped "that a phenomenon like Franklin D. Roosevelt would not recur" because, in the words of his speechwriter, Robert Sherwood, the nation must never again rely so much on "the durability of one mortal man." It could happen again because, as Sherwood pointed out in a kind of warning, "the extraordinary and solitary Constitutional powers of the President remain and, in times of crises, they are going to be asserted for better or for worse."[46]

Harry S. Truman

SUCH admonition did little to impair the widespread esteem for the executive as activist-savior. It carried over into the administration of Harry S. Truman. This politician had been born, bred, and educated in Missouri, as a biographer notes, "in a society that venerated masculine strength and leadership." Another biographer maintains he "found his model for manliness in his army experience [during the First World War], and he would never abandon this model."[47] Regardless of the source of Truman's admiration for virility, he brought it to the White House.

When Truman took over the presidency, it awed and bewildered him. He knew something of how the office functioned but little of the intricacies of Roosevelt's wartime policies. While serving as vice president, he never made it into the administration's inner circle. Roosevelt spoke to him only twice. As Truman told his daughter, he "never did talk to me confidentially about the war, or about foreign affairs or what he had in mind for peace after the war."[48] Furthermore, compared to that of his immediate predecessors, Truman's background had been provincial. He lacked in-depth knowledge about foreign policy in particular and about world affairs generally.

Despite these limitations, Truman brought to the presidency two certitudes that would guide his administration's foreign policy. First, he believed in an America of exceptional worth, a nation endowed with a worldwide mission. Secondly, he was convinced that communism, perceived mistakenly as a monolith controlled by Moscow, menaced the world much as had fascism. He also brought qualities that he believed helped him master the job—candor, a willingness to learn but also stubbornness in support of mistaken beliefs, to work at a heady pace, and to delegate responsibility. In addition, he possessed intimate knowledge of practical politics and a capacity to make and stand by tough decisions.

"I am here to make decisions," Truman said within a month in office, "and whether they prove right or wrong I am going to make them." Even in matters of life and death he claimed to act free of anxiety. "Once a decision was made," he explained, "I did not worry about it afterward." At times, though, an impulsive streak made for wrongheaded judgments. As another biographer who had observed him closely put it, "He had a weakness for rushing into action without fully weighing the consequences."[49] Various scholars perceive this quality in his decision to use atomic bombs.

Truman did not learn the details of the atomic arms project until well into his second two weeks in office when Secretary of War Stimson explained it to him. At the time no bomb had been built but Truman quickly assumed, as did his advisers, that this device of potentially vast destructive force could bring Japan to her knees. Seemingly for this reason he did not explore Japanese peace feelers intensively and did not hesitate in deciding to employ this weapon when ready. In July when he departed for two weeks of meetings with Russian and British leaders in Potsdam, outside Berlin, he learned of the successful atomic test held in New Mexico. He and his counselors decided quickly to deliver an ultimatum, which the United States and Britain did on July 26, demanding that Japan surrender unconditionally or face prompt and utter destruction. Two days later, the Japanese rejected this Potsdam declaration, as Truman put it, "with a very snotty answer." Immediately, as commander in chief, he took what many historians and others regard as the most controversial act of his presidency.[50] He ordered the dropping of the first atomic bomb on Hiroshima.

When the bomb exploded on August 6 Truman blurted out, "This is the greatest thing in history." Most Americans shared this sentiment. A poll taken two days later indicated that 85 percent of those queried approved of the deadly blast. The next day the army air force released its other atomic bomb over Nagasaki. The president was convinced that weapon "had given us great power, and . . . in the last analysis, it would control."[51] On August 14, Japan surrendered and the Second World War ended.

A critical minority, composed largely of intellectuals such as journalists and revisionist scholars, attacked the president for bombing hastily and insensitively. Among other skeptics, two of the nation's highest military leaders, Admiral William D. Leahy and General Dwight D. Eisenhower, condemned "the use of this barbarous weapon" as ethically wrong, as of "no material assistance in our war," and as "completely unnecessary." From the start, though, Truman stood firm and took full responsibility for his acts, defending them with a variety of reasons such as revenge for Pearl Harbor and as necessary to save an estimated 250,000 American and an equal number of Japanese lives that would have been lost in a planned invasion of Japan. Others estimated casualties as high as one million. Years later, he denounced the uproar about what he did or what he could have done. He denounced the supposed experts as not knowing what they are talking about. "I was there. I did it. I would do it again." He professed also, "I didn't hesitate a minute, and I've never lost any sleep over it since."[52]

In the two or three months that followed the bomb decisions, this blunt style became a characteristic of Truman's presidency. He became accustomed to wielding the authority of his office, now widely regarded as the most powerful executive post in the world. Determined to prove himself a strong, in-charge executive, he spoke of his power in the vocabulary of masculine toughness. He also compared being president to riding a tiger—keep mounted or be devoured. To remain on top of events and to exercise his authority more directly than had past presidents, he asked Congress "for increased presidential authority over executive agencies."[53] The legislators produced and passed a bill that on December 20 he signed into law. It permitted him to continue to exercise the special wartime powers of the executive into the cold war.

In waging the cold war, Truman had an almost visceral reaction to the tactics of the Russians, comparing them at times to the barbarians from the East who had shattered the Roman Empire. In March 1946 when the Soviets refused to evacuate northern Iran where they had been wartime occupiers, he took a firm stand against them, claiming later to have sent an ultimatum to Josef Stalin—Get your troops out or else. No one has found a record of the ultimatum but the Russians finally did leave Iran.

As the cold war intensified, so did Truman's distrust of the Soviets. He became convinced they intended to invade Turkey, seize the Black Sea straits, and aid communists in taking over Greece. "Unless Russia is faced with an iron fist and strong language," he declared, "another war is in the making."[54] He assumed the Soviet leaders understood only force. The crisis came to a head when the British—who had been aiding with arms and money both the Turks and Greece's conservative regime, which was engaged in a civil war against communist guerrillas—informed him they could no longer afford the subsidies. On February 24, 1947, the British asked him to take over the policing burden they had shouldered, couching their request as in keeping with the responsibility of world leadership they acknowledged the United States had assumed.

Even though the allusions to the Soviet use of force in either Greece or Turkey in the British request lacked evidence of troop buildups or of aggressive moves, the appeal touched the president's combativeness. The next day he told aides "that the United States was going to be at war with Russia, and on two fronts." After consultation with his cabinet members and others, he decided to embark on a program of containing Soviet expansion. On March 12, he announced that the aggressions of totalitarian regimes "undermine the foundations of international peace and hence the security of the United States." Therefore, "it must be the policy of the United States to support free peoples who are resisting attempted subjugation by armed minorities or by outside pressure." He wished to carry out this policy first by assisting Turkey and Greece economically and militarily. Congress passed the aid bill and on May 22 Truman signed it. Despite denials, from the start the administration had planned to use military measures in Greece as a "means for facilitating strategy."[55]

This containment policy, known usually as the Truman Doctrine, soon became the vehicle for expanding the scope of executive authority beyond anything claimed by Truman's predecessors. Of course, it had precedents, as in Theodore Roosevelt's policing of the Caribbean. Since Truman saw the communist threat as global, he asserted the right to intervene virtually anywhere in the world as he deemed proper. Skeptics, and even supporters, consequently perceived him as converting the United States military machine into the world's foremost anticommunist police force with himself as its chief. The immense growth in the nation's wealth and power gave him the capacity for such globalism, a power he used sometimes positively, sometimes negatively, but with only minor restraint.

Soon, Truman employed his doctrine to pave the way for massive economic as well as military assistance to many countries but chiefly to those in Western Europe. After some planning within the administration, this program took off when Secretary of State George C. Marshall, in a commencement address at Harvard University on June 5, proposed to help Europeans combat hunger, poverty, desperation, and chaos, along with aid that would revive the world economy and stimulate conditions "in which free institutions can exist." Later, he said, "We can act for our own good by acting for the world's good."[56]

The president backed the recovery program as a cold-war measure to contain a possible surge in Soviet power, named it the Marshall Plan, and on December 19 presented it to Congress. In March 1948 he combined his plea for the program with proposals for universal military training and resumption of the draft. In April, Congress approved the plan as the European Recovery Act and in June voted an initial funding of $4.3 billion. Later, the government poured more billions into the plan, helping to make it ultimately the most successful of the cold-war ventures to aid allies.

Earlier, in addition to addressing economic concerns in Europe, a number of the president's leading advisers had wanted to strengthen the nation's gathering of intelligence for cold-war purposes. Since the United States faced no immediate, tangible foreign danger, Truman initially resisted this idea, particularly when it came to him in the package of a centralized spying agency, or what he called "building up a gestapo." Shortly, he bowed to pressure. On January 22, 1946, through a presidential directive, he created a central intelligence group, a restructuring that moved the "primacy in intelligence from the State Department to the Executive Office of the President."[57]

Closer executive control followed on July 25, 1947, when Congress passed the National Security Act, which coordinated the armed services under the military establishment, created the National Security Council, and converted the intelligence group into the Central Intelligence Agency (CIA). It also made the CIA an independent department responsible directly to the president. Two years later, amendments to this law placed the armed services under a single Department of Defense and freed the CIA from congressional budgetary controls imposed on other agencies.

Quickly, the CIA abandoned its proposed role of intelligence analysis and became directly involved in covert activities. In 1949, it secretly attempted, but failed, to overthrow the communist regime in Albania. Regardless of the agency's failures or successes, Truman, in agreeing to create it, amplified presidential power. Furthermore, in using the CIA for clandestine endeavors, he set the precedent for shielding executive decisions, which frequently involved the use of military force, from outside scrutiny.

Meanwhile, in December 1947 Western Germany's American, British, and French occupiers had combined their zones under a central administration in a united front against the Soviet Union. In June of the following year, they introduced a common currency and began circulating it in western Berlin, 110 miles within the Soviet zone of Eastern Germany and headquarters for the four occupying powers. The Soviets then introduced their own currency in the city and restricted highway and rail traffic into it. On July 19 when the cabinet debated what to do about the blockade, Truman took a belligerent stance even though Berlin had no intrinsic strategic value. "We'll stay in Berlin—come what may," he stated. "I don't pass the buck, nor do I alibi out of any decision I make."[58]

Cynics viewed Truman's decision as an effort to preserve his containment policy as well as his presidency at stake in the forthcoming election. Cold war ideologues within the administration, however, perceived this posture as insufficiently aggressive. They urged the use of force to crash through the blockade. Recognizing this advice as too risky because it could trigger war with the Soviets, the president rejected it. He and his British and French allies chose instead to supply the city with basic necessities, such as food and coal, with a massive airlift.

As the fear of war persisted, Truman ruminated uneasily that "we must be prepared for trouble if it comes. Twice in a generation brave allies have kept the barbarian from our borders. It can't happen that way again. . . . Our friends the Russkies understand only one language—how many divisions have you—actual or potential." A month later, with tensions still high, he confided to his diary, "I have a terrible feeling . . . that we are very close to war. I hope not." Privately, he also indicated a willingness to employ atomic weapons "if it became necessary."[59] The necessity did not arise because in May 1949 the Soviets called off the blockade and the war scare passed. For Truman personally, the tough, unilateral risk taking paid off because it did not escalate into a major war; caused his public approval rating, as measured by polls, to bounce up; and gave his election campaign a needed boost.

During this crisis the Supreme Court, as usual, upheld presidential activism abroad, maintaining that "the war power does not necessarily end with the cessation of hostilities." Nonetheless, Justice Robert H. Jackson, the same man who had stretched executive authority in the destroyers-for-bases deal, expressed concern about "this vague, undefined and undefinable 'war power'" that presidents "invoked in haste" to deal with crises, often of their own making. "No one will question," he wrote, "that this power is the most dangerous one to free government in the whole catalogue of powers."[60]

The following year, after winning the presidency on his own in an unprecedented upset, Truman added more military clout to his containment policy. On April 4, 1949, in Washington, representatives from the United States, Canada, and twelve other nations, mostly from Western Europe, signed the North Atlantic Treaty, which aligned them against the Soviet Union. Congress approved it in July, thus ending America's traditional policy of avoiding alliances in times of peace. When, however, he requested $1.5 billion to arm the allied countries, he ran into trouble. Since he had developed his containment policy without much consultation with Congress, many legislators balked at voting funds for it. Arthur H. Vandenberg, the Republican senator from Michigan who had supported most of the administration's foreign policy initiatives, opposed the bill. "It's almost unbelievable in its grant of unlimited power to the Chief Executive," he commented. "It would permit the President to sell, lease or give away anything we've got at any time to any country in any way he wishes. It would virtually make him the number one war lord of the earth."[61] Congress killed the bill. The administration then drafted a measure that included changes acceptable to recalcitrant legislators but left the amount of money requested unchanged. That bill won approval.

In the months that followed, Truman took under consideration plans to build a hydrogen bomb. Most of his scientific advisers opposed the idea, fearing a "superbomb might become a weapon of genocide." Others called it "an inhumane application of force" and "an evil thing." Military and political staffers, however, urged construction of the weapon. Despite this divided counsel, the president wasted little time on further deliberation. During a seven-minute meeting on January 31, 1950, with his special committee on the problem, he asked, "Can the Russians do it?" It responded yes. "In that case," he retorted, "we have no choice. We'll go ahead."[62] The White House immediately made the H-bomb decision public.

Five months later, the president made another swift decision on a matter of worldwide significance. He jumped into the turmoil in divided Korea, a country American and Russian forces had occupied and then had withdrawn their forces from. Initially, he had regarded Korea of little strategic value to the United States and accordingly as a place where there should be no further commitment of military force. On June 25 when North Korean communists invaded the Republic of Korea, the rump nation in the south the United States had largely created, this thinking changed.

Truman reacted with alarm for a mix of reasons, such as his preconceived cold-war, anticommunist convictions and his belief that he must conduct himself in keeping with his own understanding of the diplomacy of the recent past in the Korean situation. He was convinced, for instance, that the Western democracies' lack of solid support for collective security through the League of Nations had permitted the rise of Nazi Germany. Viewing the attack on South Korea as a threat to the new collective security system, he vowed not to let the United Nations go the way of the league.

In addition, Truman perceived North Korea and Communist China as tools of Moscow. "Korea is the Greece of the Far East," he explained. "If we are tough enough now, if we stand up to [the communists], like we did in Greece three years ago, they won't take any next steps." As the CIA and others maintained, he assumed the Russians had brokered the invasion, that they were determined to follow in the path of Hitler and Mussolini, and therefore "they should be met head on in Korea." As later research would reveal, although Kim Il-sung, North Korea's dictator, was beholden to the Soviets and Chinese communists for arms and other assistance, he had launched the war on his own initiative to reunify the country. "I do not sleep at night," he explained, "thinking about unification."[63]

Not knowing of Kim's role, on the day following the invasion an incensed Truman condemned North Korea's "lawless action," warning that "willful disregard of the obligation to keep the peace cannot be tolerated by nations that support the United Nations Charter." His daughter Margaret entered in her diary, "Northern or Communist Korea is marching in on Southern Korea and we are going to fight." To his aides, the president exclaimed that to foil the attackers he would "hit them hard."[64]

On June 27, without yet having a request for help from the Republic of Korea, the president bypassed Congress, as well as his security council, to rush into hostilities. He ordered General Douglas MacArthur, in command of American forces in Japan, to give direct air and naval support to the South Koreans. On that same day, American officials manipulated the security council of the United Nations into validating the president's action by declaring the communist attack a breach of the peace and calling on the organization's members to aid the South Koreans in repelling it.

Even though, as we have seen, other presidents had used force on their own, constitutional scholars still usually maintained it was illegal for the president, or anyone but Congress, to authorize the use of the military in foreign territory. Most of them conceded, though, that the executive could in a sudden emergency act militarily on his own. Critics questioned that the Korean situation constituted such an emergency or that it threatened American security. If it did, they asked, why not declare war?

On the day of Truman's intervention order, a senator inquired if he had "arrogated to himself the authority of declaring war." The following day, June 28, Robert Taft of Ohio, in speaking for the dissenters, denied the president had "any right to precipitate any open warfare." He declared also, "We are now . . . in a de facto war with the northern Korean Communists," that "Korea itself is not vitally important to the United States," and that Truman had "no legal authority for what he has done." A day later when a journalist asked the president if the country had gone to war, he reiterated, "We are not at war." When another one queried, Is the conflict then "a police action under the United Nations?" Truman agreed, saying, "Yes. That is exactly what it amounts to."[65] The next day, he expanded the intervention by ordering ground troops to the combat zone in Korea.

The president did not go to Congress for a declaration of war even after plunging into the distant civil conflict because, among other reasons, he and his advisers perceived his credibility as an anticommunist sheriff at stake. Moreover, he had readily at his disposal the massive military power necessary to sustain that reputation. He also had public support. As a Gallup poll reported, 68 percent of those queried favored stopping presupposed Russian expansion in Asia and Europe. Truman stressed this popular sentiment when Frank Pace Jr., the secretary of the army, brought up the matter of the declaration. "Frank, it's not necessary," he responded. "They are all with me."[66]

As with the idea of declaring war, Truman spurned suggestions he should seek at least a resolution of approval from Congress. Instead, he leaned on the counsel of intimates such as Secretary of State Dean G. Acheson, his most trusted foreign policy adviser, and Tom Connally, chairman of the Senate Committee on Foreign Relations. Acheson recommended that the president "rely on his constitutional authority as Commander in Chief of the armed forces." Unlike the critics of the intervention, the secretary never had "any serious doubt . . . of the President's constitutional authority to do what he did." Nor did Connally. He told Truman, "You have the right to do it as commander-in-chief and under the UN Charter."[67]

On similar grounds on July 3 the State Department, as directed by its chief, publicly defended the president's unilateral decision. It asserted that his "power to send Armed Forces outside the country is not dependent on Congressional authority" and that it "has repeatedly been emphasized by numerous writers."[68] The memorandum listed eighty-five instances when chief executives on their own sent troops into combat. The cited precedents referred to the use of force against freebooters or against threats to the lives of Americans in weak countries. None applied to major hostilities against a sovereign nation backed by a great power.

As other scholars pointed out, reliance on previous executive breaches of constitutional restraints does not legitimate subsequent violations. In addition to citing dubious precedents to justify the president's use of large-scale force, the State Department referred to anecdotal data, to scholarly and other opinions favorable to its position, and to treaty obligations—essentially the United Nations charter. Truman's other defenders in Congress and elsewhere echoed such arguments, stressing that in deploying troops in Korea he did not commit an act of war. He merely exercised a police power he assumed the right to define.

Bolstered by such support, Truman claimed he acted with an inherent power or "within his authority as Commander in Chief." With this contention he successfully defended his independent exercise of power. Whereas other presidents had maneuvered the nation into war, they had not advanced a questionable constitutional authority to do so against a major foe. Others also had theorized about inherent power, but he became the first president to exploit the concept extensively as though fact. In addition, he boasted of his ability to expand executive authority as though unaccountable to the elected legislature. Critics such as Taft warned that if the president could intervene in Korea "without congressional approval, he can go to war in Malaya or Indonesia or Iran or South America."[69]

Dismissing such censure as isolationist, Truman and his advisers ran the war just about as they wished. He proceeded according to his belief that "when a nation is at war, its leader . . . ought to have all the tools available for that purpose."[70] Other than sponsoring the American effort, the United Nations had virtually no authority over the war's conduct. South Korea and the nations who supplied a few token forces under the United Nations flag also had no say. As in past wars and other policing interventions, initially most of Congress and the public approved of the president's take-charge behavior. Without much hesitation, the legislators voted military expenditures and extended the life of the selective service system.

This widespread endorsement followed an already established pattern, sometimes called the "rally-round-the flag" phenomenon. Initially most military ventures attract popular and congressional approval. Those who oppose the warfare earn opprobrium as appeasers, constitutional nit-pickers, or isolationists. When, however, the bloodletting runs into trouble the support erodes. This happened in the Korean War.

First, though, the American intervention registered striking success. Beginning with a daring counteroffensive on September 15, 1950, MacArthur's forces crushed the Korean Communist army. Truman and his advisers then decided to alter their war aim from defense of the south to offensive action for a total victory that would unify Korea on terms favorable to the United States. Twelve days later, the president granted MacArthur permission to pursue the war beyond the thirty-eighth parallel into North Korea. On October 1, South Korean troops crossed that line and a week later so did American forces. As though stumbling over a trip-wire, they set in motion Chinese intervention.

From the start, the People's Republic of China had viewed the presence of American forces in Korea as a menace and had threatened to enter the war. On September 30, after Kim Il-sung had requested immediate aid from Beijing, Chou En-lai, China's premier, announced his people would not "supinely tolerate seeing their neighbors savagely invaded by imperialists."[71] Truman and his advisers ignored this and other warnings. When the American and South Korean troops approached the Yalu River, which marked the border with China, the threat of Chinese communist intervention became reality. On October 25, troops that Beijing euphemistically called volunteers clashed with a South Korean regiment, practically annihilating it. More fighting followed until on November 25, in a move carefully prepared, some two hundred thousand Chinese foot soldiers slammed across the Yalu, hurling back the American and South Korean forces in what turned into a rout. *Time* called the defeat a military disaster, "the worst the United States has ever suffered."

The rout activated rumors that Truman stood ready to use the atomic bomb in Korea. When queried he responded, "There has always been active consideration of its use. I don't want to see it used. It is a terrible weapon." Ten days later, after his remarks had set off a diplomatic and political crisis, he recorded in his diary, "I've worked for peace for five years and six months and it looks like World War III is here."[72]

On December 15 the president spoke to the nation via radio and television, announcing, "Our homes, our Nation, all the things we believe in, are in great danger. This danger has been created by the rulers of the Soviet Union." On the basis of this questionable assumption, he decided to triple the armed forces, vastly increase military production, and place the nation on a war footing. The following day, he declared a national emergency that resurrected a number of special executive powers. In his State of the Union message on January 8, 1951, he summarized his war policy and the rationale for it. He repeated the need to uphold collective security; American honor, prestige, and credibility before the world; and to thwart an aggression he stubbornly persisted in perceiving as "part of the attempt of the Russian Communist dictatorship to take over the world, step by step."[73]

When in line with this thinking the president asked for Congress's support in assigning four army divisions to Western Europe, he triggered a great debate, much of it on the extent of executive power in foreign relations. Republicans, mainly, questioned his assumption that the Russians had masterminded the hostilities in Korea and were bent on war elsewhere. In particular, they denied he possessed the authority to order the troops to Western Europe just because he presumed the Soviet Union planned to attack. Dissenters also denounced Truman's claim that as commander in chief he had "the authority to send troops anywhere in the world" without congressional sanction as he had done in Korea. He countered by arguing "that power has been recognized repeatedly by the Congress and the courts." The opinions of these bodies, he added, "are all in favor of the President's exercise of the Presidential power when in his judgment it is necessary."[74]

Acheson claimed even more. He insisted the president not only had "the authority to use the Armed Forces in carrying out the broad foreign policy of the United States. . . , but it is equally clear that this authority may not be interfered with by the Congress in the exercise of powers which it has under the Constitution." Then he waffled, saying "the argument as to who has the power to do this, that, or the other thing, is not exactly what is called for from America in this very critical hour."[75] The debate continued until April. As usual in such confrontations, the Senate finally backed down. It accepted the president's plan for troops to Europe but for not more than four divisions without further congressional approval.

Meanwhile, more and more Americans became frustrated with the mounting casualties in Korea, the rising costs of the war, and the seemingly endless bloodletting. Public support for what many had come to call "Truman's war" eroded. People now sneered at the administration's notion of a police action. In January a poll had indicated that 66 percent of the public surveyed wanted to pull out of Korea and 49 percent regarded the intervention a mistake. As for Truman's presidency, 36 percent approved of it while 49 percent disapproved. Media pundits dismissed him as a spent force politically groping to find a way out of what had become an unpopular war.

This sentiment meshed with a wariness toward presidential authority, which earlier had stemmed primarily from Roosevelt's actions during his long occupancy of the White House. Early in 1947, after having captured control of both houses of Congress, Republicans had gained passage of a constitutional amendment to curb the accumulation of power in the hands of any one person by restricting any president to two terms and sent it to the states for ratification. Truman, who maintained immodestly, "I could be elected again," professed sympathy for the two-term idea stating that "eight years as President is enough and sometimes too much for any man to serve in that capacity." Despite his previous defense of expansive executive authority, at this point he spoke of the "lure of power" and its corroding influence on the executive. Still, he disliked the idea of restricting the president's tenure by law because he felt "the honor of the man in the office" should maintain the two-term tradition.[76]

Regardless of Truman's views, as discontent with the war grew so did distrust of presidential honor, giving the two-term movement in the states the impetus to reach its goal. On February 26, 1951, that limit became part of the Constitution as the Twenty-second Amendment. As time would show, it did not, as some supporters had hoped, do much to restrain presidential power in matters of war and peace.

The amendment also had little impact on Truman's exercise of power. In Korea he tried to break what had become a bloody stalemate by unleashing greater and greater force, as in the saturation bombing of the north that destroyed the rice crops and irrigation channels vital to the civilian population. He also reiterated his threat to use atomic bombs "if the North Koreans and Chinese refused to agree to an armistice." On April 6 he decided to send B-29 bombers equipped with "complete atomic weapons across the Pacific." On July 10, when the communists entered armistice negotiations, it appeared possible to end what had become to many Americans a detested entanglement, but the talks bogged down. The following month, as production of the H-bomb neared completion, Truman downplayed whatever additional leverage that superweapon might give him in coercing the communists. "I never wanted power," he said, "only what is necessary to have so as to get some things done. I'd lay it all down and get out of here right off if I could settle [the rivalry with the Soviet Union] now."[77]

In November a Gallup poll indicated that only 28 percent of the public approved of Truman's conduct. This rating for a president was the lowest in the history of the poll. It reflected the deepening public dissatisfaction with the war he had made his own. Regardless, Truman remained pugnacious. Several times shortly thereafter in his diary he sketched possible belligerent ultimata to the Soviets and Chinese. "Now do you want an end to hostilities in Korea," he asked communist leaders rhetorically, "or do you want China and Siberia destroyed? You either accept our fair and just proposal [at the armistice talks] or you will be completely destroyed." He signed, "The C. in C."[78]

At this time, too, Truman's elastic view of executive authority ran into difficulty in domestic affairs. The problem began when the United Steelworkers Union asked for a large wage increase and to achieve it scheduled a strike. He saw their demand, as well as that of the industry for an accompanying increase in the price of steel, as compromising his anti-inflation program. On April 8, 1952, he seized the steel mills, saying a work stoppage would imperil the war effort. To justify this deed, he again claimed immense authority to meet national emergencies through the inherent-power theory. He perceived himself as acting "in the interest of the people, and in order to do that," as he explained later, "the President must use whatever power the Constitution does not expressly deny him." He assumed, therefore, "that the taking of the companies' property was a valid exercise of the authority of the President," or as one analyst put it, "What the Prince has decided, let that be law."[79]

In one of its rare decisions against the executive in time of war, the

Supreme Court by a vote of six to three on June 2 pronounced the takeover unconstitutional because neither the Korean War nor the cold war was a full-scale emergency justifying the exercise of the president's war power. Speaking for the Court, Justice Hugo L. Black declared that the seizure "order cannot properly be sustained as an exercise of the President's military power as Commander in Chief."[80] In a separate opinion, Justice Jackson called the appropriating of the mills sinister and alarming because it could enlarge the president's power over internal affairs. Truman then asked Congress for authority to seize the plants, now idled by the strike, but it refused. In compliance with the Court's ruling, he relinquished control. As he did frequently, he grumbled that his opponents, not he, were out of step.

This setback for Truman, but mostly the albatross of the war in Korea, with its seemingly endless armistice negotiations, had a crucial impact on presidential politics. Even though he did not run, he became a prime issue in the electioneering. Tired of him and of the war, the voters in November turned against the Democrats. Shortly after, he penned a cautionary note to the incoming president. Be careful, he warned, the "men in Congress are forever trying to take the President's powers as Chief Executive, Commander in Chief, and Foreign Policy Chief away from him."[81] A few months later, as he prepared to surrender power, Truman commented, "The greatest part of the President's job is to make decisions. . . . He can't pass the buck to anybody. No one else can do the deciding for him. That's his job."[82] Many Americans disliked his decisions, disapproved of him, and now hated the war he left behind. It proved no menace to national security as he had claimed but it devastated Korea and devoured lives and wealth on both sides.

The war also had a lasting impact on the presidency, a matter of deep concern to Truman. He spoke often of the office as a burden and of being entrusted "with a power that appalls a thinking man." He expressed disdain for that power and for the glamour that surrounded the presidency but deplored the "abuse from liars and demagogues" the president had to endure. Biographers and students of Truman's presidency discount his protestations, noting that "unquestionably he enjoyed the power of the office and its trappings."[83] More than had his predecessors, he amplified the executive's war power. Whereas others had employed the military in hostilities on their own initiative, he did so on a larger scale and claimed he could do so as prerogative.

Truman acted in this manner because of his temperament, his black-

and-white view of the world, his simplistic, nationalist convictions, and the immense power he had at his disposal. He rationalized his raw exercise of power by citing a doubtful need to move swiftly to protect the nation in a hostile world. Despite his public expressions of humility and his accomplishments as a liberal reformer, this feisty cold warrior's wide-ranging resort to military force on his own brought presidential machismo to maturity.

CHAPTER 6

Covert Interventionism

> *When the push of a button may mean obliteration of countless humans, the President of the United States must be forever on guard against any inclination on his part to impetuosity; to arrogance; to headlong action; to expediency; to facile maneuvers; even to the popularity of an action as opposed to the rightness of an action. He cannot worry about headlines; how the next opinion poll will rate him; how his political future will be affected.*
>
> Dwight D. Eisenhower, November 4, 1960

Dwight David Eisenhower

AS a career military man, Dwight D. Eisenhower spent much of his life outside the United States. He gained fame as the general who led the Allied armies to victory in Europe in the Second World War. Except for two years as president of Columbia University, he had no experience in a major civilian occupation, never held elective office, and knew little about domestic politics even from theory or casual reading. "I was of course," he acknowledged later, "a political novice."[1] Nonetheless, in 1948 leading members of both the Republican and Democratic Parties begged him to run for president on their tickets.

These politicos wanted Eisenhower because they saw in him the hero, adored by millions, who could win elections. With a smile that radiated friendliness, he was likable and gregarious. Despite these assets, at first he resisted all pressures to seek the presidency. For instance, after completing a term as chief of staff of the army, he told reporters he had no desire for the office because a man should not reach beyond his peak. "I think I pretty well hit my peak in history when I accepted the German surrender in 1945," he explained. "Now, why should I want to get into a completely foreign field and go out and try to top that? Why should I go out and deliberately risk that historical peak by trying to push a bit higher?" At another time while in Europe as head of the North Atlantic Treaty Organization (NATO), he told others who pressed him, "I do not want to be president of the United States, and I want no other political office or political connection of any kind."[2]

Soon, the general changed his mind. Why? He did so, he told himself and others, because he discerned a revived isolationism in the nation that threatened two principles he held dear—collective security and presidential control of foreign policy. He disliked the assaults on what he regarded as "the President's constitutional rights, in peacetime, to deploy and dispose American forces according to his best judgment and without the specific approval of Congress." He thought "the President's rights were unassailable" and wanted to protect them. Conversations with conservative Republican leaders in 1951 confirmed his judgment that they "were interested, primarily, in cutting the President, or the Presidency, down to size."[3] To thwart them, as well as the perceived isolationists, he fought for the Republican presidential nomination and won it.

Eisenhower also sought the presidency out of pride, believing he could handle it as well, or better, than others who sought it. This attitude did not show up in his initial campaigning. He gave the impression of being able to take or leave power in his stride. Both his self-esteem and seeming disdain came to the surface when the electorate appeared apathetic because he spoke in platitudes, disappointing even ardent supporters. "If they don't want me," he commented in reference to the voters, "that doesn't matter very much to *me*. I've got a hell of a lot of fishing I'll be happy to do."[4]

The novice politician plodded ahead anyway until on October 24, 1952, in Detroit, he pledged "in the cause of peace," if elected he would "go to Korea" to explore ending the "tragic war."[5] Pundits claim this promise clinched the election. It merely added frosting to the cake because the Korea issue already favored him. Moreover, despite his fear of rejection, Eisenhower had such grassroots personal appeal that his oratorical fumbling hardly deflected his march to a stunning victory that gave Republicans not only the presidency but also control of both houses of Congress. Soon after the election, he made his pledged visit to the Korean battlefields.

In his inaugural, which concentrated on foreign policy, Eisenhower addressed his major interests. As had most of his predecessors, he professed love of peace but connected it to a fierce anticommunism within a cold-war context, asserting, "we hold it to be the first task of statesmanship to develop strength that will deter the forces of aggression and promote the conditions of peace."[6] This sentiment, expressed in terms of power, seemed to voice what most Americans wanted to hear from a hero they had elected in part because of his reputation as a world leader.

In addition to these convictions, Ike, as he was popularly known, brought to the White House a formidable temper, which in his public life he kept under control; an extravagant admiration for Herbert Hoover; and a conservative view of politics, government, and society. Like Hoover, and regardless of his reverence for the presidency, Ike had a conception of the office comparable to that of nineteenth-century Whigs. With a self-confidence seemingly free of arrogance, Eisenhower presumed his wartime experience in international affairs and as head of NATO, as well as his natural endowments, had prepared him for the demands of the presidency, especially in foreign affairs.

Early evaluators of Eisenhower's behavior in the White House thought differently. They perceived him either as a captive hero who came to the presidency "to crown a reputation, not to make one" or as a laissez-faire executive trapped in an office beyond his depth. An adviser noted he "never lost his view of himself as standing apart from politics generally and from his own party in particular." Furthermore, he did not see himself as the dominator of political forces.[7] Instead, he stressed cooperative politics, as in the importance of collective action by Congress and the president, because he believed Franklin Roosevelt and Harry Truman had upset the proper balance between the two branches at the expense of Congress. He wished, moreover, to avoid the barrage of criticism that plagued Truman for embarking on the Korean War on his own. Therefore, despite Ike's determination to protect presidential authority, observers viewed him as opposed to executive aggrandizement.

In theory, this conjecture proved sound because Eisenhower often did govern with an eye on the constitutional limitations of presidential power. On the other hand, as had Thomas Jefferson, as he confronted specific situations he did not allow hypothetical considerations to stand in the way of actions he perceived as proper for the executive to take. We can see this placing of practice above abstract principle in Ike's handling of the Korean War, in its thirty-first month when he took office and still stalemated. During his visit to Korea, he had been sympathetic to a forced military conclusion to the conflict but he put that idea aside because he felt he had "a mandate from the American people to stop this fighting."[8]

For several months in resumed talks with the communists the president tried to work out a truce but the negotiations broke up over repatriation of prisoners. Frustrated, he spoke privately of employing nuclear weapons against North Korea and China. In a meeting of the National Security Council on February 11, 1953, he indicated "we should consider the use of tactical atomic weapons on the Kaesong area" because "we could not go on the way we were indefinitely." On March 31, "somehow or other" he wanted to destroy "the tabu which surrounds the use of atomic weapons." Five days later he "reached the point" of considering "the atomic bomb as simply another weapon in our arsenal" and then decided to force a settlement with the threat "that the United States was prepared to use atomic weapons to end the Korean War." Through various sources, including India's prime minister, the president let the communist adversaries know that "without satisfactory progress" in the armistice talks, "we intended to move decisively, without inhibitions in our use of weapons, and would no longer be responsible for confining hostilities to the Korean Peninsula."[9]

Eisenhower claimed this rattling of nuclear bombs brought the North Koreans and Chinese into line. Researchers since his time dissent. They view the decision, taken secretly on his own authority, as less significant than averred and as bringing the nation to the verge of another, larger war. They contend he acted out of an exaggerated belief in the efficacy of military threat as well as to satisfy certain personal needs, such as a compulsion for action that could later appear virile to both friends and foes. In April the truce talks resumed and, on July 27, the negotiators signed an armistice. Still, the threat of more violence remained because of the president's release, a week later, of a menacing statement from the National Security Council. It declared that if the armistice did not hold "it would not be possible to confine hostilities within the frontiers of Korea."[10] In all, though, the outcome pleased the public, enhanced the president's stature as a decisive leader, and bolstered his faith in the value of macho diplomacy.

Ironically, unilateral action of this kind in matters of war and peace, as well as executive negotiation of international agreements such as those Franklin Roosevelt had concluded at Yalta, had long bothered the most conservative members in Eisenhower's own party. Three years earlier it had prompted Senator John W. Bricker of Ohio, a well-known foe of executive activism who had been the Republican candidate for vice president in 1944, to attack the problem. He sponsored a constitutional amendment designed to prohibit the president from concluding treaties or agreements that abridged "any of the rights recognized" in the Constitution.[11] Support for this measure cut across party lines. In Congress it aroused considerable emotion but became entangled in political and legal controversy. On January 7, 1953, after the squabbling had subsided, he introduced a vague redaction cosponsored by sixty-one senators, most of them Republicans.

While sympathizing with the idea of constitutional restraints on the authority to conclude far-reaching agreements, Eisenhower deplored the basic features of the Bricker Amendment because it would diminish the executive power he wished to protect. He told his brother Edgar, an attorney and a constitutional conservative who favored a tough version of the amendment, that it would "cripple the executive power to the point that we [would] become helpless in world affairs." To placate Bricker and other Republican conservatives, however, the president was willing to compromise. In July, therefore, he endorsed a watered-down form of the measure but Bricker rejected it as woefully inadequate. "The whole damn thing," Eisenhower fumed, "is senseless and plain damaging to the prestige of the United States."[12]

In January 1954, as the showdown approached, the president got mad and "agreed to fight up and down the country" against this "stupid, blind violation of Constitution by stupid, blind isolationists." He would not accept any impairment of his authority to conduct foreign affairs. "The President," he insisted, "must not be deprived of his historic position as spokesman for the nation in its relations with other countries." He now fought the proposal vigorously with speeches, letters, and pressure on members of Congress, stressing it invaded presidential powers. When the Senate on February 26 voted sixty in favor and thirty-one against the amendment, it lost by only one vote short of the needed two-thirds majority. Ike's opposition, backed by his own "convictions and conscience," proved crucial in the measure's narrow defeat.[13]

Soon, Eisenhower's concern for undiminished presidential authority resurfaced over independence struggles in Southeast Asia. Since the end of the Second World War various nationalist and communist groups in Indochina had been resisting French efforts to reimpose colonial rule. Instead of seeing the French struggle as an effort to prop up a discredited colonialism, Truman had perceived it as part of the cold-war crusade he was leading against communism. Accordingly, he aided the French with money and arms. Viewing the Indochina warfare in similar terms, Eisenhower greatly increased assistance to the French. He acted on the theory that if communists or anticolonialists triumphed in Indochina, other states in the region, like a row of upright dominoes, would also fall to communism.

The American assistance did not prevent the warfare in Vietnam, France's most powerful former colony in the region, from taking a disastrous turn for the French. So, in January 1954, they asked Eisenhower for more help. At this point he saw no sense in a deeper involvement that could push the Vietnamese into transferring "their hatred of the French to us." Nonetheless, he sent twenty military aircraft and two hundred American technicians to service them, to French forces in Vietnam. To congressional leaders he explained this limited commitment as necessary because "we can't get anywhere in Asia by just sitting here in Washington and doing nothing. My God, we must not lose Asia."[14]

In March the Vietminh, or Vietnamese communists representing widespread nationalist aspirations, trapped some twenty thousand French and supporting colonial troops in Dien Bien Phu, a remote fortress in northern Vietnam. The French now pleaded for American military intervention against the Vietminh. Reacting cautiously, Eisenhower was willing to consider "the possibility of a single strike, if it were almost certain to produce decisive results." He refused, however, to send ground troops merely to reinforce French units. "Part of my fundamental concept of the Presidency," he explained, "is that we have a constitutional government and only when there is a sudden, unforeseen emergency should the President put us into war without congressional action."[15] When the French plea became public, alarming many Americans, he recoiled from action solely on his initiative.

A short time later when reporters brought up the question of intervention, as they had a number of times, the president reiterated his opposition. He stated, "there is going to be no involvement of America in war unless it is the result of the constitutional process that is placed on Congress to declare it." The following month, he repeated this conviction to hawkish advisers who urged, as the French requested, air strikes against the Vietminh. He knew that congressional leaders had just stated "we want no more Koreas with the United States furnishing 90% of the manpower." Again Eisenhower insisted "there was no possibility whatever of U.S. unilateral intervention in Indochina, and we had best face that fact. Even if we tried such a course, we would have to take it to Congress and fight for it like dogs, with very little hope of success."[16]

Ten days later Vice President Richard M. Nixon contradicted his chief, suggesting that troops should go to Indochina to stem communist expansion. "I think the Executive has to take the politically unpopular decision," he said, "and do it."[17] In addition to causing a furor, this supposedly off-the-record remark revived talk of restricting the president's authority to deploy armed forces on his own. Then on April 23 in desperation the French again appealed to Eisenhower, this time to intervene with a nuclear air strike from carriers against the besiegers at Dien Bien Phu. As before, he refused unilateral action.

The president did, however, suggest a concerted approach involving Britain, France, Australia, and others to meet the crisis. If these countries agreed to united action in a coalition and Congress approved, he would authorize American intervention. The potential allies refused with Winston Churchill, again Britain's prime minister, declaring he would not risk a nuclear holocaust to save Indochina for the French. The plan failed. When hawkish advisers urged Eisenhower to intervene anyway, he again said no to an air strike or to any other military action. "Unilateral intervention," he told them, "would mean a general war with China and perhaps the USSR, which the United States would have to prosecute separated from its allies" and that would amount to sheer folly.[18]

As revealed in opinion polls, this stance placed the president in line with the popular sentiment that strongly opposed intervention. He was not however, as many assumed, a dove who from the start skillfully maneuvered to keep the country out of war. He had been willing to employ air and naval forces, and even a limited number of marines on the ground, against the Vietminh on his own terms. Still, as in the Bricker issue, he would not allow pressure, even from his closest advisers, to force him to act against his own convictions and, in this instance, to utilize the war power impulsively. As a number of analysts maintain, if he had desired he could have bucked popular opinion successfully and involved the nation in the war because "an administration appeal to Congress for support of multilateral intervention undoubtedly would have been persuasive."[19] In both his willingness to intervene and in his refusal to do so without allies, he had again acted decisively in a manner outsiders could not observe. On May 7 the Vietminh overran Dien Bien Phu. Thereafter, Eisenhower did everything within his means, aside from war, to prevent communist control of South Vietnam.

At the same time, we can see another aspect of Eisenhower's use of armed power in his expanding the CIA into a major weapon of the cold war. As historians have noted, he "took an active role in defining policies and erecting mechanisms for conducting covert operations." In these ventures, he used the CIA, which he spoke of as the agency of "a very great aggressiveness," as his instrument for unilateral armed interventionism. Keeping his personal involvement secret "on the theory of why put burdens on people that they don't need to know about," he defended undercover wars as necessary to combat communism.[20] In these cold-war operations he even put aside the constitutional restraints on the presidency that he professed to value.

Eisenhower first resorted to significant undercover violence in dealing with Iran's Mohammad Mossadegh, a landlord who, as a legislator in April 1951, had engineered the nationalization of the British-owned Anglo-Iranian Oil Company. In the following month Mossadegh became prime minister. Within the next two years, he assumed dictatorial powers with the aim of converting Iran to a republic or to reducing Shah Mohammad Reza Pahlavi to a figurehead.

Eisenhower and his advisers presumed the prime minister would then establish a communist regime. To prevent such a possibility, on June 22, 1953, the president ordered the CIA to topple him. Agency operatives informed the shah, who wanted to rid himself of Mossadegh, of the plan. The shah approved, issued a decree dismissing his prime minister, who nonetheless continued to hold office, and fled Teheran. Then in covert operation Ajax, American agents bribed mobs to demonstrate against Mossadegh and supplied the shah's supporters with guns and other equipment. On August 13 this uprising, backed by army units and other groups loyal to the monarchy, forced the prime minister from power.

The ease of this operation pleased Eisenhower, leading him to misjudge the efficiency of the CIA. He did not realize that agency operatives could not have overthrown Mossadegh without the cooperation of weighty segments of the population that had lost faith in his leadership. Regardless, the outcome of the Teheran affair strengthened the president's determination to go ahead with planned covert violence against Guatemala, an even less powerful country seemingly ripe for manipulation. It had a regime that he, as had Truman, found objectionable.

Accordingly, the CIA engaged in a number of secret destabilizing activities to overthrow Guatemala's agrarian populist president, Jacobo Arbenz Guzmán, including plots to assassinate those in high positions of the government. Shortly after Ajax had succeeded, this effort accelerated, particularly in December when Arbenz began expropriating lands belonging to the United Fruit Company, a North American corporation. To Eisenhower and his advisers, the seizures confirmed their set convictions that communists ran the government. He told the Guatemalan ambassador, for instance, that Arbenz's government was "infiltrated with communists, and we couldn't cooperate with a Government which openly favored communists."

In March 1954 administration officials pressured the Organization of American States to condemn communism as a threat to peace and security in the Americas. The crisis came to a head on May 17 when arms from

Czechoslovakia arrived at Puerto Barrios, Guatemala. Secretary of State John Foster Dulles announced that Arbenz's government "has come into a position to dominate militarily the Central American area." Eisenhower averred, the United States is "not going to sit around and do nothing."[21] So on his own authority and in violation of international law, the president quickly ordered the navy to search vessels on the high seas bound for Guatemala for arms. He also placed in motion a larger armed covert intervention.

The operation began in the early morning hours of June 18 when Colonel Carlos Castillo Armas, an exiled Guatemalan conservative, led a makeshift force of 150 mercenaries assembled by CIA operatives, out of Honduras into Guatemala to attack the government. In less than two weeks, Castillo Armas, aided by Americans piloting old bombers, overturned Arbenz and seized power. Eisenhower praised Guatemalans for freeing "themselves from the shackles of international Communist direction" but believed also his aid to Castillo Armas had been critical in the victory. In addition, he assumed the rest of Latin America approved of what he regarded as a valuable achievement. He was wrong. In various cities to the south, demonstrators denounced the revival of big stick diplomacy, burned the Stars and Stripes, and hanged him in effigy.

This episode revealed once more that despite what pundits perceived as passive qualities in Eisenhower, when determined to attain his own foreign-policy objectives he could and would use force with a heavy hand. Within his policy agenda, he elevated anticommunism to such a high status that even if Marxists posed no plausible threat to the United States, their mere presence in positions of authority or their infiltration in weak states justified secret violence against them. Two months after Arbenz fell, Eisenhower created a special group to study covert operations. It concluded that in waging cold war against "an implacable enemy whose avowed objective is world domination by whatever means . . . [the] hitherto acceptable norms of human conduct do not apply." From its perspective, survival in this struggle dictated that "long standing American concepts of 'fair play' must be reconsidered."[22]

While leaving the undercover dirty work involved in this cold-war strategy to the CIA, the president brandished military power openly in another international crisis. It started to unfold in August 1954 when Chou En-lai, the Chinese premier, announced his government's determination to wrest Taiwan from Chiang Kai-shek, its nationalist leader. "Any invasion of Formosa," Eisenhower countered, "would have to run over the

7th Fleet." The mainland Chinese did not invade, but commencing on September 3, they bombarded nationalist troops on two islands of the Quemoy group located five miles off Amoy. To aid Chiang, the president's military advisers recommended retaliatory bombing of the mainland. Some even urged an attack with nuclear weapons. Eisenhower disagreed. "We're not talking now about a limited brush-fire war," he pointed out. "We're talking about going to the threshold of World War III." Moreover, "if we get into a general war, the logical enemy will be Russia, not China, and we'll have to strike there." As his closest aide observed, he "rejected a hot-headed plunge into atomic war as a solution to the Chinese problem" and thus showed again he would not use the war power lightly, particularly against a major foe.[23]

The president did not, however, just back away from confrontation. In December he concluded an alliance with Chiang, implying he would provide aid in the defense of Taiwan and its territories. On January 18, 1955, communist troops seized the Tachens, the offshore islands he had persuaded Chiang to evacuate because of the difficulty of defending them. Five days later, Eisenhower asked Congress for authority to deal with any emergency that might arise in Taiwan Strait. Although in this situation he assumed he had authority to act on his own, he wanted to avoid the harsh congressional debate that had followed Truman's intervention in Korea. On January 28 Congress approved a joint resolution authorizing the president to use the armed forces to protect Taiwan. To allay fear that Chiang or some military office might trigger hostilities, Eisenhower announced he alone would decide when and how to invoke this enhanced war power.

Public sentiment, the media, and academic observers generally approved of the resolution but diverged as to its significance. Some of them believed that with it Eisenhower had taken Congress as a partner in the making of foreign policy and hence had weakened presidential power. Others viewed the resolution as a blank check that allowed the executive to proceed as he saw fit. These critics denounced it as an open-ended commitment that diminished Congress's authority because once the president acted within the scope of the resolution it had no choice. It had to go along with him.

On March 6 Eisenhower and Dulles agreed that in order to defend Quemoy and Matsu we might "have to go to war" and "use atomic weapons." Ten days later, the president publicly endorsed the use of "tactical small atomic weapons" for military purposes. He remarked, "I see no reason why they shouldn't be used just exactly as you would use a bullet or anything else."[24] Even though Ike expressed a determination to fight if necessary and later admitted he had come to the "edge of war," the extent of his willingness to risk nuclear conflict was not made apparent because in April Chou backed off from his threat to invade Taiwan and tensions eased.

As this crisis passed, Dulles boasted of the administration's aggressive stance, asserting he and the president "had walked to the brink of war" deliberately to advance their planned deterrence. He claimed this policy had "not only prevented the 'big' hydrogen war but the little wars as well." He called this brinkmanship "a necessary art" that if not mastered inevitably brought on war. "We've had to look it square in the face—on the question of enlarging the Korean War, on the question of getting into the Indo-China war, on the question of Formosa. . . . We took strong action." In each crisis, he added, "the President never flinched for a minute . . . he came up taut."[25]

Other administration leaders, and the president, too, regarded Dulles's words as hyperbole. Others, including historians, praised Eisenhower's "crisis management" in the Taiwan episode as "a *tour de force*," seeing in it "beauty" because of its "ambiguity." Skeptics viewed the crisis as "self-inflicted," meaning by the president himself, and as an example of machismo. They also found it "hard to be dazzled by policies that brought the world to the brink of nuclear war" over "a piece of real estate of little consequence" to American or even Taiwanese security.[26]

The president's muscle-flexing in this case appeared also to contradict his repeated concern for peace. Even while threatening China with war, he told reporters "there is no place on this earth to which I would not travel, there is no chore I would not undertake if I had the faintest hope, that by so doing, I would promote the general cause of world peace." Polls indicated most Americans liked his focus on peace more than any other aspect of his policies.

Six months later, while in Denver, Eisenhower suffered a heart attack, leaving many with the fear his commitment to peace would falter. Seemingly, it did not because the presidential staff worked well, carrying out his policies as though he were still directly in charge. Nixon told reporters the president had set up "the business of government . . . in such a way that it can go ahead despite the temporary absence of anyone."[27]

In January 1956 Eisenhower returned to a full schedule. Despite his heart problem, he decided to run for a second term because he believed, as others told him, "no man of our times has had the standing throughout the world that seems to be mine" and hence he "must try to carry on." During the campaign, his health and his delegating of duties became issues. Opponents attacked him for entrusting foreign-policy decisions to Dulles, whom at various times he called "indispensable" and "brilliant . . . in foreign affairs" with a "technical competence" in diplomacy probably unmatched in the world. The president admitted allowing Dulles considerable authority but insisted the two of them always recognized that "the final decision had to be mine."[28] Still, Democrats criticized Ike for delegating too much and charged that with his impaired heart he could serve only as a part-time president. In refutation, he insisted that if reelected he would continue personally to handle all the important duties of his office.

In the next three months, Eisenhower focused a good part of his attention on rising Soviet influence in the Middle East. Earlier, to counter it, he had agreed to help finance the plan of Egypt's strong man, Gamal Abdel Nasser, to build a huge hydroelectric dam on the Nile River at Aswan. When Nasser flirted with the Soviets and appeared to be preparing for hostilities with Israel, Ike shifted gears. He pressured Nasser to moderate his seemingly procommunist activities, which the Egyptian refused to do.

Journalists talked of force, possibly "the covert overthrow of the Nasser regime." One newsman asked the president if he would order marines "to war, without asking the Congress first." Eisenhower replied, "I have announced time and time again I will never be guilty of any kind of action that can be interpreted as war until Congress, which has the constitutional authority, says so." He added that to defend themselves American troops may "undertake local warlike acts, but that is not going to be war and I am not going to order any troops into anything that can be interpreted as war until Congress directs it." Six months later he repeated privately that except for "a direct attack on the United States itself . . . we could not possibly go to war without a declaration of war by the Congress."[29] He did not, however, confront the issue of covert military actions that failed to meet his test of constitutionality because Congress did not authorize them. He got around the problem by excluding the covert actions from his definition of war.

Even so, on October 23 while Eisenhower campaigned for reelection, the intervention issue came up again. Hungarians led by students in Budapest revolted against their Soviet masters. Earlier he had announced a project of liberation for Eastern Europe that hypothetically went beyond the containment of communism. He backed this policy with a covert program code-named Red Sox/Red Cap that trained East European émigrés for paramilitary missions against the Soviets. With this activity, CIA agents helped spark the revolt and joined the local freedom fighters. Understandably, the Hungarians expected more assistance and appealed to Eisenhower for it.

The request placed the president in a bind because beginning on November 4 some two hundred thousand troops and twenty-five hundred tanks under Soviet leadership battered Budapest and crushed the uprising. He decided reluctantly that regardless of his sympathy for the Hungarians and his support of past undercover backing, he could do nothing worthwhile militarily to aid them without risking a third world war. Much of the public as well as political leaders commended the decision as proper. Critics, and even some of his usual defenders, believed that because of his liberation policy "Eisenhower himself . . . was the man most responsible for the debacle."[30] Nonetheless, he did curb possibly impulsive behavior even when pressured to use force unilaterally for a commendable cause. He also realistically recognized the limitations of executive power. The use of that power came up again in a concurrent crisis.

The problem stemmed from the escalation of the president's quarrel with Egypt's Nasser. Profoundly upset because the Egyptian had turned to the Soviets for arms, Dulles in July 1956 had abruptly withdrawn the American financing for the Aswan dam. Nasser retaliated by nationalizing the Universal Suez Canal Company, owned by British and French stockholders. He announced that henceforth Egyptians would operate the canal. On October 29, after three months of muddled diplomacy, Israeli troops, followed shortly by British and French forces, invaded Egypt without their governments informing their American ally beforehand.

The attack angered Eisenhower. Regarding it as wrong, he joined Russia in condemning it. "We cannot—in the world, any more than in our own nation," he announced, "subscribe to one law for the weak, another for the strong; one law for those who oppose us, another for those allied with us." He worried also about the Soviets. If they openly assisted Nasser, the president and his advisers agreed the United States would be drawn into the war. Otherwise he saw no sense "in getting into a fight to which there can be no satisfactory end, and in which the whole world believes you are playing the part of the bully."[31] When the Soviets spoke menacingly of intervening with volunteers and even of raining missiles on London and Paris, he countered with his own threat of war. On November 5, he ordered a partial mobilization of the armed forces.

At the same time, the president exerted economic and diplomatic pressure that compelled the British, the French, and ultimately the Israelis to withdraw from Egypt. In this situation, he exercised executive power unilaterally, swiftly, and effectively. Even so, he found his stance against allies, in what he termed a family fight, so distasteful he considered this week of decisions, aside from periods of sickness, the worst in his presidency. Despite this feeling and the Hungarian and Egyptian crises, on November 6 he won reelection overwhelmingly. "The American people's love affair with Eisenhower overlooks all faults," a columnist observed shortly thereafter. "The less he does the more they love him. That, probably, is the secret. Here is a man who doesn't rock the boat."[32] In foreign affairs he had rocked it, however he did so again when after the Suez war the Soviets moved into the Middle East with heightened influence.

Fearing the Russians might resort to force in an effort to dominate the region, Eisenhower decided to issue a warning designed to deter them. Before taking that step, he appeared before a joint session of Congress to ask, as he had during the earlier Taiwan crisis, for a resolution authorizing him "to employ the armed forces . . . to defend the territorial integrity and political independence of any" Middle Eastern nation "against Communist armed aggression." He realized, as he had noted during the Bricker Amendment ruckus, that lawyers in the executive branch, as elsewhere, could justify unilateral presidential action because they were "trained to take either side of any case and make the most intelligent and impassioned defense of their adopted viewpoint." In doing so, they submerged "conviction in favor of plausible argument."[33] In this instance, however, he desired more than persuasive legal reasoning from his hired hands. He wanted to work with Congress to minimize contention and to convey a sense of national unity.

Despite the soundness of the president's logic, he encountered some opposition because a few senators regarded the request as merely another effort to compel Congress to share responsibility for a decision he should make. In direct contrast, others argued he really sought "a predated declaration of war" or power rightfully belonging to Congress.[34] Finally, after two months of debate, Congress approved a resolution that on March 9, 1957, he signed into law. This new blank check, which quickly became known as the Eisenhower doctrine, authorized the president to aid Middle Eastern nations in combating armed attack from communist states. In essence, it endorsed his role as an anti-Marxist police officer with discretionary power to exert military force.

In May of the following year, a civil war in Lebanon between Muslims and Maronite Christians exposed the difficulty of applying the doctrine to a specific situation. Camille Chamoun, the embattled Maronite president who sought to perpetuate his power through an illegal second term, appealed for American help. Eisenhower hesitated because he did not wish to become involved in this essentially local conflict. "How can you save a country from its own leaders?" he fumed at an emergency White House meeting. "We would be intervening to save a nation; and yet the nation is the people, and the people don't want our intervention."[35]

This attitude changed after army officers in Baghdad on July 14, 1958, overthrew the pro-Western monarchy in Iraq in a coup that appeared to menace Lebanon. Again a frightened Chamoun pleaded for assistance. Out of motivation that still appears hazy, Eisenhower at this point seemed eager to use force. He contended that "to lose this area [to communists] by inaction would be far worse than the loss of China, because of the strategic position and resources of the Middle East." A few hours later, he went through the motions of consulting some members of Congress who opposed getting in a civil war.

Then, on his own authority as commander in chief and in his only overt military intervention, Eisenhower ordered troops to invade. The following day, in operation Blue Bat, seventeen thousand American marines splashed ashore at Beirut. As they did so, he described Lebanon in a television address as the victim of internal aggression. This characterization prevented him logically from invoking the Eisenhower doctrine directed specifically against external aggression. Therefore, he offered other explanations. He claimed a need to protect twenty-five hundred American lives, declared Lebanon's "territorial integrity and independence . . . vital to United States national interests and world peace," and asserted a necessity to uphold that nation's "safety and security."[36]

Privately, the president expressed macho feelings, telling a State Department official he wished to disprove sentiment in the Middle East "that Americans were capable only of words" and would not take "military action" because they feared the Soviet reaction. This diplomat reported him as wanting also "to demonstrate . . . that the United States was capable of supporting its friends."[37] At the same time, another Middle Eastern friend, Jordan's King Hussein, requested American and British military assistance against internal pro-Nasser forces he labeled communist. So three days after the initial American landing, thirty-seven hundred British troops protected by American jet fighters swarmed into Amman to bolster the sagging monarchy.

In the wake of this armed toughness, Eisenhower insisted he had not committed an act of war. He contended that the deploying of troops on foreign soil fell within the scope of his constitutional authority and was in keeping with executive precedents. Critics viewed his behavior differently. They portrayed him as waging "a limited but undeclared presidential war" without specific congressional authorization and for vague objectives, such as to preserve American credibility. He thereby set "some dangerous precedents."[38] They pointed out also that he could document no communist or other tangible threat to American interests and hence had resorted to armed force on the basis of nebulous assumption. In addition, they maintained he had misled the American public and Congress by publicly attributing Lebanon's turmoil to communist subversion while knowing it stemmed from Arab nationalism.

From the viewpoint of the White House and of later admiring chroniclers, however, the operation succeeded beautifully, even to the point of its defenders hailing it as Eisenhower's "finest hour." They praised him for shoring up pro-Western regimes in Beirut and Amman, protecting oil sources, and for pulling out the troops in October, after a conflict during which "not a shot was fired in anger, not a single American died in combat."[39]

During this Middle Eastern entanglement, the president also employed the CIA in a clandestine armed intervention in Indonesia. He and his advisers considered Achmad Sukarno, the neutralist president, too cozy with communists, so American agents fomented political turmoil to destabilize his regime. Later they expanded their undercover activity by encouraging dissatisfied local leaders to rise against Sukarno. Then, on February 5, 1958, in Sumatra some of the discontented launched a civil war. Washington supplied the rebels with bombing planes and pilots to fly them. In April, when Sukarno protested, Eisenhower denied the charge, insisting that "our policy is one of careful neutrality . . . so as not to be taking sides where it is none of our business."[40] In May Indonesian government gunners shot down one of the bombers, captured the American pilot, and exposed Ike's lie. He then backed away from the venture. Soon after the rebellion collapsed.

In August, the president had to deal with another crisis in the Taiwan Strait that grew out of the Chinese communists' resumption of massive shelling of the nationalist-held offshore islands of Quemoy and Matsu. Ike had assigned American warships to convoy Chiang's supply vessels to within three miles of the communist guns trained on the islands. This time he announced he would meet any attack with force. He took this posture because Chiang had committed one hundred thousand troops, or one-third of his army, to those islands, making them, in the president's outlook, increasingly related to the defense of Taiwan. In September, as the situation festered, Soviet premier Nikita Khrushchev warned he would support his ally if the United States struck at China's mainland.

In turn, Eisenhower announced there would be no appeasement of communism because somehow he still had fixed in his mind "that Quemoy and Matsu were essential to America's security." Privately, he did not shrink from the possibility of using force, even with small-yield atomic weapons, but he also thought the Chinese communists would not "risk war with us." Even so, many Americans, as well as allies, regarded his actions as courting war or at least as provocative. Gloomily he noted that "as much as two-thirds of the world, and 50 percent of U.S. opinion, opposes the course which we have been following."[41] What he considered a test of prestige, others perceived as a demonstration of machismo over islands of no consequence to American security. As though having second thoughts, he turned to negotiations and in October this crisis, too, passed without hostilities.

The following month the president faced another confrontation with the Soviets. Khrushchev threatened to terminate Allied rights in West Berlin. Eisenhower insisted those rights rested on wartime agreements that neither the Soviets nor the East Germans could abrogate. He met this challenge firmly through diplomacy but also with measures to employ force if necessary, hinting at the possible use of nuclear weapons. He did not persist on this course, turning instead to negotiations. After that, this trouble faded also without bloodshed.

Concurrently, the president had to deal with still another problem with a potential for his unilateral use of force. The matrix for it had taken form earlier, after Fidel Castro, a young, left-leaning revolutionary, in Cuba on January 1, 1959, had seized power from the right-wing dictator Fulgencio Batista y Zaldívar. Within weeks Castro eliminated opponents in public executions before firing squads, a form of revolutionary justice that horrified Eisenhower. The Cuban leader spewed anti-Americanism and tried to export his revolution to neighboring countries, leading the president and his advisers in November to back anti-Castro groups to replace his revolutionary regime. When Castro in February 1960 concluded trade agreements with the Soviets, Ike assumed he had succumbed fully to communism. Believing this intolerable, the president decided to take measures that would overthrow the Cuban as he had toppled Arbenz in Guatemala. "Let's get a program," he told advisers, "that will really do something about Castro."[42]

The president did his something by ordering the CIA to train Cuban exiles in south Florida for operation Pluto, a military invasion of their former homeland. In addition, the agency hatched schemes to assassinate the dictator and directed commando strikes on Cuba's shores. In August, with the intent of disrupting Cuba's economy, Eisenhower imposed a trade embargo. Castro retaliated by nationalizing American businesses in Cuba and drawing closer to the Soviets. On January 3, 1961, Eisenhower severed diplomatic relations, but before he could launch his last covert operation against Cuba his presidency ended.

As president, Eisenhower left a controversial legacy. Numerous contemporary academics, intellectuals, and others regarded him as a do-nothing executive, markedly in domestic affairs. They were wrong. As he later pointed out, for six years of his administration, "to get things done" he had to work with "a politically hostile Congress" and hence could not employ the methods of a president with a large legislative majority behind him. "For me," he explained, "persuasion, friendly conference, and even cajolery had to be used to accomplish the constructive things in domestic affairs that we thought best for the country. In foreign affairs my independence was naturally far more pronounced."[43]

A generation later, revisionists came around to an appreciation of this viewpoint, lauding Eisenhower, especially for his exercise of power in foreign affairs. They depict him, as did Richard Nixon, as a keen, analytical thinker who in making final decisions was "deliberate and careful," cold and "unemotional." They perceive him as personally "the engine of his presidency," a leader who "fully appreciated the complicated relationship between using military instruments and achieving sound diplomatic goals." Rather than shunning power, they claim, he used it quietly but vigorously behind the scenes to shape policy in his own way through "hidden-hand leadership." In specific instances, the revisionists make a good case but they claim too much.[44]

Ike himself laid the foundation for this conception of hidden executive leadership. "I believe," he explained publicly several times, "the Presidency should be relieved of detail and many of its activities by proper officials who can take delegated authority and exercise it in his name." In contrast to revisionists, critics view this approach to the office negatively. They point out that "Eisenhower consciously apportioned responsibility to trusted subordinates to a greater degree than any president in the last half century" or practiced a failed hands-off, procrastinating approach in matters of national security. To the end of his life Eisenhower resented any implication he did not make foreign policy. He stated many times he alone retained "the final word on every major question" and that his secretary of state "made no important move without consulting the President."[45]

Although not a hands-on executive in the day-to-day business of running the country, in matters of war and peace Eisenhower regarded himself as an activist who used the armed forces "to defend a 'way of life,' not merely land, property or lives." He insisted, too, that the president as commander in chief "is in a very definite sense responsible for all measures that are taken to defend the United States and provide for securing its rights everywhere in the world."[46] On this premise, as we have seen, in the larger matters of war and peace he often proceeded cautiously.

At times, though, in lesser matters Eisenhower acted aggressively, launching covert interventions in countries across the globe that offered no credible threat to the United States. Still, he claimed with pride that "the United States never lost a soldier or a foot of ground in my administration. We kept the peace." In the large picture, as in his behavior toward Hungary, he did guard peace commendably but in assassination plots in Cuba and the Congo against the revolutionary Patrice Lumumba, and in secret CIA wars, people died as a result of his policies. He also deepened the involvement in Vietnam where he retained the conviction "that military intervention was a tenable U.S. option."[47]

Eisenhower believed also that he had curbed executive aggrandizement. During his tenure, though, the staff of the executive office proliferated as never before and the president's use of the war power as commander in chief continued to rise. It rose for a number of reasons but particularly because of his conception of the president's role in foreign affairs—that he must lead—and because of his cold-war conviction that he must combat communism with the full resources of his office. As a cold warrior, fighting for what he regarded as a noble cause, he flexed muscle in the macho style well beyond what he himself once regarded as constitutional limitations.

John Fitzgerald Kennedy

UNLIKE Eisenhower, John F. Kennedy was a professional politician who, to observers, appeared to have been "born to politics."[48] His two grandfathers had been prominent in Boston politics; his father Joseph had held several important posts under Franklin Roosevelt; and John himself as a schoolboy had engaged in precinct work. Young Kennedy started his public career by winning a seat in the House of Representatives and then moving up to the Senate. Ambition and impatience moved him in 1956 to seek the Democratic nomination for vice president, but he failed to obtain it.

Undeterred by this defeat and bankrolled by his wealthy father, John, his family, and close friends laid out plans for him to gain his party's presidential nomination in 1960. They succeeded. During the election campaign that followed, Jack Kennedy offered himself as a man of energy who would recapture the country's allegedly slipping greatness. He attacked what he called "a restricted concept of the Presidency," indicated he would "be the Chief Executive in every sense of the word," and asserted the president should "exercise the fullest powers of his office—all that are specified and some that are not."[49] Most of all, he strove to overcome anti-Catholic sentiment by portraying himself not as the Catholic candidate but as the candidate who happened to be a Catholic. He won the election by a paper-thin margin, with 49.7 percent of the popular vote.

At age forty-three, Kennedy entered the White House as the nation's youngest elected president. Even though he had no executive experience, he felt confident he could handle the "big job," commenting, "I don't know anybody who can do it any better than I can." Like most of his predecessors, he expressed love for peace but pursued power in the raw, or in the view of detractors, compulsively. Aware that the public admired the virile, decisive, take-charge leader, he strove to fit that model. Accordingly, as journalists and friends noted, he embraced "the values of the masculine mystique . . . toward women, sexuality, and weakness in men" and "similar 'macho' values toward male politicians."[50]

In all, Kennedy cultivated an image of boldness and vigor, being careful, as had Franklin Roosevelt, to show publicly no sign of weakness. Shortly before his inauguration, for instance, Kennedy even lied to protect that image, stating flatly, "I never had Addison's disease," an often-fatal adrenal gland failure.[51] He not only had the disease but also kept himself alive by submitting daily to a combination of pills, pellets implanted in his thighs, and painful cortisone injections.

In line with his concern for activism, especially in foreign affairs, Kennedy brought into his official family a group of individuals, as one of them, former Undersecretary of State Chester B. Bowles, recalled, "full of belligerence" and "sort of looking for a chance to prove their muscle." Kennedy also carried with him a decided preference for foreign over domestic affairs. Accordingly, he devoted most of his inaugural address to the cold war. As a theme, he stated, "Let every nation know, whether it wishes us well or ill, that we shall pay any price, bear any burden, meet any hardship, support any friend, oppose any foe to assure the survival and success of liberty." He vowed to "oppose aggression or subversion," saying, "I do not shrink from this responsibility—I welcome it."[52]

From this point on the president immersed himself in the details of foreign policy. "Domestic policy," he would repeat, "can only defeat us; foreign policy can kill us." Those close to him reported that he "dealt personally with almost every aspect of policy around the globe," as with problems in Southeast Asia and Cuba. His obvious involvement with the Cuban situation began during his campaign when, in nationally televised debates with his Republican opponent, Richard Nixon, he took a tough anti-Castro stance. Kennedy blasted Republicans for promising to roll back the Iron Curtain in Europe and not doing so. "Today," he stated, "the Iron Curtain is 90 miles off the coast of the United States," and we should do something about it. In January 1961 when Eisenhower explained that something was being done, mainly the secretly planned invasion of Cuba to overthrow Fidel Castro, Kennedy asked, "Should we support guerrilla operations in Cuba?" Eisenhower responded, "To the utmost."[53] Since this advice corresponded essentially with what Kennedy had already advocated, he promptly agreed.

Neither man sought congressional approval for this covert activity. Kennedy did consult military and other advisers and a few congressional leaders but only after he had decided to continue the venture. Although neither public sentiment nor dire danger demanded armed intervention, most of the mavens around the president gave his strategy a green light. Secretary of State Dean Rusk disapproved but not openly. Another dissenter, J. William Fulbright, chairman of the Senate Committee on Foreign Relations, objected vehemently. He called the plan "a piece with the hypocrisy for which the United States is constantly denouncing the Soviet Union." After all, he stressed, "the Castro regime is a thorn in the flesh; but it is not a dagger in the heart."[54]

The following week when newspaper people asked the president how far he would go to overthrow Castro, he replied, "there will not be, under any conditions, any intervention in Cuba by United States armed forces." He added that "the basic issue in Cuba is not one between the United States and Cuba; it is between the Cubans themselves."[55] The president thus lied to retain the secrecy of his commitment to use force. Fundamentally he did not want, as this denial might suggest, to appear soft on communism, indecisive, or weak-kneed. He proceeded, therefore, with the clandestine training of the Cuban exiles as a strike force against Castro while the CIA continued to plot Castro's assassination and to harass Cubans.

As planned, at dawn on April 17, with more than fourteen hundred men of the exile brigade, Kennedy launched the invasion on Cuba's south coast at Bahía de Cochinos, or Bay of Pigs. As is well known, the supposedly secret operation turned into a widely publicized fiasco. Although shaken by his own stupidity and furious over what he perceived as bad advice, he admitted responsibility; but he did spread blame even while saying he wanted no "passing of the buck." "I was assured by every son of a bitch I checked with—all the military experts and the CIA—that the plan would succeed," he told Nixon. Then he cogitated, "It really is true that foreign affairs is the only important issue for a President to handle, isn't it? . . . I mean who gives a shit if the minimum wage is $1.15 or $1.25 in comparison to something like this?"[56]

Despite this blunder, Kennedy's popularity rating, according to a Gallup poll, rose to a high of 82 percent. Even in failure, Americans registered approval of a macho endeavor against a demonized adversary. As though in tune with such sentiment, the president expressed contrition while behaving as though he had acted properly but had run into bad luck. Neither he nor most of his advisers questioned the premise of the whole operation—that the unilateral use of force was ethically wrong and unnecessary for the security of the nation. As skeptics noticed, the Kennedy team seemed imbued with "the military machismo and cold-war view of the world that led to the Bay of Pigs" and underlay its attachment to globalism.[57]

Kennedy set the tone for this pugnaciousness. He wanted to invade Cuba, to use surrogates to do the fighting, and spurned advice not to proceed. Students of his presidency have described his behavior as characteristic in cases of exaggerated manliness or as a touch of machismo that persisted after the failure.[58] To him, Castro's regime had become an obsession, a personal affront he transmuted into a threat to American security. Secretary of Defense Robert S. McNamara recalled, "We were hysterical about Castro at the time of the Bay of Pigs and thereafter."[59] The president believed he could remedy what he perceived as a mere mistake with bravado because he realized that executives who display weakness earned scorn. He persevered, therefore, in using covert force (as in CIA-staged hit-and-run attacks on Cuban soil), economic pressure, and other means to overthrow Castro.

At this time Kennedy also had to deal with an emergency over the fate of Berlin that had the potential for escalating into nuclear war. Khrushchev renewed earlier demands that the Allied occupiers leave the city. Under this threat Kennedy agreed to meet the Soviet leader in Vienna to discuss this situation along with other matters. For various reasons, including the Bay of Pigs fiasco, Khrushchev considered Kennedy weak. Knowing this, the president left for Europe determined to prove otherwise. "I have to show him that we can be just as tough as he is," Kennedy told his aides.[60] He arrived in Vienna on June 3 for two days of what turned out to be sober, intense conversations. The Soviet leader set a deadline of six months for settling the status of the divided metropolis, saying that if the United States preferred war to negotiation he could do nothing about it. Kennedy left chastened, alarmed, and convinced that Khrushchev had challenged his will and manhood.

After returning home the president took a comparably truculent stance, declaring he would not placate the Russians even under the menace of war. "We cannot and will not permit the Communists," he emphasized, "to drive us out of Berlin, either gradually or by force." He inflated the crisis by linking American security to Western Europe's defense and to "our presence and access rights to West Berlin." He gave warning he was "determined to maintain those rights at any risk."[61] In preparation for possible hostilities, he expanded the armed forces, called reservists to active duty, and asked Congress for an additional $3 billion in military spending, which it granted.

On August 13 Khrushchev countered by erecting a barrier that divided East from West Berlin. He later expanded it into a concrete-block wall twenty-eight miles long that blocked East Germans from readily fleeing west. All the while Congress and the public backed Kennedy's tough stand. When, however, he faced up to the reality of war with a major foe, he put aside his harsh rhetoric to demonstrate an admirable restraint. So did Khrushchev, who in October retreated from his menacing position to allow the most dangerous aspect of the crisis to pass without hostilities.

Immediately, the president again focused on Castro, authorizing on November 30 operation Mongoose, a top-secret program sometimes called the "Kennedy vendetta," designed to "help Cuba overthrow the Communist regime."[62] He also proceeded with plans for an open military intervention, possibly an air strike or even an invasion. Between April 9 and 24, 1962, the armed forces staged massive maneuvers in the Caribbean that raised fears of an attack in Havana and Moscow. Castro appealed to the Soviets for help. They responded with a flow of arms, planes, naval craft, and other military equipment. In August anonymous State Department officials leaked reports of Soviet troops and missiles in Cuba. Republicans and anticommunist hawks urged Kennedy to blockade the island, threatening to make any hesitation a foremost issue in the forthcoming congressional elections. This political assault on his image of virility, still battered by the Bay of Pigs failure, placed him on the defensive.

Aides pressed for a demonstration of "presidential firmness toward Cuba." They played on Kennedy's fixation with vigor, cautioning him against appearing "weak and indecisive." They urged him to take control of the situation with "a very clear and aggressive explanation" of his policy. As an involved military official, Lieutenant General Samuel W. Wilson, later put it, "The Kennedy people wanted to be known as people with balls, and this was a chance to show whether they had them or not." Even so, on September 13 the president announced he would not undertake unilateral military intervention but added a warning. If "the Communist buildup in Cuba were to endanger or interfere with our security," he said, he would do "whatever must be done." He pointed out that "as President and Commander in Chief I have full authority now to take such action."[63]

For this reason, based in part on the dubious inherent powers theory, Kennedy did not seek congressional backing to act. But he did request legislation empowering him to muster 150,000 military reservists for one year of service. Congress passed the mobilization bill he desired and on October 3 again followed his wishes by voting overwhelmingly for a joint resolution endorsing but not authorizing the "use of arms . . . to prevent in Cuba the creation or use of an externally supported military capability endangering" American security. Some senators were willing, uncritically, to leave the whole matter of force in the president's hands. For example, George Smathers, a Democrat from Florida, tried to turn the fundamental war-power clause on its head. "We all recognize," he averred, "that the final decision is left to the President of the United States by the Constitution."[64]

The reason for an armed presidential intervention changed when on October 14 an American U-2 surveillance plane photographed, near San Cristóbal, Cuba, launching pads built by the Soviets for medium-range missiles targeted on American cities. Two days later when Kennedy viewed the pictures he expressed puzzlement as to why Khrushchev had taken this risk and had lied to him about not deploying missiles. Kennedy also interpreted the action as a personal affront, an assault on his virility, and as a threat to his leadership as well as to the country. He assumed the Soviet leader was again trying to test his toughness. The president maintained this attitude even during the height of the crisis when the Soviets still did not mobilize their military forces.

Meanwhile, Kennedy had decided to move swiftly before the missiles became operational. "We are probably going to have to bomb them," he professed. His national security adviser, McGeorge Bundy, told the president, "No question. If this thing goes on, an attack on Cuba becomes general war."[65]

Later, Khrushchev and other Soviets explained they deployed the missiles to help Cuba guard against invasion and, perhaps more importantly, to counter United States nuclear superiority. The Soviets knew that many in Washington wanted to invade. Indeed, some presidential advisers believed Khrushchev was justified in concluding "that there was a great risk of a U.S. invasion" but claimed nonetheless, "we had absolutely no intention of invading Cuba."[66] Meanwhile, the president had formulated a response to the Soviets. He now cooled his initial feeling to react with massive force because he realized the crisis had turned into a confrontation with a potential for nuclear disaster.

By October 22, after six days of discussion with his closest advisers, the president resisted the recommendations to invade or to strike at Cuba by air. He decided instead to blockade the island with what he euphemistically called a quarantine to keep out more Soviet arms and to make clear that the installed missiles must go. Still, he saw himself in a dilemma. "If we stop one Russian ship, it means war," he told advisers. "If we invade Cuba, it means war."[67]

In that state of mind on that evening, Kennedy delivered a surprise television broadcast to the nation. Again he assumed a belligerent posture. He described the Soviet missiles as "clearly offensive weapons of sudden mass destruction" and denounced their clandestine placement as a "deliberately provocative and unjustified change in the status quo," a change he would not accept. Then he threatened war, announcing he would "regard any nuclear missile launched from Cuba against any nation in the Western Hemisphere as an attack by the Soviet Union on the United States, requiring a full retaliatory response upon the Soviet Union."[68] He did not mention his own clandestine actions against Castro that had contributed to the crisis.

On the following morning, as the quarantine went into effect, the president told his brother Robert, "It looks really mean, doesn't it? But then, really there was no choice." Robert reinforced this view with some fanciful reasoning, saying, "if you hadn't acted, you would have been impeached." The president agreed.[69]

More than sixty naval vessels, backed by planes of the strategic air command placed on nuclear alert, enforced the blockade. Other aircraft stood ready for a strike as did troops for an invasion of Cuba. Except for the few members Kennedy had informed, Congress played no role in these measures or in the fundamental decisions in this, the world's first nuclear confrontation. Furthermore, at this point Kennedy did not seek to negotiate with either Khrushchev or Castro to resolve the crisis because, as critics assert, he insisted on demonstrating unrestrained strength. Even so, his immediate aides advised a more hawkish response. He overrode them, refused to court war impulsively, and preferred peace if he could have it without appeasement.

At this point Khrushchev deplored Kennedy's ultimatum, denied deploying offensive weapons, and asked the president, "What good would a war do you? You threaten us with war." He added, "do you really seriously think" Cuba can attack the United States or "that even we together with Cuba could advance against you from Cuban territory? . . . Only lunatics or suicides, who themselves want to perish and before they die destroy the world, could do this." Kennedy now had thoughts along a similar line. "It is insane," he wisely admitted, "that two men, sitting on opposite sides of the world, should be able to decide to bring an end to civilization."[70]

On the next day, October 28, the Soviet leader who unilaterally made Soviet decisions and, according to his own ambassador in Washington, misunderstood the psychology of his opponents now told colleagues, we are "face to face with the danger of war and of nuclear catastrophe. In order to save the world, we must retreat."[71]

The next day, after more diplomatic maneuvering, Khrushchev backed down, agreeing to remove the missiles if the United States would not invade Cuba. Sobered by how close he had come to a possible nuclear holocaust, Kennedy moderated his toughest demands, promised not to invade, and agreed to remove the intermediate-range Jupiter missiles from Italy and Turkey. The immediate crisis passed. As Rusk put it to journalist John Scali, in a macho metaphor, "Remember when you report this—that eyeball to eyeball, they blinked first."[72] Accordingly, the president appeared to have won a great diplomatic victory.

Kennedy admirers who accept this view of the crisis have described his performance as masterly; brilliant; his finest hour; "a model of American managerial skill," leadership, and judgment; as an example of "genuine statesmanship"; and as the greatest achievement of his presidency. They maintain that he and his aides "performed superbly in the thirteen critical days," demonstrating a "combination of toughness and restraint, of will, nerve and wisdom, so brilliantly controlled, so matchlessly calibrated, that dazzled the world."[73]

Does the record justify such claims? Did the missiles in Cuba pose such a danger to American security that Cuba and Russia merited nuclear retaliation? Hardly. Even presidential confidants, such as McNamara and Dean Acheson, did not think so. British critics, too, perceived no significant military threat to the United States. One of them wrote in harsh judgment, "It may well be that Kennedy is risking blowing the world to hell in order to sweep a few Democrats into office," a reference to the November congressional elections that later research largely substantiated.[74]

Harsher critics contend the president forced the confrontation to boost declining popularity and to "promote his carefully cultivated macho image." They regard his rattling of nuclear arms as "irresponsible and reckless to a supreme degree." They accuse him of acting on his own on the basis of the dubious inherent powers doctrine to bring the nation to the brink of a nuclear inferno. Later, when accessible Soviet sources indicated Moscow had nuclear weapons in Cuba and would have used them "rather than lose them," Kennedy's conduct appeared more prudent than detractors had thought. Still, at the time, to maintain his public image of a virile leader, he insisted on keeping secret his compromise with Khrushchev to avoid war.[75]

As for the public, even though it did not know how close to disaster the nation had come, it liked Kennedy's macho behavior. His rating of approval in opinion polls shot up from 61 percent to 84 percent. While basking in this popular triumph, he abandoned operation Mongoose. Less than a month later, though, concerned that his no-invasion pledge might "allow Castro to operate from an invulnerable base," he considered reinstating the plan. He wanted to reserve "the right to invade Cuba in the event of civil war, if there were guerrilla activities or if offensive weapons were reintroduced in Cuba."[76]

Kennedy also refused to forsake covert intervention as policy, as against Rafael Leónidas Trujillo Molina, the aging dictator who had ruled the Dominican Republic for thirty-one years. Eisenhower had severed relations with him because of his brutal regime. On taking office, Kennedy had refused to resume them. Presidential aides, shortly thereafter, suggested eliminating the dictator through force because they regarded the republic a potential second Cuba. On the heels of the Bay of Pigs fiasco, however, the president was cautious, avowing, "we must not run the risk of U.S. association with political assassination."[77] The next evening, May 30, 1961, Dominican dissidents, apparently using weapons supplied by the CIA, murdered Trujillo. A henchman, Joaquín Balaguer, succeeded him. During the next year, Washington monitored his regime carefully, hoping it would move toward self-government.

In November 1962 when remaining members of the Trujillo family appeared poised to regain power, Kennedy decided to "forcibly intervene if necessary" to prevent that from happening. He ordered a naval task force, which included an aircraft carrier and a complement of eighteen hundred marines, to the Dominican shore to save Balaguer, whom Kennedy still regarded as the only tool for edging the republic toward democracy.[78] With this tactic, Kennedy succeeded in prodding the Dominicans to hold an open presidential election in December that brought to power Juan Bosch, a liberal intellectual living in exile. Seven months later, when right-wing militarists menaced his regime, he sought American assistance. Kennedy refused to intervene. The rebels then deposed Bosch and reimposed a military dictatorship on the republic. Kennedy had not hesitated to flaunt force on his own for a commendable purpose in the case of Balaguer, a pliable client. He refused to do so for Bosch, however, because he perceived him as tainted with communism. Again, the personal perception of a president, as much as overall policy considerations, governed how and when he used military force abroad.

A similar anticommunist persuasion motivated Kennedy's resort to covert activity in Southeast Asia. From the start, he had accepted the domino theory as applied to the region, especially after Eisenhower told him "if Laos is lost to the free world, in the long run we will lose all of Southeast Asia." Kennedy and most of his aides perceived Ike's advice as favoring unilateral military action because it would be "preferable to a communist success in Laos." Six weeks after receiving this counsel, when Laotian communist forces or Pathet Lao appeared ready to take over Laos, Kennedy authorized military preparations for possible intervention. He explained this mobilization on television, announcing that "Laos is far away from America, but the world is small. . . . Its own safety runs with the safety of us all." Despite his veiled threat, he insisted he wanted "peace, not war."[79]

During the next year, the president tried to resolve the fate of Laos through diplomacy with the Soviets but in May 1962 Pathet Lao troops surged to the border of Thailand. To demonstrate strength and resolve, Kennedy rushed naval forces, two air squadrons, and five thousand combat troops to Thailand, deploying them along the Laos border. This unilateral exercise of the war power did not prompt a negative statement by anyone in Congress on the presidential usurpation of the legislature's authority.[80] Kennedy also told Andrei Gromyko, the Soviet foreign minister, that if Laos could not be neutralized, a confrontation there between their two countries could lead to a third world war. Finally, in July, representatives from fourteen interested governments met in Geneva and agreed to a wobbly neutralization of Laos. With that, the president recalled the troops in Thailand.

At the same time, Kennedy tried to curb the spread of communist power in neighboring South Vietnam. Earlier he had created a special task force on Southeast Asia to deal with such a problem. In April it recommended committing regular combat troops to Vietnam. Suspicious of such advice because of the Bay of Pigs experience, he refused to do so but went ahead with a more limited intervention. He approved, "on an accelerated basis, a series of mutually supporting actions of a military, political, economic, and psychological covert character" designed purportedly to create a democratic society in South Vietnam. Despite this commitment, more than once he told a friend the United States could not prevail there. "But," he added, "I can't give up a piece of territory like that to the Communists and then get the American people to reelect me."[81] He increased economic assistance, enlarged the dependent South Vietnamese military forces, and immediately tripled the six hundred or so American military advisers in the Republic of Vietnam. These Americans secretly ferried troops into battle against the local communists or Vietcong and northern communists and at times even engaged in combat. The president also launched an undercover counterinsurgency program that involved the training, support, and guidance of South Vietnamese forces.

When rumors of this military involvement reached the American public, a journalist asked the president, "Are Americans now in combat in Viet-Nam?" He responded tersely, "No." Steadily though, the covert operation increased until ultimately, without congressional authorization, he committed more than sixteen thousand troops, one hundred of whom died, to that distant land. Under him, also, the CIA tampered in the internal politics of the Republic of Vietnam even to the extent of promoting a coup that culminated on November 2, 1963, in the assassination of the reactionary president Ngo Dinh Diem, basically because he resisted puppet status. Kennedy lamented the murder, saying "Diem had fought for his country for twenty years and it should not have ended like this."[82] In all, Kennedy had intervened secretly, forcefully, and, to a greater extent than had his two predecessors, in civil wars in Laos and Vietnam, which did not menace any vital American interest.

Even though Kennedy had to deal with frustrating, back-to-back foreign-policy crises, as had Roosevelt, Truman, and Eisenhower, he liked being president. Supposedly, the presidency sobered him, but he relished the power it gave him to demonstrate virility on a global scale. When a reporter asked if he enjoyed the office, he responded, "Well, I find the work rewarding" and the presidency a source of "some happiness."[83] Twenty-three days later, on November 22, before he could explore more of the executive powers, an assassin's bullet cut him down.

Assessments on Kennedy vary. Partisans praise him as "a strong President primarily because he was a strong person," a hero, and a farsighted leader who understood "the true art of statecraft" and used it with great skill. More critical investigators of his presidency charge him "with crisis mongering, with escalating the arms race," with being "more enamored with military than with diplomatic means," and, in Vietnam, with being focused on "winning the war" rather than on peace. They maintain "his escalation of the defense budget, his intervention in Vietnam and his enthusiasm for the space race were all attempts to prove his machismo" in what some categorize as "the phallic presidency" because of his sexual escapades.[84]

As critics argue, Kennedy did tend to view the international crises in personal terms as a test of his courage or nerve, and by implication as challenges to the nation's willingness to use its immense power. He also employed intelligence and military agencies covertly for political purposes more than had most presidents up to his time in a comparable period and behaved as a macho cold warrior. These unilateral actions, his conviction that he must make his mark through foreign policy, and his conception of exceptional executive authority in foreign affairs, all contributed to the expansion of presidential power. In major confrontations as in Cuba, however, in contrast to his more belligerent advisers who urged war, he moderated his machismo. Despite his tough language, he chose diplomacy and peace. In these instances, when he believed he had a choice, he did not recklessly plunge the nation into a war or an extended police action.

CHAPTER 7

The Watershed

In short, there have been—and will be in the future—circumstances in which Presidents may authorize lawfully actions in the interests of the security of this country, which if undertaken by other persons, or even the President under different circumstances, would be illegal.

Richard M. Nixon, 1976

Lyndon Baines Johnson

WHEN Jack Kennedy's assassination thrust Lyndon B. Johnson into the presidency, his strength lay in domestic politics. His work as Senate majority leader had earned him recognition as one of the nation's most accomplished politicians. Although as vice president he had dealt with some foreign policy issues, he had little direct experience in foreign affairs. Close observers commented he had a leery view of the outer world. Scholars echoed this assessment, pointing out that his lack of solid knowledge in international matters made him feel vulnerable in directing foreign policy. Even so, other presidents had started out with even less comprehension of foreign relations and with no less insecurity and had handled them well.

Knowing this record, Johnson did not allow inexperience to deter him from quickly taking personal command of foreign policy. With a macho sense of the importance of standing up to evil in the world, he assumed he could do as well as, and probably better than, his predecessors. He expressed no uncertainty in his resolve to demonstrate virility with a willingness to use military force. This attitude befitted his determination to dominate all aspects of his presidency and his love of power.

A number of Johnson's predecessors had similar qualities but none of them, as biographers relate, "became President with a greater relish for power." Those who knew him well or observed him closely describe him as "a power house, a mover," a "man with extraordinary shrewdness, phenomenal driving force, and an implacable will," yet insecure and at times emotionally unstable.[1]

A subordinate who worked closely with Johnson for nearly two decades characterized him as cruel, and "a colossal son of a bitch" not given to sublimating "his macho instincts." Another analyst of his character maintained he had "a hunger for power in its most naked form, for power not to improve the lives of others, but to manipulate and dominate them, to bend them to his will." For instance, Johnson told an aide, "Just you remember this: There's only two kinds at the White House. There's elephants and there's pissants. And I'm the only elephant."[2]

This attitude encapsulated Johnson's conception of the presidency, a subject he talked about frequently. Virtually as a matter of faith, he believed in strong executive leadership. He saw the president as the initiator of major legislation, the creator of the national agenda, and the dominator of foreign policy. As he put it, "the congressional role in national security is not to act but to respond to the executive." He believed "that the possession of presidential authority included possession of unequaled information, understanding and skill." He maintained that congressional and popular efforts to give direction to policymaking, especially in foreign affairs, were just plain wrong. For public consumption he could also assert, "the Presidency brings no special gift of prophecy or foresight. . . . A President does not shape a new and personal vision of America."[3]

Johnson revealed his stronger perception of the presidency, as well as his impulse to dominate, shortly after taking office when he met with Henry Cabot Lodge, the ambassador to the Republic of Vietnam, then on a visit to Washington, and several of his advisers. Lodge presented his view of the American role in the conflict in Southeast Asia, stressing it would require difficult decisions. "Mr. President, he said, you will have to make them." "I am not going to lose Vietnam," Johnson responded, "I am not going to be the President who saw Southeast Asia go the way China went." He also alluded to political support for this tough stance, adding, "I don't think Congress wants us to let the Communists take over Vietnam." At a meeting with other subordinates in the matter of Vietnam, he announced he alone exercised command. He wanted "no more divisions of opinion, no more bickering, and any person that did not conform to policy should be removed."[4] This personal identification with toughness came to characterize various aspects of his dealing with international politics, especially toward Vietnam and Laos. He took extraordinary pains to portray himself as the leader of steel who would not back down from a communist challenge, however wrongly or rightly perceived.

Initially Johnson's actions and public comments were cautious. He played down the impression of "getting involved in a war" because he assumed a massive, publicized escalation would endanger his strategy for winning election to the presidency on his own in 1964. However, he did act.[5] He spoke of wanting peace, moved slowly in expanding the involvement in Southeast Asia, and held back in stretching presidential authority. On February 1, though, he intensified the covert warfare initiated by Kennedy against the Pathet Lao in Laos and against communists along the North Vietnamese coast.

At the same time, Johnson could not avoid doubt about the value of what he was doing, fearing "we're getting into another Korea." He grumbled privately to his national security adviser, "What the hell is Vietnam worth to me? What is Laos worth to me? What is it worth to this country? Of course if you start running from the Communists, they may just chase you right into your own kitchen." He spoke also of Congress impeaching a president who would not defend South Vietnam. So, in the following weeks he plowed ahead, establishing a committee to carry out, in his words, "an energetic, unified, and skillful prosecution of the only war we face at present."[6]

By July the president had increased the American troop strength in South Vietnam by twenty-five hundred and some 200 Americans had died. While inflicting these casualties, the North Vietnamese protested the raids of South Vietnamese commandos assisted by American military personnel and naval patrols in the Gulf of Tonkin. On August 2, in apparent retaliation, North Vietnamese torpedo boats fired on the American destroyer *Maddox* as it returned from a provocative electronic spying mission along the coast. The attack caused no damage. The president immediately doubled the patrols in the gulf and ordered the navy to demolish future attackers.

Two nights later, Vietnamese communists allegedly struck again, this time at the destroyer *C. Turner Joy* as well as at the *Maddox*. Immediately, before receiving all pertinent data and having a chance to weigh it, the president decided to respond openly with force. "I want . . . those patrol boats that attacked the *Maddox* destroyed, I want everything at that harbor destroyed; I want the whole works destroyed," he told subordinates. "I want to give them a real dose."[7] Accordingly, in sixty-four sorties American bombers blasted four North Vietnamese coastal bases, destroyed 90 percent of that country's oil storage, and sank or damaged twenty-five patrol boats.

Hanoi admitted involvement in the first clash but denied its torpedo boats had attacked a second time. In addition, the personnel on the destroyers never sighted enemy naval craft. Indeed, within a few days Johnson himself admitted to a State Department official, "Hell, those dumb, stupid sailors were just shooting at flying fish!" Later he said, "For all I know" they were "shooting at whales out there."[8] Moreover, naval investigations indicated no second attack had occurred.

The doubts had made no difference to the president. He had been waiting for an excuse to strike hard at the North Vietnamese communists. They aided the National Liberation Front made up of nationalists and communists in the south, called pejoratively Vietcong, who sought to unify with the north. He perceived the incident as an opportunity to demonstrate virility without alienating the significant segment of the electorate that wanted peace.

Shortly before midnight with the attack in progress, the president appeared on national television to explain his use of force. In hyperbolic language, he characterized it as a response to "repeated acts of violence against the Armed Forces of the United States" and by implication to "aggression by terror" against peaceful South Vietnamese villagers. He did not mention the covert raids on North Vietnamese territory. Despite this deception and his rush to violence, he announced that his government's "mission is peace." On the next day, though professing "no rashness" or desire for a "wider war" but the need "to end communist subversion and aggression" in Southeast Asia, he asked Congress for a resolution modeled on that granted Dwight Eisenhower during the Taiwan Strait crisis.[9]

Johnson also had Harry Truman's precedent in mind. When he would actually decide to employ substantial military force in the Truman manner he wanted to avoid the bitter congressional debate that followed the intervention in the Korean hostilities. Indeed, for this reason and in anticipation of the precipitating incident, Johnson had the text of the resolution already prepared. This macho posturing dazzled Congress. So, even though it had no knowledge that a second assault on American naval vessels had in fact occurred, on August 7 it passed the Tonkin Gulf resolution. Even administration partisans characterized this action as a "terrifyingly open-ended grant of power." It promised support for "all necessary measures to repel any armed attack against the forces of the United States and to prevent further aggression."[10]

In the whole Congress, only two senators dissented. One of them, Wayne Morse of Oregon, asked, "Why should we give arbitrary discretion to mere men who happen to hold office at a given time, when the American people and their lives are at the mercy of the discretion of those mere men?" The other opponent, Ernest Gruening of Alaska, maintained correctly that "the Constitution does not permit the President to wage war at his discretion." Even if there had been greater opposition to the resolution, it apparently would not have deterred Johnson. Projecting a seemingly unbridled pride in his manliness, he pointed out that in his capacity as commander in chief, he had already taken military action against North Vietnam and that the decision "was mine—and mine alone." In his perspective, the resolution, which he said privately "was like Grandma's nightshirt—it covered everything," merely reinforced authority he already possessed.[11]

Nonetheless, the president regarded the resolution as personally reassuring. It buttressed his confidence in the course he had chosen because the American people through their elected representatives backed him and not his critics. Moreover, his approval rating in the Louis Harris opinion poll shot up from 42 to 72 percent. Also, when Morse and Gruening sought reelection, they failed. As we saw earlier during the Korean War, such public support can be fickle. Almost as a matter of course in such situations, out of patriotism and awe for the office, people rally around the president. When the urgency passes, often so does the approbation.

Despite these bellicose measures, during the presidential campaign that soon followed, Johnson portrayed himself as a sensible leader devoted to peace who had rebuffed those "eager to enlarge the conflict." He disparaged them as calling "upon us to supply American boys to do the job that Asian boys should do . . . to take reckless action which might risk the lives of millions and engulf much of Asia and certainly threaten the peace of the entire world." The next month, he restated his peace promise. "We don't want our American boys to do the fighting for Asian boys," he said. "We don't want to get involved in a nation with 700 million people and get tied down in a land war in Asia." To another audience he preached, "You don't get peace by rattling your rockets. You don't get peace by threatening to drop your bombs." You must "do anything that is honorable, in order to avoid pulling the trigger . . . that will blow up the world." Then he repeated his theme that "there can be and will be, as long as I am President, peace for all Americans."[12]

A number of Washington insiders familiar with Johnson's temperament doubted his commitment to peace. They were few and their views made no difference in the campaign because his Republican opponent, Barry M. Goldwater, a senator from Arizona, came across as more of a hawk than the president. He gave the impression of being a trigger-happy warrior eager to start a nuclear war, quipping several times he would settle the Vietnam conflict by lobbing a nuclear bomb into the men's toilet room of the Kremlin. Such rhetoric contributed to Johnson's landslide victory. Moreover, party stalwarts, many in the media, and much of the public portrayed him as a talented president who carried out policies beneficial for the nation.

Even though Johnson had campaigned as the peace candidate, this sentiment, as well as the gulf resolution, gave him reason to assume he had considerable support for his publicly muffled aggressiveness in Vietnam. Sampling by opinion polls indicated that 50 percent of the public "felt that the United States had been right in becoming involved with its military forces in Southeast Asia." The polls also hinted caution because 28 percent of those queried opposed the involvement and 22 percent expressed no opinion.[13] Now standing at the pinnacle of his power, with *Time* in January 1965 designating him Man of the Year, the president understandably could dismiss the minority timidity among Americans as less than significant.

Earlier, Johnson had secretly stepped up the military involvement by authorizing the bombing of routes in Laos that northern communist fighters used to infiltrate South Vietnam. With renewed confidence he now more openly asserted his determination to turn back the communists. On February 7 when Vietcong forces attacked the American airfield and army barracks at Pleiku, near the Laotian and Cambodian borders, killing nine and wounding over one hundred men, he had a pretext for going full steam ahead with his planned escalation. Within fourteen hours, he retaliated with carrier-based bombing raids against barracks and other installations in the north.

Many in Congress, the media, and most other Americans endorsed the air strikes. Various polls indicated that 60 percent or more of the public approved of the president's "handling of Vietnam."[14] Heeding this apparent popular appetite for aggressive force while ignoring the less-evident opposition, he continued the bombings systematically and ordered more marines to Vietnam. On March 8, some thirty-five hundred of them in full battle gear scrambled ashore at Da Nang Bay to protect the air base there.

Shortly though at home signs of trouble became more discernible. Beginning on March 24, those belonging to the minority opposed to the intervention launched an antiwar movement at the University of Michigan with teach-ins and other demonstrations. Some three thousand faculty and students denounced the president's war policy. As polls indicated, this peace sentiment soon rose and spread over the country. To counter this now visible but still-weak opposition, Johnson employed his usual anticommunist and other generalized rhetoric.

The president asked an audience at Johns Hopkins University rhetorically, "Why are we in South Viet-Nam?" We are there, he stressed, to help "defend its independence" and "to strengthen world order." As had his two predecessors, he portrayed that rump country's survival vital to the national interest but could demonstrate no tangible reason for that judgment. As he admitted privately, neither the Vietcong nor the North Vietnamese threatened the United States with invasion or with other perceivable physical harm. Regardless, that April he increased the marine ground forces in Vietnam by twenty thousand for a more active mission, meaning they "would now directly enter the war." He also ordered his advisers and others to avoid premature publicity. Simultaneously, he told the press he planned "no far-reaching" change in policy. This "*lying to the public*," as a leading student of the presidency contends, "*was not a matter of the President's reacting in response to criticism, but a carefully thought through part of administration planning*."[15]

At this point Johnson's response to events in the Dominican Republic for a time diverted attention from the deepening Vietnam commitment. On April 24 young military officers favorable to the deposed Juan Bosch attempted a coup against the conservative regime headed by Donald Reid Cabral whom Washington favored. The rebels failed to gain power but ignited a civil war. Johnson assumed that communists dominated the opposition movement. Four days later he ordered marines into the island republic, the first open military intervention in Latin America in nearly a half century.

That evening in another televised address to the nation, the president explained his action as a response to a request from military authorities in the Dominican Republic. They told him "American lives are in danger" and that they could no longer "guarantee their safety." He announced the troops would "give protection to hundreds of Americans." To others, he commented the "American people hadn't elected their President to dodge and duck and refuse to face up to the unpleasant."[16] Within ten days, as the internal struggle continued, he committed twenty-three thousand troops to the venture, or about a hundred times more than were needed for protection duty. An aide described it as Texan overkill. Owing to its violation of international law, the intervention aroused indignation worldwide and outrage in Latin America, where many denounced it as a mockery of the inter-American system.

In the United States, Congress and most of the public backed the president. Angry liberals, however, condemned the invasion on legal as well as moral grounds, pointing out he had resorted to force without seeking congressional authority. He dismissed such consent as not required because he merely exercised traditional executive power to protect American lives when endangered. Because the massive deployment of troops did not accord with the small numbers mentioned, on May 2 he offered another explanation. This time he claimed "a band of Communist conspirators" had taken over leadership of the rebel movement, threatening "the lives of thousands." He added, "the American nations cannot, must not, and will not permit the establishment of another Communist government in the Western Hemisphere." The next day he declared, what's important is "that everybody knows we don't propose to sit here in our rocking chair with our hands folded and let the Communists set up any government in the Western Hemisphere."[17] The occupiers found no communist peril or danger to American lives, and he offered no convincing evidence of communist control.

Again, Johnson fell back on traditional explanations for such interventionism, stating that "99 percent of our reason for going in there was to try to provide protection for these American lives and for the lives of other nationals." Despite his vacillating reasoning, fundamentally this employment of force, as in Vietnam, fit within his expansive conception of the presidency.

Johnson elucidated this view two weeks later at a press conference in response to an apparently set-up question on Vietnam. While citing the Tonkin Gulf resolution as providing congressional support for the war there, he asserted he did not need legislative approval because the "Commander in Chief has all the authority that I am exercising."[18] Under this pretension, the executive could keep the nation's military forces constantly entangled because Americans were scattered over the globe with many or a few always endangered by some kind of upheaval. He could, therefore, choose—as it suited him in the Dominican case as well as in Vietnam—when and where to employ force.

Notwithstanding Johnson's stated reasons for the Dominican intervention, abundant data reveal no threat to any vital United States interest. It indicates instead he had resorted to armed force impulsively to maintain his status as a virile, no-nonsense, anticommunist leader. "What can we do in Vietnam," he asked, "if we can't clean up the Dominican Republic?" Through what he had made his "personal policy," he wanted to erase whatever doubt persisted about his ability to meet the standards of strong leadership. He got away with this unilateral use of force, which critics compared to Teddy Roosevelt's big stick chauvinism, owing to the immense power of the United States and to a public that applauded successful macho behavior, even against a puny foe. Some 76 percent of the Americans polled approved of this military venture while only 17 percent objected. The foray ended in September 1966 but Johnson never recognized its harmful consequences or immorality. In his memoirs he stated, "I would do it again to protect American lives."[19]

As for the Vietnam War, even though the dissent had continued to mount, most Americans still supported it, much as they did the Dominican venture. Johnson refused to negotiate meaningfully with the Vietnamese adversaries, fearing he might look weak. Eisenhower, Kennedy, "and your present President," he explained, "have made a commitment . . . and our national honor is at stake in southeast Asia. And we are going to protect it, and you just might as well be prepared for it." If he did not stay the course, he maintained later, "I'd be the first American President to put my tail between my legs and run out because I didn't have the courage to stand up and support a treaty and support the policy of two other Presidents."

On July 28, 1965, the president again escalated the involvement by announcing he would increase American forces in Vietnam from 75,000 to 125,000 and would send more troops as the field commander requested them. On his own he thus converted what had started as a limited intervention in a civil conflict into an essentially American crusade against the National Liberation Front and the North Vietnamese. "Now," he explained in his memoirs, "we were committed to major combat in Vietnam." He also declared, "This is the most agonizing and the most painful duty of your President."[20]

Soon, as had Americans in the past during unpopular wars or those of questionable purpose, many began attaching the president's name to the conflict—Lyndon Johnson's war, as they called it. While personalizing the struggle, he also tried to internationalize it with assistance from allies. Most of them held back. Australia, New Zealand, the Philippines, and others sent token forces but only the South Koreans provided a substantial number of troops.

In August, as opposition to the war mounted, the public's rating of Johnson's performance plummeted to 39 percent. Still, he persisted in viewing the conflict largely in terms of his own stake in it, which he identified with the national interest. "When I land troops they call me an interventionist," he complained, "and if I do nothing I'll be impeached." We must hang on, he said in another instance, to thwart the Vietcong because they "actually thought that pressure on an American President would be so great that he'd pull out of Vietnam. They don't know the President of the United States. He's not pulling out." He told journalists several times, "I'm not going down in history as the first American President who lost a war."[21]

This concern for self came out in numerous other ways. Johnson assumed he had a right to expect patriotic support. When confronted with dissent over presidential decisions in foreign policy, which he tried to suppress, he perceived it as verging on treason. He spoke of "my security council," "my State Department," and "my troops," conveying to many the impression that he alone, rather than those who fought and died, mattered in the war making. He reiterated that this was "his war and he would run it his way" and that he was determined to win it. This attitude riled the critics. As the casualties mounted, they became more vociferous, denouncing the conflict as unnecessary and immoral, and Johnson as a "slob" and "murderer." This disdain for the man unavoidably rubbed off on the presidency. Public reverence for it declined.

In an effort to refute the critics, Johnson directed the State Department's legal adviser, Leonard C. Meeker, to prepare a tract justifying the intervention. Fully backing his boss's position, Meeker stated the president needed "no declaration of war" for launching hostilities in Vietnam. He claimed "the President has ample authority" to use the military forces on his own, to decide what constituted an attack on the United States, and to commit troops anywhere in the world for such defense. The adviser cited various precedents, such as the Quasi-War and the Korean War, for Johnson's action. Meeker concluded, "If the President could act in Korea without a declaration of war, *a fortiori* he is empowered to do so now in Viet-Nam."[22] He thus used a case of doubtful constitutionality to sanction another of questionable validity.

This defense of expansive executive power fit an established pattern. As we have seen, members of the executive branch regularly behaved as sycophants or hired guns who bent data to produce whatever rationale their client desired. Even though at times they acted out of conviction, they could hardly escape the reality of being dependent on the president for their jobs, their status, and possibly their future. Johnson exploited this power more than had most presidents to awe his staff, members of Congress, and even popular opposition. "Now, there are many, many, who can recommend, advise and sometimes a few of them consent," he reminded the skeptics of his authority. "But there is only one that has been chosen by the American people to decide."[23] Even so, as demonstrated in polls and elsewhere, he could not check the unraveling of his credibility with the public.

During this declining popular perception of presidential trustworthiness, Johnson turned his attention to the Middle East where he tried to prevent another Arab-Israeli war. He failed. On June 5, in retaliation for Arab raids on their territory and other menaces, the Israelis attacked Egypt and battled Jordan and Syria, defeating all three in a six-day war. The president sided openly with Israel. Despite a publicly proclaimed embargo on arms to the Middle East, he supplied it with guns and other equipment. In consequence, the Arabs and their Soviet backers regarded "the United States a de facto belligerent." On June 10, when the Israeli conquest of Damascus appeared imminent, Alexei Kosygin, the Soviet premier, told Johnson, "If you want war, you will get war." The president then ordered the Sixth Fleet, cruising on alert in the Mediterranean, to within sixty miles of Syria's shoreline. He did this as a warning "that the United States was prepared to resist Soviet intrusion in the Middle East." In this instance, he brandished force unilaterally in keeping with his personal sentiment without concern over a possible backlash. Not only did the Israelis enjoy enormous support from the public and Congress but also this venture ended quickly, successfully, and with no American lives expended.[24]

In contrast, the war in Vietnam continued to devour blood and wealth. On October 26, 1966, from a conference in Manila, Johnson secretly journeyed to the huge American base at Cam Ranh Bay where he tried to boost morale, praising the troops for defending the nation's security. He also enjoined them to "nail the coonskin to the wall," a comment that became the butt of ridicule. More and more Americans also mocked him and the war itself. It had come to overshadow all else in his presidency—the Great Society or fight against poverty, the struggle for civil rights, and other domestic programs.

The rising opposition took many forms—ever larger antiwar demonstrations, bitter letters to editors, critical appraisals by journalists, and organized pleas by intellectuals and others to withdraw from Southeast Asia. In 1967 protesters, frequently chanting "Hey, hey LBJ, how many kids did you kill today," organized 116 antiwar demonstrations outside the White House. By midyear, polls indicated that nearly half the nation viewed the intervention as a mistake and a "little more than a quarter of the population approved of his handling of the war."[25]

In response, Johnson persisted in his pro-war rhetoric but also took the criticism personally, denouncing it as immoral and unpatriotic. He belittled those who disagreed with him as "nervous nellies," "half-brights," and "knee-jerk liberals" and tried to dismiss the peace movement as communist dominated. To confirm his suspicions, he ordered the Central Intelligence Agency and the Federal Bureau of Investigation to place the movement's leaders and other prominent antiwar activists under surveillance. He listened mainly to those who told him what he wanted to hear. Few around him dared dissent from his views because as "servants of the president" they perceived their loyalties belonging "to him and *his* policies" rather than to principles or to the people. If they dared disagree with him, did not give him unquestioning support, or attempted to reflect popular sentiment, he sacked them. He castigated them also for being weaklings rather than real men. When, for instance, he learned that an adviser had become a "dove," he dismissed him as feminine, saying, "Hell, he has to squat to piss." He had the justice department also investigate some of these "trouble-makers."[26]

A number of earlier presidents had similarly violated civil liberties, but more than others, Johnson did so under the guise of national security to further his own partisan agenda. He also used fright tactics, such as telling Americans that if we quit in Vietnam we would soon be fighting in Hawaii and San Francisco, and our freedom would be swept away in a flood of conquest. This depiction had no basis in fact. Neither the Vietcong nor their allies had the resources for such overseas warfare.

Johnson continued to speak often about courage, of his concern for the presidency, of his commitment to peace, and of his compassion for the dying as the result of his decisions. "There is no American killed or wounded in battle for whom I do not feel a sense of personal responsibility," he wrote to the parents of one such casualty.[27] Critics perceived such commiseration as crocodile tears, as slighting the slaughter of Vietnamese, and as immoral. In all, the more he talked, the more he fueled dissent, even in Congress.

Again, the State Department came to Johnson's defense, with Nicholas deB. Katzenbach, the undersecretary of state, on August 17, 1967, taking on the task. "Today," he told the Senate Foreign Relations Committee, the interaction between Congress and the executive branch "requires that the President fill the preeminent role." As had other employees of the executive branch, he maintained that with the Tonkin Gulf resolution, Johnson "had all the authority that a declaration of war would have given any President."[28] He called it the "functional equivalent" to a declaration of war. The resort to such circuitous reasoning to justify the executive's claim to an unrestricted war power appeared to reflect Katzenbach's role as the administration's mouthpiece rather than constitutional reality.

All the while the war lurched toward a stalemate, costing thousands of lives and destroying much of the country that Johnson proclaimed he wanted to save. He blamed his difficulties on ultraliberals and others whom he perceived as conspiring against his beneficent crusade. He saw himself as right and everyone else as wrong. "It is hell," he said, "when a President has to spend all of his time keeping his own people juiced up. But it doesn't matter whether the poll is 10 or 40, I am going to do the right thing." Imagining the media pundits as hostile, he was convinced they "want me to be the son-of-a-bitch." As the result of the press and television coverage, he added, many Americans refused "to see the enemy as the enemy." He lashed out further at a journalist, shouting, "This is not Johnson's war. This is America's war."[29]

Much of the public, including prominent legislators in the president's own party, thought differently. In particular, they resented Johnson's and Secretary of State Dean Rusk's continual references to the nation's commitment in Vietnam. In August Senator Sam J. Ervin Jr. of North Carolina, a conservative Democrat, had expressed this indignation succinctly. The president, he stated, has come to exercise "virtually plenary power to determine foreign policy and decide on war and peace," and "it is time for us to end the continual erosion of legislative authority." He stressed the executive could employ the armed forces on his own only defensively "against sudden armed attack." In line with this attitude, in November the Senate Foreign Relations Committee urged passage of a resolution stating that "the Commitment of the armed forces . . . to hostilities on foreign territory for any purpose other than to repel an attack" requires "affirmative action by Congress."[30]

Two months later, while the Senate had this national commitments resolution under consideration, Americans gained further insight on Johnson's war. Beginning on January 30, 1968, during the Vietnamese new year Tet holiday, Vietcong and North Vietnamese troops assaulted virtually every major city and military installation in South Vietnam. Despite suffering huge losses, they demonstrated a capability that mocked the president's claims to an upper hand in the hostilities. This offensive not only destroyed what credibility he still retained but also emboldened the doubters in his inner circle, in his party, and in the country as a whole to speak out. In the weeks that followed, Gallup polls indicated that 79 percent of the public regarded the Southeast Asian entanglement as wrong.

This dissatisfaction spilled over into Johnson's handling of the presidency. Sixty-four percent disapproved. This turn in popular sentiment, coupled with his poor showing in the New Hampshire presidential primary, indicated his bid for a second elected term would fail. On March 31, therefore, while still maintaining unrealistically that "what we are doing now in Vietnam, is vital . . . to the security of every American," he made a startling announcement. He told the nation he would stop bombarding North Vietnam with the hope Hanoi would begin peace talks promptly, that he would "not permit the Presidency to become involved in the partisan divisions that are developing in this political year," and that he would not seek reelection.[31]

In response, Hanoi proposed direct peace talks. They began in Paris on May 13 but quickly deadlocked. As for Johnson, he had decided publicly to give up another run for the presidency not because he recognized the depth of his folly or felt guilt for his war policy but because he had lost most of his constituency and what he cherished most—personal power. Furthermore, according to biographer Robert Dallek, he tried later to retain the presidency by secretly promoting a draft for himself at the Chicago Democratic National Convention. The plan flopped.

Those Americans who turned against Johnson did so for a plethora of reasons. They did not, however, abandon him for using power illegitimately, for lying, or for waging unilateral war in part at least out of a massive ego and a "flamboyant . . . brand of military minded machismo."[32] The public had tolerated comparable behavior in other presidents but none had commanded authority as outrageously as he did. He acted as though his will and his power stood preeminent in the fate of the presidency, of the nation. Dissenters challenged these presumptions but they did not, as he and some analysts asserted, seek to weaken the office. Most of the public, and the pundits, too, even during this unpopular war, continued to approve of the virile presidency.

Of course, much of the public rejected Johnson because it considered his war immoral or because he could not show "that American physical security was actually endangered." Most Americans, though, wanted him out because of the war's mounting casualties, high costs, and his failure to crush an ostensibly weak foe as he had promised he would. In retrospect some aides tried to shift blame for the unnecessary bloodletting away from Johnson. Charitably, as one contended, "he might have steered a wiser Vietnam course had his erudite advisers not all given him the same advice"—fight to win.[33]

Such commentary overlooks Johnson's determined personalizing of a struggle in a land where the very people he sought to protect from the perdition of communism regarded Americans as alien intruders. Even when at times doubtful of the worthiness of his cause, he went ahead with decisions that led to the burning of bodies with napalm, the defoliating of farmlands, the torturing of prisoners, and the deaths and maiming of thousands. Still, several recent biographers have claimed redeeming qualities in this man often depicted as emotionally unstable, paranoid, and "a monster of ambition," claiming he "has been short-changed" by earlier chroniclers.[34] Other scholars have observed that in one way or another, with his ego and machismo, "Johnson was the cause of his ultimate undoing," and even worse, the chief architect of the nation's tragedy up to this point.[35]

Richard Milhous Nixon

As had Johnson, Richard M. Nixon came to the presidency with a reputation as a ruthless politician driven by vaulting ambition. Unlike Johnson, he had acquired considerable experience in foreign affairs, primarily while serving eight years as Dwight Eisenhower's vice president. This background did not help much in his first run for president, which he lost to Kennedy. Nonetheless, in 1968 he again won the Republican nomination.

In the campaign that followed, foreign policy, or how to end the entanglement in Vietnam, became the crucial issue, virtually tearing apart the Democratic Party. Even though well known for his hawkish views on the war, at this point Nixon tempered his sails to the winds of popular sentiment. He played down his bellicosity; promised to terminate the American involvement with a secret plan he never revealed because, as he admitted later, he never had one; and repeated often he would end the war on an honorable basis. He also emphasized, as though Johnson had been a weakling, that "the next President must take an activist view of his office."[36] Nixon's liberal opponent, Vice President Hubert H. Humphrey, could shake off neither Johnson's distrust of him based on a fear he "would abandon the war the minute he took the oath of office" nor his connection to Johnson's war policy.[37] Largely for these reasons Humphrey lost to Nixon by a thin margin.

Nixon brought to the presidency the standard views of a cold warrior, a combative temperament, a tyrannical streak, a preoccupation with self, frequent single-handed decision making, and a resolve to exercise power in the tradition of the strong executive. He reiterated this conviction often but summed it up in his retirement years, stating the common view that the "great initiatives both abroad and home have always been undertaken when we have had strong Presidents in the White House." He believed "the successful leader has a strong will of his own, and he knows how to mobilize the will of others," stressing that "to wish is passive; to will is active." Above all, he was determined to conduct an activist foreign policy, an area where he felt most comfortable, and where he considered himself an accomplished strategist. Accordingly, in policymaking he chose to bypass the State Department, which he distrusted in part because "its personnel had no loyalty to him," and to concentrate control of foreign affairs in the White House.[38]

Neither those who knew Nixon well nor the public that observed him from a distance were indifferent to him. George Ball, the foreign affairs specialist who for a time worked for him, characterized him as "the archetypal hawk, ready at slight provocation to dispatch Americans to kill and be killed." Others described Nixon as a leader who lied to the public, to Congress, to foreign leaders, and even to his closest aides. A biographer concerned with his psychological makeup perceived him as paranoid with "a severely defective or almost nonexistent conscience."[39]

While admitting flaws in the man, admirers usually view him from a different perspective, primarily because they, unlike his enemies, focus on the positive aspects of his character. Friends recall exceptional consideration for others, sentimentality, kindness, and generosity. They portray him as "a warm and religious person under a cold-appearing shell," a president whose "decisions were courageous and strong."[40] Members of his entourage point out other qualities, such as his determination to keep in tune with public sentiment in any way he could, and his financing private polls on almost all aspects of his administration but above all in matters of foreign policy. They, as well as some critical observers, maintain also he took office under a handicap because Johnson had virtually destroyed the customary public reverence for the presidency. They believed the office had become a target for unjustified attacks that undermined its foreign-policy powers. In all, though, chroniclers exaggerate the harm, if any, done to the presidency as they do Nixon's flaws and virtues.

At his inaugural, Nixon gave no indication he regarded the presidency as crippled by his predecessor. Indeed, he saw it as a source of immense power, some of which had yet to be tapped. As had other presidents on their debut, he made peace his major theme. "The greatest honor history can bestow is the title of peacemaker," he announced. "This honor now beckons America—the chance to help lead the world at last out of the valley of turmoil and onto that high ground of peace." In dealing with the opposition to the Vietnam War, he referred to dissent as a "crisis of the spirit" but revealed nothing about his peace plan.[41]

This vagueness upset antiwar activists. They demanded specifics. Right after the address, some of them who had congregated in Washington vented their distrust by disrupting the inaugural parade, shouting, "Four more years of death! Four more years of death!," spitting obscenities, lighting smoke bombs, and hurling debris at the presidential limousine. Never before had such violence marred the inaugural ceremony. Thus, from the start, Vietnam came to overshadow virtually everything in the administration, every discussion, every decision, every other problem.

In this atmosphere, Nixon reshaped Johnson's Vietnam policy without changing the substance. For example, he continued the secret air and proxy war in Laos—kept secret primarily from the American people—and the formal peace talks with North Vietnamese representatives in Paris. In February 1969 when the North Vietnamese launched a new offensive, he reacted in personal terms, believing they had done so to ascertain whether or not he would be a determined adversary. To demonstrate his vigor as well as his might to them and to Russia and China, he began sustained bombing of North Vietnam. On March 18, he also ordered heavy strikes on the northerners' bases in supposedly neutral Cambodia but kept that air war, too, secret from the American public. In addition, he took an unyielding stance toward the discussions at Paris, asserting we must "negotiate from strength" and hence not withdraw unilaterally from Southeast Asia. "I have not," he emphasized, "ordered and do not intend to order any reduction of our own activities."[42]

This belligerent attitude carried over into the president's initial reaction to a provocation by North Koreans. On April 15, their jet-fighters shot down an American naval reconnaissance plane, purportedly because it violated their coastal air space. The thirty-one men aboard the craft perished. Ostensibly, Nixon felt compelled to hang tough because earlier he had lambasted Johnson for not using military force against the Korean communists when, in January of the previous year, they had seized the navy's electronic spy ship *Pueblo*, which was operating off their coast. Denouncing the attack on the navy plane as unprovoked, Nixon immediately assumed, as he had with the North Vietnamese, that "we were being tested, and therefore force must be met with force." He then deployed a naval task force to the Sea of Japan for possible retaliatory attacks against North Korea. When an adviser pointed out he would be courting further hostilities, Nixon retorted, "So you've sold out to the doves too."[43]

Nonetheless, when the president learned that logistics could not support a swift, reactive air strike, he drew back. He decided also not to gamble with a possible communist retaliatory attack on South Korea that would, or could, ignite a second Asian war and more protests at home. Even so, this episode and his desire to follow a hard line, along with the New York *Time*'s exposure on May 9 of the air war in Cambodia, alarmed domestic doves. He therefore cooled off on Korea and spoke of reducing the American involvement in Southeast Asia without moving openly to terminate the war there.

Despite Nixon's bellicosity in word and deed, this nebulous promise and other comments led many in Congress to hope he would not follow in the path of his predecessor in exploiting the war power. Senators in particular wanted to make it clear to him they recognized no kind of presidential commitment or other obligation to continue the war. So on June 25 by a vote of seventy to sixteen, they passed the national commitments resolution. Although it did not have the force of law, the Senate Foreign Relations Committee viewed the resolution as "an invitation to the executive to reconsider its excesses, and to the legislature to reconsider its omissions, in the making of foreign policy."[44]

The president, who claimed that as commander in chief he possessed sole authority over the armed forces and could order them abroad without specific congressional approval, ignored the invitation. He thereby placed himself on a collision course with Congress. A month later at Guam, while on a visit to six Asian countries, he announced the first of several vague, ambiguous, and contradictory policies he and his aides called the Nixon doctrine. On this occasion he stated he would provide Asian allies with "the matériel and the military and economic assistance . . . to defend themselves" but would not aid them with American troops. Thus, he expected "that this problem will be increasingly handled by . . . the Asian nations themselves."[45] By indicating the war in Southeast Asia would continue but with a modified strategy, this pronouncement dashed hopes in the Senate for a cooperative effort to terminate it.

Both the tactic of evading peace and the Guam version of Nixon's doctrine offered nothing new. The doctrine merely repeated Johnson's pledge to leave Asians to do their own fighting, a principle that in practice the Texan had ignored. Nixon called his version of the defunct policy "Vietnamization." It would, he stressed, trim the war's cost in dollars and in blood to the United States. He backed the policy with a promise to withdraw twenty-five thousand troops from Vietnam but also with the threat that Hanoi should negotiate to end the war because "Saigon could win it." At the same time, he initiated secret negotiations with the North Vietnamese that his national security adviser, Henry A. Kissinger, began on August 4 in Paris. At home, the president denounced his critics in the media and elsewhere as aiding the enemy, dismissed pursuit of peace except on his own terms as suggesting evidence of weakness, and under the guise of protecting national security, grasped more power.

This strategy aggravated the rising discontent with the president's policies. Opponents grumbled about the slow pace of the promised withdrawal of troops from Vietnam and then denounced the president for it. In September, therefore, Nixon pulled out sixty thousand more military personnel. Still, the critics assailed Vietnamization as well as his pledge to end the war as semantic hoaxes. Nixon bristled, insisting as had Johnson that he did not intend to be the "first American President to lose a war" or to "retreat from the world."[46] He also announced that the mounting peace demonstrations would not force him to modify his Vietnam policy.

Shortly after, on October 15, defiant dissenters in more than two hundred cities staged a Vietnam moratorium involving some four million Americans. The president dug in his heels, determined to demonstrate he "was not going to be pushed around by the rabble in the streets." Five weeks later, in a nationally televised speech, he scorned the protesters as making up a disloyal minority. He reemphasized, in contradictory terms, that he wanted to end the war while "winning" the peace. Furthermore, American forces would have to remain in Southeast Asia until the South Vietnamese could defend themselves. A "precipitate withdrawal," he warned, "would be a disaster of immense magnitude. A nation cannot remain great if it destroys its allies and lets down its friends." He went on to ask "the great silent majority of my fellow Americans" for support. "Let us be united against defeat," he concluded, because "North Vietnam cannot defeat or humiliate the United States. Only Americans can do that."[47]

Polls taken immediately after the address indicated his approval rating had zoomed to a high of 64 percent. He consequently regarded the speech as the most effective of his presidency and as assuring him of "the public support" he felt he needed "to continue a policy of waging war in Vietnam."[48] The protests continued but more subdued and on a smaller scale than previously. On November 15, some 250,000 people joined in a "march against death" from Arlington National Cemetery to the White House. The mainstream media gave it scant coverage because, demonstrators alleged, the media bowed to administration pressure against publicizing the peace movement.

Meanwhile, the secret peace negotiations with the Vietnamese adversaries had broken down. To make some kind of a breakthrough in his quest for peace with honor, the president, late in February 1970, sent Kissinger to Paris to resume the interrupted talks. Nixon decided also to do something to prevent a perceived communist takeover of Laos and Cambodia. He regarded the North Vietnamese military presence in Cambodia as exceptionally troublesome. Seemingly, he could employ force there with limited American casualties and without provoking a resurgence of massive demonstrations at home, which he wished to avoid. He could also display virile leadership and enhance his bargaining position in Paris. On this basis on April 28, without consulting Congress, he thrust twenty thousand American along with South Vietnamese troops into neutral Cambodia. The next morning in a briefing with Pentagon officials he declared, "You have to electrify people with bold decisions. Bold decisions make history."[49]

The following day, in a televised national address, Nixon defended the incursion, which he insisted was not an invasion. He explained it as designed to disperse North Vietnamese forces poised in "privileged sanctuaries" they used for attacking the Republic of Vietnam. He struck, he added, also "to protect our men who are in Vietnam" as well as to end the war and win "the just peace we desire." To placate critics, he promised to scrupulously respect Cambodian neutrality, an assertion journalists labeled "an outright lie." At the same time he warned them, "If, when the chips are down, the world's most powerful nation, the United States of America, acts like a pitiful, helpless giant, the forces of totalitarianism will threaten free nations and free institutions throughout the world." He insisted he would not allow that to happen because he "would rather be a one-term President . . . than to be a two-term President at the cost of seeing America . . . accept the first defeat in its proud 190-year history."[50] Nowhere, though, did he make clear that his action countered any tangible threat to American security.

In contrast to the president's depiction, a substantial portion of the public saw the Cambodia invasion as simply a widening of the war. It set off protests and riots in colleges and universities across the nation. On May 1, in disgust, Nixon characterized the student demonstrators as "these bums, you know, blowing up the campuses." As had Johnson, because of the protests he became something of a White House prisoner. He no longer dared show his face on a college campus, notably after a tragedy on May 4 at Kent State University in Ohio. National Guardsmen had fired point-blank at unarmed protesters, killing four and wounding eleven students. The bloodletting horrified moderates as well as administration critics. The situation worsened when the father of one of the girls killed protested, "My child was not a bum," and the president did not express sympathy for the dead students and their families.[51]

Nonetheless, Nixon's war policy still played well with numerous supporters. Polls recorded that 50 percent of those queried backed the Cambodian invasion whereas 39 percent disapproved. On May 20, in New York City, one hundred thousand people led by hard-hat construction workers paraded to show solidarity with the president. Mail to Congress, however, ran overwhelmingly against his unilateral initiative. Most of the doves now dubbed the Vietnam conflict Mr. Nixon's war and described it as no longer a Vietnam war but an Indochina war.

Four days after the start of the Cambodia invasion, in response to the furor it had created the president had asked the State Department to make a constitutional case for it. The task fell to William H. Rehnquist, at the time an assistant attorney general. He interpreted the Commander in Chief Clause as "a grant of substantive authority" that had always enabled presidents to order troops "into conflict with foreign powers on their own initiative" and even to deploy them "in a way which invited hostile retaliation." Accordingly, he argued, Nixon had made "precisely the sort of tactical decision traditionally confided to the commander-in-chief in the conduct of armed conflict." Scholar Arthur M. Schlesinger Jr. dismissed Rehnquist's contention as "persiflage," averring he had compromised his legal scholarship as well as historical knowledge in service to his mentor.[52]

In another attempt to confound critics, on June 3 the president stepped up troop withdrawals from Vietnam and promised to remove fifty thousand within five months. This effort to pacify opponents failed, in part because overall, as in Cambodia, he had bypassed Congress. Discontented legislators charged him with usurping Congress's war authority by conducting a constitutionally unauthorized war. They then relaunched a campaign to restrain the president's self-assumed power to make unilateral war. Republican senator John S. Cooper of Kentucky and Democrat Frank Church of Idaho sponsored an amendment to a military appropriations bill that forbade military involvement in Cambodia without consent of the legislative branch. This measure marked the first legislative effort to restrict the president's use of the military in Indochina. On June 24, the Senate repealed the Tonkin Gulf resolution, leaving Nixon, according to critics, without legal sanction to continue military operations in Southeast Asia. In response, he dismissed the resolution, avowing that as commander in chief he possessed the authority to maintain the warfare on his own.

Six days later, as the last American troops departed Cambodia, the Senate passed the Cooper-Church Amendment, thus actually moving to check the executive war power under the Commander in Chief clause. The House, however, rejected the measure, thus allowing Nixon to continue air operations in Cambodia. Nonetheless, the Senate's vote reflected a mounting reaction against the deceptions and bloodlettings of cold-war presidents. It also manifested a distrust of Nixon personally.

Unlike his critics, the president believed the Cambodia incursion had been successful. So, in February 1971 he again expanded the war by providing air and artillery support for Republic of Vietnam troops who invaded Laos. Now though, to a greater extent than ever before, various litigants—taxpayers, servicemen, members of Congress, and others—challenged the president's authority to initiate and conduct hostilities without Congress's declaring war. Nixon fought these suits. They all failed because invariably the federal courts sustained or legitimated presidential initiative in decisions to wage undeclared war. In addition, as a rule Congress accepted this executive preeminence spelled out in the courts.

Regardless of this kind of solidarity by the three branches of government on the war-making issue, that summer public disillusionment with the Vietnam conflict reached a peak. Polls indicated that 71 percent of the people considered it a mistake. Doves in Congress tried numerous times to restrict the president's authority to wage the war or to persuade their colleagues to set a date for bringing all the American troops home, but without success. Nixon reacted by asking for public support as a matter of patriotism. The tactic worked. Despite widespread grumbling, again according to the pollsters most Americans—wealthy and poor, white-collar and blue—responded with approval of Nixon's stance. A minority composed of the young, intellectuals, blacks, and others, however, continued to oppose him vehemently.

Soon that mix changed. Polls in September reported a deeper dissatisfaction with the war than in the past. A majority of those questioned now favored termination within the year. The following month, the president announced a peace program along with accelerated troop withdrawals, thereby regaining some of his lost goodwill. Basically, though, in Paris, where through negotiation he had the opportunity to make peace quickly, he had his representative stick to his hard line.

At this juncture, as Pakistan, an American ally, and India slid toward war, Nixon also took a tough stand against India. The confrontation began over the status of the Muslim part of Bengal, known then as East Pakistan, in revolt against the West Pakistani establishment that ruled the country. These leaders resented India's siding with the Bengali rebels. On December 3, 1971, therefore, they launched a war with an attack on Indian airfields. Disliking the Indians and their prime minister, Indira Gandhi, Nixon stepped up pressure against them with economic sanctions. He also squeezed Kissinger, who handled details of this diplomacy, to make sure he carried out this personal policy without falter. "I'm getting hell every half hour from the President that we are not being tough enough on India," Kissinger told a National Security Council group. "He wants to tilt in favor of Pakistan."[53]

Regardless of Nixon's hubris, Indian forces quickly gained the upper hand, defeating the Pakistanis in the east. Seemingly out of a personal vendetta against Indira Gandhi, Nixon then exerted whatever coercion he could, short of armed intervention, to prevent India from going ahead with a rumored invasion of western Pakistan, which he wished to preserve as an independent nation. Impulsively, he ordered a naval task force spearheaded by the aircraft carrier *Enterprise*, the navy's most powerful ship with a nuclear capability, into the Bay of Bengal close to Pakistani shores. Thus, on his own authority, in the absence of any emergency or threat to the United States or to American forces, he intervened in this limited regional conflict at the risk of nuclear war with the Russians, who had made clear they sided with India.

This saber rattling had no direct effect on the war's result or the peace terms. When the conflict ended on December 17 Pakistan had to accept dismemberment. Its eastern half emerged as the independent state of Bangladesh. A poll indicated the American public, by a margin of two to one, disapproved of the president's handling of the crisis. Despite this lack of support for his bravado, he remained convinced, on the basis of "our intelligence reports" but without hard substantiating evidence, that his threat to use force saved "West Pakistan from the imminent threat of Indian aggression and domination."[54]

All the while, the president had been making overtures to the People's

Republic of China even though its leaders had said repeatedly that relations with the United States could not truly improve until he pulled out of Indochina. After being bloodied in a series of border clashes with Soviet forces, the Chinese government reversed this attitude, sought to use the United States to offset Russian power, and invited Nixon to Peking. On July 15, 1971, nine months before another presidential election, the former communist-basher announced he would visit China to seek normalization of the relations between the two countries. He arrived on February 14, 1972, and remained for seven days. Although the mission accomplished nothing tangible diplomatically, it initiated a détente between these former foes. For Nixon personally, it proved a political triumph, obscuring his stumbling in Vietnam and enhancing his image as a world statesman.

After returning to Washington, the president still had to confront the problem of Vietnam, which he did indirectly by boycotting the Paris talks. Then in April the North Vietnamese made a shambles of what remained of Vietnamization by invading the south across a previously demilitarized zone and routing the defenders. Tossing aside restraint, an angered Nixon told aides "the bastards [North Vietnamese] have never been bombed like they're going to be bombed this time."[55] He ordered massive air raids over much of North Vietnam and the mining of Haiphong and other ports. Despite this raised level of violence, in October, in resumed talks in Paris, Kissinger worked out a truce with the communist negotiators. It fell apart in the midst of the presidential campaign but the negotiations continued.

Meanwhile, Nixon had become deeply concerned about unauthorized disclosures of confidential documents revealing deceptive practices within the executive branch in the conduct of the Vietnam War. More than a year earlier, in an effort to plug the leaking of such information, he had ordered lie-detector tests of staff and the wiretapping of seventeen government officials and journalists. In addition, he had created a special group of agents called "plumbers," responsible only to him, and had installed a voice-operated tape-recording system in several White House offices. "I don't give a damn how it is done," he told an aide, "do whatever has to be done to stop these leaks. I don't want to be told why it can't be done." Nixon had become "convinced that he was faced with a hostile conspiracy" that threatened his foreign policy.[56] He assumed also that in the interest of national security, as president he possessed an inherent authority to take even illegal actions, such as the wiretapping without warrants, to foil the imagined conspirators.

As the election campaign picked up momentum, several of the plumbers joined the Committee to Reelect the President, known as CRP or

CREEP, and expanded their undercover activities to the sabotaging of Nixon's political opponents. Through chance in the early-morning hours of June 17, 1972, at gunpoint police caught five of the CREEP agents burglarizing the headquarters of the Democratic National Committee in Washington's Watergate hotel and office complex. George McGovern, the Democratic candidate who campaigned with the promise that if elected he would immediately withdraw from Vietnam, asked embarrassing questions about the caper but they had no influence on the election. Viewing him as a radical on many issues, not just Vietnam, most voters distrusted him and ignored the Watergate episode. Seemingly they found Nixon's contradictory posturing, as warrior and tough peacemaker who would end the conflict in Vietnam with honor, more appealing. In November he won reelection with the greatest sweep of electoral votes in the twentieth century.

Nixon then pressed on with the war with renewed confidence and an enhanced ego. He repeated his various reasons for doing so, such as the need "to stand by allies," to demonstrate "confidence in ourselves," and to show he would not "succumb to the fashionable debunking of 'prestige' or 'honor' or 'credibility.'" Within two weeks after the election, he again pressed his case with the Vietnamese enemy in the Paris negotiations but they soon stalemated. On December 18, therefore, he began twelve days of around-the-clock bombing of the north, the most destructive pummeling of the war, with the intent of crippling daily life in Hanoi and Haiphong. Critics called him a maddened tyrant but he ignored them. If "the Russians and Chinese" thought "they were dealing with a madman," he told a reporter, then they might "force North Vietnam into a settlement before the world was consumed by a larger war."[57]

The horror these massive raids inflicted on the Vietnamese seemed to bother Nixon much less than concerns about self. As had Johnson, he spoke of the burden of the presidency, the crushing work load, his personal suffering, how he detested war, and how he hated "to make decisions ordering brave young men into battles in which I knew many would lose their lives."[58] He called his bombing decision "my terrible personal ordeal" and "heartrending," and deplored the American casualties it caused. He rationalized them by saying, "We simply have to take losses if we are going to accomplish our objectives."[59] Reality indicated, however, that his willingness to bomb ruthlessly to achieve minor diplomatic gains again demonstrated that as president he regarded himself unaccountable to anyone but himself.

In light of this behavior, more and more Americans began questioning the wisdom of permitting such a man, or any president, to wield unrestrained power over life and death for millions. Friendly governments, members of Congress, and even leaders from Nixon's own party begged him to terminate the carpet bombing, which they and others called "a stone age tactic," "war by tantrum," or violence "beyond all reason." Even though the protests did not deter him, they raised the issue of the justiciability of presidential war to a level never before reached, a concern that cut through various layers of society. Some defenders of the strong presidency, such as Senator Barry Goldwater, even misconstrued the Constitution and mangled history. He and others claimed "the Framers intended to leave the 'making of war' with the President."[60] Viewing the question as political, the courts, too, disregarded the evidence on original intent and upheld the legality of the war.

Finally, the publicly expressed opposition to the conflict became so intense the president could no longer defy it. On January 23, 1973, in Paris, Kissinger concluded cease-fire accords with North Vietnam even though they fell short of winning the peace as the president had previously demanded. That night Nixon announced "an agreement to end the war and bring peace with honor in Vietnam and Southeast Asia." The accords committed him to terminate the ground hostilities in Vietnam, Laos, and Cambodia and to withdraw American troops from Vietnam by March 28. A week later he told reporters, "we have finally achieved peace with honor," adding bitterly, "I know it gags some of you to write that phrase, but it is true, and most Americans realize it is true."[61]

Nixon contradicted his own version of the peace by maintaining a macho posture and by persisting with secret bombing raids in Cambodia and Laos. He regarded this toughness important because, in his view, a leader who gave the appearance of timidity would lose popular support. This would encourage people to go after him. On the basis of past executive experience, this theory had some validity but in this case members of the executive branch used it to support the assumption that the president could do no wrong. They overlooked the high costs and meager achievements of America's longest war. Some three million Americans served in that conflict and more than fifty-seven thousand lost their lives in it, whereas the Vietnamese suffered more than one million dead. Regardless of their ideology, in fighting outsiders in a civil war in their own land, the Vietnamese could not imperil American security except mainly in the eyes of hubristic presidents and cold-war zealots.

As for the peace accords, even though Kissinger received a Nobel Peace Prize for negotiating them, they did not work. When the president withdrew the American troops from Vietnam, the ground hostilities between north and south continued with North Vietnam still determined to unify the country on its terms. Nixon therefore perpetuated the American involvement by aiding Indochina's anticommunist regimes with weapons, money, and air power. Finally, Congress became bolder in challenging presidential war making. Legislators now insisted that the Vietnam experience pointed to the need for "definite, unmistakable procedures to prevent future undeclared wars."[62] That summer Congress voted to cut off funds for Nixon's air war in Cambodia. He vetoed the legislation but Congress compelled him on August 15 to end that bombing as well as other hostile actions in Indochina.

Meanwhile, the practice of Nixon and his cold-war predecessors of aiding conservative candidates for high office in foreign countries backfired, notably in Chile, a nation with a century-old tradition of democracy. This intervention had begun in 1970 when the administration siphoned millions of dollars to the two opponents of Salvador Allende Gossens, a socialist physician in his third try for president. In a secret appraisal of the operation, the CIA concluded "the United States had no vital interests within Chile," that an Allende victory would not alter "the world military balance of power," and that it would not threaten peace in the Western Hemisphere. Nevertheless, when on September 4 Allende won by a narrow plurality, "Nixon was beside himself," convinced "another Cuba had come into being," and that he must do "something, *anything*, that would reverse" the election result.[63] Kissinger summed up this paternalistic globalism. "I don't see why," he said, "we need to stand by and watch a country go Communist due to the irresponsibility of its own people."

On September 15 an angered president gave the head of the CIA, Richard M. Helms, a blank check to keep Allende out of power, telling the director, "If there is one chance in ten of getting rid of Allende we should try it." Helms recalled that Nixon "wanted something done, and he didn't much care how." Six days later the CIA chief of station in Santiago received orders "to work toward a military solution of the problem."[64]

This clandestine effort failed. On November 3 Allende took office. Nixon then ordered the CIA, without being specific as to details, to organize a military coup against him. Within the next three years, Chile's economy collapsed in part because of Allende's policies and because American agents abetted the internal opposition to him. In a coup on September 12, 1973, military leaders reputedly murdered him though they insisted he committed suicide. They then imposed a dictatorship on the country. As Nixon claimed, Allende had stumbled on his own but the American involvement in the coup contributed to his downfall.

During the course of this entanglement, a special committee in the Senate uncovered nasty details on the purpose of the Watergate burglary. When the committee appeared ready to subpoena White House documents with a demand that the president testify, Nixon informed its chairman, Sam Ervin, that he would neither testify nor permit access to his papers. The president explained his position with a number of reasons but essentially as based on his "Constitutional obligation to preserve intact the powers and prerogatives of the Presidency." Five days later, he cited foreign policy as his foremost justification, pointing out that "here in this office is where the great decisions are going to be made that are going to determine whether we have peace in this world for years to come."[65] Contending he had been elected to make those decisions, he insisted he would do so regardless of Watergate.

While the president maintained his defiance of the legislature, the Justice Department prepared to file charges of extortion and tax fraud against Vice President Spiro T. Agnew, who had taken bribes from Maryland businessmen. On October 6, as these internal crises rocked the administration and as Jews prepared to celebrate their religious holiday of Yom Kippur, Egypt and Syria attacked Israeli forces occupying the Sinai Peninsula and the Golan Heights, territory they had conquered five years earlier. The Arab troops, equipped with Soviet arms, quickly overran front-line Israeli positions, inflicted heavy casualties, and destroyed much of their equipment.

The president had known of the planned assault through intelligence sources but not when it would happen. He told the Israelis he would make good their losses but did not carry out his promise until after Agnew, on October 10, resigned. That same day the Soviets began replacing destroyed Arab armaments with an airlift and other means. On October 12 Nixon ordered an all-out airlift of arms worth more than $2 billion to Israel that beefed up its counteroffensive three days later. Because of this aid, Arab countries, through the Organization of Petroleum Export Countries (OPEC), embargoed oil exports to the United States. Prices in American gasoline stations tripled or quadrupled. Concurrently, the Soviets warned they would not tolerate another Egyptian defeat. The president countered by announcing he would resist by force any Soviet intervention. At this point, though, the extent of his direct control of policy is ambiguous.

Three weeks earlier, Kissinger had replaced William P. Rogers, an amiable attorney who lacked background in foreign affairs, as secretary of state. On October 25, acting in the distracted president's name, the new secretary placed American forces on a nuclear alert. Accounts vary as to whether Nixon or Kissinger actually instituted the alert but the order had to go out under the president's authority. Later, Kissinger alluded to this confrontation with the Soviets and his role in it in terms of a teenage macho game, commenting that "two could play chicken."[66] Contemporary analysts and historians have perceived this display of toughness, whether emanating from the president or Kissinger, as designed to demonstrate that Nixon's Watergate troubles had not weakened his command of foreign policy. Nixon and sympathetic biographers who place the president in direct command claim more, or that his decisiveness saved Israel.

This spurt of global activism proved only a temporary diversion from Nixon's troubles over his abuse of executive power. On November 7, after four decades of debate on the president's unilateral war-making capacity, Congress overrode his veto to adopt the War Powers Resolution designed to curb or place precise limits on it. Proponents wanted to ensure the participation of Congress as well as of the president in the deployment of armed forces into hostile situations and to curb the executive's secret, unauthorized military activities as in Indochina. Nixon later condemned the legislation as hamstringing the president with "Marquis of Queensberry rules in a world where good manners are potentially fatal hindrances."[67]

Regardless of its flaws, the resolution stands out as the most significant attempt to curb the excesses of presidential machismo. By permitting the executive to introduce armed forces abroad without congressional authorization, however, it contradicted the aim of assuring collective decisions in such matters. Those who desired a clear-cut restriction on the deployment of military force saw the resolution as delegating congressional authority to the president and according him a power greater than that allowed in the Constitution. It would, Senator John Culver of Iowa predicted accurately, present the president with "a blank check to wage war anywhere in the world for any reason of his choosing for a period of 60 to 90 days." Even so, according to a Gallup poll conducted shortly after the passage of the new law, 80 percent of the people approved of it.[68]

As we shall see, the resolution failed to control presidents' unilateral use of military force. Those who believed in permitting the executive considerable leeway in employing the military attacked the legislation as serving no beneficial purpose. They perceived it as amounting to little more than a license for congressional recrimination after the event, and as "the most dramatic example of a congressional attempt to weaken the presidency."[69] In keeping with this attitude, later presidents would maneuver around the resolution with armed covert operations against foreign governments or with open, short-term military strikes.

Meantime, the probing of the select Senate committee, of Washington *Post* journalists, and of John J. Sirica, a Republican federal judge in Washington, revealed that the Watergate burglars had connections with the White House and the CIA. The investigators also exposed Nixon's use of the CIA to spy on Americans opposed to the war and to block the Federal Bureau of Investigation's examination of the Watergate affair. Testimony by witnesses and information on tapes from secret recording devices in the Oval Office showed that for two years he had tried to cover up the illegalities by lying to the public, to Congress, and to others. He destroyed evidence and deceived even his own staff. In defense of this conduct, the president claimed to have acted to protect national security. Repeatedly, he linked this behavior with what he regarded as his major accomplishments in foreign policy—notably the détente with the Soviets, the rapprochement with China, and the peace in Vietnam—and cited them as reasons that he should remain in office. This record could not, however, excuse his wrongdoing.

Mounting evidence indicated what administration insiders knew. As an aide put it, "We have a cancer—within—close to the Presidency that's growing. It's growing daily. It's compounding." Nixon believed that as president he alone could determine the extent of his power as long as he acted in the name of an ill-defined national security. This conception, along with the revelations of his lying and illegalities, inspired a movement within the House of Representatives to impeach him. In recommending impeachment, its Judiciary Committee accused him of obstructing justice and abusing presidential authority. Several members wished to charge him with more, such as corrupting the process of using the military. As William Hungate, a Democrat from Missouri, put it, "It's kind of hard to live with yourself when you impeach a guy for tapping telephones and not for making war without authorization."[70]

Given the depth of such feelings, even friends urged Nixon to resign. He loved being president and gloried in it, so he resisted, saying he would have to be dragged from power. He contended repeatedly that he must "be always thinking in terms of the presidency," and that the President must not be hurt in a cover-up. Fifteen months later he cautioned, "We must not let this office be destroyed or let it fall easy prey to those who would exult in the breaking of the president."[71] When his various arguments failed to persuade even legislators of his own party, rather than face impeachment proceedings and probable loss of pensions and allowances, on August 9, 1974, he resigned, becoming the first president to do so.

Nixon left office without admitting any abuses of trust, saying simply he now lacked the political base needed to govern. This fall from the pinnacle of power came not as the result of built-up outrage over his warmongering or breach of laws but virtually by accident. If his ego had not demanded the secret taping of his conversations, he might well have gotten away with his transgressions. Despair over this blunder led him to claim that he had acted much as had other presidents. Like him, Truman, Eisenhower, Kennedy, and Johnson had overestimated the power of communism and underestimated that of nationalism, especially in Southeast Asia. All had behaved as though they possessed an ordained right to intervene in the affairs of other nations, particularly weak ones. All, on their own authority, had used armed force, openly or covertly, on a global basis without effective opposition from Congress or public sentiment. All, as the nation's power rose to immense height, had expanded executive power beyond constitutional and other limits. All thereby contributed to converting what remained of the balance between the branches of government to an imbalance. For such behavior, only Nixon suffered a mortal wound because, as his defenders claim, he was caught.

More obviously than most of his predecessors, Nixon identified self with his office and abused power more than had any of them. He inflated their precedents to make his own conception of national security cover almost any employment of force. Enamored of military power, he claimed a more sweeping authority to order troops into battle than had any of his predecessors. For a time, his application of the old theory of an inherent presidential war power seemed to fit well the militarized aspects of life in cold-war America but ultimately it did not work. It failed because he trapped himself in a commitment to continue waging an undeclared war that seemed endless and had alienated most Americans. Neither he nor his defenders saw his plight in these terms. Kissinger, for instance, who privately had denigrated him as having a "meatball mind," claimed his "decisions reflected a remarkable self-discipline and dedication." Nixon blamed Congress for his woes, never ceasing to allege he had "won the war in Vietnam" and that "congressional irresponsibility" had lost the peace.[72]

This attitude reflected Nixon's perception of himself as the virile, puissant leader—the sovereign who dominated the legislature, reigned over an executive office of five thousand people, and deserved popular support for his activism virtually as a matter of patriotism. Skeptics challenged this assumption, pointing out that "unlike a monarch, the President is not the Sovereign."[73] Finally, though, even a public accustomed to admiring strong presidents and a Congress with a record of bending to their will turned against him, for his illegalities as well as for his record in prolonging the war in Southeast Asia.

In his retirement Nixon continued to defend his extravagant conception of the strong executive—that in his use of power he was accountable mostly to himself. To justify his Watergate actions, for instance, he compared himself to Abraham Lincoln wrestling with a great national crisis. Nixon contended that at times leaders have to deceive, as with "covert activities," to get things done and "that secrecy that leads to good results is not necessarily bad."[74] This happens in wartime, he claimed, when the president has "certain extraordinary powers" that make otherwise unlawful acts lawful if taken to preserve the nation and the Constitution. He explained this hypothesis in a Senate interrogatory in 1976 and repeated it a year later in a television interview. When asked if "the President can decide that it's in the best interest of the nation . . . to do something illegal," he gave a sweeping response. "Well, when the President does it, that means it is not illegal."[75]

With such views and related behavior, more than had any other executive Nixon demonstrated that power in the hands of a paranoid, pugnacious president could endanger democratic government. His conduct also debunked several popular myths about the presidency, that Americans invariably choose the best person to lead them and that somehow the office ennobles even the meanest of its occupants. Of course, the behavior of other presidents such as Pierce, Buchanan, Harding, and Lyndon Johnson had already exposed these platitudes as meaningless, but Nixon's negative example had a deeper impact on society as a whole. Regardless of to what extent he behaved rationally or irrationally, his administration in the context of the Vietnam War marks a watershed in the history of presidential machismo. For the first time, Congress moved decisively against such conduct, disabused an executive of the notion that the war making belonged to him alone, forced him to resign in disgrace, and for a time reasserted its constitutional authority over the basic war power.

CHAPTER 8

Preeminence Regained

Every nickel-and-dime dictator the world over knows that if it [sic] *tangles with the United States of America, he will pay a price.*
Ronald Reagan, Grand Forks, North Dakota, October 17, 1986

Gerald R. Ford Jr.

WHEN Richard Nixon had to choose a candidate for vice president to replace the disgraced Spiro Agnew, he nominated Gerald R. Ford Jr., the minority leader of the House of Representatives who had served there for twenty-five years. Many in the executive entourage and in Congress regarded Ford as a decent but dumb politician loyal to his party and to the president, useful mostly in lining up Republican votes against an impeachment resolution. They assumed he lacked the qualities to make a good president. Nixon stuck by him anyway because "there was no question that he would be the easiest to get confirmed."[1]

As expected, Congress readily accepted Ford, so on Nixon's departure the Michigan congressman entered the White House without having run for statewide office or having been elected vice president. On taking the presidential oath, Ford acknowledged this gap in his experience. In keeping with pro forma rhetoric on this occasion, he pledged "an uninterrupted search for peace." He announced also that "our long national nightmare is over," that the "Constitution works," and that ours "is a government of laws and not of men."[2]

Ford took office without a popular constituency beyond his Grand Rapids Fifth Congressional District. Consequently, he had to build political support and loyalty to himself within the executive branch as best he could, primarily among those who had served Nixon. Almost all who knew Ford personally liked him, but the White House staffers and others often referred condescendingly to his alleged lack of intellect. In his public life, however, he had shown as much mental competence as had many of his predecessors when they took office. Sensitive president-watchers who were acquainted with him and his career regarded him as intelligent enough for the job and as possessing "a lot of leadership ability." They perceived him as differing from most other presidents primarily in having no pretensions of grandeur and no "fire in the belly" driving him to amass power.[3]

Ford also lacked in-depth experience in foreign affairs but so initially had other executives. Defensively, he denied paucity of knowledge in the area. He claimed to have learned much from travel to Europe and Southeast Asia while in Congress and from his duties as vice president, primarily as a member of the National Security Council. On the basis of this exposure and of crammed reading on the subject, he was confident he "knew as much about foreign policy as any member of Congress."[4] Even so, he recognized the need for help. To strengthen his hand in dealing with foreign issues and to demonstrate continuity in policy, he retained Henry Kissinger as secretary of state as well as national security adviser.

Kissinger's admirers claim he instructed the president on the intricacies of international matters and that Ford relied so heavily on him that in practice the secretary charted the course of foreign policy. Ford disputed this presumption, insisting often "that the final decisions" in matters of foreign policy "are made by me."[5] He was correct because, as with all presidents, he could reject his secretary of state's advice, accept it, or decide to make it his policy. He could not, however, evade responsibility for the foreign policy decisions of his administration regardless of their intellectual origin. The two men understood this relationship and the true source of its power. They tried, therefore, to work as a team to preserve from the wreckage they inherited as much executive authority as possible, particularly in foreign affairs. Loyalties to Nixon within the White House staff frustrated this effort.

Kissinger and most of the other holdovers from the previous administration urged Ford to protect their former boss from prosecution and possible imprisonment. For example, the American Bar Association wanted Nixon put on trial. A month later, on September 8, as though succumbing to the pressure from Nixon's friends, Ford pardoned him for all federal crimes he "committed or may have committed or taken part in" while in office. In less than a week, polls indicated public approval of Ford as president had plummeted from 71 to 50 percent, largely because of the pardon. Many Americans, in Congress and elsewhere, believed he had struck a bargain with Nixon—the presidency for the pardon. Ford angrily countered the charge. "There was no deal, period," he insisted, "under no circumstances." The skeptics, who still viewed him as a nonentity beholden to his predecessor, remained unconvinced. "We have always cherished the promise that any one of us could be president," one of them commented. "Any of us now is."[6]

The pervasiveness of the Nixon influence became evident again the day after the pardon when the Senate Foreign Relations Committee quizzed Kissinger on the CIA's efforts to destabilize Chile's Allende government. The secretary responded that Nixon had approved that strategy. On the heels of this disclosure, Seymour M. Hersh, a New York *Times* journalist, revealed Nixon had misled or lied to Congress about the Chilean operation. Ford blundered into the controversy that followed when a reporter asked him if the United States had the right to subvert the constitutionally elected government of another country. Ignoring the question of legality, Ford maintained the covert policy served the interests of the countries involved. As when Nixon and Kissinger had advanced the same notion, few could understand how the backing of violence against a legitimate executive benefited Chile. Still, Ford asserted that as long as he remained president and deemed such covert efforts in the national interest, they would continue.

Ford's position, as well as the *Times* exposé, angered many legislators. Congress as a whole, though, despite the Nixon experience, still retained much of its traditional reluctance to challenge presidential authority in foreign affairs. It refused, therefore, to ban covert operations. With the Hughes-Ryan Amendment to the Foreign Assistance Act of 1974, it did, however, vote to restrict executive discretion by changing the CIA's operating rules. That legislation permitted the president to retain control over the agency but for each covert intervention he had to certify in writing he found it "important to the national security of the United States." The bill directed him to report this judgment, called a "finding," to Congress in a "timely fashion." The president thus had "to put his name, and his reputation, on the line."[7] Ironically, this legislation also augmented the executive's propensity to make war unilaterally because, for the first time, Congress openly recognized his assumed power to engage in covert operations in the name of national security.

In the course of this legislative pondering, the public learned of more presidential abuses of power. On December 22, Hersh published another disclosure of the CIA's shady activities as authorized by Nixon to serve executive purposes. This time Hersh revealed illegal domestic spying, with break-ins, wiretaps, and mail-openings, on thousands of antiwar dissidents and other Americans. Ford then felt compelled to sign the Hughes-Ryan bill into law, which he did reluctantly eight days later. Still, popular sentiment demanded he do more to curb the abuses of the intelligence agency. In an effort to deflect a congressional inquiry, which might expose too much of the CIA's dirty linen, he responded to the pressure. On January 14, 1975, he appointed Vice President Nelson A. Rockefeller to head a special commission to investigate the charges against the agency.

Ford believed he must protect the presidency, so he limited the commission's inquiry to the CIA's activities conducted within the United States. Twelve days later, he explained this restriction to senior executives of the New York *Times*. He stated in essence that if the commission should "stray into the area of covert operations abroad" and "dug too deeply" it would stumble upon disturbing activities, including assassinations. He expressed surprise over learning "things that could blacken the name of every President after Harry Truman."[8] Nonetheless, his effort to preempt Congress failed. The Senate and House appointed committees of their own to deal with the problem of covert intervention without imposing geographical limitations on their investigations.

Ford also encountered difficulties with Congress owing to his attitude toward Southeast Asia. Out of conviction, he had always supported the Vietnam War. Accordingly, from the start of his presidency, he made Nixon's war policy his own. On the day he took office, Ford announced to the South Vietnamese leaders "the existing commitments this nation has made in the past are still valid and will be honored in my administration."[9] Thereafter, he thrust his personal support behind the regimes in South Vietnam and Cambodia that were hard put to defend themselves against heavy assault by communist forces. In the following six months, he tried time after time to persuade Congress to back his policy. It refused to approve any action that would continue the old involvement or would initiate fresh intervention in the Asian wars.

The crunch in this executive-congressional confrontation came on March 20, 1975, when Da Nang, South Vietnam's second-largest city, fell to the North Vietnamese. Thousands of anticommunist Vietnamese sought to flee. In view of what the president called a severe emergency, he announced he would employ naval and other vessels to assist in the evacuation of the refugees. A congressional critic denounced the move as violating the prohibitions against meddling in Indochinese hostilities. Others believed this intrusion fell within the authority of the commander in chief. The latter attitude prevailed.

This congressional backing permitted the president to deal directly first with the situation in Cambodia where the Khmer Rouge, a local communist faction, had conquered most of the country. When these troops attacked Phnom Penh, the capital, he authorized on April 11 the helicopter evacuation of American personnel and others from the city. Seventeen days later, as other communist forces stormed the perimeters of Saigon, he launched a similar but larger operation. Two days after that, the communists captured the city, thus ending what remained of the war in Vietnam. In using the military for these rescue operations, the president had prevailed over dissenters but failed to save the larger interventionist Southeast Asian policy he advocated. In all, though, as he told his cabinet, he felt good about coming "out of a very difficult situation better than we had any right to expect."[10]

Shortly, Ford had another opportunity to show he could hang tough. On May 12, the Khmer Rouge seized the SS *Mayaguez*, an American merchant vessel en route from Hong Kong to Sattahip, Thailand, and its crew of forty men. The Rouge regime accused the Americans of spying on their territory. Within nine hours the president denounced the capture as piracy. In the wake of a series of foreign policy mishaps, he and his advisers deemed a swift, vigorous reaction to this minor crisis necessary to demonstrate the commander in chief could still flex muscle meaningfully. Without seeking to negotiate, Ford warned the Cambodians to release the ship and crew promptly or suffer serious consequences. When this threat did not deter them, he turned to force. In disregard of the original intent of the War Powers Resolution requiring him to "consult" with Congress on his plan, he merely "informed" it. He asserted the right to employ the military on his own under his assumed power as president and commander in chief. Again, even though he had a weak claim to this authority, Congress went along, albeit with some dissent.

Through surveillance of the *Mayaguez* by American military aircraft the president knew the Khmer Rouge had moved the ship and captives to Koh Tang, a heavily fortified island thirty miles off the Cambodian mainland. This prompted Senate Minority Leader Mike Mansfield to ask, "Why are we going into the mainland of Asia again when we practically have the boat in our custody?" After more questioning Ford shot back, "I have a right to protect American citizens." Another legislator inquired why he had not consulted Senate leaders before deciding to strike. "It is my constitutional responsibility to command the forces and to protect Americans," the president responded. "It was my judgment . . . that this was the prudent course of action."[11]

Meanwhile the Cambodians broadcast they would free the ship and crew, which they did but too late. On the evening of May 14, one and a half hours after the president had made the final decision to use force, American planes struck at the mainland and marines assaulted the island in search of the crew. They met fierce resistance. The commandos who boarded the *Mayaguez* found it abandoned. After the assault team accomplished its task, the air force continued to bomb Cambodians as though to show the president's ability to turn a rescue mission into a punitive expedition. During this operation to rescue forty crew members already out of danger, eighteen marines died in combat and twenty-three air force personnel perished in a related crash in Thailand. Moreover, this unilateral resort to violence against an insignificant foe had not been necessary to rescue the released hostages.

To many Americans, the losses and sad aspect of this affair did not seem to matter much because Ford had displayed manly vigor. As Barry Goldwater put it, he had not allowed "some half-assed country" to kick him around. Other admirers of the strong presidency viewed it as Ford's finest moment in the White House. *Time* gave the escapade its ultimate accolade, saying it "had many of the gung-ho elements of a John Wayne movie." The president's popularity, as measured by letters and polls, shot upward. He perceived himself as having given the American people a significant "psychological boost."[12] Many in Congress and much of the public now regarded him as a dynamic leader who had taken quick, bold action to uphold national credibility and prestige.

Critics, though, saw this "indulgence in machismo diplomacy" as meaningless, "foolhardy and arrogant," and "another example of military overkill and trigger happiness." They called it "folly," reflecting "no general principle of law, diplomacy, or morals," and noted that other small countries, such as Ecuador, had seized American vessels and had not suffered such violence. One columnist found it "impossible to imagine the United States behaving that way toward anyone other than a weak, ruined country of little yellow people who have frustrated us."[13]

When another journalist asked Ford how he felt about the use of force, he replied, "I have always been on the side of stronger rather than weaker action, and I think my comments, for example, during the early stages of the Vietnam War reflect that."[14] He continued to defend his actions as constitutional. As usual, a federal court supported presidential machismo, holding his resort to force immune from judicial review.

As this episode and the overall military involvement in Southeast Asia ended, Ford and Kissinger turned to another foreign venture involving the president's unilateral use of force, this time by proxy. They intervened in a civil war that broke out in Angola on the eve of its freedom from Portugal. Once more, the president wanted to demonstrate toughness, anticommunism, and skill in managing a globalist foreign policy. In July and August 1975, he allotted more than $35 million to a CIA program that supported conservative factions battling Angolan communists and the Cuban troops backing them. Furthermore, as the press reported in September, when armed forces from apartheid South Africa entered the warfare against these left-wing fighters, the administration collaborated with the invaders.

This de facto but supposedly undercover American alliance with Pretoria's racist government, in what CIA officials dubbed an "economy-sized war," failed to halt the communist guerrillas. They captured Luanda, the capital, and on November 11 proclaimed Angola independent. Congress disliked the connection with South Africa but could not end it with the Hughes-Ryan law. Therefore, in January 1976, it passed legislation that flatly prohibited any kind of covert activity in Angola. Certain that Congress would override a veto, Ford, on February 9, signed the act into law and reluctantly ended the intervention in Angola. Thus, for the first time Congress intervened directly to stop a covert military operation.

In addition, the legislators moved to restrict the executive's emergency powers, as in the right to seize private property or institute martial law. Presidents had exercised this authority often in conjunction with military operations, as during the Korean and Vietnam Wars. So Congress passed the National Emergencies Act that on September 14 became law. It required the president to report any plans for meeting what he perceived as a national emergency directly to the legislature. At this point Congress could approve his declaration of such an emergency and then, every six months, could review its grant of authority. If Congress saw fit, it could at that time terminate the emergency. In theory, this law ended the series of executive proclamations that since 1933 had frequently placed the nation on a crisis footing. In practice, the legislation had slight impact on the exercise of presidential power in situations involving military force.

Meanwhile, the Select Committee to Study Government Operations with Respect to Intelligence Activities, headed by Frank Church of Idaho and known as the Church Committee, had proceeded with its investigation. In the matter of covert military operations, he noted, the "pressures on Presidents to use" such force "were immense." They engaged in these ventures because, with the CIA, they had clandestine force readily available, because they could direct it as they saw fit, and because they assumed they could "control other countries through the covert manipulation of their affairs." Church concluded this attitude "formed part of a greater illusion that entrapped and enthralled our Presidents—the illusion of American omnipotence."[15]

Even the usually modest Ford could not escape the attraction of such might. He loved being president—the pomp, the perquisites, and the power of the office. "I never enjoyed an experience more," he recorded in his memoirs. Eager to continue in office, he now focused on the 1976 presidential campaign, presenting himself as a decent man who had healed the wounds of the Vietnam era. Foreign policy, the pardon, and the Nixon legacy became prominent issues.

Ford stressed his activism in foreign affairs but the popular approval of his macho conduct did not carry over into the campaign. It did not, in part, because in discussing foreign affairs he made several gaffes, the most egregious in a nationally televised debate. "There is no Soviet domination of Eastern Europe," he stated wrongly, "and there never will be under a Ford Administration." When he tried to explain away the blunder, he made it worse. He also had difficulty in dispelling the notion that he did not himself take charge of international affairs. He was the architect of foreign policy, he insisted; Kissinger served as his messenger. "It is the President—and only the President—who can decide where to send our troops," Ford reiterated, "who can decide how many missiles and bombers and ships we need to protect our security."[16] Despite this counteroffensive, he could not overcome his handicaps. He lost by a narrow margin.

James Earl Carter Jr.

THE victor, James Earl Carter Jr., known usually and later officially as Jimmy, also had no experience in foreign affairs. While serving as governor of Georgia he had his eye on the presidency, so he tried to acquire knowledge on current foreign concerns by joining the Trilateral Commission. This private internationalist organization dominated by the Eastern establishment lobbied for maintaining close connections with industrialized Western Europe and Japan. He viewed the commission's meetings as classes in foreign policy.

In his presidential campaigning, Carter promised a foreign policy that would distinguish the United States as "a beacon light for human rights throughout the world." He attacked military adventurism, stating "never again should our country become militarily involved in the internal affairs of another country unless there is a direct and obvious threat" to American security. He also denounced the use of covert military operations to change any government. As for executive authority, he followed conventional attitudes, declaring "our country is best served by a strong, independent and aggressive president" because Congress "is inherently incapable of leadership."[17]

At his inaugural, Carter repeated his commitment to strong leadership and to the elimination of "all nuclear weapons from this Earth." In special remarks, he promised, "We will not seek to dominate nor dictate to others."[18] These objectives, as well as his intelligence, compassion, and openness struck many president-watchers as commendable. They soon noted, however, he could be mean, ruthless, "tough, cool, and determined," impulsive and opportunistic, and have difficulty controlling a penchant for exaggeration.

From the start, in keeping with his ideas on executive power, Carter indicated he would dominate the conduct of foreign affairs. "The final decisions on basic foreign policy," he told aides, will be "made by me in the Oval Office, and not in the State Department." As his national security adviser, Zbigniew Brzezinski, a political scientist from Columbia University, observed, he not only "wanted to be the decision maker" but also "to be perceived as" such. Soon, as had most presidents, from practical experience Carter realized he had "much more authority in foreign affairs" than in domestic matters.[19] For this and other reasons, he came to prefer dealing with foreign policy and even, purportedly, to disdain domestic policy matters.

During his initial year, Carter faced no major foreign-policy crisis. Nor did he exhibit macho qualities. This brief record prompted leading media commentators to suggest he had put to rest lingering concerns about a continuation of an imperial presidency, a concept popular at this time. When one of them asked, "How do you feel about this first year?" he responded, "I feel good about it. It's been an exciting and stimulating and challenging and sometimes frustrating experience for me." Notably, he spoke of his satisfaction with what he called one of his "most popular" foreign-policy endeavors—"to express to the world our own people's commitment to basic human rights."[20]

Three days later, Carter carried this message to Mohammad Reza Pahlavi, the shah of Iran whom he had entertained two months earlier. In an exchange of New Year's Eve toasts with the shah, the president praised the leadership of his royal host as providing "an island of stability in one of the more troubled areas of the world." Then Carter announced, "The cause of human rights is one that is shared deeply by our people and by the leaders of our two nations."

A week later, while flying back home, the president told reporters, "the Shah is very deeply concerned about human rights." What he did in Iran was the "equivalent to what we've done in the last 20 years."[21] This effusiveness may have been, as Carter's defenders argue, mere social talk. Nonetheless, it was foolish, wrong, and suggested naïveté in the comprehension of international affairs. Moreover, when this rhetoric reached the ears of Iranians who suffered under the shah's authoritarian rule it aroused outrage.

Carter's words contributed to the making of his first major foreign-policy confrontation. In the months following his trip to Iran, the discontent with the reign of the shah rose. The Ayatollah Ruhollah Khomeini, the spiritual head of Iran's thirty-two million Shi'ite Muslims, preaching from exile in France to the Iranians, heated the antishah sentiment to a boiling point. When the ayatollah's fundamentalist followers resorted to antigovernment violence, Carter in October reassured the shah of his friendship. Soon the violence escalated into a civil war that the shah's troops and secret police attempted to suppress with a brutality that took thousands of lives, but to no avail. On January 16, 1979, the shah fled to Egypt.

Two weeks later, Khomeini returned to Iran to assume control of the Islamic revolution he had kindled. He labeled Carter an enemy of Iran because he had supported the shah and by extension condemned the United States as the Great Satan. As though in keeping with such sentiment, on February 14 Muslim guerrillas stormed the American embassy in Teheran, killed one Iranian, and took the ambassador and one hundred others hostage. They called for the shah's return to face punishment for misdeeds, alleged and real. Several hours later, police units under the ayatollah's control persuaded the invaders to go home and this confrontation ended.

A new crisis erupted when on October 23 Carter permitted the deposed shah, now living in Mexico, to enter the United States for medical treatment. Khomeini militants regarded the president's act as an affront to their cause. In retaliation, on November 4, a student-led mob invaded the embassy in Teheran, took a hundred hostages, and again demanded deportation of the shah, with his wealth, to Iran. Khomeini backed this violence. Reacting in anger at "those bastards holding our people," the president refused the demand. His ratings in the polls, which had been declining, sprang upward. "At any time," observers believed, "Carter could have found massive domestic support for bombing Iran" or for other military action.[22] He calmed down, though; resorted to an array of economic and other pressures on Iran, such as sending naval units to the Arabian Sea; and strove to resolve the crisis through diplomacy. Despite this effort, the holding of the hostages stretched over months. All the while America's sense of outrage mounted.

As for Carter, as he looked forward to reelection, what to do about the hostages, as aides put it, "got to be a real trap." Advisers such as Secretary of State Cyrus Vance urged continued patience, warning against doing anything rash such as resorting to force. Others, such as Hal Saunders, assistant secretary of state, thought differently. "If we don't get those people out quickly and safely," he warned, "I don't see how he can be reelected." The president despaired. "Nothing we have tried diplomatically has worked," he told a close political confidant. "The UN can't do anything, our allies have tried and struck out, everything imaginable has been attempted. We've got to take some risks."[23]

As the hostage crisis deepened, the president became embroiled also in a civil war in Nicaragua between the guerrillas of the *Frente Sandinista de Liberación Nacional* (FSLN), a coalition of Marxist groups, and the troops of the right-wing dictatorship of Anastasio Somoza. The rebels, who had long been battling Somoza, took their name and part of their political philosophy from Augusto César Sandino, the revolutionary who had fought American marines in the twenties and early thirties. On June 17, 1979, the Sandinistas forced Somoza to resign. They then formed a Marxist government headed by Daniel Ortega Saavedra. These revolutionaries spewed anti-Americanism, expressed friendliness to the Soviets, formed close ties to Fidel Castro's Cuba, and in 1980 supplied military aid to left-wing guerrillas in El Salvador. All this alarmed Carter. While deeply concerned for human rights and theoretically opposed to the clandestine use of force, he worried more about communism and how to combat its expansion than he did about the tactics he employed. With this consideration foremost, he terminated economic aid to Nicaragua and expended nearly one million dollars in covert assistance through the CIA to forces there battling the Sandinista regime.

Tumult in Afghanistan also persuaded Carter to shift his position on dealing with aggressive communists. In April 1978, Marxist army officers had overthrown an anti-Russian regime, proclaimed the Democratic Republic of Afghanistan, and brought the country within the Soviet orbit. Thousands of Soviet military advisers moved into the country to aid the new government. Even so, in the following year, rival communist politicians and a fundamentalist Islamic insurgency undermined the regime. At the invitation of the communist prime minister, in the last week of December 1979 some eighty-five thousand Soviet troops poured into Afghanistan. They came to help fight the insurgents in the bitter civil war and to bolster the government. They thus internationalized the conflict.

Immediately Carter denounced this Soviet resort to massive force as scandalous, as a grab for 90 percent of the world's exportable oil, and as aggression against a freedom-loving people. Putatively, this fresh crisis steeled, toughened, and made him more forceful. On January 4, 1980, he imposed economic sanctions, the most effective being an embargo on exports of grain to the Soviet Union. Soon, the embargo proved sticky because it also harmed the American economy.

Meanwhile, four days after the sanctions, the president exaggerated the total effect of the crisis on the United States. He told congressmen that in his opinion as well as that of many "of the world's leaders . . . the Soviet invasion of Afghanistan is the greatest threat to peace since the Second World War" and that it "directly threatened" the nation's security. He even considered military action to drive the Soviets out of Afghanistan.[24] Quickly, though, he abandoned that idea as inappropriate.

Within five days, with equal implausibility, Leonid I. Brezhnev, Russia's premier, announced publicly he had intervened in Afghanistan because he could not watch passively the rise on the southern border "of serious danger to the security of the Soviet state."[25] As had American presidents, he bent the concept of national security to conform to his immediate purpose. Like them also, he explained his military intervention in a weak state with platitudes. Regardless of the danger that their inflated rhetoric and warrior posturing could provoke conflict, the two leaders continued this behavior.

On January 23 Carter declared the "Soviet Union is now attempting to consolidate a strategic position . . . that poses a grave threat to the free movement of Middle East oil." Then he enunciated what journalists dubbed the Carter doctrine. "Let our position be absolutely clear," he warned. "An attempt by any outside force to gain control of the Persian Gulf region will be regarded as an assault on the vital interests of the United States of America, and such an assault will be repelled by any means necessary, including military force."[26] He also asked Congress to restore compulsory draft registration for youths, a requirement Nixon had ended. Congress complied.

The president thus abandoned what remained of a détente with the Soviet Union and reverted to the conventional cold-war strategy of trying to contain communism on a global scale. Advisers such as Brzezinski, who reminded him "that the Soviets have only contempt for weakness," urged him to hang tough. Vance and the European allies on whom the president had counted for support disagreed with his visceral bellicosity and "sense of urgency in responding to the Afghan invasion." Carter then reevaluated his rash courting of war with the Soviets to embark on a program of covert assistance to Afghans designed to aid while punishing the Russians "for their unwarranted aggression."[27] Analysts viewed this switch to a muscular foreign policy as a response to perceived shifts in public sentiment which, in the main, favored belligerent leadership. In a broader sense, it indicated also that even a mild-mannered executive could not in specific instances resist the pressure for macho behavior.

Concurrently, Carter felt a similar if not greater urgency to do something decisive about the hostages languishing in Iran. Their fate had become increasingly important politically and the gaining of their freedom had become intensely personal or, as he admitted later, "had almost become an obsession with me." These pressures caused him to magnify what had started as a minor confrontation into a major crisis. On April 10, 1980, he noted in his diary that "*the Iranian terrorists are making all kinds of crazy threats to kill the American hostages if they are invaded by Iraq—whom they identify as an American puppet.*" He exaggerated the peril to the captives. Nonetheless, to meet the demands of domestic politics as well as to retain his claim to strong leadership, he decided to act. The following day he moved ahead with plans for a military rescue mission. Among his advisers only Vance opposed it, maintaining "that the decision was wrong and that it carried great risks for the hostages and our national interests."[28] Carter decided to proceed anyway, on his own authority.

On the president's orders, on the night of April 24, a commando force ferried into Iran by helicopters attempted to rescue the Americans held prisoners in Teheran. A series of mishaps, including the crash of a helicopter with a refueling aircraft that killed eight crew members and wounded five, bedeviled the mission. It failed within a few hours. As with the Bay of Pigs and *Mayaguez* operations, many Americans viewed the rescue attempt as a fiasco. Being a long shot, it might have misfired under any circumstance but hard-line activists blamed Carter for its failure, alleging he had delayed a military response too long. Four days later Vance, who earlier had tendered his resignation but held off acting on his discontent with the president's policy during the operation, resigned.

As had his predecessors in unilateral military ventures, Carter had acted in his capacity as commander in chief. He had, however, violated the War Powers Resolution by not consulting Congress beforehand. Despite his previous criticism of covert operations, he defended the secrecy that enveloped this rescue mission with the argument that leaks about it could have harmed national security. As had Truman and other presidents involved in questionable military strikes, he also claimed an unsubstantiated "inherent constitutional right" to act unilaterally. Through a legal adviser, he rebutted congressional attacks on this theory, reiterating he possessed the "constitutional power to use armed forces to rescue Americans illegally detained abroad." He contended also that the War Powers law did not apply "under the precise circumstances of this case."[29]

To his credit, Carter refused to cover up his failure with massive unilateral military action or call for a crusade that would bring on another deadly war. For a while, though, he listened skeptically to Brzezinski, who believed "We must go back in" and approved planning a second armed rescue. When, however, available data indicated chances for success were extremely dim, that scheme died. Khomeini's regime exulted over the American defeat but it did continue to negotiate with the Carter administration over the hostages.

As had other presidents, Carter showed less reluctance in the use of force on a global scale in what he perceived as low-risk interventions. He engaged in "a wide variety of covert operations" in Africa as well as Central America, Afghanistan, and Iran. The public did not know about this undercover activism but what it did know, such as his pugnacious rhetoric toward the Iranians and the Soviets, failed to satisfy admirers of the tough executive. They labeled him a "wimp" who had been "weak, indecisive, and ineffective as a guardian of American national security."[30] The characterization stuck, contributing to the crushing electoral defeat in his bid for reelection. He remained convinced, as he asserted fifteen years later, that if he had used massive force and other macho tactics, such as incinerating Teheran to gain release of the hostages, he would have been reelected.

Skeptics disagree while scholarly revisionists praise Carter for holding back. They contend that unrestrained violence "was too morally repugnant" for him even to consider it. His comments as a lame duck contradict this estimate. He confided in his diary that if the negotiations for release of the hostages collapsed, he would "declare a state of belligerency or ask Congress to declare war against Iran." Finally, on his last day in office, in exchange for nine billion dollars of Iranian assets frozen in American banks and their overseas branches, Khomeini freed the hostages unharmed.[31]

Even this, Carter's peaceful conclusion of the major crisis of his administration, could not dispel his image as an ineffective president with a naïve understanding of power politics. A public accustomed to admiring the virile executive continued to perceive him as irresolute, a leader who allowed the Soviets to push him around and Iranian fanatics to thumb their noses at the most powerful nation in the world. One later critic even denounced him for having a "true feminine spirit," arguing that "in a sense, we've already had a 'woman' president: Jimmy Carter. And his feminine style of leadership nearly drove us crazy."[32] Despite such acerbic attacks and his macho moments, Carter could boast as his partisans have that during his term no Americans perished in direct combat and no foreign peoples died in open battle with American military forces. Among his recent predecessors, only Hoover and Eisenhower could claim a similar record.

Ronald Wilson Reagan

AS had Carter, Ronald Reagan came to big-time politics late in life. He achieved considerable success as a film actor but never rose to star status. During his Hollywood years, as a New Deal Democrat and an anticommunist, he involved himself in advocacy politics. When his film career lagged, he hosted a national prime-time television show sponsored by the General Electric Company. He became increasingly conservative, politically ambitious, and switched to the Republican Party. Capitalizing on his celebrity status, he won two terms as governor of California. Influential friends promoted him for the presidency. In 1976, he came close to capturing the Republican nomination and in 1980 did so.

In his campaign, Reagan criticized Carter for bungling the Iranian hostage crisis, described the Vietnam War as a noble cause, promised to deal harshly with terrorists, and announced he would regenerate American pride. In a counterattack in September, Carter dubbed him a hawk because he repeatedly called "for the use of military force." He would, Carter stressed, set off a "massive nuclear arms race" that could trigger war with the Soviets. "I think it is inconceivable," Reagan rejoined, "that anyone, and particularly a President of the United States, would imply . . . that anyone, any person, in this country would want war. And that's what he has been charging and I think it is unforgivable." After that, as his foremost biographer points out, "Reagan mentioned 'peace' so often it sounded like he had invented the word." In a televised debate on October 28, he announced "that I believe with all my heart that our first priority must be world peace, and that the use of force is always and only a last resort when everything else has failed."[33]

Reagan's ability to convey such sentiment with a persuasive sincerity, polished oratory, and masculine charm made him a formidable candidate. To pundits, however, his views on international affairs, economics, and social issues came across as banal. That mattered little to the public. He won with more than 90 percent of the electoral vote.

As with Ford, consequently, when Reagan entered the White House, president-watchers dismissed him as a simplistic thinker, "a retired film actor and professional after-dinner speaker" who had difficulty conceptualizing. They underestimated him. He was smart in a practical way, a quick study who could transmit ideas simply and convincingly. He did so in his inaugural address, which dealt mostly with the economy but also touched on the old exceptionalist theme of "what makes us special among the nations of the Earth." As usual on these occasions, he paid homage to peace, saying "we will negotiate for it, sacrifice for it," but promised also "when action is required to preserve our national security, we will act."[34]

As indicated by the anecdotes in the address, Reagan liked to tell stories. Critics dismissed this penchant as a ploy to build support for his policies while avoiding hard analysis. In addition, as observers noted, he pursued pet policies, especially in foreign affairs, out of "nonrational impulses."[35] He could do so without significant political harm to himself or to his party because of his upbeat personality, his self-effacing demeanor, and his warmth—comparable to that of Eisenhower—which at times disarmed even staunch opponents.

Reagan was also a fierce ideologue, a tough-minded cold warrior who still thought in terms of wrestling with a monolithic communist enemy he pictured as "the focus of evil in the modern world" or as "an evil empire." He often spoke with conviction about matters that had no factual basis, or as one adviser put it, "He could rearrange facts to make a good story better." He "made so many errors, misstatements, gaffes, and blunders, 'bonehead' remarks, and blatant lies" that some observers characterized his administration as the "reign of error." Various biographers and former executive staffers characterize him as a passive president, "an enigmatic monarch who reigned rather than ruled," the great delegator who "suffered from the delusion he was a 'hands-on president.'" He admitted delegating authority and not interfering with subordinates "as long as the overall policy . . . is being carried out." He insisted, though as virtually all presidents have, that ultimately "I make the decision" or that "the decisions about policy are mine, and I make them." He claimed to "set broad policy and general ground rules" and to bear responsibility for the results of his policies.[36]

At times, as we shall see, Reagan tried to avoid such responsibility, markedly in the minefield of foreign policy. Even formerly close advisers point out he "really didn't know much about foreign affairs or national security policy" and needed help in making informed decisions. Of course, other incoming presidents had not comprehended much more. Others who knew him maintain he lacked interest in international problems, distanced himself from them, disdained details, and usually accepted whatever his staff advised. However, he did not remain aloof in foreign-policy matters that interested him either for personal or ideological reasons.

In these instances, regardless of the depth of his knowledge or lack thereof, Reagan was hands-on, "an activist President," the final decision-maker, the individual who "himself made the big decisions." For example, he rid himself of Alexander Haig as secretary of state because "he didn't want to carry out the president's foreign policy; he wanted to formulate it and carry it out himself."[37] Regardless of who or what pushed Reagan, or whether he decided foreign policy-matters actively or passively, those decisions came out as his.

In addition, even though the president portrayed himself as an apostle of peace, in each of his terms he resorted to covert military force more often and with greater persistence than had Carter. Reagan began this course of action quickly by easing restraints on the CIA. He allowed it to engage in domestic spying, clandestine foreign operations, and surveillance of Americans abroad, especially when they were administration opponents. Indeed, he seemed to regard the CIA as his own secret army.

Within three years Reagan launched more than fifty covert operations, more than half of them in Central and South America. Foreign-policy pundits frequently referred to this clandestine use of force and to more open violence against radical regimes in small countries as the Reagan doctrine. Academics described the unilateral armed intervention in third-world countries to overthrow Marxist-Leninist regimes as ideologically focused. Supposedly these ventures involved little risk for involvement in a major war, as in Vietnam. The president first articulated what became this malleable doctrine in May 1985, as a form of militarist globalism or support for "people fighting for their freedom against Communism wherever they were."[38] Most international jurists regard it as "untenable in law."[39]

From the beginning, Reagan and his advisers applied the concept to Cuba, a country they perceived as bent on targeting "all of Central America for a Communist takeover." Hotheads among them urged strong-arm tactics to resolve the problem. Reputedly, Secretary Haig told the president, "Give me the word and I'll make that island a fucking parking lot."[40] Reagan backed away from such open violence but as others who shared Haig's outlook urged, he drew the line against communist expansionism in Latin America. He intervened in small countries in Central America such as El Salvador, where he beefed up the number of United States military advisers sent there to aid the government combat a leftist insurgency. In that region, though, he focused primarily on Nicaragua because he saw the warfare there as connected directly to the larger cold-war struggle with the Soviet Union.

The president started the Nicaragua program promptly merely by continuing Carter's secret use of force. On March 9, 1981, Reagan strengthened it by ordering "the CIA to undertake covert actions in Central America to interdict arms trafficking to Marxist guerrillas." With a "finding" in December, he expanded the intervention by authorizing the agency to "support and conduct paramilitary operations" in Nicaragua.[41] The CIA then created an army in Honduras composed of Somoza loyalists, military adventurers, and anti-Sandinistas—known as Contras from the abbreviation in Spanish for counterrevolutionaries—to harass and destroy the Ortega government. In this surrogate war the president set the policy and the CIA, as his private strike force, executed it. William J. Casey, the agency's director who had been Reagan's campaign manager, had the role of commanding general.

In March 1982 the Washington *Post*, the New York *Times*, and the *Nation* ripped the veil of secrecy from this unilateral exercise of military force. Dismayed by the disclosure, a number of congressmen charged the president in court with violating the War Powers law. At this time they got nowhere. Since no effective legal restraint stood in its way, in the following month the administration stepped up its campaign of holding the Sandinistas' feet to the fire.

The extent of this intervention aggravated the discontent of legislators who disliked the president's policy. In an effort to prevent it from escalating into another open presidential war, Congress passed what came to be known as the first Boland Amendment. This legislation, named after Edward P. Boland, the Democrat who chaired the House Intelligence Committee, and signed into law on December 21, blocked funding for agencies involved in financing the Contras.

The statute had no immediate effect on the CIA's guerrilla strike team in Nicaragua, which grew twentyfold into a major military force. Reagan announced nevertheless, "We are complying with the law, the Boland amendment, which is the law." When pressed, he added, "We are not doing anything to try to overthrow the Nicaraguan Government."[42] Two weeks later, to preclude loss of funding for the Contras and to mobilize support for aid to El Salvador's conservative government, he went public with his no-longer-secret and controversial military program.

In an address to a joint session of Congress the president declared "the Government of Nicaragua has treated us as an enemy." He exaggerated the significance of the confrontation. Without factual basis, he claimed, "The national security of all the Americas is at stake in Central America." In July, with the CIA in charge, he ordered "a program of expanded U.S. military activities" in the area. This expanded warfare led Boland in August to characterize the agency as "a rogue elephant, doing what it wanted to."[43] So in December a second Boland Amendment placed a financial cap on military aid to the Contras.

While pushing ahead with this tough policy in Central America, the president employed force more openly in North Africa against Libya's Muammar al-Qaddafi. As had others, Reagan portrayed him as a madman, the Satan behind international terrorism. This attitude and Qaddafi's claim to sovereignty over the Gulf of Sidra, regarded usually as an international waterway, paved the way to a violent confrontation. In June 1981 Reagan decided to test what the Libyan dictator designated the line of death in the gulf by authorizing naval maneuvers there. On August 20, after ships of the Sixth Fleet crossed the line, two Libyan warplanes attacked fighter planes from a carrier. The Americans promptly shot them down. Without doubt, Reagan demonstrated toughness and initiative in dealing with notably obnoxious, weak foreigners. In his words, he had sent a message to the world "that the United States wasn't going to hesitate any longer to act when its legitimate interests were at stake."[44]

A year later, in his capacity as commander in chief, Reagan again employed force, this time in the Middle East. He agreed to help Lebanon's government, then embroiled in internecine warfare, with American troops to evacuate troublesome Palestinian forces from Beirut. He got around the War Powers law and congressional concerns over the proposed intervention by promising to station the troops in the war zone for a very short period. Essentially, though, as had predecessors, he took the questionable position that Congress had no constitutional basis for establishing precise periods for the presidential deployment of the military. In any case, on August 24, 1982, he ordered eight hundred marines to Beirut to join French and Italian troops in a multinational force. The marines carried out the mission and on September 10 departed.

When assassination, mass murder, and other turmoil followed, the Lebanese government requested the return of the multinational force. Assuming the legislative approval of the first intervention still stood, the president agreed. He did so on his own without consulting Congress and ignoring the War Powers Resolution. On September 20 he deployed twelve hundred troops, stressing as before that they would stay in Beirut for a limited period of time to keep the peace and to protect American and other lives. The marines took up positions near the international airport, and in June 1983 Congress approved the venture.

In the months that followed, the civil war intensified. Muslim Arabs battling the government came to view the American troops as combatants hostile to their side rather than neutral peacekeepers and hence as legitimate targets. In August these rebels attacked the Americans with rocket and artillery fire, killing several marines. In retaliation, American warships shelled the Arabs on the ridge of the Chouf Mountains above Beirut. This violence climaxed on October 23 when a large truck bulging with explosives and driven by a suicide bomber crashed through the perimeter of the American compound. It plunged into the barracks and exploded, slaughtering 241 sleeping marines and injuring more than a hundred others.

"This is an obvious attempt to run us out of Lebanon," the president told advisers. "The first thing I want to do is to find out who did it and go after them with everything we've got." On the following day, he acknowledged that "many Americans are wondering why we must keep our forces in Lebanon." Shifting from an earlier explanation, he stated, "Well, the reason they must stay there until the situation is under control is quite clear: we have vital interests in Lebanon" and our actions there "are in the cause of world peace." Few Americans could understand what those interests were or how they affected the country's welfare. Robert C. McFarlane, recently the president's personal representative in the Middle East and now the national security adviser, noted, "If Lebanon disappeared, it wouldn't affect the United States' security interests very much." Furthermore, the president did not carry out planned retaliatory air strikes because his intelligence experts "were not absolutely sure" who the culprits were.[45]

In December, Reagan received another chance for he-man retaliation. Syrian troops in Beirut fired a missile at an American reconnaissance plane. Immediately, disregarding opposition from the secretary of defense and the Joint Chiefs of Staff, he ordered air strikes against Syrian antiaircraft sites. Despite this pummeling, the Syrians fired at another American plane. This time the president struck at them with a bombardment from the sixteen-inch guns of the battleship *New Jersey*, which was stationed off the coast. Even so, Syrian defiance continued.

Reagan's advisers feared that this Lebanon affray, with the continuing casualties among the marines there, would become a damaging issue in the forthcoming presidential election. They persuaded him to back off. Reluctantly, on February 7, 1984, he removed the troops from the city to offshore vessels and sent them home. The withdrawal defused a minor quarrel that had the potential of escalating into protracted violence and into an embarrassing campaign problem.

Earlier, during the height of the Beirut confrontation, the president manufactured another crisis out of events on the small Caribbean island of Grenada, part of the British Commonwealth of Nations. On October 13, 1983, a far-left military council had toppled the island's left-wing regime. In the view of Reagan's staff, the coup endangered the lives of one thousand Americans there, most of them medical students. Immediately the president wanted to invade. "He was very unequivocal," his national security adviser noted. "He couldn't wait." Tip O'Neill, the leader of the Democratic majority in the House, tried to stop the president by warning, "You're going to take a lot of heat over this. Americans don't want their kids put at risk for something that's none of our business."[46] Reagan ignored the advice.

Some forty-eight hours after the Beirut slaughter, the president ordered nineteen hundred troops, joined by three hundred others from nearby islands, to invade Grenada because, he explained, "American lives are at stake." The forces involved in this "operation urgent fury" encountered tougher resistance than expected. Nineteen died and 115 suffered wounds.

Notwithstanding the casualties, he said later that "I probably never felt better during my presidency than" on the day of the ousting of the unpopular radical regime. He had achieved that satisfying emotion by circumventing the War Powers Resolution. When confronted with this transgression, he once more defended his unilateral violence as within his power as commander in chief. Later, he admitted acting in total secrecy to prevent leaks from Congress. "We didn't ask anybody," he explained, "we just did it."[47]

With similar bravado, Reagan justified his use of force with a variety of arguments beyond his original explanation, such as to protect the students from being seized as hostages. Critics belittled this contention as the first known preemptive rescue, that is to save hostages before they were taken. At other times he explained the assault as necessary to "defend freedom and democracy," to forestall "further chaos," to assist in restoring law and order, and to safeguard United States credibility in the Americas and the world. He also characterized the intervention as a response to an appeal from neighboring states to disarm a communist regime backed by at least eleven hundred Cuban mercenaries impersonating construction workers. He described Grenada as "a Soviet-Cuban colony, being readied as a major military bastion to export terror and undermine democracy." Later the Pentagon conceded that there were about a hundred combatants. In all, the president claimed, he "had no choice but to act strongly and decisively."[48]

None of Reagan's reasons could stand logical scrutiny. Noting this, the New York *Times* saw no reason for the occupation. It commented that "people around the world who do not automatically assume American virtue are left to conclude that the United States is either a bully or a paranoid—quick to attack where it can do so safely or when it feels compelled to demonstrate muscle." Reagan's special friend, British prime minister Margaret Thatcher, stated publicly that Western democracies do not use force against small countries. In a similar vein, others criticized him for bashing a straw enemy to divert attention "from the failure of Beirut" with "the victory of Grenada." He denied this charge but nonetheless linked the two interventions. "The events in Lebanon and Grenada, though oceans apart," he told the nation, "are closely related." He claimed "Moscow assisted and encouraged the violence in both countries . . . through a network of surrogates and terrorists."[49]

Regardless of the muddled reasoning behind the Grenada affair, the skirting of "international legal norms," and the trampling of the War Powers Resolution, the president's macho conduct gave him another victory with the American people. By a margin of 90 percent polls indicated they approved of his quick success against an insignificant foe. Members of Congress read the polls, too. Democratic critics demanded enforcement of the War Powers law, condemned the invasion as gunboat diplomacy, and seven members asked the House of Representatives to impeach Reagan. Congress as a whole, though, termed the use of force justified and dropped proposed inquiries into his conduct. As in past episodes, he emerged unscathed, free to use unilateral force for his own purposes, as in his continuing quarrel with Qaddafi.

In December 1985, when terrorists set off bombs at the Rome and Vienna airports that massacred nineteen people, including five Americans, Reagan officials held Qaddafi responsible. No violent countermeasures followed but in March 1986 the Sixth Fleet again menacingly held maneuvers in the Gulf of Sidra with orders to strike back if attacked. When Libyan forces fired missiles at carrier-based planes and missed, the Americans retaliated by sinking three Libyan patrol boats and destroying a radar installation. Still the clashes continued.

On April 4 radicals bombed a West Berlin disco frequented by American servicemen, killing one of them and injuring about 230 people. The president claimed Libya had sponsored the outrage and that "our evidence is direct; it is precise; it is irrefutable." So, ten days later he launched air attacks on Benghazi and on Qaddafi's headquarters near Tripoli, killing scores of civilians but not the dictator. In addition, Reagan pledged, "When our citizens are abused or attacked anywhere in the world on the direct orders of a hostile regime, we will respond so long as I'm in the Oval Office. Self-defense is not only our right, it is our duty."[50]

Those knowledgeable in international law maintained the bombings "constituted a unilateral act of war" that "violated all international conventions, the War Powers Act, and both the Ford and Reagan orders on assassination plots."[51] Most intelligence officials in Western Europe refuted Reagan's alleged evidence. Many denounced the bombings and critics lampooned him as a trigger-happy cowboy. Regardless, he felt satisfaction in having demonstrated he would not take flack from a third-rate dictator. As a result of his bold actions, he boasted, America once more was standing tall. Congress remained quiet but the public and most of the media again applauded his machismo, sending his approval ratings in the polls to their highest levels.

All the while, the president had pushed ahead with his proxy warfare in Nicaragua. In addition to carrying out the military operations and sabotage he had previously approved, beginning in January 1984 the CIA attempted to destroy that nation's seaborne commerce by laying magnetic mines in three of its harbors. In April the *Wall Street Journal* and others exposed this secret warfare to the public, surprising Congress and even high-ranking members of the administration's foreign-policy team. All disapproved.

Secretary of State George P. Shultz called the escapade, which damaged a number of ships belonging to foreign nations, outrageous. Barry Goldwater, now chairman of the Senate Intelligence Committee, complained, "The President has asked us to back his foreign policy" but how can we "when we don't know what the hell he is doing? This is an act violating international law. It is an act of war."[52] On a bipartisan basis both the House and Senate passed resolutions condemning the operation.

This furor raised the question of the CIA's authority to engage in hostilities. Since it could act only at the direction of the president, again Reagan had defied the War Powers Resolution. Furthermore, Ortega's government challenged the mining on a broader scale. It brought suit in the International Court of Justice at The Hague against the United States, charging illegal violence. In November the court accepted the case.

This setback did not diminish Reagan's obsession with Nicaragua. He persisted in trying to persuade Congress to approve $21 million in additional aid to the Contras. Several months later, he tried to build public support for the funding and for his interventionism by depicting Sandinista rule as "a Communist reign of terror." He argued that "Communist subversion is not an irreversible tide. We've seen it rolled back in Venezuela and, most recently, in Grenada . . . All it takes is the will and resources to get the job done."[53] He persuaded neither the public nor Congress.

Noting the legislative and other opposition to this bellicose program, Shultz obtained Reagan's left-handed approval to open talks with the Sandinistas for a possible peaceful solution of their differences. For more than two hours on June 1, he met with Ortega at the Managua airport. They agreed to continue the negotiations but White House aides, particularly those in the National Security Council, dismissed this effort as a publicity stunt. As one of them, Jeanne Kirkpatrick, put it, "It's vital for the administration to stand tough." Since this sentiment appealed to the president more than did quiet diplomacy, the negotiations and the secretary's overture collapsed.[54]

Shortly after, Reagan's campaign for more direct aid to the Contras also crumpled. On October 10 Congress terminated that assistance with a third Boland Amendment. It prohibited the use of funds, "directly or indirectly," for any kind of military or paramilitary operations in Nicaragua "by any nation, group, organization, movement or individual."[55] The president circumvented this law by secretly shifting control of the Contra operation to the staff of the National Security Council. He also put aside lobbying for what he called his freedom fighters to concentrate his energy mostly on his campaign for reelection.

Walter Mondale, the Democratic candidate, argued that four more years of Reagan would mire the nation in an enlarged war in Central America. Even though critics belittled the president as "Ronnie Rambo," he countered by posing as the peace candidate while still posturing as the no-nonsense strong leader. Among other factors, this strategy worked. Since few voters appeared to comprehend the illegal aspects of the entanglement in Nicaragua, it had little impact on the election. Reagan won hands down.

Promptly, with renewed confidence and patched relations with Congress, Reagan resumed active involvement in the back-door Nicaragua war. He proceeded on the assumption that when the president knew all the facts about a situation "he should be permitted to lead the nation and make decisions based on what he knows and the trust placed in him by the voters." In addition, he refused to acknowledge the world court's jurisdiction in the harbor-mining case. Well into his second term he was devoting more time and giving "more speeches on Nicaragua than on any other single issue."[56] He behaved as though this personal, minor vendetta had become the nation's foremost foreign-policy concern.

The president called the Contras "lovers of freedom and democracy" and insisted he would support them until the Sandinistas would "say: Uncle." With inept analogies from the past, he also described the Contras as "the moral equal of our Founding Fathers and the brave men and women of the French resistance." He praised them as patriots struggling to bring "democracy to Nicaragua in the same way that the freedom fighters who led the American Revolution brought democracy to our people." Again turning reality upside down, on April 1, 1985, he told the nation, "U.S. support for the freedom fighters is morally right and intimately linked to our own security."[57]

On May 1 the president declared a national emergency that enabled him to impose a trade embargo against Nicaragua. Without any substantive basis, he insisted on characterizing its government as an "urgent threat . . . to the security and foreign policy of the United States." In the following month Congress responded by voting $27 million for humanitarian aid to the Contras. Ten months later, Reagan pressed for more assistance, declaring "you can't fight attack helicopters piloted by Cubans with Band-Aids and mosquito nets."[58]

On March 8, 1986, as Congress prepared to vote on more aid to the Contras, the president described the Sandinistas as a "cruel clique of deeply committed Communists at war with God and man from their very first days." A week later in a major television address he continued the demonization of Nicaragua as "a Soviet ally on the American mainland" and as "a privileged sanctuary" for communist use against the United States.[59] He referred to a map of Latin America that turned red as he detailed the alleged spread of communism out of Managua. In February Congress approved an additional $70 million in military assistance. He immediately accelerated the surrogate war, spreading more death and destruction over Nicaragua.

Then on June 27 the Hague court found the United States guilty of "an unlawful use of force," of breaching treaties, and of violating international law in its intervention in Nicaragua. It dismissed the American claim to a right of "collective defence" in this case as unjustified.[60] The ruling had no impact on Reagan. He refused to accept it, continuing his Contra policy and defying federal and international law to advance it.

The administration's most egregious illegalities began after Congress had prohibited funding of the Contras. The CIA ceased supporting them outright but continued intelligence gathering in Nicaragua, which remained legal. Officials in the National Security Council who reported directly to the president, however, went beyond the collecting of data. They raised money from private right-wing individuals and groups within the country, from foreign governments, and from the sale of arms to Iranians through Israeli intermediaries. With these funds the president's operatives expanded the military operation.

Because the government had categorized Iran officially as a source of terrorism and had embargoed the export of weapons to her, these sales were illegal. On January 17, 1986, the president signed a "finding" that authorized the sale of "arms, equipment and related materiel" to Iran. He did this despite the law, the vigorous opposition from the secretaries of state and defense George Shultz and Caspar Weinberger, and his own well-publicized words that "America will never make concessions to terrorists."[61]

This activity remained secret until October 5 when Sandinistas shot down an American cargo plane delivering arms to the Contras. The captured survivor admitted he worked for United States officials. The administration then closed its no longer clandestine program and denied involvement in the sale of arms, claiming that private initiative supplied the money for the Contras. Rumors circulated indicating that from the start the government had also used some of the money as ransom to obtain release of hostages held by Hezbollah, or Party of God, an organization of pro-Iranian militants in Lebanon.

After the press substantiated the rumors, the president on November 13 admitted secret negotiations with allegedly moderate Iranians to help end the Iran-Iraq War, then in its seventh year. While conceding he had authorized "the transfer of small amounts of defensive weapons" to Iran, he claimed ample precedent for such diplomacy, emphasizing he had proceeded according to federal law. "We did not—repeat—did not," he insisted, "trade weapons or anything else for hostages, nor will we."[62] In reality, he had violated his own embargo against what he had labeled a terrorist nation at war with Iraq, the adversary he had covertly aided.

Within two weeks, details of the administration's confusing policy of trying to skirt federal law in this case, which became known as the Iran-Contra affair, became public. The disclosures revealed that National Security Advisers McFarlane and John M. Poindexter, and a member of their staff, Oliver L. North, a retired marine lieutenant colonel, had solicited millions of dollars for supplying the Contras with arms and other equipment while the Boland law still forbade such aid. This news caused the president's approval rating in the public opinion polls to plummet 16 to 20 percent. When he denied knowledge of the operation, few believed him. In Congress and out, many even talked of impeachment.

Reagan defended himself on national television, announcing that the decision on the arms operation "is mine and mine alone" and that he believed deeply in the endeavor's correctness. There would be, he added, "no further sales of arms of any kind . . . to Iran." Six days later he asserted, "I was not fully informed on the nature of one of the initiatives." His credibility plunged deeper when in response to a query of why oligarchs in Saudi Arabia, Brunei, and Taiwan contributed to the Contra fund, he responded, because they "share our feeling about democracy." Furthermore, after dismissing North under investigation as a suspected lawbreaker, the president praised him as a "national hero."[63]

Shultz, who did not "want Ronald Reagan to be yet another American president destroyed in office," advised him, "You must not continue to say we made no deals for hostages." Unwilling to accept fact, the president ignored him. Later, the testimony of his subordinates indicated he personally signaled "go ahead" with the Iran operation, saying he would take "all the heat for that." McFarlane, for instance, told Reagan that one "would have to be a fool not to see that, whatever our intentions were, the reality apparently was arms for hostages."[64] While still insisting the shady activities were undertaken without his knowledge, Reagan finally admitted that "what began as a strategic opening to Iran deteriorated, in its implementation, into trading arms for hostages."[65]

Despite this acknowledgment and the depth of the scandal, and regardless of how aid to the Contras was funded, polls indicated public opinion ran two to one against arms to them. Nonetheless, the president continued to back them and on his own decided the extent of the assistance. When others in the administration faltered or opposed his policy, he kept the initiative going. Even though Congress sharply curtailed the military activity, he persisted in it well after his Iran-Contra policy had been discredited or until he left office.

As for the scandal itself, one commission, two committees, and an independent counsel investigated it. The President's Commission, which Reagan appointed and was known usually as the Tower Commission, exonerated him on the theory that his appointees, as rogues, had acted "on their own initiative" without his knowledge. The Senate and House committees held the president responsible for both the "policies and lawlessness within his administration." They concluded that "It was the President's policy—not an isolated decision by North or Poindexter—to sell arms secretly to Iran and to maintain the Contras 'body and soul.'" Still, Reagan refused to accept accountability for the illicit activities, and neither Congress nor the courts held him accountable. The courts convicted several executive officials for illegal activities but later higher tribunals overturned the verdicts. Other executive officers who were involved later received a presidential pardon. Lawrence E. Walsh, the independent counsel investigating the scandal, denounced this act as undermining "the principle that no man is above the law."[66]

While the affair was still capturing headlines, Reagan again tangled with Iran. The confrontation grew out of the seemingly endless Iran-Iraq War. In January 1987 as part of a major offensive against Iraq, Iran mined the Persian Gulf, threatening, as the administration claimed, to throttle the commerce of the states of the Arabian peninsula. Kuwait then asked the president to allow the reregistering of a number of its oil tankers under the American flag, thereby entitling them to United States naval protection. In March on his own authority Reagan agreed, primarily on the premise that Iran could not close down an international waterway and block the flow of oil through it. Critics dismissed this justification as bogus because Iraq launched most of the attacks on the shipping, as in a clash on May 17 that took the lives of thirty-seven American servicemen.[67] Then on July 21 a reflagged Kuwaiti tanker escorted by American naval vessels struck a floating mine, suffering heavy damage.

Reagan beefed up the American presence in the Persian Gulf with forty ships, supplemented by allied seacraft and planes under orders to block with force Iranian efforts to control Persian waters. In this tense situation on July 30 gunners on the cruiser *Vincennes* accidentally shot down an Iranian passenger plane, killing 290 people. Other clashes with Iranian forces followed until October 8, when American helicopters sank three of their gunboats. Eight days later, an Iranian missile struck an American-flagged tanker while anchored at Kuwait. On October 19 American naval guns destroyed an Iranian oil rig used as a gunboat base and the president banned all imports from Iran.

Once more Reagan had used force as a global policeman in a distant land that posed no tangible threat to United States security, not even with an amorphous connection to international communism. Despite the widespread criticism, he and his advisers viewed the intervention differently. They saw it as an expression of tough, proper executive resolve in leading a multinational effort to protect transit rights and petroleum sources in an international waterway.[68]

Similar resolve laced with anticommunist zeal had contributed to Reagan's decision at the start of his presidency to continue Carter's supposedly secret, but generally known, intervention in the war in Afghanistan. Reagan increased the flow of arms and other aid to the *mujaheddin*, the guerrillas who battled the communist regime as well as the Soviet invaders. Publicly, with considerable emotion, he denounced the brutalities of the Soviet occupiers. This attitude, along with his backing of the guerrillas, raised no significant problems politically because both the American people and Congress approved of his limited assistance program. They presumed correctly that with it the Afghans could do well enough without direct American military participation, an involvement with the potential for triggering a major war.

Ultimately, in this surrogate confrontation with the Soviets, notwithstanding years of anticommunist rhetoric, Reagan revealed he could moderate his bellicosity to achieve a practical goal. His change in behavior, but not in bombast, began in September 1986, when Mikhail Gorbachev, the pragmatic Soviet leader, indicated he wanted to end the bloodshed in

Afghanistan. Reagan responded graciously. "If you really want to withdraw from Afghanistan," he told the Russian, "you'll have my cooperation in every reasonable way. We've no desire to exploit a Soviet military withdrawal from Afghanistan to the detriment of Soviet interests."[69] As Gorbachev had promised, in May 1988 he began pulling out combat forces, completing the task the following February.

The president and his aides touted this withdrawal as a triumph for the Reagan doctrine and his ability to project an image of decisive leadership. When coupled with his tremendous popularity, the perception helped the presidency regain much of the preeminence it had presumably lost with the Watergate scandal. Close and even friendly president-watchers noted, though, that "too often, Reagan was a performer and presidential leadership an empty shell."[70] Harsher critics never ceased depicting him as an amiable dunce. On the other hand, after eight years, quite a few of the earlier skeptics raised their estimates of his intelligence or found him no worse in brain power than a number of his predecessors. Most important, the larger public perceived him as competent.

That public ignored or forgave Reagan's lawless and unaccountable behavior. It appeared mesmerized by his ability to manipulate the media and to dodge responsibility for wrongheaded policies. For example, scholars who appraised his conduct of foreign policy condemned his bombing of Libya "as both unlawful *and* contrary to the nation's best interests." They viewed his invasion of Grenada as even more detrimental. This criticism made no difference in Reagan's popularity. Astonishing both friends and foes with his ability to shed responsibility for his actions, people spoke of him as the "Teflon president," the leader on whom blame could not stick. Other observers who noted his "affection for men of action" on and off the screen and his ready resort to force against weak foes characterized him also as "the quintessential macho president"[71]

As did a number of his predecessors, Reagan did not speak of the presidency as a killing job and his power as a burden too heavy for mere mortals to bear. He demonstrated that a person of ordinary intelligence could handle it. Like Ford, he "enjoyed being president very much," even liked its "ceremonial aspects," and often considered it "fun."[72] Even though he had been driven by ambition and had misused power, he conveyed the impression of being a patriot-warrior with whom millions of Americans could identify. Thus, despite his blunders, and especially the Iran-Contra scandal, he remained popular to the day he left the White House. For him, machismo paid off handsomely.

CHAPTER 9

Machismo Still Rewarded

As President I wasn't reckless in the use of force. But I was not afraid to commit people to battle, and that is the toughest decision a President makes.

George Bush, December 1, 1996

George Herbert Walker Bush

UNLIKE Ronald Reagan, George Bush belonged to Washington's governing elite. He served two terms in the House of Representatives, held diplomatic posts in the United Nations and China, chaired the Republican National Committee, and headed the Central Intelligence Agency. In 1980, he made a failed run for president but gained the vice presidency where he remained for eight years, becoming friendly with many of the world's top political leaders. Initially, Reagan had "doubted his toughness," a quality he considered essential for a president. Later, though, Reagan backed him for the office, pointing out that "no vice-president had been more involved at the highest level in our policy-making than George."[1]

In 1988, after winning the Republican presidential nomination, Bush conducted a nasty but effective campaign revolving around domestic issues such as no new taxes and no mercy for criminals. Despite his macho rhetoric at this time, he failed to overcome the popular perception of him as not "strong enough or tough enough for the challenges of the Oval Office" or that he was a wimp.[2] This image stuck to him in part because, in contrast to Reagan's he-man posturing, he seemed bland. Even so, Bush won the election with 53.4 percent of the popular vote, but Democrats retained control of Congress.

Bush assumed office with a fascination for the scope and details of foreign policy. Immediately, he made it his major concern even, as critics charged, to the neglect of important domestic issues. In his inaugural, though, he barely alluded to foreign relations, promising vaguely "we will stay strong to protect the peace." He offered pragmatic leadership, as he said, with no "high drama" or "the sound of trumpets calling."[3] These words appeared to fit his temperament as an anticommunist who had avoided being pegged also as a cold-war ideologue. His intimacy with the executive branch contributed to set attitudes toward the presidency and what he believed should be his place in it. He viewed its powers as expansive, his role as activist, and his foreign policy as globalist. He also approached the office with possessiveness, especially toward its real or imagined prerogatives.

These perspectives, along with a determination to show backbone and a penchant for impulsive action, came into play in Bush's clash with Manuel Antonio Noriega, Panama's de facto ruler and head of its armed forces. For several decades, Noriega had been on the payrolls of Washington's intelligence agencies. He lost this support when American officials concluded he participated in criminal dealings. In February 1988, an American court indicted him on drug trafficking charges. The next month, in an effort to eject the wheeling-and-dealing general from power, the Reagan administration imposed economic sanctions against Panama.

Bush continued the sanctions, stepped up covert operations in Panama, which Congress readily funded, and made Noriega's removal a priority item in his foreign-policy agenda. Still, the *caudillo* clung to power. Indeed, he used fraud to annul elections held on May 7, 1989, that went against his own candidate for president. Announcing "we will not be intimidated by the bullying tactics . . . of the dictator Noriega," an angry Bush began augmenting the American troops in the canal zone. "I have a profound obligation as Commander in Chief of the Armed Forces and as President," he explained, "and that is to protect American life. And I'm going to do what is prudent and necessary to do this." Two days later, he added, "the problem is Noriega." Bush said he would love to see the Panamanian people "get him out," indicating he would back an uprising for this purpose. On October 3, a few Panamanians, aided by American troops, did attempt a coup but it fizzled. The president felt chagrined because, as a supporter pointed out, "we look indecisive, vacillating, and weak."[4]

To White House insiders, the quarrel between the president and the dictator appeared motivated by personal animus. Bush belittled Noriega as "an indicted drug trafficker" and a "thug." Since the American public also perceived the Panamanian as a demon, the president assumed he could use force against him as he deemed necessary. When questioned on this point, Bush responded, "Well, I want as broad a power as possible, and I think under the Constitution the President has it." The executive "has broad powers, broader than some in the Senate or the House might think." In the weeks that followed, Bush relied heavily on the covert operations to "topple Noriega," to "snatch" him, and to "return him to the United States for trial." These efforts failed. The president then proceeded with operation Blue Spoon, an invasion plan for eliminating the entire Panama defense force as well as for removing Noriega.[5]

Beginning on December 15, when Noriega took more direct power as chief of government with the title of "maximum leader," Bush's assumed need for open military intervention took on a sense of urgency. On the next night, Panamanian soldiers shot and killed an American marine lieutenant who had attempted to run a roadblock. They also beat up a naval officer and threatened his wife with sexual abuse. In the recent past Panamanian military police frequently had harassed and mistreated Americans without triggering a confrontation with the president. Bush, however, refused to tolerate this abuse of American rights.

Holding Noriega himself responsible for this outrage, the president now decided to use the roadblock incident to justify placing in motion his plan for military force. On December 17 when his advisers concurred, Bush told them, "Let's do it."[6] The following day on his own authority as commander in chief he ordered the invasion of Panama. On the night of December 20 while Congress stood adjourned, eleven thousand fresh troops joined the thirteen thousand already in the canal zone to launch the president's operation now given the name Just Cause. The following day, he informed congressional leaders of his action, designating it "an exercise of the right of self-defense recognized in . . . the United Nations Charter."

Seeing no peril to national security or to the canal in Panama, political commentators, many ordinary Americans, and others asked, Why this resort to massive force? The president contended he had to act to defend the United States against possible attack by Panama, "to protect American lives in imminent danger and to fulfill our responsibilities under the Panama Canal Treaties." He spoke also of defending democracy in Panama and of apprehending Noriega to bring him to trial on the drug-related charges filed two years earlier. Analysts dismissed both the self-defense and protection arguments as flimsy because "Americans are harassed and/or killed in different parts of the world every day."[7] To safeguard them everywhere with force or to uphold, no matter how feeble, nascent democracy abroad with bayonets would involve virtually constant hostilities.

Critics called the drug charge equally ludicrous. If the United States were to police foreign traffickers as a matter of policy, they pointed out, "it would have a right to intervene militarily in South America, Mexico, Turkey, the Golden Triangle, and other regions in the world." The dissenters accused Bush of wanting to invade "because he and his advisers concluded Panama was too weak and isolated to resist American force," that a show of might would help "to dispel the 'wimp factor,'" and would, as well, "augment his image as a strong president."[8]

In crushing a despised but virtually defenseless foe, the president sacrificed twenty-three American and five hundred Panamanian lives and destroyed the homes of eighteen thousand Panamanians at a cost of more than a billion dollars. On January 29, 1990, Noriega surrendered. Federal authorities shipped him to Florida where ultimately an American court tried him on criminal charges, convicted him, and jailed him.

At home, meanwhile, the quick, successful strike brought Bush applause throughout the media. In the polls, his popularity skyrocketed with four out of five people approving his no-nonsense virility. A senior Pentagon officer called the invasion "a test of manhood" while the president's political strategist characterized it as a domestic "jackpot."[9] Faced with this ground swell of acclaim for the president's machismo, few in Congress dared challenge his defiance of the War Powers Resolution or his failure to obtain legislative approval of the invasion beforehand as constitutionally mandated. Indeed, on February 7, the House of Representatives passed a resolution praising him for his decisive action.

Although only a few Americans protested, those who did were vocal. Some dissenters viewed the assault on "an independent and sovereign nation" as irresponsible. Foreigners shrugged it off disapprovingly as more North American imperialist arrogance. The Organization of American States condemned the intervention by a vote of twenty to one, the first time it formally criticized the United States in this manner. An American, British, and French veto blocked a move for censure in the United Nations Security Council. By a vote of seventy-two to twenty, however, the general assembly condemned the invasion as a "flagrant violation" of international law. Attorneys who worked in the executive branch defended Bush against these charges. Independent jurists who were troubled by the president's actions could find no "legal justification for the use of force" against Panama. In a formal report, they agreed with their foreign colleagues, denouncing the invasion as illegal "under existing standards of international law."[10]

While the criticisms seemed to have little effect on the administration, the approbation had an intoxicating influence that carried over into Bush's next resort to military force, this time in the Middle East. Initially in that region, he had continued Reagan's policy of supporting Iraq's president, Saddam Hussein, as a counterforce to Iran. Soon, Hussein's expansionist posturing alarmed the president. On July 20, 1990, American intelligence agents reported that thousands of Iraqi trucks filled with troops were rolling toward the Kuwaiti border. The president then placed an aircraft carrier, the *Independence*, in the Arabian Sea to deter a possible assault.

This show of force did not work. On August 2, some eighty thousand Iraqis slammed into Kuwait, quickly overrunning the country. The United States had no treaty or other commitment to defend Kuwait. Nevertheless, the president wanted to reverse that invasion. He promptly obtained passage of a resolution in the U.N. Security Council condemning Iraq and calling for its withdrawal from Kuwait. Departing from Washington for a meeting in Aspen, Colorado, he denounced the assault as "naked aggression" but also said "We're not discussing intervention. . . . I'm not contemplating such action."[11] The next day, however, he declared a national emergency and imposed sanctions against Iraq.

At Aspen, Bush spoke to Britain's prime minister, Margaret Thatcher, a hawk who agreed they should not tolerate this aggression. She did not, as rumor maintained, have to perform a "backbone transplant" on Bush to make him hang tough. On that same day he ordered covert operations against Iraq, announcing, "I view very seriously our determination to reverse this awful aggression. . . . This will not stand, this aggression against Kuwait."[12]

Believing in the efficacy of force, the president now took upon himself the role of avenger-savior in the tradition of predecessors who had perceived themselves as international policemen. Stressing the need to protect neighboring Saudi Arabia against possible but uncertain aggression from Hussein, he persuaded the reluctant Saudi king to accept American troops. So on August 6, on his own authority, Bush ordered their deployment. At the same time, he persuaded the U.N. Security Council, which shared his concerns over Kuwait, to call for economic sanctions against Iraq. He proceeded also with organizing an international coalition for possible war. Two days later he informed the nation, via television, of his planned second venture to cage a foreign monster. Although Bush intended to intervene to evict Hussein from Kuwait, he called the operation Desert Shield to convey the impression of defensive action. Essentially, though, he sought to safeguard an autocratic monarch from the menace of another autocrat.

On August 11, as though again personalizing an international confrontation, the president denounced Hussein as evil itself. Eleven days later, a journalist asked Bush, "Are you preparing Americans for the possibility of war and American deaths?" Evasively and without regard for his own previous disdain for international legalities, he replied, "anytime you move American forces and are up against . . . an outrageous violator of international law . . . the best thing is to be prepared."[13] Subsequently, he talked also about the need to stand by friends, to combat appeasement, and to draw a line in the sand against aggression. Polls indicated strong support throughout the country for this policy, including the deployment of one hundred thousand troops. On August 15, he received further backing from another United Nations resolution, this time for the use of military force.

Heartened by such approval for his now well publicized hard-line position and by a conversation with Mrs. Thatcher, who at this point told him "this was no time to go wobbly," Bush shortly indicated the United States and Iraq were on the brink of war. He then authorized the CIA to get rid of Hussein. "No one—not the American people, not this President—wants war," he announced shortly. "But there are times when a country, when all countries who value the principles of sovereignty and independence—must stand against aggression."[14]

Some legislators, and military leaders such as Colin L. Powell, chairman of the Joint Chiefs of Staff, and privately even other advisers, counseled patience. In late September Powell suggested allowing more time for the sanctions to take effect. Bush responded, "I really don't think we have time for sanctions to work."[15]

The president then shifted from his alleged defensive posture to one of preparing for an offensive war but cautioned his subordinates to keep this strategy secret until after the upcoming congressional elections. Nonetheless, state and defense secretaries James A. Baker III and Richard B. Cheney, in appearances before Congress, echoed his claim that the executive did not need congressional approval before taking military action. On constitutional grounds, both Republican and Democratic legislators challenged this assertion. On November 3, Baker embarked on a three-week trip abroad to lobby a coalition of nations to support a United Nations resolution in favor of force. On November 8, two days after the midterm balloting, Bush announced an increase in personnel and arms in the gulf—actually a doubling to four hundred thousand troops—along with his changed objective of ensuring "an adequate offensive military option."[16]

Legislators, journalists, and many of those in the segment of the concerned public who had been reluctant to buck a well-liked president pursuing a popular course now began asking, Why this one-man rush to war? "It's as if that great armed force which was created to fight the Cold War," Senator Daniel P. Moynihan of New York pointed out, "is at the president's own disposal for any diversion he may wish, no matter what it costs." Another legislator professed the president "must come to Congress and ask for a declaration. If he does not get it, then there is no legal authority for the United States to go to war."[17]

Bush blunted some of this criticism by promising to consult congressional leaders before acting. He insisted, though, "I have the right, as commander in chief, to fulfill my responsibilities, and I'm going to safeguard those executive powers" and "to see that this aggression is not rewarded."[18] On November 18, he left for a weeklong trip to Europe to rally members of his coalition behind the planned hostilities.

Two days later, forty-five Democratic members of Congress, joined ultimately by eight others and a senator, filed suit in a federal court for an injunction prohibiting the president from employing force against Hussein without legislative authorization. The initiator of the suit, Congressman Ronald V. Dellums, contended, "War is a very solemn act, and the decision to go to war should not be granted to one person."[19]

Within less than two weeks, the judge, Harold H. Green, ruled the suit premature because Congress as a whole had not come to grips with the issue. In marked contrast to the string of judicial decisions upholding the executive war power as interpreted by presidents, however, he rejected the administration's contention that the president could go to war on his own authority, needing only to consult with Congress. The judge stood by the constitutional "clause granting to Congress, and to it alone, the authority 'to declare war.'" Shortly before, Bush had tried to counter the charges in the suit by presenting his case directly to the public. In a brief magazine essay spiced with emotional appeal, he asked, "Can the world afford to allow Saddam Hussein a stranglehold around the world's economic lifeline?"[20] The president pointedly failed to mention Congress.

By this time Bush had succeeded in his diplomacy of forging a coalition for offensive war. With assurances of some allied support now in hand, he turned to the United Nations. On November 29 the U.N. Security Council agreed to his desire by authorizing, but not directing, member nations "to use all necessary means" to eject the Iraqis from Kuwait if by January 15, 1991, they did not withdraw. The following day he announced, "We're in the Gulf because the world must not and cannot reward aggression. And we're there because our vital interests are at stake. And we're in the Gulf because of the brutality of Saddam Hussein."[21] As his invective indicated, he perceived Hussein as a Hitler who had to go. Bush boasted that the Iraqi was going to get his ass kicked.

As in the Panama affair, this swagger played well at home. Public opinion polls indicated Bush had retained his considerable popular support for determined action. So, on January 2 he announced he would himself decide for or against war no matter what Congress or the people had to say. He claimed that with United Nations backing and with his power as commander in chief he could commence hostilities "without a formal declaration of war by Congress."[22] He also did everything in his power to solidify the public sentiment for war and to stifle opposition. Virtually all of the media sided with him.

Even so, some legislative as well as public protest arose. One congressman even urged Bush's impeachment for initiating belligerent acts. Critics charged him with orchestrating a war to counter his lingering reputation as a wimp and to demonstrate his masculinity. Furthermore, as in the Panama venture, they noted his stated reasons for charging ahead with military force readily shifted. He had defined the intervention variously as defending human rights, as keeping "the world's great oil resources" out of Hussein's hands, as protecting Saudi Arabia, as returning 'legitimate' rulers to Kuwait, and as ousting Hussein.[23] Each rationale had difficulty standing on its own.

At times, when reminded of the inconsistencies in his belligerence, Bush would attempt to explain it in terms of a global mission. "The U.S. has a disproportionate responsibility when it comes to helping secure the world," he contended. "I would not call it the world's policeman because there are certain areas where we wouldn't be in a position to act or want to act." Nevertheless, he added, we have responsibility for the "security of various countries" as in the case of those in the Persian Gulf. When asked publicly, "Don't you need an authorization from Congress, in effect, for war?" he cited flawed precedents, much as had his Vietnam and other predecessors. "We have used military force 200 times in history," he responded. "I think there have been five declarations of war."[24] His defenders argued along similar lines, echoing his view that in this instance war was appropriate.

Bush believed also that his desire to crush Hussein, a goal he equated with the national interest, outweighed constitutional niceties. "For me it boils down to a very moral case of good versus evil, black versus white," he asserted. "If I have to go, it's not going to matter to me if there isn't one congressman who supports this, or what happens to public opinion. If it's right, it's gotta be done."[25]

The president perceived himself as obligated to overcome legal obstacles in order to do right. On this basis, much as had macho predecessors, he resorted to the old "inherent power" theory to justify acting on his own regardless of legislative opposition. Worried over the possibility he might trigger a divisive quarrel over the war power, advisers stepped in, urging him, "as a practical political matter," not to defy Congress but to persuade it to fall in line with him. Giving in to this pressure, on January 8 he requested a resolution approving the use of force but did not ask for a declaration of war. He also directed the staff of the National Security Council to prepare a "historic document" detailing constitutional authorization for what he contended "permitted the president to use military force against Iraq without a declaration of war from Congress."[26]

Against this backdrop, two days later Congress took up the war resolution question. It immediately became a partisan issue with the argumentation carried live on television. Most Democrats opposed the request but virtually all of the Republicans, along with crucial Democratic defectors, favored it. The final version of the measure passed in the House by a vote of 250 to 183 and in the Senate 52 to 47. Dated January 14, the joint resolution authorized the president to initiate military action on the condition he would inform legislative leaders he had "used all appropriate diplomatic and other peaceful means to obtain compliance by Iraq with the United Nations Security Council resolutions."[27] The Iraqis refused to comply.

Technically, Congress sanctioned a presidential war. Substantively, it accepted a fait accompli. The president alone had made the decisions that set the country on the course to war. He had sent more than five hundred thousand troops to Saudi Arabia, had shaped a United Nations coalition, and had in effect set the deadline for the hostilities to start. His behavior fitted well within the conception "of the President as a king-general who exercises prerogative or discretionary power to make foreign policy, initiate war, and conclude peace treaties."[28] Few could fault the ideal of penalizing aggression but the United States had never followed that standard consistently. It had not, for instance, gone to war to punish Soviet violence against Hungary or Afghanistan, the Chinese conquest of Tibet, or Iraq's assault on Iran. Bush claimed that in assuming the role of gendarme against a weak power, he had followed precedent. True enough, but that precedent rested essentially on the dubious ideological reasoning of cold-war presidents.

The day following passage of the resolution, the president declared, "As a democracy we've debated this issue openly and in good faith. And as President I have had extensive consultation with the Congress." He also reiterated that Congress could not impinge on "the President's constitutional authority to use the Armed Forces to defend vital U.S. interests."[29] On January 16, just hours after Iraq had allowed the deadline set by the United Nations ultimatum to pass unheeded, he led the nation into war. In an operation dubbed Desert Storm, mostly American forces struck at Iraq. Two days later, the president informed Congress of his action, in a manner, he asserted, "consistent with the War Powers Resolution."

Bush benefited immediately from his bravado. As usual in past conflicts, at the start of hostilities the president's popularity zoomed. In the polls, his "approval rating jumped to 82 percent, an increase of 24 percent from the beginning of the month." For a while, it soared even higher. "The polls, by which we live and die, are up in astronomical heights," Bush told his diary, "and the country is together."[30] His assessment appeared correct. Public sentiment virtually muzzled Americans who dared oppose the war. If they spoke up, superpatriots denounced them as traitors.

As for the war itself, even though Hussein fielded about one million troops, immediately it became a turkey shoot. America's military machine blasted Iraq by air for forty-three days while engaging in ground combat—with little effective resistance—for only one hundred hours. On February 27 Bush announced, "Kuwait is liberated. Iraq's army is defeated. Our military objectives are met."[31]

In all, 137 Americans died, nearly one in four from friendly fire. Administration spokespeople maintained that the air force, using "smart" bombs with alleged pinpoint accuracy, blasted only military targets and hence avoided killing civilians. In reality, the military relied heavily on traditional ordnance that often missed its targets, inflicting injury mainly on noncombatants. The Iraqis absorbed the most lopsided defeat of any people in modern times. They suffered more than five hundred thousand military personnel and civilians killed or wounded as well as massive destruction of property. Bush bathed in the glory of a Caesar. Immediately after the victory, his approval rating with fellow Americans rose again, now to 89 percent of those queried—"the highest figure ever in the history of the Gallup poll."[32]

Some outsiders, such as the Russians and the Japanese, who in the past had been themselves quick to resort to the sword, perceived the conflict differently. At the start of the ground war, a Soviet official expressed official regret that the "instinct for a military solution had prevailed" and that a "real chance to solve the conflict peacefully has been missed." In their media, the Japanese depicted the United States as "war-loving" and "extremist." They read booklets titled "Why Does America Like War?" and "Scary America." Moreover, even in terms of Bush's varied objectives, such as ensuring "the security and stability of the Persian Gulf," the hostilities accomplished little. One incensed academician described it as a "nothing war" that "resolved nothing and settled nothing."[33]

Bush, however, believed the war did a great deal for him personally as well as for his conception of the presidency. In the course of the Iraq confrontation, he explained, "I felt after studying the [war] question that I had the inherent power to commit our forces to battle after the U. N. resolution." He reminded his audience that the president "is responsible for guiding and directing the nation's foreign policy," so he should be permitted to perform "this duty with 'secrecy and dispatch' when necessary." In other words, he desired no truly effective legislative oversight of his deployment of military forces. He viewed himself and his office as locked in battle with a Congress that "has taken aggressive action against specific Presidential powers" and "sometimes tries to manage the executive branch—micromanage the executive branch." When that happens, he added, "the President has a constitutional obligation to protect the Office."[34]

Regardless of the questionable quality of Bush's constitutional perspective, in making war on the basis of an indefinable inherent power, he went beyond safeguarding presidential authority as he perceived it. As usual with macho leaders, he had acted instead in a manner that aggrandized the president's already inflated power.

Bush did not, however, further exploit his power by occupying Iraq and destroying Hussein. The United Nations sanctions against Iraq remained in force but turmoil in the Persian Gulf area continued and the dictator remained in power. The United States stood as the primary guarantor of the Gulf sheikdoms, which had appeared threatened by Iraq. The United States also continued deploying some thousands of troops in the region at huge cost to the taxpayer. It still had a few friends in the Middle East but most Iraqis and various Arab sympathizers hated it.

From a skeptical outlook, an outstanding characteristic of Bush's war, aside from its selective punishment of aggression, is that it satisfied one man's self-esteem. He won endorsement from a public that admired martial virility, especially when it brought a quick victory and involved no tangible menace to the nation's security. For example, a *Time/CNN* poll in March 1991 showed that 58 percent of the respondents believed the United States should "use military force to protect its interests around the world." As for Bush, in later years he would bristle at criticism of his Iraq escapade, giving still another disputable reason for it. "We did it right," he insisted, "and we restored the honor and credibility of the United States."[35] No tangible evidence from the period indicates that such honor had been at stake.

During the course of Bush's martial ventures, the Soviet Union broke up, the cold war ended, and ethnic strife tore apart Yugoslavia. The fiercest Balkan fighting broke out in March 1992 when Bosnia-Herzegovina declared independence and the Bosnian Serbs who desired union with Serbia, still called Yugoslavia, rebelled against the new regime. The United Nations applied an arms embargo against all sides but the Bosnian Serbs received weapons from the Yugoslav army while the Bosnian Muslims obtained arms from Iran. Bush supported United Nations efforts to pressure the warring Serbs, Croats, and Muslims into a cease-fire. He even threatened to intervene with military force against the Bosnian Serbs besieging the city of Sarajevo. He did not do so because, as his secretary of state reported, "our vital national interests were not at stake."[36] As Bush sought reelection, the ethnic fighting continued unabated.

The president campaigned as a successful war leader, as the man at the helm when the United States "won the Cold War," and as the master of an activist, no-nonsense foreign policy. His rhetoric saddened former Soviet leader Mikhail Gorbachev. "The end of the Cold War is our common victory," he contended. "We should give credit to all politicians who participated in that victory." This admonition had no discernible effect on Bush. In turn, his exaggerated claims meant little to the electorate because the rally-around-the-flag effect, which usually benefits incumbents engaged in hostilities, had worn off. Economic issues dominated the campaign. With the cold war ended, only 6 percent of the voters "included foreign policy among the issues that mattered most."[37] In this ambiance, Bush lost the election but still clung to his conception of the president as a savior sovereign.

Therefore, even as a lame duck Bush decided to take on another foreign entanglement, this time in Somalia. For years that African state's feuding clans had spilled blood, produced a famine that took several hundred thousand lives, and virtually destroyed the country. As he prepared to leave office, Somalia's misery became worse. The embattled warlords blocked humanitarian agencies from breaking the famine with cargoes of food and other supplies.

Commendably, Bush had backed these relief efforts while realizing they alone could not bring stability to Somalia. Nonetheless, for one more time he seemed unable to resist the compulsion to use his vast power as commander in chief. Now, though, he chose to act unilaterally in an obviously humanitarian cause he called—in the redeemer tradition—"God's work." In December he ordered an armed intervention named operation Restore Hope of more than thirty thousand American troops. They were to feed the starving and pave the way for a United Nations effort that would keep the peace in devastated Somalia.

The president also gave the troops "the authority to take whatever military action is necessary" to accomplish their mission. To the American people he announced, "This operation is not open-ended. We will not stay one day longer than is absolutely necessary." He promised not to become involved in hostilities or "to dictate political outcomes." Even though few legislators dared fault his intervention, which had wide popular support, several commentators saw this humanitarianism as "an exercise in rescue of a damaged image."[38]

Two days before leaving office, Bush also launched two air strikes and missile attacks on southern Iraq and Baghdad to punish the Iraqis for violating terms of the Gulf War armistice. Joined by British and French planes, the attackers killed twenty-one people and injured more than fifteen. The president called these assaults "the right thing" but others, even in allied countries, differed. Tony Benn, of Britain's opposition Labor Party, summed up the view of such dissenters. "President Bush," he stated, "is not licensed to kill nor to speak on behalf of the international community."[39] So Bush left the presidency he relished as he began, with a "sense of wonder and majesty" it allegedly instilled and as a macho activist given to globalism.[40]

In all, Bush's eagerness to use military force against small powers stands out as a characteristic of his presidency. He took pride in this record. Retrospectively, he commented, "As President I wasn't reckless in the use of force. But I was not afraid to commit people to battle, and that is the toughest decision a President makes." As others noted, he had "pushed to the very outer limits, and beyond, the case for presidential primacy in war-making." Since he had at his disposal the overwhelming might of the world's only superpower, he employed force because it could bring quicker results and initially more political rewards personally than could patient diplomatic negotiations. Skeptics pointed out that the benefits to the nation of this behavior were questionable. Some of them viewed the Grenada, Panama, and Iraq wars as "unnecessary" and as having been "fought essentially to prop the egos of Presidents Reagan and Bush."[41]

William Jefferson Clinton

IN contrast to Bush, Bill Clinton had no family tradition of public service but possessed an intense ambition that early in life he focused on politics. He began seeking public office at age twenty-eight, lost, tried again, and in 1976 won the post of attorney general of Arkansas. Two years later he moved up, becoming the youngest governor in the nation. When he lost his bid for reelection, a constituent asked, Given the uncertainties of a life in politics, why have you chosen this livelihood and why have you stuck with it? Clinton replied, "It's the only track I ever wanted to run on."[42] Within two years he regained the governor's office and held it for four more terms. In 1992, after a grueling campaign, he emerged as the Democratic presidential candidate.

Clinton campaigned on a domestic program calling for improved social welfare and for a drastic reduction of the military budget while promising also to preserve "a strong America." He pledged "to focus like a laser beam" on the economy. When he referred to foreign policy he tried to outflank Bush's machismo by also talking tough. For instance, Clinton urged forceful intervention in the Bosnian civil war to punish Serb aggressors against hard-pressed Muslims. With these tactics he won the presidency with only 43 percent of the popular vote.

As during the campaign, in his inaugural Clinton concentrated on the domestic economy but did speak with the usual generalities of the occasion about war and peace. "There is no longer," he announced as many knew, "a clear division between what is foreign and what is domestic." He maintained "America must continue to lead the world" but warned that when "our vital interests are challenged . . . we will act, with peaceful diplomacy whenever possible, with force when necessary."[43] In all, he indicated a determination to become a hands-on president, even in foreign affairs where he had little experience and supposedly a limited desire for deep involvement.

This approach to the office fitted Clinton's temperament, which he characterized as "almost compulsively overactive." Immediately he immersed himself in detail, much of which, owing to his eagerness to produce results, he mastered. Even so, he quickly became bogged down in minutiae. Early in his administration, therefore, Treasury Secretary Lloyd Bentsen spoke up. "Mr. President," he said, "you want to make every decision. You can't. You've got to delegate more."[44] Clinton agreed but a seemingly boundless confidence in his own ability, in his charm, and in the magic of executive power led him to think he knew more about complex issues than he did.

As experience would show, this inflated self-confidence could and did produce an arrogance, frequently evident in presidents, that magnified Clinton's own importance and that of his decisions. He also acquired a reputation for being "indecisive by nature" but it did not impede his continued personal involvement even in minor matters. In all, as close observers noted, "Bill Clinton loved the Presidency . . . the trappings and the unmatchable opportunity to put his ideas into national policy."[45] It permitted him to do what he liked best—to call the shots, and on a grand scale.

Initially this style of governing applied primarily to domestic policy. As Clinton explained in retrospect, "I came here as a Governor. . . . My exposure to foreign policy, as an adult at least, was largely through international economic measures." He concentrated on the economic program, he added, "because I was afraid that unless we reversed our economic course, nothing I did in foreign policy would permit the U.S. to really succeed."[46] Despite this inward focus, he did not remain aloof from decisions involving the use of force abroad. Owing to his temperament, his responsibility for guiding policy, and the inherited Somalia peacekeeping venture, which Bush had not terminated as he had promised, Clinton had to grapple with foreign problems.

At first Clinton expected no difficulties with the peacekeeping because he planned to withdraw the troops from Somalia gradually and hand the operation to the United Nations. That goal changed when on June 5, 1993, warriors of clan leader Mohammed Farah Aidid in Mogadishu killed twenty-three Pakistani peacekeepers and injured three Americans. Immediately the president denounced Aidid as a murderer. A week later he authorized the American troops to use force against the Somalis who provoked "terror and chaos." In keeping with a United Nations resolution drafted largely in the State Department, he also ordered the warlord's arrest. When an American military force went after Aidid with air and ground attacks, his urban guerrillas fought back, killing six soldiers. This defiance, as though directed at him personally, infuriated Clinton, eliciting from him a private flare-up of macho arrogance. "We're not inflicting pain on these fuckers," he said as recalled by White House aide George Stephanopoulos. "When people kill us, they should be killed in greater numbers." As his anger rose, he added, "I believe in killing people who try to hurt you, and I can't believe we're being pushed around by these two-bit pricks."[47] What had started as a humanitarian mission now took on the trappings of a military occupation ordered by one man who saw it largely in personal terms.

Although at this point the president exhibited no public militant swagger as had immediate predecessors, this confrontation marked the first of his macho moments. Like Reagan and Bush, Clinton exercised his military authority rashly. He ignored the obvious but generally sound principle that in interventions to maintain peace there can be no real stability when some of the parties involved view the armed peacekeepers as unwanted or as hostile.

Clinton's second display of military force followed quickly after he learned of a plot, hatched allegedly in April of that year, to assassinate Bush while he was visiting Kuwait City. Through what the president called "compelling evidence" from the CIA, he attributed the conspiracy to Hussein. In hyperbolic rhetoric he characterized it as "particularly loathsome and cowardly" and as "an attack against our country and against all Americans." He could not, he insisted, allow it to "go unanswered." In retaliation, on June 26 he ordered the launching of twenty-three missiles from ships in the Persian Gulf and the Red Sea against an already battered Baghdad. Among other reasons, he justified this assault publicly as "essential to protect our sovereignty" and to show his determination "to head off emerging threats." Constitutional lawyers commented that "calling the U.S. bombing of Iraq an act of self-defense for an assassination plot that had been averted two months previously is quite a stretch."[48]

Leaks from the White House indicated that as had Bush, Clinton used force for personal reasons, mainly to counter a reputation for indecisiveness summarized in the caricature "William the Waffler" and to build an image of a strong and assertive leader. Aides explained the assault as notifying the nation of the president's willingness to exercise leadership with military might measured out as he thought proper. The tactic paid off. Polls indicated Americans approved of the raid by a large margin.

A few months later, though, the public attitude toward the presidential exercise of force soured because of an episode in Somalia. On August 8, a remote-controlled land mine operated by warlord guerrillas killed three American soldiers on patrol in Mogadishu. The president responded by deploying a special assault team, known as Delta Force, to Somalia. The Delta troops staged several blundering raids on Somali dissidents to flush out the attackers as well as to capture Aidid but failed in both objectives. On a foray on October 3, the occupiers met fierce resistance from his warriors. These Somalis killed eighteen Americans, wounded seventy-four, captured one, and dragged the body of another soldier through the streets of Mogadishu, a scene millions in the United States witnessed on television. Official American estimates placed the Somali dead at three hundred or more.

Up to this point Clinton and his advisers had expressed a desire to go beyond humanitarianism. They spoke ambiguously about nation building and of creating stability in Somalia through force. This talk, the firefight, and the casualties alarmed not only many in Congress but also significant segments of the public. Concerned legislators who called for removal of the troops from Somalia discussed the placing of restrictions on how the president could employ them there and in Haiti, another trouble spot. He resisted restraints, claiming questionably that the president possessed the ultimate authority on the deployment of troops. "We started this mission for the right reasons," he stressed, "and we're going to finish it in the right way." He added, "We need more armor, more air power, to ensure that our people are safe and that we can do our job." So he ordered more than five thousand fresh troops, heavy armor, and additional warships to Somalia.[49] He also announced he would consult with members of Congress on the matter.

Six days later, after stating that "without us a million people would have died," Clinton reacted to some of the criticism he had received. He announced the Somali mission was never "one of 'nation building'" but now he backed off from what critics called mission creep, promising to withdraw the armed forces within six months. By March 25, 1994, he did so. Despite the bloody nose the president received in this venture, he still embraced the policy of sending troops to trouble spots overseas. His national security adviser, Anthony Lake, tried to place this unilateral policy in a positive light by claiming that "peacekeeping . . . is rooted in American interests."[50]

Meanwhile, a crisis in poverty-stricken Haiti had festered into a minor foreign-policy concern and then, for Clinton personally, into a sticky political issue. The problem revolved around the fate of Jean-Bertrand Aristide, who in February 1991 had become Haiti's first elected president. In September, a military coup forced him out of office. He obtained refuge in the United States where prominent liberals, media pundits, and notably the congressional black caucus made his fate, despite his spotty credentials as a democratic leader, a cause célèbre. These groups demanded that Clinton restore him to power, with force if the situation required it, and they believed it did. The president responded by denouncing Haiti's military junta and, in conjunction with the United Nations, imposed sanctions on the country. He also made it a "high priority to return democracy to Haiti" by restoring Aristide to office. Few Americans took issue with the goal of upholding democratic principles. Critics, however, perceived this policy as emanating from a "very narrow constituency" that had succeeded in making "the restoration of Aristide a 'litmus test' for the administration." These opponents, primarily in Congress, threatened to "withhold critical support for the president's domestic initiatives on health care, welfare reform, and crime."[51]

Regardless, Clinton stuck to his policy. On July 3, 1993, he brokered a plan for the resignation of Haiti's militarists that would by the end of October clear the way for Aristide's resumption of power. To assist in the transfer of authority, Clinton sent two hundred lightly armed soldiers, accompanied by a few Canadian police, to Haiti. When their ship arrived, armed bands of Haitians hostile to Aristide prevented the troops from landing. In addition, the junta refused to resign. Immediately, the president implied he might use force, citing "important American interests at stake in Haiti," the need to protect the Americans living there, and his "interest in promoting democracy in this hemisphere."[52]

Clinton now tightened the economic sanctions, ordered warships to patrol the island's waters, and placed military units on alert. Those in Congress who questioned his authority to commit troops on his own in this situation proposed legislation to prevent him from doing so. He objected to the proposals as encroaching "on the President's foreign policy powers."[53] After debating the issue, Congress avoided a direct confrontation by settling for a nonbinding resolution against the unilateral deployment of troops.

In the months that followed, the political pressure on Clinton for intervention became more intense. As the humorist Art Buchwald put it, "Every so often the United States decides to show every one that it supports democratic forms of government even if they aren't exactly what we had in mind." Such caricature of his policy did not deter the president. He said several times that "we cannot remove the military option. We have to keep that as an option." Like Woodrow Wilson in his Caribbean interventions, Clinton professed a desire "to find other ways to do it" but decided to plant democracy with bayonets where previously it had not flowered.[54]

Why, various skeptics asked, should the United States assume as its business how the rest of the world, or good portions of it, governs itself? Should a president intervene whenever dictators seize or hold power by force, as in Nigeria, Algeria, Korea, Iraq, and elsewhere? Pundits noted also that personal or domestic political considerations rather than any menace to the national interest motivated those in the administration eager to intervene. They urged invasion because it would demonstrate to the public "the President's decision making capability and the firmness of leadership in international political matters."[55] Some of them believed it would serve also as a means of stopping at the source the flow of unwanted Haitian refugees into Miami.

In one aspect of this analysis, however, the president and his advisers miscalculated. As measured in the polls, majority public sentiment opposed the planned employment of force. In a formal resolution, so did the Senate. Furthermore, an administration-sponsored poll in the House of Representatives "over whether or not to intervene . . . came back 219 against and 17 for." Still, Clinton persisted, obtaining on July 31 a United Nations resolution authorizing a multinational force "to use all necessary means" to eject the junta. Four days later, he indicated that his determination to exert force had not abated. As on previous occasions, he announced that like his "predecessors of both parties" he did not regard himself as "constitutionally mandated" to obtain congressional approval before invading Haiti. "We have kept force on the table," he emphasized. "We have continued to move it up as an option as the dictators there have been more obstinate."[56]

To justify this defiance of public and congressional sentiment, the president repeated muddled arguments. For instance, he maintained that duty required him to "secure our borders," to safeguard national security allegedly endangered by the situation in Haiti, and to carry out the will of the United Nations. Critics refuted much of his reasoning. They even cited self-serving Raoul Cédras, the head of Haiti's discredited junta, who claimed there was "no threat against any American on Haitian soil." Nonetheless, Clinton announced that the message "to the Haitian dictators is clear: Your time is up. Leave now, or we will force you from power."

He asserted also "that the United States cannot, indeed we should not be the world's policeman . . . but when brutality occurs close to our shores it affects our national interests. And we have a responsibility to act." George J. Mitchell, the Republican leader in the Senate, questioned this reasoning. He declared that "restoring Jean-Bertrand Aristide to power was not worth a single American life and that the American people wanted more restraint on the use of troops abroad."[57]

Given this opposition to presidential force, at the last minute Clinton half-heartedly appointed a three-man commission headed by former president Jimmy Carter to negotiate with Haiti's military dictators. On September 18 Carter concluded an arrangement that allowed the militarists to step down peacefully, provided for Aristide's return, and made the hostile invasion unnecessary. American troops then entered the country, disarmed junta supporters, policed city and village streets, and placed Aristide back in Haiti's presidency.

Upset by the president's handling of the situation in Haiti as well as the peacekeeping in Somalia, a Republican Congress in February 1995 moved to restrict his authority to deploy troops abroad. As with other similar moves, Clinton opposed the measure as an encroachment on the executive's conduct of foreign policy. The proposal soon faded away. The discontent over the Haiti intervention and over the hundreds of millions of lives expended for it also dissolved because the occupation ended officially on March 18, 1996, without a major violent incident to mar it. Clinton and his advisers touted this venture as a foreign-policy triumph but skeptics continued to view it as resurrected big-stick executive paternalism.

Meanwhile, the president had become the center of controversy over policy toward the persisting ethnic warfare in Bosnia-Herzegovina. Since he had taken office the rebelling Bosnian Serbs had bombarded the besieged Muslim-controlled city of Sarajevo, defying a United Nations resolution that had declared it a safe area for civilians. He had quickly retreated from his campaign rhetoric calling for tough action in Bosnia to protect basic human rights. Nonetheless, in seeking to end the conflict he wavered between using diplomacy or force and whether to act unilaterally or in cooperation with the United Nations and NATO allies.

Early in 1993 when the president took it upon himself to order food and medicine drops by air into Muslim-held areas of Bosnia, he explained the involvement as an emergency measure. "These airdrops are being carried out strictly for humanitarian purposes," he announced; "no combat aircraft will be used in this operation." Two months later, he intervened militarily as part of a NATO operation to stop Serb bombings of Muslim Bosnian villages. He stated that American "fighter aircraft are equipped for combat to accomplish their mission and for self-defense." Within a few days, he hinted at a broader military commitment, saying, "We have an interest in standing up against the principle of ethnic cleansing." He advocated air strikes against Bosnia's Serbs, the most aggressive of the ethnic cleansers, but ruled out "the question of ground troops." He did so because powerful Democratic legislators such as Lee Hamilton of Indiana opposed sending young Americans "to give their lives in the Balkans" where one could not detect "a vital American interest."[58] Furthermore, at this time the president's British and French allies objected to an air offensive because they had peacekeeping troops on the ground who were vulnerable to Serb retaliation.

Clinton held back on the bombing but late in May stepped up his intervention in the Balkan troubles by sending three hundred troops to Macedonia as part of a United Nations war monitoring force already there. He explained this deployment as an effort to "limit the conflict." Skeptics scoffed. They argued he acted largely to demonstrate to hawkish constituents that he "was doing something about the war in the Balkans." Several months later, he announced the "enforcement" of peace in Bosnia "potentially could include American military personnel as part of a NATO operation." He added "it would be helpful to have a strong expression of support" from Congress for the "military involvement" but did not consider its consent essential.[59]

In February 1994, following a deadly Serb mortar attack on civilians in Sarajevo, Clinton's involvement turned violent. As part of a NATO operation, American jet-fighters shot down four Serb bombers over Bosnia. The president defended this use of armed might as within his power as commander in chief. In April, he exercised that power again when, at the request of United Nations officials, he unleashed American bombers against the Serbs attacking the Muslim-held city of Gorazde. On August 5, he bombed them once more. He also gave tacit approval to the clandestine shipment of Iranian arms through Croatia to Bosnia.

Despite the president's tough stance, the public still appeared to lack confidence in his management of the Bosnian situation and of foreign policy as a whole. It perceived him as indecisive, as when Serb gunners on June 2, 1995, shot down an American plane. Holding back on substantial armed retaliation, he announced, "I am determined that we certainly should not have ground forces there." Public dissatisfaction with his wavering, as evident in negative polls, appeared to advisers to jeopardize his presidency. So he reshuffled his White House entourage, bringing in as chief of staff Leon Panetta, an aide and former congressman from California. Panetta urged him to pay more attention to the stature of the office. Clinton agreed, saying, "I've got to be more like John Wayne," thus viewing the advice as a call for more red, white, and blue machismo.[60]

Even though the president changed his demeanor, it did not affect the Balkan situation much. The Bosnia warfare came up virtually every time he alluded to international affairs. So on July 21, at a meeting of allied leaders in London, Secretary of State Warren Christopher presented a contingent activist strategy for dealing with the Balkan situation. They accepted it. Once again Western diplomats warned the Bosnian Serbs to discuss peace seriously or face military retaliation. When, therefore, besieging Serbs on August 28 lobbed mortars into Sarajevo, killing thirty-seven people, wounding more than a hundred, and outraging Americans and others, Clinton and his aides "seized the moment" to go ahead with "a tougher posture on Bosnia." As one of them reported, "the mood that we had to go for it was quite emphatic" and there was "no doubt" that Clinton now "wanted to see tough action taken."[61]

Accordingly, the team put together a plan for immediate robust action and the president adopted it. By phone he lobbied his European counterparts to go along with it. Joined by his NATO allies, he then ordered a massive strike by seventy-three bombers, most of them American, that blasted Serb positions in Bosnia. This air offensive continued for days, becoming in the eyes of many observers "the U.S.-packaged war."[62]

Most Western observers believed that the Bosnian Serbs merited such punishment but the Russians thought otherwise. Moscow denounced the bombings as genocide, saying it could not "remain indifferent to the tragic fate of the children of our brother Slavs."[63] It threatened a rupture of recent cordial relations with the United States. In any case, at home Clinton's key role in the decisions to use such force immediately boosted his sagging popularity. Advocates of a macho policy against the Serbs, however, gave him only faint praise. They believed he should have acted in this manner much sooner. Others applauded because at last he was beginning to look "presidential," meaning that a president perceived as weak could still gain approbation by appearing decisive in using force on his own, albeit against a weak opponent.

Congress as a body seemed less impressed because in part Clinton's secret assistance to the Bosnian Muslims touched on the sensitive issue of the executive's use of the war power. As we have seen, numerous academics and others had excused the cold-war presidents' abuse of that power, as in supposedly covert operations in Afghanistan and Central America, as necessary to meet dire emergencies. When the cold war ended, skeptics asked, therefore, "Do we still need the CIA?"[64] They pointed out it no longer had a powerful communist foe to thwart, that it had become scandal-ridden, and that it had a record of ineptness. They argued that much of its intelligence activities duplicated what could be obtained through ambassadors and from unclassified sources in universities and newspapers such as the New York *Times* and the Los Angeles *Times.* Others concerned about the war power attacked the agency because they saw it as an instrument of executive adventurism accountable to no one but the president.

Of course, like most government agencies the CIA had acquired a constituency in Congress as well as in the executive branch.[65] Supporters wished to revamp the agency but critics who wanted to disband it perceived the reorganizing as an effort to shuffle a self-perpetuating bureaucracy into "a brave new world for spies." The agency's constituents won this battle because Presidents Reagan, Bush, and Clinton had no desire to lose a virtually private strike force funded with a massive annual budget, estimated at this time to be $28 billion. Presidents could and did use it in unilateral interventions abroad essentially without oversight or other constraints by Congress and the public.

The executive reluctance to dismantle the CIA bothered those Americans who regarded "a new check on presidential war-making," policing, or even peacekeeping as imperative. They maintained that with the demise of superpower confrontations, the recurring lesser foreign crises, as in Bosnia, had "only local implications utterly irrelevant to America's safety or well-being." This argument failed to persuade presidents. They appeared incapable of resisting intervention, "even in the world's backwaters," particularly because Congress invariably acquiesced in their global policing. As had the isolationists of the thirties, critics of the executive in the nineties urged a "radical fix" on his use of force.[66] They called for a popular vote on presidential initiatives that would commit the nation to military action but failed to build a grassroots movement for their proposal.

As for Bosnia's civil war, the secret arming of the Muslims who fought the Orthodox Serbs to a standstill, along with the American and NATO air strikes, finally forced the Serbs to negotiate. Under pressure from the United States, representatives of the rival Serb, Croatian, and Muslim factions meeting in Dayton, Ohio, on November 21, 1995, initialed peace agreements. Thus, after nearly four years of bloodletting that took 250,000 lives, spawned numerous atrocities, and created two million refugees, hostilities ceased. The outcome produced the most glittering foreign policy success yet for Clinton. It also again brought him into conflict with Congress because the arrangement called for the deployment of as many as twenty-three thousand ground troops in Bosnia as part of a NATO peacekeeping mission. He insisted, however, that "the United States as NATO's leader must play an essential rôle in this mission. Without us, the hard won peace would be lost." He also emphasized, "Our leadership made this peace. . . . Our values, our interests, and our leadership all over the world are at stake."[67]

A majority in Congress and most Americans—61 percent according to a Los Angeles *Times* poll in June—opposed the deployment of the troops as not in the national interest. Why, many of them asked, should we embark on another precarious foreign policing mission costing millions, probably billions, of dollars when at home health care, education, urban crime, borders patrols to prevent crossings by drug smugglers and illegal immigrants, and environmental programs all suffer from lack of funding?

While this attitude dealt with real concerns, it produced no effective change in presidential behavior. In dealing with Congress on this issue, as had other activist presidents, Clinton relied on flawed precedent. He claimed the right as commander in chief to deploy troops wherever and whenever he thought necessary regardless of legislative opposition. In July, therefore, he again decided to bypass Congress and buck public sentiment by going ahead with the military commitment. He counted on the usual patriotic approval of Americans once the troops were in place. He and his supporters also raised now-traditional arguments. They warned that the nation must not retreat into isolationism, that as the world leader it had a moral obligation to participate in peacekeeping, and that peace in Europe served the national interest.

The president and his aides could not, however, disguise his personal stake in the venture, particularly in an election year. As they admitted, his decision had a political dimension. By employing American military might in Bosnia, he could increase his stature as a bold leader. "One of the things he has realized over the last two years," a staffer asserted, "is that foreign policy can help your image. It makes him look like a President." Another added that "people respect a tough, straightforward decision."[68] In other words, whether or not the controversial troop deployment was in the national interest, or defied the will of Congress, he expected the usual reward for tough behavior.

In November, the president presented his case to the nation via television. He asked for support but not permission to station troops in Bosnia, making it clear he would go ahead regardless of their dissent. He contended that the United States as the world's lone superpower had a moral and political obligation to lead the peacekeeping. As had previous interventionist presidents, he justified this military action as the burden of world leadership the nation must bear. He also repeated that "America cannot and must not be the world's policeman" but he had assumed that role in the Balkans, Somalia, and Haiti.

As gendarme, Clinton put his credibility on the line. He also identified his personal agenda with the national interest. If the nation did not support him, he stated, then its prestige as well as his would suffer. As had James Madison, James Polk, Lyndon Johnson, and others, he asserted a presidential authority of questionable legality. Then he acted on it. Despite the polls indicating widespread popular and congressional opposition to his initiative, in January 1996 he unilaterally began deploying twenty thousand ground troops in Bosnia backed by an equivalent support force.

Clinton defended this deployment as within his constitutional authority, a doubtful interpretation of prerogative. He had acted, however, in keeping with precedents set by strong presidents. In roughly comparable situations they, too, had claimed the right to use force unilaterally to defend national honor or to carry out a personal commitment to allies. Constitutional scholars and others dismissed such precedent as irrelevant. They argued that again a president had placed American lives in harm's way where no vital national interest existed. The Serbs, Croats, and Bosnians were fighting a civil war that, regardless of interventionist rhetoric, posed no danger to the welfare of the United States or to that of its allies.

After prolonged debate in the media and elsewhere, the House of Representatives denounced the president's decision to send the troops. Emotions ran high. When supporters of the deployment insisted that out of patriotic duty Americans must support their men and women in uniform, a congresswoman shot back that the opposition was not directed "to our boys. It's a message to our president, who is acting like a dictator." Regardless, the Senate on December 13 voted sixty-nine to thirty to back the commitment of the troops. As in the past, numerous senators disliked the policy but refused to reject it for fear of being accused of lacking patriotism or of being labeled isolationists.

Moreover, as usual in such circumstances, and as the administration had anticipated, the public's resistance to sending soldiers into action soon diminished. It rallied behind the president, a phenomenon confirmed by Clinton's rising approval ratings in the opinion polls. In January he strengthened his blooming popular image by visiting the troops stationed in Bosnia and telling them, "You are defending our Nation's values and our Nation's interests."[69] Later, as the peacekeeping missions increased, stretched out without a deadline, gobbled up more and more of the nation's military resources, and required the pressing of army reservists into active duty, critics grumbled about this policing. They asked how often and for how long will civilians "put up with being taken away from their families and careers and dispatched to hazardous, low-paying jobs in other countries?"[70] Three years later American troops still policed Bosnia.

Meanwhile, in several more confrontations the president again rattled sabers while keeping his eye on the polls. The first encounter occurred on February 24, 1996, when Cuban warplanes shot down two civilian aircraft operated by an émigré organization based in Florida. Four Americans died. Accusing Fidel Castro of violating American rights in international waters, Clinton threatened to retaliate with force. In this instance, he wanted to project toughness to avoid being outflanked by his Republican rivals in the current presidential campaign and also to make points with Cuban American voters in Florida. He demonstrated strength through tough posturing and tightening the screws on the economic sanctions already in force against Cuba.

The following month, Clinton flexed muscle in a disagreement with China over Taiwan. The mainland communists had mounted a campaign of threat, backed by a buildup of military force, to disrupt scheduled first-time democratic elections on the island state they regarded as a renegade province. To deter a possible invasion of Taiwan, Clinton beefed up naval forces stationed in Asian waters with a second aircraft carrier battle group geared for combat. China's foreign minister warned against intervention in what he termed an internal dispute. He reiterated his government's standard position "that Taiwan is a part of China and not a protectorate of the United States."[71]

Both the Cuban and the Taiwan confrontations passed without resort to military force but another clash with Iraq did not. Clinton had continued Bush's policy of trying to bring Hussein down through a covert CIA operation. After several botched attempts to do so, that campaign failed. When the defiant Hussein launched a military offensive against a Kurdish enclave in northern Iraq the president promptly turned to overt force. On September 3 and 4 Clinton ordered missile attacks on Iraq. On national television, he announced, "We must make it clear that reckless acts have consequences, or those acts will increase . . . And we must increase America's ability to contain Iraq over the long run."[72]

Skeptics lampooned the assaults as selective machismo that did nothing for the country but much for Clinton's image. He had again punished Hussein, ostensibly to protect an armed minority. Simultaneously, however, Clinton tolerated Russian attacks on minority Chechens and Chinese oppression of Tibetans because he could not intervene with relative impunity in Chechnya or Tibet as he could in Iraq. A Republican critic, Senator John McCain, called the Iraq action part of a "feckless photo-op foreign policy." According to opinion polls, however, the public approved of this unilateral policing venture by a margin of more than three to one.

This approbation contrasted sharply with the foreign reaction. Other than a few close allies who expressed tepid support, most countries criticized Clinton. Russia, China, and Arab states condemned his resort to force. Kuwait, for example, refused to accept additional American troops on its soil even though Clinton offered them for its protection against Iraq. Saudi Arabia announced it would not permit the United States to mount more attacks on Iraq from its territory. A journalist in friendly Egypt commented, "Since it reached the apex of the pyramid in the new world order, the United States has been adopting the behavior of the cowboy and the quarrelsome bully in every international crisis."[73]

In these three crises, Clinton portrayed himself as a crusader with a global commitment to combating evil. This depiction drew a warm response from the public but did not have a significant impact on his reelection campaign. Domestic issues dominated the contest. Nonetheless, throughout the campaign as during most of his presidency he seemed compelled to act tough to overcome his record of having evaded military service as a youth during the Vietnam War. His political opponents never allowed the public to forget it. In addition, like Bush, he wanted to parade himself as a strong president to dispel traces of wimpishness while reaping political reward from his behavior. Had he not shown toughness in using military force, the reelection victory he achieved in November 1996 might well have eluded him.

To be fair, we should recognize that Clinton's readiness to assume the role of international gendarme did not always stem from a desire for personal benefit. As noted earlier, several times he employed the military to alleviate human suffering. Even in such instances the intended recipients of his do-good interventionism on occasion resisted it. Moreover, in his policing endeavors when he defied public and congressional sentiment, he sometimes miscalculated, as in the Middle East and Somalia, and almost in Haiti. Except for the confrontation with China over Taiwan, his machismo succeeded without a crippling backlash because he exercised it mainly against weak foes in situations where the United States could suffer no vital injury. Critics contended, therefore, that his toughness tended to serve no fundamental purpose other than to boost his political stature.

Clinton cloaked his interventions with altruistic rhetoric. He claimed that as the leader of the world's chosen nation, he could not shirk the responsibility of striking at evil and of spreading democracy even if it required armed might. At the start of his second term, he explained this variation of the stewardship theory by announcing that "taking reasonable risks for peace keeps us from being drawn into far more costly conflicts later." Consequently, he added, "we must maintain a strong and ready military" and "do what it takes to remain the indispensable nation . . . for another 50 years."[74]

Words such as these, as well as his behavior, suggested that Clinton, like Woodrow Wilson, wanted to bring peoples his kind of salvation whether or not they desired it. In April 1997, for instance, when he deployed about a thousand marines along Zaire's border to evacuate some five hundred Americans from that country torn by civil war should the need arise, the rebel leader, Laurent Kabila, suspected a broader intent. He viewed those troops as more than necessary for the task Clinton had proclaimed. Kabila said "they could move in at any time" and posed "a threat to our territorial integrity."[75] Despite the protest, the troops remained poised for action.

American troops also stayed in Bosnia primarily because of presidential will. Originally Clinton had announced they would remain only until the end of 1996. Then, after his reelection, when he adopted a more aggressive interventionism, he announced they would remain longer. With mushrooming numbers and influence, Americans came to control the principal monitoring agencies. This Americanization of the peacekeeping reflected an awareness that it had stagnated and threatened to unravel what the president regarded as a major foreign-policy success. In some instances, as in trying to make the Dayton Accords work, the mission had succeeded. It also had placed American troops under attack. In October 1997 angry Serbs, who regarded the American presence in Bosnia as an occupation, denounced the troops with epithets and pelted them with stones.

In the next year, when Clinton again asked Congress to extend the deployment, critics cited the Serb opposition, arguing the mission had failed to lay a solid groundwork for permanent peace and should end. As president, he countered, he had a constitutional right to station thousands of Americans on duty without a pullout deadline. So he not only kept the troops in Bosnia but also expanded their policing responsibilities.

All the while, the president had maintained the sanctions and other pressures on Iraq. Also, a special United Nations commission monitored Iraq's progress in eliminating its weapons of mass destruction. The Iraqi government never fully cooperated, playing hide and seek with the commission's inspectors, but it still sought relief from sanctions. Early in 1997, therefore, Clinton embarked on a tougher policy against Iraq. In March Secretary of State Madeleine Albright announced the United States would not allow the lifting of sanctions until Hussein was gone.

On October 29 Hussein informed the United Nations he would no longer accept American participation in the weapons commission inspections and demanded the United States terminate its flights of U-2 surveillance planes over Iraq. He denied possessing weapons of mass destruction, labeled the United Nations commission a pawn of the United States, and placed large government installations, including presidential compounds, off limits to the United Nations commissioners. Dismissing Hussein's charges as nonsense and his intransigence as rendering the weapons inspection program useless, an irate Clinton announced that only force through air strikes would compel his compliance with the United Nations monitoring program.

Russia, China and, to a lesser degree, France and the Arab nations argued against the president's reasons for using force. They favored peaceful diplomacy. Despite their differences in many matters, Russia and China in this instance even cooperated in denouncing what they termed the American "hegemony and power politics" in world affairs. This opposition did not deter Clinton. Maintaining he had tried diplomacy but it had failed, he lined up a few allies, primarily Britain, to intervene with massive force. Critics at home and abroad perceived this saber-rattling as another bullying presidential police action, an extension of the idea of the United States as "the world's indispensable nation."

On January 28, 1998, Secretary Albright swept aside the concerns of hesitant allies to announce the United States would launch air strikes against Iraq on its own: "While we prefer always to go multilaterally and have as much support as possible, we are prepared to go unilaterally."[76] This hard line disconcerted even close allies but Clinton pressed on with it in his State of the Union Message. Congress supported him.

Internationally, though, the president stood almost alone as the sheriff determined to punish a defiant but toothless villain. With the eyes of the world focused on him, Clinton built up a vast military force within striking distance of Iraq. On February 4 Russia's president, Boris Yeltsin, warned that if Clinton proceeded with the air strikes he could provoke a world war. Minority critics at home also spoke in favor of a peaceful solution, denouncing the president's "testosterone-driven foreign policy." On February 12 in a televised address Russia's defense minister, Igor D. Sergeyev, denounced the United States's "uncompromising and tough" stand on Iraq. He warned that air strikes on Baghdad could have "grave consequences" for American-Russian military cooperation.

The next day Samuel R. "Sandy" Berger, the national security advisor, declared Hussein's chemical and biological weapons capabilities a direct security threat to the American people. The Iraqi government rebutted the contention, stating Clinton was itching for a fight. The president stated, "We don't believe it is acceptable, if diplomacy fails, to walk away." Some congressional skeptics doubted the morality of an attack on Iraq. Seven Catholic cardinals and the president of the National Conference of Catholic Bishops sent Clinton a letter, stating "this action . . . could be exceedingly difficult if not impossible to justify."

Neither this opposition nor that of Russia dissuaded Clinton. On February 13 he said if Hussein did not allow the United Nations weapons inspectors unfettered access to Iraq he would strike. He and his top aides embarked on a campaign to prepare the nation for war. They quickly encountered opposition in Congress and among the clergy and others. Arab kingdoms near Iraq refused American access to their air bases; allies in Europe, Asia, and Africa warned against the use of force; and members of the United Nations Security Council could not agree on a new resolution condemning Baghdad for obstructing the weapons inspections. Anti-American demonstrations erupted in Britain, Italy, Egypt, and elsewhere. Again, the president's eagerness to act as the indispensable global sheriff provoked more opposition than approval.

On February 17 Clinton addressed the nation via television. "Our purpose is clear," he stated. "We want to seriously diminish the threat posed by Iraq's weapons of mass destruction program. We want to seriously reduce [Hussein's] capacity to menace his neighbors." If we do not stop him now, the president warned, "I guarantee you" he will someday unleash an arsenal of destruction. He depicted Hussein as the embodiment of a twenty-first-century predator.

Public opinion polls indicated that if Hussein did not comply with the inspection demands, most Americans favored air strikes. However, only 45 percent supported military action if the United States were forced to go it alone. Misgivings over possible war mounted. Student demonstrators termed the planned action "United States aggression." Even Britain had qualms, wishing for a stronger United Nations endorsement of military force. President Nelson Mandela of South Africa sided with Hussein's view of the inspections and cautioned that Clinton's stance might confirm the perception of many "that America is trying to be a policeman of the world." A journalist, William Pfaff, commented, "The affair no longer has a connection to common reality. It is a matter of symbolic action and gesture, related to political power, policy investment and status inside Washington. . . . The war plan fails the morality test."[77]

The next day, in an effort to build support for military action, the president's foreign-policy aides held a town hall meeting in Columbus, Ohio. Some six thousand people made up the audience at Ohio State University but television beamed the proceedings to two hundred million homes around the world. Protesters heckled, denounced, and sharply questioned the morality, legality, and purpose of the proposed intervention, shouting, "One, two, three, four! We don't want your dirty war!" They denounced Clinton's goals as contradictory. Why punish Iraqis to get at a dictator while supporting authoritarian regimes in Indonesia, Turkey, and elsewhere? Uncomfortably, the administration's top guns responded evasively. Secretary of State Albright depicted Hussein as the most evil man since Hitler, who must be punished, yet not destroyed. "You're not answering my question, Madam Albright," an interrogator snapped at her.[78]

Observers termed the meeting a public relations disaster. One White House staffer tried to put a positive spin on the debacle. He linked it to the furor over a sex scandal involving the president and a young White House intern from California. "I think we probably bumped Monica Lewinsky from the top of the news," he commented.[79] Antiwar demonstrations erupted in San Francisco and elsewhere. In Washington three thousand marchers converged on the White House to protest the proposed bombings.

Earlier, polls had indicated considerable public support for the intervention. Now it dropped to below 50 percent. Only 41 percent approved of an air campaign against Iraq. The rally-around-the-flag phenomenon did not seem to work as smoothly as in the past. In addition, because the president had attracted only meager international support and none from the United Nations Security Council, he did not dare ask the council for a resolution of support. He knew it would not be forthcoming. Congress, too, could not agree on such a resolution of its own.

Publicly, the president persisted in going it alone, seemingly convinced the macho style would pay off regardless of the widespread dissent. He could not resist using the world's most powerful military machine even for trivial purposes. As Albright had put it to General Colin Powell in advocating air strikes in Bosnia, "What's the point in having this superb military you're always talking about if we can't use it?"[80]

Fortunately, at the last minute as during the Haitian crisis, the president backed away from military force. On February 22 Secretary-General Kofi Annan of the United Nations brokered an arrangement with Hussein in which he capitulated to Clinton's threat. Iraq agreed to allow the weapons inspectors immediate and unconditional access throughout the country. Clinton accepted the deal. The next day he told the nation, "If [Iraq] does not keep its word this time, everyone would understand that then the United States and hopefully all of our allies would have the unilateral right to respond at a time, place, and manner of our own choosing." In other words, he reserved what he regarded as his personal right to respond with military force. He indicated also that diplomacy would not have worked without his military buildup, calling it essential in compelling Hussein to capitulate. "Once again, we have seen that diplomacy must be backed by strength and resolve," the president said. As though programmed, his advisers repeated this traditional big stick sentiment popular with the powerful who coerce the weak.

Skeptics portrayed the outcome as a victory of the United Nations Security Council members who were unhappy with the idea of an American-led war against Hussein. Russia and China, for instance, had agreed "no country should claim absolute dominance in resolving international matters." Mandela explained, "It was of great concern, the threat to strike, because we knew it's not going to hit any military targets, it's going to kill children, women, the aged—very innocent people—and that is something we cannot tolerate."[81] Other foreign commentators painted Clinton and his foreign-policy team as arrogant, highhanded, and trigger happy.

Months later the president again flexed muscle abroad while ostensibly weakened by scandal at home. The trouble began on August 7 when terrorists bombed American embassies in Kenya and Tanzania, killing twelve Americans and nearly three hundred Africans. Ten days later Clinton admitted to a federal grand jury and to the public his relationship with Monica Lewinsky. Within three days, on his own, he ordered missile attacks on suspected terrorist installations in Sudan and Afghanistan. He described the swift and unprecedented action against sovereign states as self-defense, commenting, "Countries that persistently host terrorists have no right to be safe havens."[82]

As is typical in this kind of military action, political leaders rallied behind the president and urged more toughness. This time, though, some Republican legislators suggested he had resorted to violence to divert attention from his domestic problem. Clinton and his aides denied any motivation other than to protect the American people from terrorist attacks. Polls indicated that 75 percent of the public supported the president and largely dismissed the notion he had ordered the strikes for political reasons. A minority of 38 percent believed his problems had at least some consideration in his decision to use force.[83] This approval of the macho style followed the textbook description of the rally-around-the-flag phenomenon. Skeptics, though, perceived the president's behavior as in keeping with the scenario in the movie *Wag the Dog*.

This skepticism spread when Clinton, suddenly and with no warning on December 16, on his own initiative but with British support, launched a fierce aerial attack—dubbed operation Desert Fox—on Iraq. In a televised address to the nation he accused Hussein of thwarting the United Nations inspection program because he wanted to continue building a deadly arsenal of nuclear, biological, and chemical weapons. Clinton's third mauling of Iraq stunned lawmakers and political observers. Senior Republicans accused him of rushing to launch a military offensive less than twenty-four hours before the House of Representatives was scheduled to begin debating his impeachment on charges of perjury, abuse of power, and obstruction of justice in the Lewinsky affair. The legislators grudgingly postponed the debate for a day to avoid undermining the military action.

As usual in an act of war by the president, the public and Congress rallied behind him. This time, though, cynics popped up everywhere to attack Clinton's motives. "Never underestimate a desperate president," a Republican congressman from New York, Gerald B. H. Solomon, commented bitterly. "What option is left for getting impeachment off the front page and maybe even postponed? And how else to explain the appearance of a backbone that has been invisible up to now?" Former secretary of state Lawrence S. Eagleburger said the timing of the attack "stinks to high heaven." Others again referred to another repeat of the *Wag the Dog* syndrome.

The president defended his behavior, insisting he had set the timing for the punishment a month before. "I am convinced the decision I made to order this military action, though difficult, was absolutely the right thing to do. It is in our interest and in the interest of people all around the world." In all, he launched more than four hundred bomb and missile strikes over four nights, killing or injuring uncounted numbers of civilians as well as soldiers. Although Hussein took the punishment helplessly, he remained defiant. What the assaults accomplished remained vague, though the president claimed, "Our mission is clear—to degrade Saddam's capacity to develop and deliver weapons of mass destruction and threaten the region."[84] Critics at home and abroad called Iraq's pummeling a callous disregard for civilian lives. France and other allies distanced themselves from the attacks while Russia and China criticized them.

On December 19 the House of Representatives voted to impeach Clinton. Scholars and others argued that his behavior toward women leading to this second impeachment in the nation's history has tarnished the grandeur of the presidency and eroded its strength. It did not, however, diminish the capacity of the president to use military force unilaterally. Clinton continued to bristle with machismo against puny foreign adversaries. He threatened to blast Serbia and Iraq into misery, and administration apologists and much of the public applauded. At the end of the year, when Iraqis fired ineffective surface-to-air missiles at American planes as they patrolled the no-fly zone of southern Iraq, he struck again at Hussein's missile sites. The president described the raids as measures of self-defense.

This machismo with its continual bashing of weak foes had become increasingly difficult to justify internationally. Other peoples perceived presidents, even when acting righteously, as superbullies, inebriated with power and too violent. Most Americans approved of the macho style abroad and revered the presidency. For instance, Henry J. Hyde of Illinois, the leader in the House of Representatives in the impeachment proceedings, demanded Clinton's conviction not for his machismo in international affairs but for its exposure in a sexual affair. In lying to hide "private pleasure," Hyde charged, he had debased and diminished "the office of the president of the United States in an unprecedented and unacceptable way."[85]

On that same day a journalist asked the president if the impeachment trial had damaged his office. Clinton responded, "I hope the presidency has not been harmed. I don't believe it has been."[86] As though to demonstrate the office's unimpaired power in foreign relations and his own virility, he again resorted to unilateral force, cloaked in humanitarian rhetoric, against a small country.

The humanitarian concerns that were real and substantial had long bothered Americans who followed foreign affairs seemingly as much as they had Clinton. He condemned the brutal tactics of ethnic cleansing used by Slobodan Milosevic, the hard-line nationalist president of what remained of Yugoslavia, against Albanian residents of the Serb province of Kosovo. These Albanians, called often Kosovars, made up 90 percent of its population. In a final attempt to resolve the province's ethnic problem, which had erupted into civil war, Clinton brokered talks between Serbs and Kosovars held in February 1999 at Rambouillet, France. His diplomats fashioned an arrangement calling for a high level of autonomy for the Kosovars to be enforced by twenty-eight thousand NATO-led troops. Milosevic viewed these terms as leading to the amputation of Serbia. He also regarded as an ultimatum the American insistence under the threat of force that he must accept the fixed conditions. He refused. Even though Kosovars desired independence, after intense pressure from Washington their leaders on March 18 agreed to the terms.

The next day Clinton told Americans why they must support the use of force against Serbia. "Make no mistake," he said, "if we and our allies do not have the will to act, there will be more massacres. In dealing with aggressors in the Balkans, hesitation is a license to kill."[87] In the next few days, and later, he explained his decision to intervene with what a skeptic called an "orgy of analogy" and contradictions. On various occasions the president and administration hawks compared dealing with the Serbs without the threat of force to appeasement in the thirties, to failure to prevent the Holocaust, to a possible failure to maintain the stability of Europe, and to a necessity to maintain America's and NATO's credibility. He claimed that "inaction in the face of brutality simply invites more brutality," that he had a "moral imperative" to act, an obligation to humanity to halt genocide, a right to defend America's national and strategic interests, and a need to abort Serb aggression and enforce democratic values.

Critics pointed out that these and other justifications, or some of them, were quite a stretch, particularly when Serbia threatened no neighbors, no territory of another state, and no tangible American interests. Those wary of presidential machismo also asked, Why the selective humanitarianism? Did not the reasoning in the call for military action apply to the genocide in Rwanda, Chinese ethnic brutalities in Tibet, Russian suppression in Chechnya, the ethnic and religious horrors in the Sudan, and the brutalities of the Taliban in Afghanistan?

Despite the inconsistencies in the president's case, on the night of March 24 the United States, supported by eighteen other countries of the North Atlantic Treaty Organization he had pressured into line, launched its armed intervention on a massive scale. Cruise missiles from American warships and mostly American warplanes slammed targets from Belgrade to Montenegro. Clinton and his aides tried to avoid using the words "war" or "killing," to apply to their violence. They resorted to impersonal euphemisms such as "degrading" and "collateral damage." They characterized the bombings as a degrading of Milosevic's capacity to wage war and labeled the killing of civilians and others inevitable collateral damage even for a virtuous cause.

Clinton, the former peacenik again acting as a "wag-dog" the leader, initiated war on his own and acted with dubious legality. The United Nations charter prohibited any nation's use of armed force against another sovereign nation except for defense of itself or allies, or when the Security Council authorized force. Clinton and his hired legalists argued that the charter authorized collective self-defense as in the "degrading" campaign. They knew also they could not obtain United Nations support because in the Security Council Russia and China would veto this undeclared presidential war.

In the United States, however, the bombing missions, as has been usual in the initial stages of hostilities, received public and congressional support. Once the air strikes began, both the people and the lawmakers, having been fed a daily diet of pictures and stories of Serb atrocities, rallied round the president but with less enthusiasm than in previous presidential wars. The Senate, largely along party lines with Democrats in favor and Republicans opposed, voted 58 to 41 to support the war. Public opinion polls indicated that Americans divided approximately equally over reaction to the air assault. Of those polled, 46 percent approved and 43 percent disapproved.[88]

Elsewhere, disapproval registered more visibly. Through much of Europe, even in NATO counties, people vented anger in the streets against the United States. In Athens, fifteen thousand demonstrators marched on the American embassy chanting, "Clinton, Fascist, Murderer." Greek newspapers ran cartoons depicting Clinton as a Hitler.[89] Ironically, the president, American newspapers, and hawk propagandists often portrayed Hussein and Milosevic as Hitlers.

Clinton had assumed that with enough bombing, Milosevic would capitulate. Instead, he gained strength. Even his political enemies rallied to his side. In turn, Clinton expanded the air war by striking at factories, government buildings, power stations, bridges, prisons, and other targets. As should have been expected, this escalation led to more collateral damage or the slaughter of civilians, men, women, and children, sometimes with cluster bombs designed to maim and kill indiscriminately. Still, he persisted on the assumption that with enough bombing the Serbs would capitulate. In a sense, he was correct. He had the means, as the head of the most powerful military machine on earth, to obliterate Serbia. Obviously, if the suffering of the Serbs became unbearable, like any people, they would have to meet the conqueror's terms.

Similar reasoning applied to Iraq, where at the same time Clinton continued to bomb, virtually on a daily basis, and lay waste to the country. He claimed he had no quarrel with the Iraqi people, only with Hussein, as also with Milosevic and not the Serb people. These contentions struck skeptics as clichés, or at least as another stretch because the Iraqi and Serb peoples, not their leaders, did all the suffering and dying, and because Clinton had a penchant for mouthing moral sentiments, and for tossing bombs, as though confetti, at weak peoples. He got away with this violence because Americans seemingly had become hardened or numbed by the war in Iraq and few questioned the horror their pilots inflicted. A minority in Congress, however, urged even heavier devastation. Clinton and his war counselors took care, however, to keep talk about this long sustained air war low-key. They avoided the word "war." Instead, they called the bombings a "campaign" and "enforcement actions."

In the other war in Serbia when so-called "smart" bombs and other technologically advanced surgical strikes wiped out nonmilitary installations, administration spokesmen dismissed them as mistakes outweighed by the virtues of Clinton's moral crusade. In one instance, American bombers destroyed the Chinese embassy in Belgrade, killing three people and injuring twenty. Apologists tried to explain the mistake as the result of pilots using outmoded maps, an explanation that even American supporters of the air war found "ludicrous." In addition, the war not only failed to stop the expulsion of Kosovars but pushed the Serbs into increasing it.

As political opposition to the air war rose, Clinton, the State Department, and other presidential spokespeople contended that as commander in chief he needed no declaration of war to use force. They argued mainly on the basis of precedent set by predecessors who had on questionable authority defied the original intent in the constitutional requirement on war making. They stated also that the president could not now pull out of the conflict because that would "cede victory" to Yugoslavia. Nonetheless, on April 28 the House of Representatives, mainly along party lines, voted against a declaration of war, against withdrawal from the conflict, against a resolution in support of the air campaign by a vote of 213 to 213, and with a vote of 249 to 180 for another resolution requiring congressional approval for the deploying of ground forces. Also, a bipartisan group of seventeen legislators filed suit in federal court seeking a ruling that the continued bombing violated the Constitution and laws of the United States such as the War Powers act.

As the president did often, he reversed himself. During the impeachment ordeal, Clinton and his supporters had touted the importance of public opinion in avoiding conviction. Now they discounted it, asserting he could not fight a war with an eye constantly on the polls. So, as the push-button bludgeoning of the Serbs continued throughout May, hawks such as Secretary of State Albright, with her dubious reasoning about the need for the "indispensable nation," urged more toughness, and Britain's prime minister, Tony Blair, called for the war's expansion into an invasion with ground troops.[90] Other members of the alliance, however, refused to go along. Some even demanded an end to this presidentially manufactured conflict in which Americans did approximately 90 percent of the bombing and provided a similar amount of the financing to the tune of billions of dollars.

Polls began showing that about 50 percent of the American public regarded the bombing campaign a failure and a majority opposed further hostilities in favor of a negotiated settlement. In late May a new bipartisan antiwar movement began taking shape. Across the country small but growing groups of demonstrators denounced Mr. Clinton's war. In other parts of the world, such as Germany, Italy, China, and Russia, opinion ran more strongly against the United States and its macho president. The Japanese, for instance, viewed Clinton as "an international bully."[91]

Still, the president disregarded both the external and internal opposition to his war making, rejected Serb peace feelers, and persisted in demanding full Serb surrender to his demands. As had predecessors, he liked the taste of power, had become addicted to the role of global policeman, refused to acknowledge fallibility, and despite occasional apologies for lying and deceptive behavior seemed to relish his macho style in carrying and arrogantly using the world's biggest stick on a selective basis.

In all, Clinton's bellicosity and his attitude as the world's policeman conformed well to both the arrogant and the leader-as-servant aspects of presidential machismo. Up until June 1999 these qualities appeared also to accord with political practicality. Using force for humanitarian purposes, voicing the rhetoric of a global mission, and projecting an image of strong leadership usually played well with a public hooked on admiring strong activist presidents and rewarding their macho ventures abroad.

CHAPTER 10

Must Presidents Prevail?

As Commander-in-Chief, the President can deploy the armed forces and order them into active operations. In an age of missiles and hydrogen warheads, his powers are as large as the situation requires.

Dean Rusk, April 1960

As we have seen, the president's right to send young men to their deaths, for reasons other than to defend the nation against assault, has always been a source of contention. Despite the considerable attention paid to this problem, we do not know with reasonable certainty what drives an individual, when he becomes president and when he has the choice, to initiate such violence on his own. Nothing in the Constitution or its amendments grants him authority to employ military force to defend national honor, financial interests, humanitarian values, or to promote other laudable intangibles such as democracy and peacekeeping.

Philosophers and others have long noted that leaders everywhere often behaved in the macho manner because they became enthralled with power. This hypothesis accords with the conviction common among the leaders of the founding generation such as John Adams, who thought deeply about the nature of the presidency. "Power naturally grows," he wrote. "Why? Because human passions are insatiable."[1] He and many of his contemporaries perceived the taste for power as innate in humans. They believed that because of this propensity the presidency would attract primarily ambitious men who loved to wield power.

The records, the deeds, and the words of presidents themselves bear out the soundness of the power and ambition hypothesis. As a rule, these men wanted the office because they regarded it rightfully as the pinnacle of power within the nation and, in our time, within the world. They realized that to achieve conventional success in foreign affairs they had to exercise power with strength, virility, and decisiveness. Some executives, therefore, turned to macho behavior as though it were expected of them, whereas others appeared to take to it as naturally as the sex drive. In addition, most of them seemed to hunger for the glory that often flowed out of military ventures.

Numerous observers have commented on the nature of this truculence, noting its gender aspect. For instance, Carrie Chapman Catt, the suffragist and peace activist, maintained, "War is in the blood of men; they can't help it. They have been fighting since the days of the cavemen. There is a sort of honor about it."[2]

Contemporary social scientists, however, discount biological programming as an explanation for the warrior streak in men. Along with feminists, these thinkers depict this behavior as rooted in a patriarchal society that breeds men "to violence and authoritarianism: to cope with it and to impose it." They assert that "men are socialized to be warriors" or, in brief, "that masculinity is socially constructed."[3]

Most presidents denied, even to themselves, that either an inborn characteristic or socialized conditioning drove their belligerent conduct. As a matter of course, when they took office they avowed selfless qualities, such as devotion to peace and democracy. Soon, though, the power that allowed them to tower above other mortals and to influence relationships with other nations intoxicated many of them. Acting as though constitutional restraints threatened their power, they often personalized it, guarded it jealously, battled the limitations on their authority, and gloried in maintaining or extending their office's power. As Richard Nixon remarked, "No one who has been in the Presidency with the capacity and power to affect the course of events can ever be satisfied with not being there."[4]

Those who have been there used force with the honest conviction they were serving the nation's best interests. Most, though, praised masculine aggressiveness while cloaking their bellicosity with selfless generalities, such as employing force to advance the nation's, or even humanity's, welfare. At times, they acted tough as part of a power trip to enhance their own agenda. With military force, they could test their virility, seemingly prove it, and usually benefit from it. Expected reward from a public that admired martial virtues provided motivation. Consequently, few presidents have been able to resist the temptation of using the military machine at their disposal or, when the opportunity arose, of exulting in the role of warrior.

Grover Cleveland, for one, rejected playing warrior even when under pressure from Congress and substantial public sentiment to order military force against Spain in Cuba. In other instances, however, he acted as though he were a macho sheriff. Among the other presidents who had ample opportunity to use force in significant foreign crises, only two, as we have seen, defied pressures to do so. Primarily out of resentment against the hawks of his own party, John Adams abandoned efforts to escalate the Quasi-War. Personal conviction, however, moved Herbert Hoover to refuse to intervene militarily in Latin America and to agree to sanctions against Japan that he believed would lead to war. Both men rank low on virtually any scale that attempts to measure presidential esteem.

In contrast to these presidents, most other chief executives regarded as strong stretched their foreign-policy authority to its constitutional limit as they perceived it. Frequently they ordered the military into action to coerce weak countries near and distant or, in some instances, to conquer. As the United States rose to the rank of world power and then superpower, the tools of destruction at the fingertips of presidents became so extensive that even a mediocrity in the White House could toy with the idea of becoming a Caesar. Fortunately, none has yet taken on that role.

However, even executives who contemporaries or historians regarded as weak at times found the office so empowering that they used force in the macho manner and got away with inconsequential accountability. They and other presidents transcended constitutional authority in foreign affairs often enough to alarm even dedicated exponents of the strong executive. One articulate believer in strong behavior, the historian Henry S. Commager, noted that such readily available "power encourages and even creates conditions which seem to require its use." Indeed, he maintained, "the greater and more conclusive the power the stronger the argument for its use."[5]

This abuse of power has not been just an aberration within a history of generally successful democratic government. As we have noted, presidential machismo has been prominent among the causes that contributed to the nation's involvement in armed clashes with numerous foreign peoples but, of course, not a sole determinant. In the case of the Vietnam War, those given to defending the system of virile executive leadership admit that "presidents constituted the main force behind establishing the Vietnam commitment and the main stumbling block to extrication from the war."[6] Now, virtually as routine, presidents affirm effectively that the Constitution's Commander-in-Chief Clause allows them to send troops anywhere in the world, including into hostilities, without seeking legislative approval. They justify this inflating of legal authority as necessary to maintain the nation's prestige and credibility abroad, to bring freedom to benighted peoples, or to defend endangered American lives, property, and interests. Rarely has this stratagem failed to attract popular approval.

Presidents have been able to aggrandize their power in this manner for a number of reasons but especially because the Constitution and the courts permitted them greater leeway in conducting foreign affairs than in managing domestic matters. Seizing this advantage often with bulldog tenacity, strong chief executives pursued power incrementally as an individual goal. They expanded their circumscribed authority to repel sudden attacks into their presumed power to use armed force as they saw fit. Repeatedly, such executives identified "self" with the national interest, a concept they shaped seemingly to mean what suited them.

As vigorous presidents expanded the scale of policing other countries or of plunging the nation into undeclared wars, so also did they amplify rationalizing their motivation in using force as a kind of personal benevolence. The people who experienced their violence, and many Americans, too, perceived the presidents' deportment differently. These victims saw it as a throwback to the unrestrained behavior of monarchs and dictators who launched military violence out of arrogance, for wealth, or for psychological gratification. In specific circumstances, critics of presidential machismo regarded it as shameful because they saw no true honor deriving from blasting poor, backward peoples with massive bombing, defoliation, and other horrors.

Such belligerency coming from the decision of one man fulfilled the fears of the Constitution makers who had prognosticated that ambitious presidents would be biased toward their own interests. This conduct in foreign relations, which at times mocked democratic theory, thrived, as we have seen, under an elastic conception of the preindependence doctrine of inherent power. No such power exists in the Constitution or in later law though the courts have on occasion held that the executive enjoys powers inherent in nationhood and sovereignty. Only on occasion, also, has Congress questioned the use of the inherent-power doctrine as permitting the executive's unilateral exercise of military force. Furthermore, the legislative branch has never refused a president's initial request for support in employing force and has never declared war except when the executive requested it or already had engaged the armed forces in hostilities. When dissenters questioned the basis for such violence, the president had ample resources through in-house attorneys in explaining away irregularities. In addition, if he were determined to employ force and to dominate its use, he could take the initiative in ways that gave his decisions an aura of necessity.

Except in 1812, this maneuvering usually left Congress with no real alternative to backing the president and no true opportunity for uninhibited debate in choosing between war and peace. Regardless of presidents' success in using military force unilaterally, if Congress had the collective will to oppose them, it had the authority to curb executive faits accomplis, international policing, or warfare. On the rare occasions when legislators did demonstrate such will, it did not last long. Invariably, the president's decision prevailed.

Moreover, when the people and/or a majority in Congress showed signs of wanting war, as in 1898, or of favoring some kind of military deployment, the legislators could hardly go ahead without presidential approval. Once an executive decided to use military force on his own, he usually found the means to do so. He could proceed without great furor because he had at his disposal the tools to bend the Constitution or to transcend its restraints in a manner that few would question.

Although this behavior and the drive to maximize power have always been ingredients of presidential machismo, conventional wisdom holds that this conduct started with the cold war. Actually, cold-war presidents differed from most of their predecessors primarily in their ability to accelerate the growth of their truculence. They not only claimed the right to commit the armed forces to sustained war on their own authority but also exercised that right.

Supported by sympathetic politicians and public sentiment, these activist executives exploited their conception of national security as the criterion of right or wrong. They argued American democracy could survive the perils of the nuclear age only with tough leadership. Pointing out that the difference between destruction and survival could hinge on hours or even minutes, they claimed nuclear technology had in effect enlarged their legal authority. They averred as well that the nuclear danger compelled them to take the broadest possible view of their powers, meaning essentially that they should have open-ended authority over military decisions.

Shortly before Dean Rusk became secretary of state, he summarized this pretension to august authority. He and others of similar persuasion maintained that "the modern Presidency cannot limit itself to a national interest narrowly defined." They claimed the Commander-in-Chief Clause freed the president from congressional restraints by somehow conferring on him an independent source of constitutional power. "In an age of missiles and hydrogen warheads," Rusk wrote, the executive's "powers are as large as the situation requires." In a similar vein, the historian Thomas A. Bailey contended that "the yielding of some of our democratic control of foreign affairs is the price that we may have to pay for greater physical security."[7]

With such reasoning, with huge standing armed forces at their disposal, and with a feared ideological foe to confront, cold-war executives found ready support for breathing new life into the inherent-power doctrine. On this basis, they used force quickly in virtually any part of the world. They cited their predecessors' actions, regardless of how unconstitutional or wrong as precedents, for legalizing forceful interventions in other countries. They and their advisers contended that executive practices and judicial rulings legitimated presidential war making, international policing, or the use of military force under other names. They argued that historical practice nullified the exclusive power of Congress to declare war.

Critics, however, countered that unconstitutional acts could not acquire validity by repetition or by having been condoned in the past. Moreover, in the American legal system bad precedents could be reversed. Nonetheless, in two centuries Congress's war power has eroded significantly. Many Americans, perhaps most, accepted without complaint the aggrandizement of executive authority over the vital issue of life and death affecting many of them, their children, or their grandchildren. "Oh well," went a widespread comment, "everybody knows that the President has the power to fight a war anytime he wants."[8]

Ironically, when the cold war ended that attitude continued to prevail. It did so largely because Congress did not reclaim its lost authority and tough-minded presidents still presented their unilateral actions in terms of real or contrived crises that supposedly demanded prompt response. Skeptics asked why the president should continue to make war on his own, why he should have vast de facto power beyond the Constitution, why he should still ask Americans to bear the burden of supporting covert armed interventions and the world's greatest military forces, and in effect perpetuate presidential machismo. Casting aside stale cold-war arguments, Bill Clinton offered his own answer couched in terms of the old redeemer-nation concept with its leader as savior. He claimed the president must have extensive military authority "because we still have interests; we still face threats; we still have responsibilities. The world has not seen the end of evil, and America can lead" the struggle against it. He added that "we cannot be the world's policeman, but we are, and we must continue to be, the world's leader."[9] Essentially, international policing against alleged evil or for interests the executive himself defines is just what he prescribed. Because the world has never been without evil, and probably never will be, crusading in this guise could go on indefinitely.

Clinton coupled this interventionist formula with an updated globalism in keeping with the caregiving aspect of machismo. This conception placed the president at the head of a haven of goodness in a world fraught with immorality, much as in the older, never-credible doctrine of exceptionalism that theoretically endowed Americans with a moral superiority over other peoples. Individual presidents have long exploited this idea, but markedly since Woodrow Wilson's time. With it they sought to justify their projecting American authority, money, and military power over the globe to uphold their own conception of moral order. Even though this crusader role rested mainly on myth, White House sycophants, hagiographers, and believers in the strong executive advanced it in speeches, journals, and newspapers.

Myth and reality soon came to seem as one because, as various scholars point out, "the President stands virtually unchallenged in his unilateral ability to commit the United States to war."[10] Through flawed precedent he has come to dominate, choosing on his own when and where to use force, frequently at great cost for inconsequential gains. This power has accrued to him for many reasons but particularly because in matters of foreign policy, he could initiate hostile activity both clandestinely and openly. Neither the people nor Congress has his global reach or leeway to choose the enemy, the time, or the place in deciding on police actions or war. As a whole, Americans have approved of this redistribution of power because they perceive the president as at his best in dealing with international affairs. Opinion surveys, anecdotal data, and scholarly literature indicate also that they have been overawed by the unwarranted hype on presidential expertise in matters of war and peace. This hype led many to believe that in this vital area the president's judgment is superior to that of Congress and hence must prevail.

Devotees of the strong presidency have helped perpetuate this reverence for executive authority by dismissing Congress as a body of windbags, deriding "government by Congress" as "no government at all," and claiming as though fact that the president is the final judge of what constitutes the malleable national interest. These executive partisans often point to Franklin Roosevelt as the wise leader who understood this problem far better than did the legislators, contending his "strong presidential leadership . . . saved American freedom."[11] On the other hand, earlier students of the executive branch, such as the British scholar James Bryce, regarded American presidents as commonplace. Although this judgment is too harsh, Bryce's well-known observation that brilliant or "great and striking men" in the office have been rare still carries credibility.[12]

Furthermore, no substantial body of evidence sustains the assumption that, in matters of life and death, one man can decide better than many or that the presidency ennobles the incumbent. As in the personal behavior of Jefferson, Harding, Kennedy, Johnson, and Clinton, considerable data suggest opposite conclusions. Often, the wisdom of presidents failed to equal their elevated status. Although Congress also has been irresponsible in backing rash uses of force, generally it has been more deliberate in dealing with such matters. Concerned scholars and others, therefore, echo the often expressed warning that no individual should hold in his or her hands alone the power of plunging the nation into war or police actions and maintaining the violence.

Most presidents have been decent men who tried to govern well but, in the words of the historian Henry Adams, like most humans often they could not "bear the strain of seizing unlimited force." Some of them, such as Lyndon Johnson, explained their problem by depicting the presidency as a crushing burden, "an office of almost unbearable responsibility." Andrew Jackson called it "dignified slavery"; James Polk saw it as "no bed of roses"; and Grover Cleveland characterized it as "dreadful self-inflicted penance for the good of my country."[13] Despite such deprecation, those who vied for the office went almost to any length to attain it and, from the start of their first term, incumbents plotted constantly to win a second.

Most men who reached the White House, among them Theodore and Franklin Roosevelt, Harry Truman, Gerald Ford, Richard Nixon, George Bush, and Bill Clinton, loved being president, luxuriated in its perquisites, and relished the deference and the power it gave them. They defended executive prerogative and stood firm against efforts to limit their power, especially their assumed capability of employing military force unilaterally.

Although articulate and savvy politically, a number of presidents were ignorant of law and history. Those on the darker side were liars, deceivers, or just plain unworthy of wielding the immense power over life and death placed in their trust. They besmirched their office by unwisely or illegally using the military force at their disposal, by violating civil rights with domestic spying, and by other unethical or scandalous behavior. On this point, the commentary of Leonard Garment, a recent White House adviser, though hyperbolic, is worth noting. "The presidential gene," he contends, "is filled with sociopathic qualities—brilliant, erratic, lying, cheating, expert at mendacity, generous, loony, driven by a sense of mission, a very unusual person."[14]

Regardless of the flaws in their presidents, in times of real or imagined international crises Americans rallied around them as though they were father figures. When a president employed force, whether or not justified by customary international standards for such conduct, usually his ratings in the Gallup and other polls surged upward. As a rule, though, this instant popularity faded about as fast as it rose. In drawn-out wars, the public withdrew its support or turned against its warrior chiefs. It reacted in this hot and cold manner in part because it accepted the wisdom of the cult that touted muscular leadership in foreign policy. When macho presidents failed to produce prompt, heady results, the public felt duped.

As a whole, Americans appear to have been too willing to accept the executive branch's arguments regarding the president's legal authority to launch police actions or to initiate and conduct war. Relying on this public trust, the most recent presidents unleashed the military in quick, low-cost strikes against weak adversaries they could easily characterize as monsters. Although in several instances these executives struck with what appeared obviously noble motivation, at other times they acted because they sought personal gain, especially if they were engaged in reelection campaigns. In the main, they had no constitutional, statutory, or moral right to intervene forcefully in the affairs of other nations but they persisted because they knew that unless they fumbled they could do so with impunity. In each instance when they did not blunder, the public applauded their machismo as they anticipated.

This behavior highlights an incongruity in executive leadership. In the domestic context, presidents speak of moral values, urge respect for the legal process, and proclaim, as have many historians, that Americans have been and are a peaceful and exceptionally law-abiding people. In dealing with foreign affairs, presidents and their aides, too, frequently circumvent laws, embellish executive authority, refuse to admit even self-evident mistakes, wrap themselves in the flag, and condemn their opponents as subversive, unpatriotic, neoisolationist, or worse. Except in extreme instances, when critics note these contradictions in word and behavior, it makes little difference to the macho presidents or to the public.

Even intellectuals who express concern about the ambivalence in presidential conduct go along, arguing that Americans can take comfort in knowing that "history lends no support to the specter of the power-drunk, reckless chief executive." Dissenters respond, "Where is the guarantee that this luck will hold?"[15] The skeptics have a point because when crises strike we cannot always count on having sensible rulers, let alone wise ones. Of course, Congress, too, can blunder. The greater danger to democracy, however, lurks in executive machismo in the conduct of foreign affairs because it breeds contempt for law, can subvert democratic institutions, and could lead to tyranny. As political thinkers since the time of Plato have noted, "Too much power given to anything . . . is dangerous."[16] Although it is true that the American presidential system has worked better than most other executive arrangements, in recent years in matters of war and peace, its preeminence appears tarnished.

Only Congress, with its power to oversee the activities of the executive branch, to demand accountability from presidents, to raise taxes that maintain the armed forces, and to enact legislation that the president must faithfully execute, possesses sufficient constitutional authority to restrain presidential machismo. The media and investigative journalists can expose the president's excesses but only Congress, aside from outraged popular will, can stop them. A democracy remains strongest when its legislative body upholds its own and the executive's constitutional role.

Congress attempted to do so a number of times markedly, as we have noted, in a reaction against Lyndon Johnson's and Richard Nixon's martial conduct. Aroused senators publicly deplored these and other presidents' almost "absolute power over the life or death of every living American" as well as "of millions of people all over the world." They characterized the "concentration in the hands of the President of virtually unlimited authority over matters of war and peace" as having "all but removed the limits to executive power in the most important single area of our national life." They perceived this development as threatening the nation "with tyranny or disaster."[17]

Only three times has Congress asserted its impeachment authority decisively against presidents. In each instance it did so for real or alleged abuses in domestic matters, though the Nixon case did touch on war policy issues. Efforts to restrain presidential machismo in the conduct of foreign policy, as with the War Powers Resolution of 1973, have misfired. They failed to restrain essentially because public sentiment, the media, and the cult of the presidency sided with the executive rather than with Congress.

While the courts have occasionally criticized presidential use of the war power, they too usually endorsed such executive machismo. Consequently, few Americans have challenged the president when he employed force unilaterally in foreign lands. As Richard Helms, a former director of the CIA cynically put it, "We're basically a rather hypocritical nation; we like things to be done, but we don't want to have blood on our hands."[18]

Defenders of the strong presidency too often disregard the bloodletting that has accompanied its rise. They contend it has served the nation well, that holders of the office must have a will to power, and that nothing should be done to emasculate it. For those Americans troubled by the concentration of power in the executive branch, this popular attitude poses a dilemma. How can we, they ask, place precise restraints on presidential machismo and still demand bold, tough leadership? Conventional scholarship contends we cannot have both and hence strong is better than weak.

Citing usually the example of Abraham Lincoln, those who demand toughness argue that a president may have to take measures of questionable legality to save the nation. For this reason he needs flexibility in the use of military force. In contrast, critics point out we have had only one Lincoln and that as a congressman he had warned against any individual holding in his hands the power to make war. Moreover, his illegalities as president were hardly key elements in preserving the Union. Those who doubt the virtues of the tough presidency warn also against confusing strength with the deployment of the military as a political tool, with its manipulation as an instrument for advancing a personal agenda, or with its use as a kind of narcotic to satisfy the macho impulse. Congress also has the capability of responding to threats to national security with flexibility and with less emotion or personal interest in the use of military force.

Regardless of the dangers in maximizing executive power, politicians, journalists, scholars, and the public at large still seem to regard masculine muscularity a condition of fitness for the office. Even though Clinton's scandalous behavior brought cries of a bespattered, less heroic, and imperiled presidency, most Americans still venerated the office and backed him when he acted tough in international affairs. As long as this approbation continues, as long as power-hungry individuals with massive egos capture the White House, as long as advisers who owe them livelihood and status work to justify executive power-grabbing, as long as cultists exalt presidents, as long as Congress acts as a rubber stamp when the executive uses force unilaterally, and as long as the public rewards it, presidential machismo seems destined to remain a prominent feature of American foreign policy.

NOTES

INTRODUCTION

1. Alexis de Tocqueville, *Democracy in America*, ed. J. P. Mayer and Max Lerner, trans. George Lawrence (New York, 1966), 114.

2. Harry S. Truman, "My View of the Presidency," *Look*, Nov. 11, 1958, 25.

3. Merlo J. Pusey, *The Way We Go to War* (Boston, 1969), 1.

4. Quoted from Robert H. Jackson, *The Supreme Court in the American System of Government* (Cambridge, Mass., 1955), 64.

5. Address, Princeton, May 10, 1991, U.S. President, *Public Papers: George Bush, 1989* (Washington, D.C., 1990), part 1, 499.

6. Quoted from David D. Gilmore, *Manhood in the Making* (New Haven, 1990), xi; and Barbara Ehrenreich, *Blood Rites* (New York, 1997), 125.

7. See Nancy C. M. Hartsock, "Masculinity, Heroism, and the Making of War," in *Rocking the Ship of State*, ed. Adrienne Harris and Ynestra King (Boulder, Colo., 1989), 134–5; Hannah Arendt, "Imperialism, Nationalism, Chauvinism," *Review of Politics* 7 (Oct. 1945): 457; and Betty Reardon, *Sexism and the War System* (New York, 1985), 35.

8. Quoted from John E. Mueller, *War, Presidents, and Public Opinion* (New York, 1973), 70; and Clark M. Clifford, *Counsel to the President* (New York, 1991), viii.

9. At the White House, Apr. 31, 1964, quoted in James MacGregor Burns, *Presidential Government* (Boston, 1966), xii.

10. See, for example, Richard E. Neustadt, *Presidential Power*, Rev. ed. (New York, 1980), xi, 7; and Louis W. Koenig, *The Chief Executive* 3d ed., (New York, 1975), v.

11. Arthur M. Schlesinger Jr., *The Imperial Presidency* (Boston, 1973), 411.

NOTES TO CHAPTER 1

1. Edmund S. Morgan, *Inventing the People* (New York, 1988), 261.

2. Chevalier de la Luzerne to Comte de Vergennes, Philadelphia, March 2, 1781. Quoted in Mary A. Giunta, ed., *The Emerging Nation*, (Washington, D.C., 1996), vol. 1, 150.

3. Benjamin Franklin to the president of the Congress, Passy, France, Dec. 25, 1783. Quoted in ibid., 959.

4. John Jay's *Report on the Algerine Declaration of War*, New York, Oct. 20, 1785; and Louis Guillaume Otto to Comte de Vergennes, New York, Dec. 25, 1785. Quoted in ibid., vol. 2, 868, 968.

5. Quoted in Charles C. Thach, *Creation of the Presidency, 1775–1789* (Baltimore, 1969), 64, 82.

6. The quotations come from Gordon S. Wood, *Creation of the American Republic* (Chapel Hill, N.C., 1969), 551 and 135.

7. For the quotations, see Catherine D. Bowen, *Miracle at Philadelphia* (Boston, 1966), 60; Thach, *Creation of Presidency*, 81; and Pinckney, June 1, 1787, in Max Farrand, ed. *The Records of the Federal Convention of 1787*, rev. ed. (New Haven, Conn., 1966), vol. 1, 64–65.

8. The quotations come from Charles A. Lofgren, "War-Making under the Constitution," *Yale Law Journal*, 81 (Mar. 1972): 700.

9. Quoted in David Gray Adler, "The Constitution and Presidential Warmaking," *Political Science Quarterly* 103 (spring 1988): 5.

10. For the quotations, see Hamilton in Federalist no. 69, Mar. 14, 1788. In Alexander Hamilton, John Jay, and James Madison, *The Federalist*, ed. Jacob E. Cooke (Middletown, Conn., 1961), 465; Ernest R. May, "The President Shall Be Commander in Chief," in *The Ultimate Decision*, ed. May (New York, 1960), 5; and David Gray Adler, "The President's War-Making Power," in *Inventing the American Presidency*, ed. Thomas E. Cronin (Lawrence, Kans., 1989), 126.

11. Quoted from Leonard W. Levy, *Original Intent and the Framers' Constitution* (New York, 1988), 30.

12. Edward S. Corwin and others, *The President*, 5th ed. (New York, 1984), 201.

13. "Philadelphiensis," Feb. 21, 1788. Quoted in Jackson Turner Main, *The Antifederalists* (Chapel Hill, N. C., 1961), 141.

14. "Federal Farmer," quoted in Jack N. Rakove, *Original Meanings* (New York, 1996), 273–74.

15. The quotations come from the Second Treatise (1689) in John Locke, *Two Treatises of Government*, ed. Peter Laslett (Cambridge, England, 1988), 377; and Richard H. Cox, *Locke on War and Peace* (London, 1960), 128.

16. Federalist no. 70, Mar. 15, 1788. In Hamilton, *The Federalist*, 471.

17. To Marquis de Lafayette, June 15 and 26, 1788. Giunta, ed., *Emerging Nation*, vol. 3, 808.

18. To General Arthur St. Clair, New York, Oct. 6, 1789. George Washington, *Papers of George Washington*, Presidential Series, ed. W. W. Abbot and Dorothy Twohig, vol. 4 (Charlottesville, Va., 1993), 141.

19. For the quotations, see entries of Apr. 15 and Dec. 9, 1790, in William Maclay, *Journal*, ed. Edgar S. Maclay (New York, 1890), 239–40, 349.

20. See second annual message, Dec. 8, 1790. George Washington, *The Writings of George Washington*, ed. John C. Fitzpatrick (Washington, D.C., 1931–44), vol. 31, 166; and Francis D. Wormuth and Edwin B. Firmage, *To Chain the Dog of War*, 2d ed. (Urbana, Ill., 1989), 127.

21. "Veritas" in the *National Gazette* (Philadelphia), June 9, 1793. Quoted in Alexander DeConde, *Entangling Alliance* (Durham, N.C., 1958), 89.

22. "Letters of Helvidius," no. 1, Aug. 24, 1793. In James Madison, *The Mind of the Founder*, ed. Marvin Meyers (Indianapolis, 1973), 270 (italics in original).

23. Quoted in Ralph Ketcham, "James Madison and the Presidency," in Cronin, ed., *Inventing the American Presidency*, 347.

24. To Hamilton, July 2, 1794, and May 15, 1796. In Washington, *Writings*, vol. 33, 422, and vol. 35, 49.

25. Quoted from John Adams, *A Defence of the Constitutions*, 3 vols. (London, 1787–88) as reprinted in John Adams and John Quincy Adams, *The Selected Writings of John and John Quincy Adams*, eds. Adrienne Koch and William Peden (New York, 1946), 105. Adams to Roger Sherman, Richmond Hill, N.Y., July 17, 1789. In Adams, *The Works of John Adams*, ed. Charles Francis Adams, 10 vols. (Boston, 1850–56), vol. 6, 428, 430, 431.

26. Philadelphia, Mar. 13, 1798. Quoted in Alexander DeConde, *The Quasi-War* (New York, 1966), 67.

27. Quoted in ibid., 81.

28. Madison to Thomas Jefferson [Orange], May 13, 1798. In Jefferson, *The Republic of Letters*, ed. James Morton Smith, 3 vols. (New York, 1995), vol. 2, 1048. Logan's speech of May 12, 1798, quoted in Frederick B. Tolles, *George Logan of Philadelphia* (New York, 1953), 150–51.

29. To George Washington, Philadelphia, Feb. 19, 1799, in J. Adams, *Works*, vol. 8, 625–26.

30. Pickering to George Cabot, Trenton, Oct. 22 and 24, 1799, Pickering Papers, Massachusetts Historical Society and to William Vans Murray, Trenton, Oct. 25, in Worthington C. Ford, ed., "Letters of William Vans Murray to John Quincy Adams, 1797–1803," *Annual Report of the American Historical Association for the Year 1912* (Washington, D.C., 1914), 610–12.

31. Adams to James Lloyd, Quincy, Mass., Jan. 1815 in J. Adams, *Works*, vol. 10, 113.

32. For the quotations, see the first inaugural address, March 4, 1801, in James D. Richardson, ed., *A Compilation of the Messages and Papers of the Presidents, 1789–1897*, 10 vols. (Washington, D.C., 1896–97), vol. 1, 310; Gary J. Schmitt, "Thomas Jefferson and the Presidency," in Cronin, ed., *Inventing the American Presidency*, 330 and 334; and to John Adams, Paris, July 11, 1786, in Thomas Jefferson, *The Papers of Thomas Jefferson*, ed. Julian P. Boyd (Princeton, N.J., 1954), vol. 10, 123.

33. For the Gallatin and Jefferson quotations, May 15, 1801, see James R. Sofka, "The Jeffersonian Idea of National Security," *Diplomatic History*, 21 (fall 1997): 537–38. For the orders, see Samuel Smith to Richard Dale, Washington, May 20, 1801, Dudley W. Knox, ed., *Naval Documents Related to the United States Wars with the Barbary Powers*, 6 vols., (Washington, D.C., 1939–44), vol. 1, 467.

34. Quoted from James A. Field Jr., *America and the Mediterranean World, 1776–1882* (Princeton, N.J., 1969), 49.

35. Jefferson to James Madison, Monticello, Aug. 28, 1801, in Jefferson, *Republic of Letters*, vol. 2, 1193–94; and first annual message, Dec. 8, 1801, in Thomas Jefferson, *The Works of Thomas Jefferson*, ed. Paul L. Ford (New York, 1893–99), vol. 9, 332.

36. Quoted in Edward S. Corwin, *The President's Control of Foreign Relations* (Princeton, N.J., 1917), 134.

37. New York *Evening Post*, Nov. 22, 1805, cited in Robert J. Allison, *The Crescent Obscured* (New York, 1995), 31.

38. To Robert R. Livingston, Washington, Apr. 18, 1802, in Jefferson, *Works*, vol. 9, 363–68.

39. To James Monroe, Washington, Jan. 13, 1803, ibid., 419.

40. To John C. Breckinridge, Monticello, Aug. 12, 1803, quoted in Alexander DeConde, *This Affair of Louisiana* (New York, 1976), 183–84; and Aug. 18, 1803, quoted in Dumas Malone, *Jefferson the President: First Term, 1801–1805* (Boston, 1970), 316.

41. To Madison, Monticello, Aug. 4, 1805, in Jefferson, *Republic of Letters*, vol. 3, 1375; to Madison, Aug. 17, 1805, quoted in Dumas Malone, *Jefferson the President: Second Term, 1805–1809* (Boston, 1974), 56; and Sept. 12 and 18, 1805, quoted in DeConde, *Affair of Louisiana*, 225.

42. Quoted in DeConde, *Affair of Louisiana*, 229–30.

43. Confidential message on Spain, Dec. 1805, Jefferson, *Works*, vol. 10, 203–4.

44. Samuel Smith, June 27, 1807, quoted in Malone, *Jefferson: Second Term*, 425.

45. Quoted from Leonard W. Levy, *Jefferson and Civil Liberties* (Cambridge, Mass., 1963), 96.

46. To Caesar Rodney of Delaware, quoted in Edward S. Corwin, *Total War and the Constitution* (New York, 1947), 168.

47. Quoted in Doris A. Graber, *Public Opinion, the President, and Foreign Policy* (New York, 1968), 178.

48. For the quotations, see Samuel Taggart in Bradford Perkins, *Prologue to War* (Berkeley, Calif., 1963), 260; and Ralph Ketcham, *Presidents above Party* (Chapel Hill, N.C., 1984), 102.

49. For the quotations, see James Madison, *The Writings of James Madison*, ed.

Gaillard Hunt, 9 vols. (New York, 1900–1910), vol. 8, 48; and Robert A. Rutland, *The Presidency of James Madison* (Lawrence, Kans., 1990), 61.

50. Madison to Thomas Jefferson, Oct. 19, 1810, in James Madison, *Letters and Other Writings of James Madison, Fourth President of the United States*, 4 vols. (Philadelphia, 1865) vol. 2, 484–85.

51. Richmond (Virginia) *Enquirer*, Nov. 13, 1810, quoted in Irving Brant, *James Madison: The President 1809–1812* (Indianapolis, 1956), 189.

52. Second annual message, Dec. 15, 1810, in Madison, *Writings*, vol. 8, 125; Senator Outerbridge Horsey of Delaware quoted in Abraham D. Sofaer, *War, Foreign Affairs and Constitutional Power* (Cambridge, Mass., 1976), 299; and Senator John Pope quoted in Stephen F. Knott, *Secret and Sanctioned* (New York, 1996), 93.

53. The Philadelphia *Aurora* and the Boston *Chronicle*, quoted in Bernard Mayo, *Henry Clay* (Boston, 1937), 391.

54. Third annual message, Nov. 5, 1811, in Madison, *Writings*, vol. 8, 162. See also John C. A. Stagg, *Mr. Madison's War* (Princeton, N.J., 1983), 91.

55. Quoted from Roger H. Brown, *The Republic in Peril: 1812* (New York, 1964), 30, 171.

56. Quoted from Henry Adams, *History of the United States of America during the Administrations of Jefferson and Madison*, 9 vols. (New York, 1962), vol. 6, 228; and Perkins, *Prologue to War*, 377. See also p. 425.

57. Benjamin Stoddert quoted in ibid., 172 and Lowell in Samuel E. Morison, Frederick Merk, and Frank Freidel, *Dissent in Three American Wars* (Cambridge, Mass., 1970), 21–22.

58. Quoted in John K. Mahon, *The War of 1812* (Gainesville, Fla., 1972), 32.

59. See D. Webster to Ezekiel Webster, Washington, March 26, 1816, in Daniel Webster, *Papers of Daniel Webster*, ed. Charles M. Wiltse (Hanover, N. H., 1974), 196; *James Madison* (New York, 1971), 471; and Donald R. Hickey, *The War of 1812* (Urbana, Ill., 1989), 104, 301–2.

60. See Perkins, *Prologue to War*, 291, 394, 435; Brown, *Republic in Peril*, 73, 78, 189; Rutland, *Presidency of Madison*, 188; Reginald Horsman, *The Causes of the War of 1812* (Philadelphia, 1962), 267; Steven Watts, *The Republic Reborn* (Baltimore, 1987), 283–84; and Hickey, *War of 1812*, 3.

61. For the quotations, see Noble E. Cunningham Jr., *The Presidency of James Monroe* (Lawrence, Kans., 1996), 34, 118; George Dangerfield, *The Era of Good Feelings* (London, 1953), 325; and inaugural address, March 4, 1817, in James Monroe, *The Writings of James Monroe*, ed. Stanislaus M. Hamilton, 7 vols. (New York, 1898–1903), vol. 6, 10, 11.

62. Quoted in Bradford Perkins, *Castlereagh and Adams* (Berkeley, Calif., 1964), 290.

63. For the quotations, see William E. Weeks, *John Quincy Adams and American Global Empire* (Lexington, Ky., 1992), 67; Samuel F. Bemis, *John Quincy Adams and the Foundations of American Foreign Policy* (New York, 1956), 315–16 (J. Q. Adams, July 18 and 21, 1818); and Sofaer, *War, Foreign Affairs*, 350.

64. Quoted in Harry Ammon, *James Monroe* (New York, 1971), 424. See also Robert V. Remini, *Andrew Jackson and the Course of American Empire, 1767–1821* (New York, 1977), 367.

65. Thomas W. Cobb of Georgia quoted in Sofaer, *War, Foreign Affairs*, 361.

66. The quotations come from ibid., 255, 264n.

67. Quoted from Graber, *Public Opinion, the President*, 37.

NOTES TO CHAPTER 2

1. Quoted from Samuel F. Bemis, *John Quincy Adams and the Union* (New York, 1965), 18.

2. Inaugural address, Mar. 4, 1825, in J. Adams and J. Q. Adams, *Selected Writings,* 356.

3. Quoted in Mary W. M. Hargreaves, *The Presidency of John Quincy Adams* (Lawrence, Kans., 1985), 224.

4. Tocqueville, *Democracy in America*, 360.

5. March 2, 1829, Richardson, ed., *Papers of Presidents,* vol. 2, 1000.

6. For the quotations, see Robert V. Remini, *Andrew Jackson and the Course of American Democracy, 1833–1845* (New York, 1984), 197; Craig E. Klafter, "United States Involvement in the Falkand Islands Crisis of 1831–1833," *Journal of the Early Republic* 4 (winter 1984): 410; and John M. Belohlavek, *"Let the Eagle Soar!"* (Lincoln, Nebr., 1985), 184.

7. Baylies to Edward Livingston, Aug. 19, 1832, is quoted in Francis Rawle, "Edward Livingston: Secretary of State," in *The American Secretaries of State and Their Diplomacy,* ed. Samuel F. Bemis and Robert H. Ferrell, 18 vols. (New York, 1963–70), vol. 4, 253. The second quotation comes from Klafter, "Falklands Crisis," 395.

8. Fourth annual message, Dec. 4, 1832, in Fred L. Israel, ed., *The State of the Union Messages of the Presidents, 1790–1966*, 3 vols. (New York, 1966), vol. 1, 362.

9. For the quotations, see the *National Intelligencer,* July 10, 1832, and the *Salem Gazette*, July 13, 1832, in David F. Long, "'Martial Thunder': The First Official American Armed Intervention in Asia," *Pacific Historical Review* 42 (May 1973): 155, 157 and the president's message of Dec. 4.

10. Quoted from Corwin and others, *The President,* 21; and Schlesinger, *The Imperial Presidency,* 35.

11. See sixth annual message, Dec. 1, 1834, Richardson, ed., *Papers of Presidents,* vol. 2, 1325–26; and Representative Augustin Clayton of Georgia quoted in Henry B. Cox, *War, Foreign Affairs, and Constitutional Power: 1829–1901* (Cambridge, Mass., 1984), 17.

12. Private to Amos Kendall, Washington, D.C., Oct. 31, 1835, in Andrew Jackson, *Correspondence of Andrew Jackson*, ed. John S. Bassett, 7 vols. (Washington, D. C., 1926–33), vol. 5, 374–75.

13. Quoted in H. B. Cox, *War, Foreign Affairs*, 7; and John Quincy Adams, *An Eulogy on the Life and Character of James Madison* (Boston, 1836), 47.

14. The statistics come from Donald B. Cole, *The Presidency of Andrew Jackson* (Lawrence, Kans., 1993), 126.

15. Richardson, ed., *Papers of Presidents*, vol. 3, 1536.

16. Ibid., 1865.

17. John Quincy Adams quoted in Frederick Merk, *Fruits of Propaganda in the Tyler Administration* (Cambridge, Mass., 1971), 5.

18. For the quotations, William S. Murphy, Feb. 14, 1844, see David M. Pletcher, *The Diplomacy of Annexation* (Columbia, Mo., 1973), 132; and Calhoun to ministers from the Republic of Texas, Washington, D.C., Apr. 11, 1844, in John C. Calhoun, *The Papers of John C. Calhoun*, ed. Robert L. Meriwether and others, 23 vols. (Columbia, S.C., 1959–96), vol. 18, 208–9.

19. Quoted from Oliver P. Chitwood, *John Tyler* (New York, 1939, reprinted 1964), 351.

20. Quoted in Norma L. Peterson, *The Presidencies of William Henry Harrison and John Tyler* (Lawrence, Kans., 1989), 232.

21. Merk, *Tyler Administration*, 34.

22. For the quotations, see Charles G. Sellers, *James K. Polk: Continentalist* (Princeton, N.J., 1966), 163; to Cave Johnson, Dec. 21, 1844, in James K. Polk, "Letters of James K. Polk to Cave Johnson, 1833–1848," ed. St. George L. Sioussat, *Tennessee Historical Magazine* 1 (Sept. 1915): 254; and Richardson, ed., *Papers of Presidents*, vol. 3, 2224, 2229–30.

23. James K. Polk, *The Diary of James K. Polk during His Presidency, 1845 to 1849*, ed. Milo M. Quaife, 4 vols. (Chicago, 1910), vol. 1, 155; and Polk to George Bancroft, quoted in Sellers, *Polk: Continentalist*, 244.

24. See Pletcher, *Diplomacy of Annexation*, 280; and Norman A. Graebner, "The Mexican War: A Study in Causation," *Pacific Historical Review* 49 (Aug. 1980): 411–12, 419.

25. Quoted from Sellers, *Polk: Continentalist*, 399.

26. John Wentworth, May 5, 1846, quoted in Don E. Fehrenbacher, *Chicago Giant: A Biography of "Long John" Wentworth* (Madison, Wis., 1957), 64.

27. Polk, *Diary*, vol. 1, 363.

28. See Richardson, ed., *Papers of Presidents*, vol. 3, 2292–93; and the "Spot" Resolutions, Dec. 22, 1847, in Abraham Lincoln, *The Collected Works of Abraham Lincoln*, ed. Roy P. Basler, 9 vols. (New Brunswick, N.J., 1953–55), vol. 1, 421–22.

29. Remarks on the "Declaration of a State of War with Mexico," Senate, May 12, 1846, in J.C. Calhoun *Papers*, vol. 23, 100–102; and John H. Schroeder, *Mr. Polk's War* (Madison, Wis., 1973), xiv, 24.

30. Adams to Albert Gallatin, Dec. 26, 1847, quoted in Weeks, *John Quincy Adams*, 196; and Clayton quoted in Louis Fisher, *Presidential War Power* (Lawrence, Kans., 1995), 32.

31. Quoted in Sellers, *Polk: Continentalist*, 417.

32. The quotations come from Richard R. Stenberg, "Polk and Frémont, 1845–1846," *Pacific Historical Review* 7, no. 3 (1938): 223; and Andrew Rolle, *John Charles Frémont* (Norman, Okla., 1991), 80.

33. Alexander H. Stephens, a Georgia Whig, and Joshua Giddings, an Ohio abolitionist, quoted in Norman A. Graebner, *Empire on the Pacific* (New York, 1955), 151; and Ashmun, Jan. 30, 1848, in Wormuth and Firmage, *To Chain the Dog of War*, 57.

34. To William H. Herndon, Washington, D.C., Feb. 15, 1848, in Lincoln, *Collected Works*, vol. 1, 451–52.

35. Quoted in Holman Hamilton, *Zachary Taylor* (Indianapolis, 1951), 158.

36. Quoted from Robert J. Rayback, *Millard Fillmore* (Buffalo, N.Y., 1959), 314.

37. Orin Fowler, a Whig congressman from Massachusetts, Mar. 31, 1852, quoted in H. B. Cox, *War, Foreign Affairs*, 113.

38. For the quotations, see Rayback, *Fillmore*, 316; and James C. Dobbin, (Nov. 1853) in William L. Neumann, *America Encounters Japan* (Baltimore, 1963), 32.

39. Neumann, *America Encounters Japan*, 34.

40. Quoted in H. B. Cox, *War, Foreign Affairs*, 115.

41. See Chitoshi Yanaga, *Japan since Perry* (New York, 1949), 28.

42. Quoted in James G. Randall and Richard N. Current, *Lincoln the President* 4 vols. (New York, 1955), vol. 4, 76.

43. Richardson, ed., *Papers of Presidents*, vol. 4, 2733.

44. Ibid., vol. 4, 2768.

45. Quoted in Larry Gara, *The Presidency of Franklin Pierce* (Lawrence, Kans., 1991), 153.

46. The quotations come from ibid., 141; and Roy F. Nichols, *Franklin Pierce*, 2nd ed. (Philadelphia, 1958), 167.

47. Quoted from Elbert B. Smith, *The Presidency of James Buchanan* (Lawrence, Kans., 1975), 78.

48. For the quotations, see second annual message, Dec. 6, 1858, in Richardson, ed., *Papers of Presidents*, vol. 4, 3047; and E. B. Smith, *Presidency of Buchanan*, 189.

49. Address to the New Jersey General Assembly, Feb. 21, 1861, and speech in Independence Hall, Philadelphia, Feb. 22, in Lincoln, *Collected Works*, vol. 1, 237, 240–41.

50. Quoted from James G. Randall, "Lincoln in the Rôle of Dictator," *South Atlantic Quarterly*, vol. 28 (July 1929), 237 and with Richard N. Current, *Lincoln the President*, 4 vols. (New York, 1945–1955) vol. 4, 373.

51. The statistics come from James M. McPherson, *Abraham Lincoln and the Second American Revolution* (New York, 1990), 57.

52. Quoted from James M. McPherson, *Battle Cry of Freedom* (New York, 1988), 289. See also Larry Anhart, "'The God-Like Prince': John Locke, Executive Prerogative, and the American Presidency," *Presidential Studies Quarterly* 9 (spring 1979): 127.

53. Message to Congress, July 4, 1861, in Lincoln, *Collected Works*, vol. 4, 429, 430.

54. Quoted from Randall, "Lincoln in Rôle of Dictator," 237 and Edward Keynes, *Undeclared War* (University Park, Penn., 1982), 108.

55. To James C. Conkling, Washington, D.C., Aug. 26, 1863, in Lincoln, *Collected Works*, vol. 6, 208.

56. See comments in James G. Randall, *Constitutional Problems under Lincoln*, Rev. ed. (Urbana, Ill., 1951), 183.

57. Clinton Rossiter and Richard P. Longaker, *The Supreme Court and the Commander in Chief*, Expanded ed. (Ithaca, N.Y., 1976), 39.

58. Bruce Catton, *Reflections on the Civil War* (New York, 1982), 31, 33.

59. Quoted from Albert Castel, *The Presidency of Andrew Johnson* (Lawrence, Kans., 1979), 41.

60. First annual message, Dec. 4, 1865, and Johnson to Napoleon III, Washington, D.C., Jan. 25, 1866, in Andrew Johnson, *The Papers of Andrew Johnson*, ed. Leroy P. Graf and Ralph W. Haskins, 13 vols. (Knoxville, Tenn., 1967–95), vol. 9, 482 and 641.

61. The quotations come from Alfred J. Hanna and Kathryn A. Hanna, *Napoleon III and Mexico* (Chapel Hill, N.C., 1971), 267; and James E. Sefton, *Andrew Johnson and the Uses of Constitutional Power* (Boston, 1980), 158.

62. Quoted in William S. McFeely, *Grant* (New York, 1981), 179.

63. Quoted in Leonard D. White, *The Republican Era: 1869–1901* (New York, 1958), 23–24.

64. Quoted in Allan Nevins, *Hamilton Fish*, rev. ed., 2 vols (New York, 1957), vol. 1, 271.

65. For the quotations, see Grant's Memorandum (1869–70) in Ulysses S. Grant, *The Papers of Ulysses S. Grant*, ed. John Y. Simon, 22 vols. (Carbondale, Ill., 1967–98), vol. 20, 75; and Sumner Welles, *Naboth's Vineyard*, 2 vols. (New York, 1928), vol. 1, 373.

66. Welles, *Naboth's Vineyard*, 383, 384.

67. To the Senate, May 31, 1870, in Grant, *Papers*, vol. 20, 154, 156.

68. See second annual message, Dec. 5, 1870, Richardson, ed., *Papers of Presidents*, vol. 6, 4053; Welles, *Naboth's Vineyard*, 397; and David H. Donald, *Charles Sumner and the Rights of Man* (New York, 1970), 498.

69. For the quotations, see Donald, *Sumner*, 513; and H. B. Cox, *War, Foreign Affairs*, 313.

70. Oliver P. Morton of Indiana quoted in Donald, *Sumner*, 514; and Grant quoted in William B. Hesseltine, *Ulysses S. Grant: Politician* (New York, 1935), 249.

NOTES TO CHAPTER 3

1. For the quotations, see Harry Barnard, *Rutherford B. Hayes and His America* (Indianapolis, 1954), 411; and Mar. 4, 1877, first annual message, Dec. 3, 1887, in Richardson, ed., *Papers of Presidents, vol. 9*, 4399, 4424–25.

2. Quoted in Ari Hoogenboom, *The Presidency of Rutherford B. Hayes* (Lawrence, Kans., 1988), 175.

3. L. D. White, *The Republican Era*, 25.

4. Quoted in Thomas C. Reeves, *Gentleman Boss: The Life of Chester Alan Arthur* (New York, 1975), 290.

5. For the quotations, see Allan Nevins, *Grover Cleveland* (New York, 1932), 4–5; March 4, 1885, in Davis N. Lott, ed., *The Presidents Speak* (New York, 1994), 174; and Richard E. Welch Jr., *The Presidencies of Grover Cleveland* (Lawrence, Kans., 1988), 159, 11.

6. The quotations come from Daniel H. Wicks, "Dress Rehearsal: United States Intervention in the Isthmus of Panama, 1885," *Pacific Historical Review* 49 (Nov. 1980), 596–98.

7. Message of Jan. 15, 1889, Richardson, ed., *Papers of Presidents*, vol. 8, 805.

8. Donald M. Dozer, "Benjamin Harrison and the Presidential Campaign of 1892," *American Historical Review* 54 (Oct. 1948): 52.

9. Quoted from Richard Gambino, *Vendetta* (Garden City, N.Y., 1977), 118.

10. For the quotations, see Albert T. Volwiler, "Harrison, Blaine, and American Foreign Policy, 1889–1893," *Proceedings of the American Philosophical Society* 79 (Nov. 15, 1938): 640 (Cecil Spring-Rice, Jan. 19, 1892), 645; and Homer E. Socolofsky and Allan B. Spetter, *The Presidency of Benjamin Harrison* (Lawrence, Kans., 1987), 148.

11. Jan. 25, 1892, Richardson, ed. *Papers of Presidents*, additional vol. (12), 5652, 5660.

12. Quoted from H. B. Cox, *War, Foreign Affairs* 273–74; and Joyce S. Goldberg, *The Baltimore Affair* (Notre Dame, Ind., 1986), 78.

13. Jan. 30, 1892, quoted in Allan B. Spetter, "Harrison and Blaine: Foreign Policy, 1889–1893," *Indiana Magazine of History* 65 (Sept. 1969): 224.

14. To Blaine, Oct. 14, 1891, Harrison papers, quoted in ibid., 226.

15. The quotations come from David Healy, *US Expansionism* (Madison, Wis., 1970), and Socolofsky and Spetter, *Harrison*, 205.

16. To Louis Ludlow, quoted in Ernest C. Bolt Jr., *Ballots before Bullets* (Charlottesville, Va., 1977), 154.

17. Quoted in Healy, *US Expansionism*, 102–3.

18. For the quotations, see Cleveland to Congress, Dec. 4, 1893, in Fred L. Israel, ed., *The State of the Union Messages of the Presidents, 1790–1966*, 3 vols. (New York, 1966), vol. 2, 17432; and to Senator William F. Vilas, Washington, D.C., May 29, 1894, in Grover Cleveland, *Letters of Grover Cleveland 1850–1908*, ed. Allan Nevins (Boston, 1933), 353.

19. Quoted in Cleveland, *Letters*, 634–35.

20. For the quotations, see special message to Congress, Dec. 17, 1895, in Richardson, ed., *Papers of Presidents*, additional vol. (12), 6090; and Cleveland to Thomas F. Bayard, Washington, D.C., Dec. 29, 1895, in Cleveland, *Letters*, 419.

21. See Dexter Perkins, *A History of the Monroe Doctrine*, rev. ed. (Boston, 1955), 180.

22. See Walter LaFeber, *The New Empire* (Ithaca, N.Y., 1963), 270, 278–281; Nelson M. Blake, "Background of Cleveland's Venezuelan Policy," *American Historical Review* 47 (Jan. 1942): 275–76; and Robert McElroy, *Grover Cleveland*, 2 vols. (New York, 1923), vol. 2, 196.

23. To Olney, July 16, 1896, quoted in Ernest R. May, *Imperial Democracy* (New York, 1961), 91.

24. Quoted in McElroy, *Cleveland*, vol. 2, 250.

25. Geoffrey Blodgett, "The Political Leadership of Grover Cleveland," *South Atlantic Quarterly* 82 (Sept. 1983): 291, 293.

26. Lott, ed., *Presidents Speak*, 204.

27. Quoted in H. Wayne Morgan, *William McKinley and His America* (Syracuse, N.Y., 1963), 356.

28. For the quotations, see McKinley to Joe Cannon, Mar. 6, 1898, in LaFeber, *New Empire*, 349; and Kristin L. Hoganson, *Fighting for American Manhood* (New Haven, 1998), 90. The Roosevelt remark is quoted in Walter Millis, *The Martial Spirit* (New York, 1965), 130.

29. Quoted in H. W. Morgan, *McKinley*, 373.

30. April 11, 1898, Richardson, ed., *Papers of Presidents*, additional vol. (13), 6289, 6292.

31. April 12, 1898, quoted in Paul S. Holbo, "Presidential Leadership in Foreign Affairs: William McKinley and the Turpie-Foraker Amendment," *American Historical Review* 72 (July 1967): 1325.

32. For the quotations, see John Coit Spooner to C. W. Porter, May 2, 1898, Spooner papers, cited in Fisher, *Presidential War Power*, 43; and Millis, *Martial Spirit*, 317.

33. Quoted from Lewis L. Gould, *The Presidency of William McKinley* (Lawrence, Kans., 1980), 60, 88; and Margaret Leech, *In the Days of McKinley* (New York, 1959), 234.

34. The quotations come from E. R. May, *Imperial Democracy*, 159; and David F. Trask, *The War with Spain in 1898* (New York, 1981), 56.

35. McKinley to his former private secretary, autumn 1900, quoted in Gerald F. Linderman, *The Mirror of War: American Society and the Spanish-American War* (Ann Arbor, Mich., 1974), 35.

36. Joseph A. Fry, "William McKinley and the Coming of the Spanish-American War: A Study of the Besmirching and Redemption of an Historical Image," *Diplomatic History* 3 (winter 1979): 77.

37. Quoted in H. Wayne Morgan, *America's Road to Empire* (New York, 1965), 295.

38. Baltimore *Sun* quoted in LaFeber, *New Empire*, 364.

39. For the quotations, see Edward Atkinson to McKinley, Aug. 25, 1898, in Robert L. Beisner, *Twelve against Empire* (New York, 1971), 95; Stuart C. Miller, *"Benevolent Assimilation": The American Conquest of the Philippines, 1899–1903* (New Haven, Conn., 1982), 23; and Elihu Root, *The Military and Colonial Policy of the United States* (Cambridge, Mass., 1916), 37.

40. Quoted in H. B. Cox, *War, Foreign Affairs*, 323; and Gould, *Presidency of McKinley*, 101.

41. The quotations come from Gould, *Presidency of McKinley*, 187, 184.

42. For the quotations, see San Francisco *Examiner*, editorial, July 17, 1900, cited in Ian Mugridge, *The View from Xanadu* (Montréal 1995), 55; Gould, *Presidency of McKinley*, 221–22; and Theodore Roosevelt, May 1, 1901, in Howard K. Beale, *Theodore Roosevelt and the Rise of America to World Power* (Baltimore, 1956), 189.

43. Thomas A. Bailey, "Was the Presidential Election of 1900 a Mandate on Imperialism?" in Bailey, *Essays Diplomatic and Undiplomatic*, ed. Alexander DeConde and Armin Rappaport (New York, 1969), 151.

44. For the quotations, see Beale, *Roosevelt and World Power*, 37; and William H. Harbaugh, *Power and Responsibility* (New York, 1961), 21, 91.

45. Annual message to Congress, Dec. 3, 1901, and Dec. 2, 1902, in Theodore Roose-

velt, *The Works of Theodore Roosevelt*, ed. Herman Hagedorn, 20 vols. (New York, 1926), vol. 15, 111–12, 115; and Roosevelt to Charles W. Eliot, Apr. 4, 1904, in Theodore Roosevelt, *The Letters of Theodore Roosevelt*, ed. Elting E. Morison, 8 vols. (Cambridge, Mass., 1951–54), vol. 4, 70.

46. Speech, Arlington, Va., May 30, 1902, Theodore Roosevelt, *Presidential Addresses and State Papers*, 2 vols. (New York, 1904), I, 59.

47. Charles J. Bonaparte to Adam G. C. de Moltke-Hitfeldt, Nov. 6, 1902, quoted in Beale, *Roosevelt and World Power*, 17; and second annual message, Dec. 2, 1902, in T. Roosevelt, *Works*, vol. 15, 151, 155.

48. The statistics come from Richard H. Collin, *Theodore Roosevelt, Culture, Diplomacy, and Expansion* (Baton Rouge, La., 1985), 146.

49. To Albert Shaw, Oct. 7, 1903, in T. Roosevelt, *Letters*, vol. 3, 626.

50. To Shaw, Oct. 10, 1903, ibid., 628.

51. Jan. 18, 1904, quoted in Richard L. Lael, *Arrogant Diplomacy* (Wilmington, Del., 1987), 33.

52. For the quotations, see Richard H. Collin, "Symbiosis versus Hegemony: New Directions in the Foreign Relations Historiography of Theodore Roosevelt and William Howard Taft," *Diplomatic History* 19 (summer 1995): 477; and address of Mar. 23, 1911, original draft in the Theodore Roosevelt Papers cited in James F. Vivian, "The 'Taking' of the Panama Canal Zone: Myth and Reality," ibid., vol. 4 (winter 1980), 99.

53. To William Bayard Hale, Feb. 26, 1903, in T. Roosevelt, *Letters*, vol. 4, 740.

54. Fourth annual message, Dec. 6, 1904, in T. Roosevelt, *Works*, vol. 15, 257. For an earlier version, see Roosevelt to Elihu Root, May, 20, 1904, in T. Roosevelt, *Letters*, vol. 6, 801.

55. Henry M. Teller of Colorado, quoted in Lewis L. Gould, The *Presidency of Theodore Roosevelt* (Lawrence, Kans., 1991), 177.

56. The quotations, to George Trevelyan, Sept. 9, and Whitelaw Reid, Sept. 13, 1906, come from H. W. Brands Jr., *TR* (New York, 1997), 569 and 570.

57. To W. H. Taft, Sept. 13, 1906, in ibid., 573.

58. To Cecil Spring-Rice, July 24, 1905, in T. Roosevelt, *Letters*, vol. 4, 1284.

59. To Hugo Münsterberg, New York, Feb. 8, 1916, ibid., vol. 8, 1018.

60. Roosevelt to George Otto Trevelyan, Washington, June 19, 1908, ibid., vol. 6, 1086–87.

61. To Henry White, Washington, D.C., Jan. 28, 1909, ibid., 1498.

62. *Autobiography*, 1913, printed in T. Roosevelt, *Works*,, vol. 20, 347.

63. William A. Williams, *Empire As a Way of Life* (New York, 1980), 130.

64. Quoted in Judith I. Anderson, *William Howard Taft* (New York, 1981), 26.

65. March 4, 1909, Lott, ed., *Presidents Speak*, 222, 223.

66. Quoted in Walter V. Scholes and Marie V. Scholes, *The Foreign Policies of the Taft Administration* (Columbia, Mo., 1970), 56.

67. To General Leonard Wood, Mar. 12, 1911, quoted in Donald F. Anderson, *William Howard Taft: A Conservative's Conception of the Presidency* (Ithaca, N.Y., 1973), 267.

68. To F. M. Dearing, Feb. 26, 1912, quoted in P. Edward Haley, *Revolution and Intervention: The Diplomacy of Taft and Wilson with Mexico, 1910–1917* (Cambridge, Mass., 1970), 40.

69. D. F. Anderson, *Taft*, 272–73.

70. Aug. 14, 1912, Root, *Military and Colonial Policy*, 157–58.

71. William Howard Taft, *Our Chief Magistrate and His Powers* (New York, 1925), 139–40.

NOTES TO CHAPTER 4

1. Quoted from Woodrow Wilson, *Congressional Government* (Cleveland, 1956), 214, 52; and Walter Lippmann in the Introduction, 12.

2. Woodrow Wilson, *Constitutional Government in the United States* (New York, 1908), 68, 70, 77, 79.

3. For the quotations, see Alexander L. George and Juliette L. George, *Woodrow Wilson and Colonel House* (New York, 1956), 120; and Arthur Walworth, *Woodrow Wilson*, 3d. ed., 2 vols. (1978), vol. 1, 26.

4. To E. G. Conklin, quoted in Ray Stannard Baker, *Woodrow Wilson: Life and Letters*, 8 vols. (Garden City, N.Y., 1927–39), vol. 4, 55.

5. Reported conversation with William Tyrell, a British official, Nov. 13, 1913, in Harley Notter, *The Origins of the Foreign Policy of Woodrow Wilson* (Baltimore, 1937), 274.

6. For the quotations, May 22, 1913, and Edward M. House, diary entry, Oct. 30, 1913, see Arthur S. Link, *Woodrow Wilson and the Progressive Era, 1910–1917* (New York, 1954), 109; and Arthur S. Link, *Wilson: The New Freedom* (Princeton, N.J., 1956), 379.

7. For the quotations, see Mark T. Gilderhus, *Diplomacy and Revolution* (Tucson, Ariz., 1977), 10; Wilson to Congress, April 20, 1914, Woodrow Wilson, *The Papers of Woodrow Wilson*, ed. Arthur S. Link, 69 vols. (Princeton, N.J., 1966–94), vol. 39, 473–74; and James R. Mann, in Fisher, *Presidential War Power*, 50.

8. Robert E. Quirk, *An Affair of Honor* (Lexington, Ky., 1962), 76.

9. For the quotations, see Felix Frankfurter, *Felix Frankfurter Reminisces*, ed. Harlan B. Phillips (New York, 1960), 60; Taft to Gus J. Karger, July 22, 1913, in D. F. Anderson, *Taft*, 275; and Wilson, May 11, 1914, in W. Wilson, *Papers*, vol. 30, 14.

10. The quotations come from Link, *Wilson and Progressive Era*, 124.

11. "Remarks to Mexican Editors," June 7, 1918, Link, ed., in W. Wilson, *Papers*, vol. 48, 255.

12. To Lansing, Aug. 4, 1915, quoted in Arthur S. Link, *Wilson: The Struggle for Neutrality, 1914–1915* (Princeton, N.J., 1960), 536.

13. Quoted from Bruce J. Calder, *The Impact of Intervention: The Dominican Republic during the U.S. Occupation of 1916–1924* (Austin, Tex., 1984), xii, 21–22.

14. Joseph P. Tumulty, *Woodrow Wilson as I Knew Him* (Garden City, N.Y., 1921), 157–58. Italics in original.

15. Press statement and release, Mar. 10, 1916, in W. Wilson, *Papers*, vol. 36, 284, 286.

16. San Francisco *Examiner*, editorial, Apr. 15, 1916, quoted in Mugridge, *View from Xanadu*, 135.

17. Remarks to New York Press Club, June 30, 1916, in W. Wilson, *Papers*, vol. 37, 334.

18. For the quotations, see Appeal to the American People, Aug. 18, 1914, ibid., vol. 30, 294; and Walter Walworth, *Woodrow Wilson*, 3d. ed., 2 vols. (New York, 1978), vol. 1, 22.

19. To James W. Gerard, Feb. 10, 1915, in W. Wilson, *Papers*, vol. 32, 209.

20. To Wilson, June 4, 1915, quoted in ibid., 417.

21. Draft note to Lansing, July 21, 1915, ibid., 548.

22. The first quotation comes from Edward S. Corwin, *Presidential Power and the Constitution* (Ithaca, N.Y., 1976), 42; and the second, Oct. 22, 1916, from Arthur S. Link, *Wilson: Campaigns for Progressivism and Peace, 1916–1917* (Princeton, N.J., 1965), 120; and on Oct. 31, 1916, from Harvey A. DeWeerd, *President Wilson Fights His War* (New York, 1968), 21.

23. Quoted in Link, *Wilson: Progressivism and Peace*, 162.

24. Address to joint session of Congress, Feb. 26, 1917, W. Wilson, *Papers*, vol. 41, 284–85.

25. Second inaugural address, Mar. 5, 1917, ibid., 333, and MacAdoo, quoted in entry of Mar. 10, 1917, E. David Cronon, ed., *The Cabinet Diaries of Josephus Daniels, 1913–1921* (Lincoln, Nebr., 1963), 111.

26. To joint session of Congress, Apr. 2, 1917, W. Wilson, *Papers*, vol. 41, 521.

27. Quoted from Link, *Wilson: Progressivism and Peace*, 428.

28. Quoted from ibid., viii.

29. Quoted from DeWeerd, *Wilson Fights*, 8. See also Daniel D. Stid, *The President as Statesman* (Lawrence, Kans., 1998), 127.

30. Quoted in Warren W. Hassler Jr., *The President as Commander in Chief* (Menlo Park, Calif., 1971), 98.

31. William Phillips, Dec. 31, 1917, quoted in David S. Foglesong, *America's Secret War against Bolshevism* (Chapel Hill, N.C., 1995), 3 and Felix Cole, vice consul at Archangel, June 1, 1918, quoted in George F. Kennan, *Soviet-American Relations, 1917–1920* 2 vols., (Princeton, N.J., 1956–1958), 364.

32. See Walworth, *Wilson*, vol. 2, 171n; an aide-memoire, July 17, 1918, written by Wilson but issued under the signature of Robert Lansing, John W. Long, "American Intervention in Russia: The Northern Expedition, 1918–19," *Diplomatic History* 6 (winter 1982): 56; and David W. McFadden, *Alternative Paths* (New York, 1993), 166.

33. See Robert H. Ferrell, *Woodrow Wilson and World War I, 1917–1921* (New York, 1985), 147, 270–71, n. 38; Betty Miller Unterberger, "Wilson vs. the Bolsheviks," *Diplomatic History* 21 (winter 1997): 127–31; Unterberger, *America's Siberian Expedition, 1918–1920* (Durham, N.C., 1956), 231–2; Unterberger, ed., *American Intervention in the Russian Civil War* (Lexington, Mass., 1969), vi; and William A. Williams, "American Intervention in Russia, 1917–1920," *Studies on the Left* 4 (winter 1964): 55.

34. Radiogram to Edward M. House, Feb. 23, 1919, W. Wilson, *Papers*, vol. 55, 229–30.

35. The *Tribune*, Feb. 15, 1919, and Herbert Hoover to Wilson, Apr. 11, 1919, quoted in Foglesong, *America's Secret War*, 228, 235.

36. Quoted from Kennan, *Decision to Intervene*, 404.

37. Suresnes cemetery, May 30, 1919, W. Wilson, *Papers*, vol. 59, 610.

38. Quoted from Corwin, *Presidential Power and the Constitution*, 53.

39. See Link, *Wilson and Progressive Era*, 34; Kendrick A. Clements, *The Presidency of Woodrow Wilson* (Lawrence, Kans., 1992), xii; and Christopher N. May, *In the Name of War* (Cambridge, Mass., 1989), vii, 25, 254.

40. John Bassett Moore, "The Control of the Foreign Relations of the United States," Apr. 1921, in *The Collected Papers of John Bassett Moore*, 7 vols. (New Haven, Conn., 1944), vol. 5, 196.

41. Quoted from Eugene P. Trani and David L. Wilson, *The Presidency of Warren G. Harding* (Lawrence, Kans., 1977), 22.

42. Robert K. Murray, *The Harding Era* (Minneapolis, 1969), 332, 28; and William Allen White, *The Autobiography of William Allen White*, (New York, 1946), 585.

43. March 4, 1921, Lott, ed., *Presidents Speak*, 244, 246.

44. Quoted from Kenneth J. Grieb, *The Latin American Policy of Warren G. Harding* (Fort Worth, Tex., 1976), 4, 13; Betty Glad, *Charles Evans Hughes and the Illusions of Innocence* (Urbana, Ill., 1966), 1; and Selig Adler, *The Isolationist Impulse* (New York, 1957), 130.

45. The quotations come from W. A. White, *Autobiography*, 616; and Glad, *Hughes*, 138.

46. The quotations come from Donald R. McCoy, *Calvin Coolidge* (New York,

1967), 320; and Calvin Coolidge, *The Autobiography of Calvin Coolidge* (New York, 1931), 196.

47. First annual message, Dec. 6, 1923, in Israel, ed., *Messages of Presidents,* vol. 3, 2642, 2655; and Aug. 14, 1924, quoted in Claude M. Fuess, *Calvin Coolidge* (Boston, 1940), 348.

48. See Donald R. McCoy, *Coolidge,* 417; and Coolidge, *Autobiography,* 199.

49. Inaugural, Mar. 4, 1925, Lott, ed., *Presidents Speak,* 256.

50. The statistics and the quotations are in Dorothy Borg, *American Policy and the Chinese Revolution, 1925–1928* (New York, 1947), 270–72, 276.

51. Fifth annual message, Dec. 6, 1927, Israel, ed., *Messages of Presidents,* vol. 3, 2726.

52. Quoted from L. Ethan Ellis, *Frank B. Kellogg and American Foreign Relations, 1925–1929* (New Brunswick, N.J., 1961), 70.

53. See Fuess, *Coolidge,* 415; and sixth annual message, Dec. 4, 1928, Israel, ed., *Messages of Presidents,* vol. 3, 2729.

54. The statistics come from Howard H. Quint and Robert H. Ferrell, eds., *Talkative President* (Amherst, Mass., 1964), 252.

55. Excerpt from an article of Apr. 27, 1931, quoted in Fuess, *Coolidge,* 417–18n.

56. Quoted from Coolidge, *Autobiography,* 235, 173.

57. Herbert Hoover, *The Memoirs of Herbert Hoover,* 3 vols. (New York, 1952), vol. 2, 104.

58. Parker Gilbert, quoted in Joseph Brandes, *Herbert Hoover and Economic Diplomacy* (Pittsburgh, 1962), 39.

59. Quoted in Richard Hofstadter, *The American Political Tradition* (New York, 1960), 297; Martin L. Fausold, *The Presidency of Herbert C. Hoover* (Lawrence, Kans., 1985), 18; and Hoover, *Memoirs,* vol. 2, 217.

60. For the quotations, see March 4, 1929, Washington, D.C., Herbert Hoover, *The State Papers and Other Public Writings of Herbert Hoover,* ed. William S. Myers, 2 vols. (Garden City, N.Y., 1934), vol. 1, 8; and Hoover, *Memoirs,* vol. 2, 330, 338, 333, 334.

61. Quoted in Alexander DeConde, *Herbert Hoover's Latin-American Policy* (Stanford, Calif., 1951), 18; and Apr. 13, 1929, Washington, D.C., Hoover, *State Papers,* vol. 1, 30.

62. Quoted in Fausold, *Presidency of Hoover,* 184.

63. DeConde, *Hoover's Latin-American Policy,* 48.

64. See D. Perkins, *History of Monroe Doctrine,* 343, 385 and Robert H. Ferrell, "Repudiation of a Repudiation," *Journal of American History* 51 (March 1965): 669, 673.

65. Quoted from Richard N. Current, "The Stimson Doctrine and the Hoover Doctrine," *American Historical Review* 59 (April 1954), 513; Hoover, *Memoirs,* vol. 2, 166; and Henry L. Stimson and McGeorge Bundy, *On Active Service in Peace and War* (New York, 1948), 245.

66. Quoted from Hoover, *Memoirs,* vol. 2, 370; and Stimson and Bundy, *On Active Service,* 262.

67. See Hoover, *Memoirs,* vol. 2, 375; and William R. Castle Jr. diary, entry of Nov. 18, 1929, quoting Hoover, cited in Richard N. Current, *Secretary Stimson* (New Brunswick, N.J., 1954), 109n.

68. Aug. 11, 1932, Washington, D.C., U.S. President, *Public Papers: Hoover, 1932–33* (Washington, D.C., 1977), 371. See also Carl Q. Christol, "Herbert Hoover: The League of Nations and the World Court," in Hatfield, ed., *Herbert Hoover Reassessed* (Washington, D.C., 1981), 338, 339.

69. Quoted in John Hoff Wilson, *Herbert Hoover: Forgotten Progressive* (Boston, 1975), 273.

70. Alexander DeConde, "Herbert Hoover and Foreign Policy: A Retrospective Assessment," in Hatfield, ed., *Hoover Reassessed,* 316.

71. Quoted from David Burner, *Herbert Hoover* (New York, 1979), 296.

NOTES TO CHAPTER 5

1. The quotations come from Ronald Steel, *Walter Lippmann and the American Century* (Boston, 1980), 300, (Feb. 1, 1933); William E. Leuchtenburg, *The FDR Years* (New York, 1995), 48 (Feb. 11, 1933); Frederick W. Marks III, *Wind over Sand* (Athens, Ga., 1988); 7; Frank Freidel, *Franklin D. Roosevelt,* 4 vols. (Boston, 1952–1973), vol. 4, 103; and Willard Range, *Franklin D. Roosevelt's World Order* (Athens, Ga., 1959), xii.

2. Quoted from Hugh G. Gallagher, *FDR's Splendid Deception* (New York, 1985), xiii, 211.

3. William L. Langer and S. Everett Gleason, *The Challenge to Isolation, 1937–1940* (New York, 1952), 2.

4. Inaugural address, March 4, 1933, Franklin D. Roosevelt, *The Public Papers and Addresses of Franklin D. Roosevelt,* ed. Samuel I. Rosenman, 13 vols. (New York, 1938–50), vol. 2, 4, 5.

5. Quoted in Bryce Wood, *The Making of the Good Neighbor Policy* (New York, 1961), 72, 73.

6. Press Conferences, Sept. 6 and 8, 1933, in Franklin D. Roosevelt, *Franklin D. Roosevelt and Foreign Affairs,* ed. Edgar B. Nixon, 3 vols. (Cambridge, Mass., 1969), vol. 1, 386, 390.

7. The quotations are in Joel F. Paschal, *Mr. Justice Sutherland: A Man against the State* (Princeton, N.J., 1951), 93, 223.

8. See Louis Henkin, *Foreign Affairs and the United States Constitution,* 2d ed. (New York, 1996), 20, 331–32 n.16.

9. Quoted from R. H. Jackson, *The Supreme Court in the American System of Government* (Cambridge, Mass., 1955), 62; Charles A. Lofgren, "United States v. Curtiss-Wright Export Corporation: An Historical Reassessment," *Yale Law Journal* 83 (Nov. 1973): 30; and Louis Henkin, *Constitutionalism, Democracy, and Foreign Affairs* (New York, 1990), 88.

10. For the quotations, see Robert A. Divine, *The Illusion of Neutrality* (Chicago, 1962), 116–17; and Robert Dallek, *Franklin D. Roosevelt and American Foreign Policy, 1932–1945* (New York, 1979), 108–10.

11. Nov. 11, 1935, quoted in Thomas H. Greer, *What Roosevelt Thought* (East Lansing, Mich., 1958), 175.

12. March 19, 1937, F. D. Roosevelt, *Papers and Addresses,* vol. 6, 125, 133.

13. For the quotations, see Rexford G. Tugwell, *The Enlargement of the Presidency* (Garden City, N. Y., 1960), 404; John P. Burke, *The Institutional Presidency* (Baltimore, 1992), 10; and Richard Polenberg, *Reorganizing Roosevelt's Government* (Cambridge, Mass, 1966), 149, 159.

14. Chicago, Oct. 5, 1937, F. D. Roosevelt, *Papers and Addresses,* vol. 6, 407–10.

15. To Endicott Peabody, Oct. 16, 1937, in Franklin D. Roosevelt, *The Roosevelt Letters,* ed. Elliott Roosevelt, 3 vols. (London, 1949), vol. 3, 220; and Samuel I. Rosenman, *Working with Roosevelt* (New York, 1952), 167.

16. The quotations come from Bolt, *Ballots before Bullets,* 153; and J. Chalmers Vinson, "Military Force and American Foreign Policy, 1919–1939," in *Isolation and Security,* ed. Alexander DeConde (Durham, N.C., 1957), 80–81.

17. See Roosevelt to William B. Bankhead, Jan. 6, 1938, F. D. Roosevelt, *Papers and Addresses,* vol. 7, 37; and for the second quotation, Frank Freidel, *Franklin D. Roosevelt: A Rendezvous with Destiny* (Boston, 1990), 289.

18. To James Roosevelt, Jan. 20, 1938, quoted in Freidel, *Rendezvous with Destiny*, 176.

19. Conference, Jan. 31, 1939, (Extra Confidential), quoted in Greer, *What Roosevelt Thought*, 182.

20. Press conf. no. 528, Mar. 7, 1939, F. D. Roosevelt, *Papers and Addresses*, vol. 8, 156–57.

21. The quotations come from Joseph P. Lash, *Roosevelt and Churchill, 1939–1941* (New York, 1976), 124; Robert E. Sherwood, *Roosevelt and Hopkins*, rev. ed. (New York, 1950), 170, 172; and Cordell Hull, *The Memoirs of Cordell Hull*, 2 vols. (New York, 1948), vol. 1, 858, 859.

22. See Churchill to Roosevelt, May 15, 1940, quoted in Philip Goodhart, *Fifty Ships That Saved the World* (New York, 1965), 4; and F.D.R. Memorandum, Aug. 21, 1940, in F. D. Roosevelt, *Letters*, vol. 3, 326.

23. The quotations come from Robert Shogan, *Hard Bargain* (New York, 1995), 218, 219, 234.

24. Press conf. no. 677, Sept. 3, 1940, F. D. Roosevelt, *Papers and Addresses*, vol. 9, 378.

25. For the quotations see James M. Burns, *Roosevelt: The Lion and the Fox* (New York, 1956), 441; Herbert W. Briggs, "Neglected Aspects of the Destroyer Deal," *American Journal of International Law* 34 (Oct. 1940), 587; and Corwin, *Total War*, 26.

26. For the quotations see Thomas A. Bailey and Paul B. Ryan, *Hitler vs. Roosevelt* (New York, 1979), 86; and Shogan, *Hard Bargain*, 271.

27. For the Willkie speeches, Oct. 22 and 28, 1940, see Charles A. Beard, *American Foreign Policy in the Making, 1932–1940* (New Haven, 1946), 306, 308; and for Roosevelt's, see address at Philadelphia, Oct. 23, 1940, at Boston, Oct. 30, 1940, in F. D. Roosevelt, *Papers and Addresses*, vol. 9, 494–95, 517; and the comment in Rosenman, *Working with Roosevelt*, 242.

28. Fireside Chat on National Security, Dec. 29, 1940, F. D. Roosevelt, *Papers and Addresses*, vol. 9 , 634, 638, 640.

29. For the quotations, see William L. Langer and S. Everett Gleason, *The Undeclared War, 1940–1941* (New York, 1953), xi.

30. The quotations come from James M. Burns, *Roosevelt: The Soldier of Freedom* (New York, 1970), 26; Corwin, *Total War*, 29; and Corwin and others, *The President*, 272.

31. The quotations come from Dallek, *Roosevelt and Foreign Policy*, 265.

32. Quoted in Langer and Gleason, *Undeclared War*, 646.

33. Quoted from Waldo Heinrichs, *Threshold of War* (New York, 1988), 159.

34. Fireside Chat, Sept. 11, 1941, F. D. Roosevelt, *Papers and Addresses*, vol. 10, 388, 390, 391.

35. Quoted in Freidel, *Rendezvous with Destiny*, 394; and Sherwood, *Roosevelt and Hopkins*, 382.

36. Nov. 4, 1941, quoted in Arthur B. Tourtellot, *The Presidents on the Presidency* (Garden City, N.Y., 1964), 65.

37. For the quotations, see Hull, *Memoirs*, vol. 2, 1080; Paul W. Schroeder, *The Axis Alliance and Japanese-American Relations, 1941* (Ithaca, N.Y., 1958), 87; intercept of Nov. 22, 1941, in Lester H. Brune, "Considerations of Force in Cordell Hull's Diplomacy," *Diplomatic History* 2 (fall 1978): 400; and Raymond A. Esthus, "President Roosevelt's Commitment to Britain to Intervene in a Pacific War," *Mississippi Valley Historical Review* 50 (June 1963): 35.

38. Quoted in Corwin, *Total War*, 32, 34.

39. Quoted from Robert A. Divine, *The Reluctant Belligerent* (New York, 1965), 158.

40. For the quotations, see Freidel, *Rendezvous with Destiny*, 486; and Bailey and Ryan, *Hitler vs. Roosevelt*, 266.

41. Hull, *Memoirs*, vol. 2, 1111; and J. M. Burns, *Soldier of Freedom*, 491.

42. May 15, 1942, quoted in Warren F. Kimball, *The Juggler* (Princeton, N.J., 1991), 7.

43. Message to Congress, Sept. 7, 1942, F. D. Roosevelt, *Papers and Addresses*, vol. 11, 364–65.

44. The quotations come from Dallek, *Roosevelt and Foreign Policy*, 442; Doris K. Goodwin, *No Ordinary Time* (New York, 1994), 524; and Rosenman, *Working with Roosevelt*, 438.

45. Radio address, Oct. 21, 1944, F. D. Roosevelt, *Papers and Addresses*, vol. 13, 350.

45. The quotations come from Charles A. Beard, *President Roosevelt and the Coming of the War, 1941* (New Haven, Conn., 1948), 590, 598; and Sherwood, *Roosevelt and Hopkins*, 931.

47. For the quotations see Alonzo L. Hamby, "Harry S. Truman: Insecurity and Responsibility," Fred I. Greenstein, ed., in *Leadership in the Modern Presidency* (Cambridge, Mass., 1988), 60; and Donald R. McCoy, *The Presidency of Harry S. Truman* (Lawrence, Kans., 1984), 3.

48. Quoted in David McCullough, *Truman* (New York, 1992), 355.

49. The quotations come from Alonzo L. Hamby, *Man of the People* (New York, 1995), 313; James D. Barber, *The Presidential Character*, 4th ed. (Englewood Cliffs, N.J., 1992), 327; and Robert J. Donovan, *Tumultuous Years* (New York, 1982), 14. Biographers differ over Truman's impulsiveness. Hamby, "Mind and Character of Truman," in Lacey, ed., *Truman Presidency*, regards him as "neither impulsive nor prone to act in spasms of anger," p. 40. In *Man of the People*, 486–87, however, Hamby describes him as "dangerously erratic," a man whose "anger and hostility" erupted "in the fashion of a geyser."

50. Robert H. Ferrell, *Harry S. Truman* (Columbia, Mo., 1994), 210.

51. Quoted in Robert J. Donovan, *Conflict and Crisis* (New York, 1977), 96; and Melvyn P. Leffler, *A Preponderance of Power* (Stanford, Calif., 1992), 38.

52. The quotations are in Gar Alperovitz, *The Decision to Use the Atomic Bomb* (New York, 1995), 3–4; and Richard F. Haynes, *The Awesome Power* (Baton Rouge, La., 1973), 46, 57.

53. Harry S. Truman, *Memoirs*, 2 vols. (Garden City, N.Y., 1955–56), vol. 1, 486.

54. To James F. Byrnes, Jan. 5, 1946, Harry S. Truman, *Off the Record*, ed. Robert H. Ferrell (New York, 1980), 80.

55. For the quotations, see Donald R. McCoy, *Truman Presidency*, 79; special message to Congress, Mar. 12, 1947, U.S. President, *Public Papers: Harry S. Truman, 1947* (Washington, D.C., 1963), 178–79; and Howard Jones, *"A New Kind of War"* (New York, 1989), 54, 235.

56. Quoted in Ferrell, *Truman*, 256.

57. The quotations come from Rhodri Jeffreys-Jones, *The CIA and American Democracy* (New Haven, 1989), 30; and Dean G. Acheson, *Present at the Creation* (New York, 1969), 161.

58. Quoted in Ferrell, *Truman*, 258.

59. For the quotations, see draft of an undelivered speech, Aug. 1948, in Donald R. McCoy, *Truman Presidency*, 150; diary entry, Sept. 13, 1948, in Ferrell, *Truman*, 258; and entry of Sept. 13, 1948, James Forrestal, *The Forrestal Diaries*, ed. Walter Millis (New York, 1951), 487.

60. From *Woods v. Miller* (1948), quoted in Schlesinger, *Imperial Presidency*, 141.

61. July 25, 1949, Arthur H. Vandenberg, *The Private Papers of Senator Vandenburg*, ed. Arthur H. Vandenberg Jr. and Joe Alex Morris (Boston, 1952), 503–4.

62. Quoted in Donovan, *Tumultuous Years,* 151, 156.

63. For Truman's outlook, see Clifford, *Counsel to the President,* 274; Barton J. Bernstein, "The Truman Administration and the Korean War," in Lacey, ed., *Truman Presidency,* 419; and James I. Matray, *The Reluctant Crusade* (Honolulu, 1985), 236. Kim, Jan. 1950, is quoted in William Stueck, *The Korean War* (Princeton, N.J., 1995), 31.

64. For the quotations, see statement, June 26, 1950, U.S. President, *Public Papers: Truman, 1950,* 491–92; Margaret Truman, *Harry S. Truman* (New York, 1973), 251; and Glenn D. Paige, *The Korean Decision* (New York, 1968), 124.

65. For the quotations, see Charles A. Lofgren, "Mr. Truman's War: A Debate and Its Aftermath," *Review of Politics* 31 (Apr. 1969), 225–26; Athan G. Theoharis, ed., *The Truman Presidency* (Stanfordville, N. Y., 1979), 96–97; and news conf., June 29, 1950, U.S. President, *Public Papers: Truman, 1950,* 504.

66. The quotations come from Wormuth and Firmage, *To Chain the Dog of War,* 150; and Ferrell, *Truman,* 324.

67. Acheson, *Present at the Creation,* 414; and Thomas T. Connally and Alfred Steinberg, *My Name Is Tom Connally* (New York, 1954), 346.

68. Quoted from U.S. Department of State, "Authority of the President to Repel Attack," *Department of State Bulletin* 23 (July 31, 1950): 173 and 177–78 for the list.

69. Quoted in Fisher, *Presidential War Power,* 88.

70. H. S. Truman, *Memoirs,* vol. 1, 234.

71. Chen Jian, *China's Road to the Korean War* (New York, 1994), 172.

72. News conf., Nov. 30, 1950, U.S. President, *Public Papers: Truman, 1950,* 727; and Dec. 9, 1950, H. S. Truman, *Off the Record,* 204.

73. Radio and television address, Dec. 15, 1950, and news conf., Jan. 8, 1951, U.S. President, *Public Papers: Truman, 1950,* 741 and *1951,* 7.

74. News conf., Jan. 11, 1951, ibid., *1951,* 19, 20.

75. Quoted in Schlesinger, *Imperial Presidency,* 138.

76. Diary entry, Apr. 16, 1950, H. S. Truman, *Off the Record,* 177; and H. S. Truman, *Memoirs,* vol. 2, 488–89.

77. The quotations come from Gregg Herken, *The Winning Weapon* (New York, 1980), 333; Roger Dingman, "Atomic Diplomacy during the Korean War," *International Security* 13 (winter, 1988–89): 72; and Aug. 4, 1951, Eben A. Ayers Diary, Harry S. Truman Library, cited in Donald R. McCoy, *Truman Presidency,* 273.

78. Diary entry, May 18, 1952, H. S. Truman, *Off the Record,* 251.

79. H. S. Truman, *Memoirs,* vol. 2, 473, 475; and Arnold Wolfers, "The President and the Law," *Political Science Quarterly* 67 (Sept. 1952): 333.

80. *Youngstown Sheet and Tube Company et al. v. Charles Sawyer,* June 2, 1952, quoted in Theoharis, ed., *Truman Presidency,* 118. See also John P. Roche, "Executive Power and Domestic Emergency: The Quest for Prerogative," *Western Political Quarterly* 5 (Dec. 1952): 618.

81. Memo for the President of the United States, n.d. [Nov. 1952] quoted in Donald R. McCoy, *Truman Presidency,* 306.

82. The president's farewell address to the American people, Jan. 15, 1953, U.S. President, *Public Papers: Truman, 1952–53,* 1197.

83. The quotations come from H. S. Truman, *Memoirs,* vol. 2, 473; and McCullough, *Truman,* 584, 585.

NOTES TO CHAPTER 6

1. Dwight D. Eisenhower, *The White House Years: Mandate for Change, 1953–1956* (Garden City, N.Y., 1963), 28.

2. Quoted in A. Merriman Smith, *Meet Mr. Eisenhower* (New York, 1955), ix; and Oct. 29, 1951, Dwight D. Eisenhower, *The Eisenhower Diaries*, ed. Robert H. Ferrell (New York, 1981), 204.

3. Quoted from Eisenhower, *Mandate for Change*, 13, 14.

4. Quoted in Emmet J. Hughes, *The Ordeal of Power* (New York, 1963), 26.

5. Stephen E. Ambrose, *Eisenhower: Soldier and President* (New York, 1990), 285.

6. Jan. 20, 1953, U.S. President, *Public Papers: Dwight D. Eisenhower, 1953* (Washington, D.C., 1960), 5.

7. Quoted from David B. Capitanchik, *The Eisenhower Presidency and American Foreign Policy* (London, 1969), 33; Neustadt, *Presidential Power*, 139; and Barber, *Presidential Character*, 182.

8. Quoted in Rosemary Foot, *The Wrong War* (Ithaca, N.Y., 1985), 219.

9. Quoted from memorandums of National Security Council meetings, Feb. 11, Mar. 31, and May 6, 1953, U.S. Department of State, *Foreign Relations of the United States, 1952–1954*, vol. 15, part I, "Korea" (Washington, D.C., 1984), 770, 826–27, 977. See also Barton J. Bernstein, "New Light on the Korean War," *International History Review* 3 (Apr. 1981): 274; Edward C. Keefer, "President Dwight D. Eisenhower and the End of the Korean War," *Diplomatic History* 10 (summer 1986): 279; and Eisenhower, *Mandate for Change*, 181.

10. Rosemary Foot, "Nuclear Coercion and the Ending of the Korean Conflict," *International Security* 13 (winter 1988–89): 112; and NSC 154/1, July 7, 1953, cited in Foot, *Wrong War*, 231.

11. Version of Sept. 14, 1951, printed in Duane A. Tananbaum, *The Bricker Amendment Controversy* (Ithaca, N.Y., 1988), 221.

12. The first quotation, Mar. 27, 1953, is in ibid., 72; and the second comes from Hughes, *Ordeal of Power*, 144.

13. The first quotation, Jan. 14, 1954, is in James C. Hagerty, *The Diary of James C. Hagerty*, ed. Robert H. Ferrell (Bloomington, Ind., 1983), 7; the second, to William Knowland, Jan. 25, 1954, is in Robert J. Donovan, *Eisenhower* (New York, 1956), 239; and the third comes from Eisenhower, *Mandate for Change*, 281.

14. The first quotation, National Security Council minutes, Jan. 8, 1954, is in John P. Burke and Fred I. Greenstein, *How Presidents Test Reality* (New York, 1989), 32; and the second, Feb. 8, 1954, is in Hagerty, *Diary*, 15.

15. The first quotation, Mar. 24, 1954, is in Richard H. Immerman, "Between the Unattainable and the Unacceptable: Eisenhower and Dienbienphu," in Melanson and Mayers, eds., *Reevaluating Eisenhower* (Urbana, Ill., 1987), 130; and the second is in Eisenhower, *Mandate for Change*, 345.

16. The quotation and comments come from press confs., Mar. 10, Apr. 7, 1954, U.S. President, *Public Papers: Eisenhower, 1954*, 306, 387–88; David L. Anderson, *Trapped by Success* (New York, 1991), 31; and National Security Council minutes, Apr. 6, 1954, in Melanie Billings-Yun, *Decision against War* (New York, 1988), 111.

17. Apr. 16, 1954, quoted in Norman A. Graebner, *The New Isolationism* (New York, 1956), 164.

18. Apr. 29, 1954, quoted in Immerman, "Eisenhower and Dienbienphu," 143.

19. Quoted from Billings-Yun, *Decision against War*, 179–80; and Burke and Greenstein, *How Presidents Test Reality*, 113.

20. Quoted from John Prados, *Presidents' Secret Wars* (New York, 1986), 108; and conference with William Knowland, Dec. 23, 1954, in Stephen E. Ambrose, *Eisenhower: The President* (New York, 1984), 226.

21. For the quotations, see excerpts from newly declassified CIA documents, Los Angeles *Times*, May 24, 1997, A11; Eisenhower, Jan. 1954, in Charles J. Pach Jr. and

Elmo Richardson, *The Presidency of Dwight D. Eisenhower*, rev. ed. (Lawrence, Kans., 1991), 90; and Dulles and Eisenhower in Richard H. Immerman, *The CIA in Guatemala* (Austin, Tex., 1982), 157.

22. Special Study Group on the Covert Activities of the Central Intelligence Agency, Sept. 30, 1954, 6–7, (partially declassified, 1976) quoted in Fisher, *Presidential War Power*, 169.

23. For the quotations, see news conf., Aug. 17, 1954, U.S. President, *Public Papers: Eisenhower, 1954*, 200; Eisenhower, *Mandate for Change*, 464; and Sherman Adams, *First-Hand Report* (London, 1962), 108.

24. Quoted in Ambrose, *Eisenhower: President*, 238–39.

25. Quoted in James R. Shepley, "How Dulles Averted War," *Life*, Jan. 16, 1956, 70–72.

26. For the quotations, see Ambrose, *Eisenhower: President*, 245; Robert A. Divine, *Eisenhower and the Cold War* (New York, 1981), 65; Gordon H. Chang, "To the Nuclear Brink: Eisenhower, Dulles, and the Quemoy-Matsu Crisis," *International Security* 12 (spring 1988): 96; H. W. Brands Jr., "Testing Massive Retaliation: Credibility and Crisis Management in the Taiwan Strait," ibid., 148; and Pach and Richardson, *Eisenhower Presidency*, 104.

27. For the quotations, see news conf., Mar. 23, 1955, U.S. President, *Public Papers: Eisenhower, 1955*, 351; and Richard M. Nixon, *Six Crises* (Garden City, N.Y., 1962), 145.

28. See Jan. 10, 1956, Eisenhower, *Diaries*, 306; and Alexander DeConde, "Dwight D. Eisenhower: Reluctant Use of Power" in Robinson and others, *Powers of the President* (San Francisco, 1966), 94.

29. The quotations come from Diane B. Kunz, *The Economic Diplomacy of the Suez Crisis* (Chapel Hill, N.C., 1991), 65; news conf., Apr. 4, 1956, U.S. President, *Public Papers: Eisenhower, 1956*, 380; and memorandum of National Security Council meeting, Aug. 30, 1956, cited in Phillip G. Henderson, *Managing the Presidency* (Boulder, Colo., 1988), 100.

30. Quoted from Stephen E. Ambrose, *Ike's Spies* (Garden City, N.Y., 1981), 239.

31. See radio and television broadcast, Oct. 31, 1956, U.S. President, *Public Papers: Eisenhower, 1956*, 1072; and Nov. 2, 1956, Dwight D. Eisenhower, *The White House Years: Waging Peace* (Garden City, N.Y., 1965), 85.

32. T. R. B. in the *New Republic*, Feb. 18, 1957, 2.

33. For the quotations, see U.S. President, *Public Papers: Eisenhower, 1957*, Jan. 5, 1957, 15; and Apr. 1, 1953, Eisenhower, *Diaries*, 233.

34. Hubert H. Humphrey, quoted in Pach and Richardson, *Eisenhower Presidency*, 161.

35. June 15, 1958, quoted in Douglas Little, "His Finest Hour? Eisenhower, Lebanon, and the 1958 Middle East Crisis," *Diplomatic History* 20 (winter 1996): 41.

36. The quotations, July 14 and 15, 1958, come from ibid., 44 and U.S. President, *Public Papers: Eisenhower, 1958*, 549, 552.

37. Quoted from Robert Murphy, *Diplomat among Warriors* (Garden City, N.Y., 1964), 398.

38. Quoted from ibid., 28.

39. Little, "Finest Hour," 27.

40. Press conf., Apr. 30, 1958, U.S. President, *Public Papers: Eisenhower, 1958*,358.

41. The quotations come from Eisenhower, *Waging Peace*, 294–95; and (to J. F. Dulles, Sept. 23, 1958) Ambrose, *Eisenhower: President*, 484.

42. The quotations are in Thomas G. Paterson, *Contesting Castro* (New York, 1994), 258; and Prados, *Secret Wars*, 177.

43. Eisenhower to the author, Gettysburg, Penn., Aug. 1, 1967, letter in possession of the author.

44. The quotations come from Nixon, *Six Crises*, 159; Burke and Greenstein, *How Presidents Test Reality*, 11; Melanson and Mayers, eds., *Reevaluating Eisenhower*, 4; and Fred I. Greenstein, *The Hidden-Hand Presidency* (New York, 1982), 58.

45. For the quotations, see news conf., Aug. 12, 1959, U.S. President, *Public Papers: Eisenhower, 1959*, 179; H. W. Brands Jr., *Cold Warriors* (New York, 1988), ix–x; Brands, "The Age of Vulnerability: Eisenhower and the National Insecurity State," *American Historical Review* 94 (Oct. 1989): 986; Eisenhower, *Waging Peace*, 633; and Eisenhower, "Some Thoughts on the Presidency," *Reader's Digest*, Nov. 1968, 55.

46. The first quotation, to Everett E. Hazlett, Aug. 20, 1956, comes from Dwight D. Eisenhower, *Ike's Letters to a Friend, 1941–1958*, ed. Robert Griffith (Lawrence, Kans., 1984), 169; and the second (Nov. 23, 1961) from Tourtellot, *Presidents on the Presidency*, 343.

47. For the quotations, see Peter Lyon, *Eisenhower: Portrait of the Hero* (Boston, 1974), 851; and D. L. Anderson, *Trapped by Success*, 205.

48. Thomas E. Cronin, "John F. Kennedy: President and Politician," in Harper and Krieg, eds., *John F. Kennedy* (New York, 1988), 5.

49. Speech, Jan. 14, 1960, reprinted in Robert S. Hirschfield, ed., *The Power of the Presidency*, 2d ed. (Chicago, 1973), 129, 130.

50. The quotations come from Hugh Sidey, *John F. Kennedy, President* (New York, 1963), 11; and William H. Chafe, *The Unfinished Journey*, 3d ed. (New York, 1995), 180.

51. Quoted in Richard Reeves, *President Kennedy* (New York, 1993), 24.

52. Bowles is quoted in Thomas G. Paterson, "John F. Kennedy's Quest for Victory and Global Crisis," in Paterson, ed., *Kennedy's Quest for Victory* (New York, 1989), 19; and the inaugural, Jan. 20, 1961, is in U.S. President, *Public Papers: John F. Kennedy, 1961* (Washington, D.C., 1962), 1–3.

53. For the quotations, see Arthur M. Schlesinger Jr., *A Thousand Days* (New York, 1967), 394–95; Kent M. Beck, "Necessary Lies, Hidden Truths: Cuba in the 1960 Campaign," *Diplomatic History* 8 (winter 1984): 45; and R. Reeves, *President Kennedy*, 32.

54. Memorandum of Mar. 30, 1961, quoted in Schlesinger, *Thousand Days*, 236.

55. Apr. 12, 1961, quoted in Theodore C. Sorenson, *Kennedy* (New York, 1965), 298.

56. Quoted in Schlesinger, *Thousand Days*, 270; and Richard M. Nixon, *RN: The Memoirs of Richard Nixon* (New York, 1978), 234–35.

57. Quoted from Harris Wofford, *Of Kennedys and Kings* (New York, 1980), 4.

58. See Robert D. Dean, "Masculinity as Ideology: John F. Kennedy and the Domestic Politics of Foreign Policy," *Diplomatic History* 22 (winter 1998): 29–30.

59. For the quotations, see Nancy G. Clinch, *The Kennedy Neurosis* (New York, 1973), 199; Richard J. Walton, *Cold War and Counterrevolution* (Baltimore, 1973), 53; and David Detzer, *The Brink* (New York, 1979), 32.

60. Quoted in Thomas C. Reeves, *A Question of Character* (New York, 1991), 294.

61. The first quotation comes from Schlesinger, *Thousand Days*, 364; and the second, radio and television report, June 6, 1961, from U.S. President, *Public Papers: Kennedy, 1961*, 444.

62. Quoted in James G. Hershberg, "Before The 'Missiles of October': Did Kennedy Plan a Military Strike against Cuba?" *Diplomatic History* 14 (spring 1990): 173.

63. For the quotations, see ibid., 192; and news conf., Sept. 13, 1962, U.S. President, *Public Papers: Kennedy, 1962*, 674.

64. For the quotations, see Abram Chayes, *The Cuban Missile Crisis* (New York, 1974), 11; and Fisher, *Presidential War Power*, 112.

65. For the Kennedy quotation, see R. Reeves, *President Kennedy*, 370; and for the

Bundy quotation, Oct. 16, 1962, see Ernest R. May and Philip D. Zelikow, eds., *The Kennedy Tapes* (Cambridge, Mass., 1997), 91.

66. Robert S. McNamara, in Laurence Chang and Peter Kornbluh, eds., *The Cuban Missile Crisis, 1962* (New York, 1962), xii.

67. Oct. 22, 1962, May and Zekilow, eds., *Kennedy Tapes*, 275.

68. Address to the American people, Oct. 22, 1962, U.S. President, *Public Papers: Kennedy, 1962*, 806, 807, 808.

69. Oct. 24, 1962, quoted in Robert F. Kennedy, *Thirteen Days* (New York, 1969), 67.

70. Khrushchev to Kennedy, Oct. 26, 1962, in Chang and Kornbluh, eds., *Cuban Missile Crisis*, 185–86; and Kennedy quoted in R. Reeves, *President Kennedy*, 411.

71. Quoted in Aleksandr Fursenko and Timothy Naftali, *"One Hell of a Gamble"* (New York, 1997), 284.

72. Quoted in Roger Hilsman, *To Move a Nation* (Garden City, N.Y., 1967), 219.

73. For these assessments, see Harold Macmillan in ibid., 7; Michael P. Riccards, "The Dangerous Legacy: John F. Kennedy and the Cuban Missile Crisis," in Harper and Krieg, eds., *Kennedy*, 82; Carl M. Brauer, "John F. Kennedy: The Endurance of Inspirational Leadership," in Greenstein, ed., *Leadership in the Modern Presidency*, 132; Detzer, *The Brink*, 257; Sidey, *Kennedy, President*, 348; and Schlesinger, *Thousand Days*, 769.

74. See the *Tribune*, quoted in Schlesinger, *Thousand Days*, 747; and Thomas G. Paterson and William J. Brophy, "October Missiles and November Elections: The Cuban Missile Crisis and American Politics, 1962," *Journal of American History* 73 (June 1986): 111.

75. For the quotations and judgments, see Riccards, "Dangerous Legacy," 82; R. J. Walton, *Cold War and Counterrevolution*, 103; Robert S. McNamara, *In Retrospect* (New York, 1995), 341; and Seymour M. Hersh, *The Dark Side of Camelot* (New York, 1997), 371.

76. Comments to the National Security Council, Nov. 21, 1962, from documents quoted in the Santa Barbara *News-Press*, Apr. 6, 1997, A14.

77. May 29, 1961, quoted in Stephen G. Rabe, "The Caribbean Triangle: Betancourt, Castro, and Trujillo and U.S. Foreign Policy, 1958–1963," *Diplomatic History* 20 (winter 1996): 73.

78. The quotation and statistics come from Jerome N. Slater, "The Dominican Republic, 1961–1966," in Barry M. Blechman and others, *Force without War* (Washington, D.C., 1978), 296.

79. For the quotations, see Fred I. Greenstein and Richard I. Immerman. "What Did Eisenhower Tell Kennedy about Indochina? The Politics of Misperceptions," *Journal of American History* 79 (Sept. 1992): 576; R. Reeves, *President Kennedy*, 31; and Kennedy in news conf., Mar. 23, 1961, U.S. President, *Public Papers: Kennedy, 1961*, 214.

80. See David K. Hall, "The Laotian War of 1962 and the Indo-Pakistani War of 1971," in Blechman and others, *Force without War*, 170.

81. For the quotations, see National Security Action memorandum, May 11, 1961, in William C. Gibbons, *The U.S. Government and the Vietnam War*, 3 vols. (Princeton, N.J., 1986), vol. 2, 40–41; and Charles Bartlett, "Portrait of a Friend,"in Kenneth W. Thompson, ed., *The Kennedy Presidency* (Lanham, Md., 1985), 16.

82. For the quotations, see news conf., Jan. 15, 1962, U.S. President, *Public Papers: Kennedy, 1962*, 17; and John M. Newman, *JFK and Vietnam* (New York, 1992), 415.

83. Oct. 31, 1963, quoted in T. C. Sorenson, *Kennedy*, 643.

84. See Hilsman, *To Move a Nation*, 581, 582; T. C. Sorenson, *Kennedy*, 389; Brauer, "Kennedy: The Endurance of Inspirational Leadership," in Greenstein, ed., *Leadership*

in the Modern Presidency, 127; Thomas G. Paterson, "John F. Kennedy's Quest for Victory and Global Crisis," in Paterson, ed., *Kennedy's Quest for Victory,* 5; Noam Chomsky, *Rethinking Camelot* (Boston, 1993), 81; John E. Ullman, "The Expert Mismanagement of the Vietman War," *War/Peace Report* 10 (Feb. 1970): 11; Reardon, *Sexism and the War System,* 35; and Blechman and others, *Force without War,* 550–51.

NOTES TO CHAPTER 7

1. Quoted from Rowland Evans Jr. and Robert Novak, *Lyndon B. Johnson: The Exercise of Power* (London, 1967), 1; David Halberstam, *The Best and the Brightest* (New York, 1972), 305; George W. Ball, *The Past Has Another Pattern* (New York, 1982), 318; and George E. Reedy, *Lyndon B. Johnson* (New York, 1982), xii, 32, 158.

2. Quoted from Robert A. Caro, *The Path to Power* (New York, 1983), xix; and Bill Gulley, *Breaking Cover* (New York, 1980), 44–5.

3. Quoted in Doris Kearns, *Lyndon Johnson and the American Dream* (New York, 1976), 140, 143; and from State of the Union message, Jan. 4, 1965, U.S. President, *Public Papers: Lyndon B. Johnson, 1965* (Washington, D.C., 1966), 9.

4. The quotations come from Eric F. Goldman, *The Tragedy of Lyndon Johnson,* (New York, 1969), 378; Michael H. Hunt, *Lyndon Johnson's War* (New York, 1996), 76; Halberstam, *Best and Brightest,* 298; and memorandum of a meeting, Nov. 25, 1963, cited in Burke and Greenstein, *How Presidents Test Reality,* 119.

5. Quoted comment to Mike Mansfield, June 9, 1964, in Michael R. Beschloss, ed., *Taking Charge: The Johnson White House Tapes, 1963–1964,* (New York, 1997), 395.

6. The first comments, May 27, 1964, to McGeorge Bundy, are in ibid., 370; and the second is in Vaughn D. Bornet, *The Presidency of Lyndon B. Johnson* (Lawrence, Kans., 1983), 72.

7. Quoted in Robert Dallek, *Flawed Giant* (New York, 1998), 150.

8. For the quotations, see chronology of events of Aug. 4, 1964, in the Johnson Library, cited in Gibbons, *U.S. Government and Vietnam War,* vol. 2, 289; Ball, *Another Pattern,* 379; and Joseph C. Goulden, *Truth Is the First Casualty* (Chicago, 1969), 160.

9. Aug. 4 and 5, 1964, U.S. President, *Public Papers: Johnson, 1963–64,* 927–28, 931.

10. The quotations come from Lyndon B. Johnson, *The Vantage Point* (New York, 1971), 118; and Ball, *Another Pattern,* 380.

11. For the quotations, see John Orman, *Presidential Secrecy and Deception* (Westport, Conn., 1980), 8; Fisher, *Presidential War Power,* 117; and Louis Heren, *No Hail, No Farewell* (New York, 1970), 50–51.

12. New York City, Aug 12; Eufaula, Oklahoma, Sept. 25; Cleveland, Oct. 8; and Pittsburgh, Oct. 27, 1964, U.S. President, *Public Papers: Johnson, 1963–1964,* 953, 1126, 1260, and 1476.

13. The quotation and statistics come from Burke and Greenstein, *How Presidents Test Reality,* 147.

14. See Robert Dallek, "Lyndon Johnson and Vietnam: The Making of a Tragedy," *Diplomatic History* 20 (spring 1996): 148.

15. For the quotations, see Johns Hopkins University, Apr. 7, 1965, U.S. President, *Public Papers: Johnson, 1965,* 395; Brian VanDeMark, *Into the Quagmire* (New York, 1991), 109; and Barber, *Presidential Character,* 28.

16. See statement, Apr. 28, 1965, U.S. President, *Public Papers: Johnson, 1965,* 461; Piero Gleijeses, *The Dominican Crisis* (Baltimore, 1978), 256; and E. F. Goldman, *Tragedy,* 395.

17. See May 2, 1965, U.S. President, *Public Papers: Johnson, 1965*, 469–70; Slater, "Dominican Republic," in Blechman, Kaplan, and others, *Force without War*, 335; and Philip Geyelin, *Lyndon B. Johnson and the World* (New York, 1966), 238.

18. News confs., June 1 and 17, 1965, U.S. President, *Public Papers: Johnson, 1965*, 616, 680.

19. For the quotations, see Abraham F. Lowenthal, *The Dominican Intervention* (Cambridge, Mass., 1972), 116; Theodore Draper, *The Dominican Revolt* (New York, 1968), 84; and L. B. Johnson, *Vantage Point*, 195.

20. For the quotations, see July 14, 1965, U.S. President, *Public Papers: Johnson, 1965*, 751; Lyndon B. Johnson Oral History, Aug. 12, 1969, quoted in Burke and Greenstein, *How Presidents Test Reality*, 191; and L. B. Johnson, *Vantage Point*, 153.

21. Quoted in Henry F. Graff, *The Tuesday Cabinet* (Englewood Cliffs, N.J., 1970), 55; Barber, *Presidential Character*, 42–43; Hugh Sidey, *A Very Personal Presidency* (New York, 1968), 211; and Henry Brandon, *Anatomy of Error* (Boston, 1969), 46.

22. Quoted from Leonard C. Meeker, "The Legality of United States Participation in the Defense of Viet-Nam," *Department of State Bulletin* 54 (Mar. 28, 1966), 488.

23. Omaha, June 30, 1966, U.S. President, *Public Papers: Johnson, 1966*, 685.

24. For the quotations, see H. W. Brands Jr., *The Wages of Globalism* (New York, 1995), 210; McNamara, *In Retrospect*, 279; L. B. Johnson, *Vantage Point*, 302; and Warren I. Cohen, "Balancing American Interests in the Middle East: Lyndon Baines Johnson vs. Gamal Abdul Nasser," in *Lyndon Johnson Confronts the World*, ed. Cohen and Nancy B. Tucker (New York, 1994), 301–2.

25. The quotations come from L. B. Johnson, *Vantage Point*, 253; and Melvin Small, *Johnson, Nixon, and the Doves* (New Brunswick, N.J. 1988), 93.

26. For the quotations, see Larry Berman, "Lyndon B. Johnson: Paths Chosen and Opportunities Lost," in Greenstein, ed., *Leadership in the Modern Presidency*, 146; George Reedy, *The Twilight of the Presidency* (New York, 1970), 81; and John Orman, *Presidential Accountability* (New York, 1990), 31.

27. To Mr. and Mrs. Charles R. Knack, Aug. 24, 1967, quoted in George C. Herring, *LBJ and Vietnam* (Austin, Tex., 1994), 19.

28. The quotations come from Nicholas deB. Katzenbach, "Comparative Roles of the President and the Congress in Foreign Affairs," *Department of State Bulletin* 58 (Sept. 11, 1967), 336; and Katzenbach, "Johnson and Foreign Policy," in K. W. Thompson, ed., *Johnson Presidency* (Lanham, Md., 1986), 215.

29. The quotations, Sept. 20, 1967, and Oct. 13, 1967, to Chalmers Roberts, are in Berman, "Paths Chosen," in Greenstein, ed., *Leadership in the Modern Presidency*, 148–49; and Berman's *Lyndon Johnson's War* (New York, 1989), xi.

30. For the quotations, see United States Senate, "National Commitments," *Miscellaneous Reports on Public Bills*, no. 797, Nov. 20, 1967, 1, 3.

31. Mar. 31, 1968, U.S. President, *Public Papers: Johnson, 1968–69*, 474, 470, 476.

32. See Sandra C. Taylor, "Lyndon Johnson and the Vietnamese," in D. L. Anderson, ed., *Shadow on the White House* (Lawrence, Kans., 1993), 115; and Wofford, *Of Kennedys and Kings*, 341.

33. Quoted from Lloyd C. Gardner, *Pay Any Price* (Chicago, 1995), 536; and Ball, *Another Pattern*, 428.

34. See Irving Bernstein, *Guns or Butter* (New York, 1996), vii; and Robert Dallek, *Lone Star Rising* (New York, 1991), vii, 5, 10.

35. Larry Berman, *Planning a Tragedy* (New York, 1982), 145.

36. Quoted in Stanley I. Kutler, *The Wars of Watergate* (New York, 1990), 131.

37. Quoted from Dallek, *Flawed Giant*, 576.

38. For the quotations, see Richard M. Nixon, *In the Arena* (New York, 1990), 207;

Herbert S. Parmet, *Richard Nixon and His America* (Boston, 1990), 21, and Henry A. Kissinger, *White House Years* (Boston, 1979), 11.

39. Quoted from Ball, *Another Pattern*, 410; and Fawn Brodie, *Richard Nixon* (New York, 1981), 505.

40. Maurice Stans, "A Balance Sheet," in K. W. Thompson, ed., *Nixon Presidency*; (Lanham, Md., 1987), 30; and Kissinger, *White House Years*, 45.

41. Jan. 20, 1969, U.S. President, *Public Papers: Richard Nixon, 1969* (Washington, D.C., 1971), 1–2.

42. News conf., Apr. 18, 1969, ibid., 300.

43. For the quotations, see Nixon, *Memoirs*, 383; and Harry R. Haldeman, *The Haldeman Diaries* (New York, 1995), 65, entry of Apr. 19, 1969.

44. The quotations come from Pat M. Holt, *The War Powers Resolution* (Washington, D.C., 1978), 3–4.

45. The quotations come from Cecil V. Crabb Jr., *The Doctrines of American Foreign Policy* (Baton Rouge, La., 1982), 317; Nixon, *Memoirs*, 395; and July 25, 1969, U.S. President, *Public Papers: Nixon, 1969*, 549.

46. Quoted in Parmet, *Richard Nixon*, 566.

47. The statistics and quotations come from Melvin Small, "Containing Domestic Enemies: Richard L. Nixon and the War at Home," in D. L. Anderson, ed., *Shadow on the White House*, 139; M. Small, *Johnson, Nixon, and the Doves*, 189; and Nov. 3, 1969, U.S. President, *Public Papers: Nixon, 1969*, 903, 908.

48. Richard M. Nixon, *No More Vietnams* (New York, 1985), 115, 116.

49. William Shawcross, *Sideshow* (New York, 1979), 152.

50. Quoted from Tad Szulc, *The Illusion of Peace* (New York, 1978), 262; and Apr. 30, 1970, U.S. President, *Public Papers: Nixon, 1970*, 406, 409, 410.

51. Nixon, *Memoirs*, 454, 457.

52. The quotations come from Schlesinger, *Imperial Presidency*, 190–91.

53. Quoted in Henry Brandon, *The Retreat of American Power* (Garden City, N.Y., 1973), 263–64.

54. The quotations come from Robert H. Jackson, *South Asian Crisis* (New York, 1975), 140; and Nixon, *Memoirs*, 530.

55. Nixon transcript, June 29, 1972, quoted in George C. Herring, *America's Longest War*, 2nd ed. (New York, 1986), 247.

56. Charles W. Colson's recollection quoted in J. Anthony Lukas, *Nightmare* (New York, 1976), 71; and from Henry Kissinger, *Years of Upheaval* (Boston, 1982), 88.

57. For the quotations, see Kissinger, *White House Years*, 228; and Gareth Porter, *A Peace Denied* (Bloomington, Ind., 1975), 158.

58. Nixon, *In the Arena*, 337. In post-presidential writings Nixon expresses this sentiment repeatedly.

59. The quotations come from Barber, *Presidential Character*, 147; and Nixon, *Memoirs*, 735–36.

60. July 19, 1973, quoted in D. J. Adler, "The President's War-Making Power," in Cronin, ed., *Inventing the American Presidency*, 123.

61. News conf., Jan. 31, 1973, U.S. President, *Public Papers: Nixon, 1973*, 55.

62. Spark M. Matsunaga (Hawaii) quoted in Kutler, *Wars of Watergate*, 159.

63. The quotations come from Szulc, *Illusion of Peace*, 361; and Kissinger, *White House Years*, 671.

64. For the quotations, see Michael A. Genovese, *The Nixon Presidency* (New York, 1990), 149–50; Paul E. Sigmund, *The Overthrow of Allende and the Politics of Chile, 1964–1976* (Pittsburgh, 1977), 115; Emanuel Adler, "Executive Command and Control in Foreign Policy: The CIA's Covert Activities," *Orbis* 23 (fall 1979): 691.

65. Nixon, July 7, 1973, is quoted in Stephen E. Ambrose, *Nixon*, vol. 3, (New York, 1991), 188; and in Szulc, *Illusion of Peace*, 710.

66. See Nixon, *Memoirs*, 939; Kissinger, *Years of Upheaval*, 575–91 (the quotation comes from p. 589); and Joan Hoff, *Nixon Reconsidered* (New York, 1994), 268.

67. Nixon, *No More Vietnams*, 225.

68. See Arthur M. Schlesinger Jr., "After the Imperial Presidency," in his *Cycles of American History* (Boston, 1986), 290; and William F. Mullen, *Presidential Power and Politics* (New York, 1976), 102.

69. Robert H. Bork, in L. Gordon Crovitz and Jeremy A. Rabkin, eds., *The Fettered Presidency: Legal Constraints on the Executive Branch*, (Washington, D.C., 1989), xii–xiii.

70. Hungate is quoted in Shawcross, *Sideshow*, 331.

71. Remarks of John Dean, Mar. 21, 1973, H. F. Haldeman, Mar. 16; John Dean, Mar. 31; and Nixon to Alexander M. Haig, Jr., May 9, are in Stanley I. Kutler, ed., *Abuse of Power: The New Nixon Tapes* (New York, 1977), 233, 247, 424; and an excerpt from an undelivered speech, Aug. 4, 1974, Santa Barbara, *News-Press*, Dec, 16, 1996, A3.

72. For the quotations, see Los Angeles *Times*, Jan. 21, 1996, M2; and Nixon, *No More Vietnams*, 165.

73. Aug. 13, 1973, legal investigator Archibald Cox quoted in Schlesinger, *Imperial Presidency*, 272.

74. The quotations come from Richard Nixon, *The Real War* (New York, 1980), 249, 260.

75. Interview with David Frost, May 19, 1977, David Frost, *"I Gave Them a Sword"* (New York, 1978), 183.

NOTES TO CHAPTER 8

1. Nixon, *Memoirs*, 926.

2. Remarks on taking the oath of office, Aug. 9, 1974, U.S. President, *Public Papers: Gerald R. Ford, 1974* (Washington, D.C., 1975), 1, 2.

3. The quotations come from Lou Cannon, "A President Who Brought Healing," and Brent Scowcroft, "Ford as President and His Foreign Policy," in K. W. Thompson, ed., *Ford Presidency* (Lanham, Md., 1988), 349, 310.

4. Gerald R. Ford, *A Time to Heal* (New York, 1979), 129.

5. Quoted in John Osborne, *White House Watch* (Washington, D.C., 1977), 104.

6. The first quotation, Oct. 17, 1974, to a congressional committee, is in John R. Greene, *The Presidency of Gerald R. Ford* (Lawrence, Kans., 1995), 57; and the second comes from Richard Reeves, "Jerry Ford and His Flying Circus: A Presidential Diary," *New York*, Nov. 25, 1974, 46.

7. The quotations come from Gregory F. Treverton, *Covert Action* (New York, 1987), 238.

8. The recollections of Ford's remarks vary. See David Wise, *The American Police State* (New York, 1976), 211; Osborne, *White House Watch*, 148; and Greene, *Ford Presidency*, 107.

9. To Ngyen Van Thieu, Aug. 10, 1974, quoted in David L. Anderson, "Gerald R. Ford and the President's War in Vietnam," in D. L. Anderson, ed., *Shadow on the White House* (Lawrence, Kans., 1993), 188.

10. Apr. 29, 1975, quoted in Greene, *Ford Presidency*, 141.

11. Quoted in ibid., 148.

12. For the quotations, see John Orman, *Comparing Presidential Behavior* (West-

port, Conn., 1987), 15; Michael S. Sherry, *In the Shadow of War* (New Haven, Conn., 1995), 337; and Ford, *A Time to Heal*, 284.

13. The quotations come from an editorial in *The Nation*, May 31, 1975, 643; and Anthony Lewis, "The Morning After," New York *Times*, May 19, 1975, A29.

14. Interview with Hugh Sidey, May 16, 1975, quoted in D. L. Anderson, ed., *Shadow on White House*, 202–3.

15. Quoted in Prados, *Secret Wars*, 337.

16. For the comments, see Ford, *A Time to Heal*, 205 and 422 (San Francisco, Oct. 6, 1976); and Robert D. Schulzinger, *Henry Kissinger* (New York, 1989), 233.

17. Quoted in Betty Glad, *Jimmy Carter* (New York, 1980), 347; Burton I. Kaufman, *The Presidency of James Earl Carter, Jr.* (Lawrence, Kans., 1993), 38; and John Dumbrell, *The Carter Presidency*, rev. ed. (Manchester, England, 1995), 17.

18. Jan. 20, 1977, U.S. President, *Public Papers: Jimmy Carter, 1977* (Washington, D.C., 1977), book 1, 2–3, 4.

19. From Jimmy Carter, *Keeping Faith* (New York, 1982), 52, 89 and Zbigniew Brzezinski, *Power and Principle* (New York, 1983), 63.

20. Interview with radio and television reporters, Dec. 28, 1977, U.S. President, *Public Papers: Carter, 1977*, book 2, 2200.

21. Toasts at state dinner, Dec. 31, 1977, in ibid., 2221, 2222; and discussion with reporters, Jan. 6, 1978, ibid., *1978*, book 1, 47. See also Barry Rubin, *Paved with Good Intentions* (New York, 1980), 201; and Peter G. Bourne, *Jimmy Carter* (New York, 1997), 454.

22. Barber, *Presidential Character*, 449.

23. For the quotations, see Charles O. Jones, *The Trusteeship Presidency* (Baton Rouge, La., 1988), 190; and Saunders, Jan. 20, 1980, and Carter, Jan. 23, in Hamilton Jordan, *Crisis* (New York, 1982), 119, 126.

24. Briefing for members of Congress, Jan. 8, 1980, U.S. President, *Public Papers: Carter, 1980–81*, book 1, 40.

25. Pravda, Jan. 13, 1980, quoted in Raymond Garthoff, *Détente and Confrontation*, rev. ed. (Washington, D.C., 1994), 1036.

26. State of the Union message, Jan. 23, 1980, U.S. President, *Public Papers: Carter, 1980–81*, book 1, 197.

27. For the quotations, see weekly report, Feb. 29, 1980, in Brzezinski, *Power and Principle*, 567; and Milton F. Goldman, "President Carter, Western Europe, and Afghanistan in 1980: Inter-Allied Differences over Policy toward the Soviet Union," in Rosenbaum and Ugrinsky, eds., *Jimmy Carter: Foreign Policy and Post Presidential Years*, 20.

28. The quotations come from Carter, *Keeping Faith*, 594, 506, italics in the original; Cyrus R. Vance, *Hard Choices* (New York, 1983), 410; and Richard C. Thornton, *The Carter Years* (New York, 1991), 496.

29. Lloyd Cutler, quoted in John Lehman, *Making War* (New York, 1992), 101.

30. Quoted from Gaddis Smith, *Morality, Reason, and Power* (New York, 1986), 48.

31. Douglas Brinkley, "The Rising Stock of Jimmy Carter: The 'Hands on' Legacy of Our Thirty-ninth President," *Diplomatic History* 20 (fall 1996): 511; and diary entry of Jan. 2, 1981, in Carter, *Keeping Faith*, 591. The timing of the release sparked rumors of a secret deal between the Republicans and the Iranians to delay the completion of the host arrangement until after the presidential election. See Gary Sick, *October Surprise* (New York, 1991), 4.

32. John Mihalec, "Hair on the President's Chest," *Wall Street Journal*, May 11, 1984, 30, cited in Orman, *Comparing Presidential Behavior*, 168.

33. The quotations come from Garland A. Haas, *Jimmy Carter and the Politics of*

Frustration (Jefferson, N.C., 1992), 160–61; and Lou Cannon, *Reagan* (New York, 1982), 283, 295.

34. For the quotations, see Fred I. Greenstein, "The Need for an Early Appraisal of the Reagan Presidency," in Greenstein, ed., *Reagan Presidency* (Baltimore, 1983), 9; Ronnie Dugger, *On Reagan* (New York, 1983), xiii; and Jan. 20, 1981, U.S. President, *Public Papers: Ronald Reagan, 1981* (Washington, D.C., 1982), 2, 3.

35. Robert Dallek, *Ronald Reagan* (Cambridge, Mass., 1984), ix.

36. For the quotations, see speech, Orlando, Florida, Mar. 8, 1983, U.S. President, *Public Papers: Reagan, 1983*, book 1, 363–64; George P. Shultz, *Turmoil and Triumph* (New York, 1993), 1133; Orman, *Presidential Accountability*, 51; Lou Cannon, *President Reagan* (New York, 1991), 176, 181–82; David Mervin, *Ronald Reagan and the American Presidency* (London, 1990), 188; and Ronald Reagan, *An American Life* (New York, 1990), 161.

37. Paul H. Nitze and John C. Whitehead quoted in Kenneth W. Thompson, ed., *Foreign Policy in the Reagan Presidency* (Lanham, Md., 1993), 22, 66; Laurence I. Barrett, *Gambling with History* (Harmondsworth, England, 1984), 9, 23; and Reagan, *An American Life*, 270.

38. The quotations come from Prados, *Secret Wars*, 370; Kenneth A. Oye, "Constrained Confidence and the Evolution of Reagan Foreign Policy," in Oye and others, eds., *Eagle Resurgent?* (Boston, 1987), 6; and Reagan, *An American Life*, 552.

39. See Louis Henkin, "The Use of Force: Law and U.S. Policy" in Henkin and others, *Right v. Might: International Law and the Use of Force*, 2nd ed. (New York, 1991), 56.

40. Reagan, *An American Life*, 238; and Cannon, *President Reagan*, 196.

41. For the quotations, see Robert A. Pastor, *Condemned to Repetition* (Princeton, N.J., 1987), 237; and Presidential Finding on Covert Operations in Nicaragua, Dec. 1, 1981, photocopy in *The Iran-Contra Scandal*, ed. Peter Kornbluh and Malcolm Byrne (New York, 1993), 11.

42. Stansfield Turner, *Secrecy and Democracy* (Boston, 1985), 166; and news conf., Apr. 14, 1983, U.S. President, *Public Papers: Reagan, 1983*, part 1, 539, 541.

43. See Apr. 27, 1983, ibid., 603, 607; president's national security directive, July 28, 1983 (photocopy), in Christopher Simpson, ed., *National Security Directives of the Reagan and Bush Administrations* (Boulder, Colo., 1995), 313; and Turner, *Secrecy and Democracy*, 168.

44. Reagan, *An American Life*, 291.

45. For the quotations, see, Robert C. McFarlane, *Special Trust* (New York, 1994), 267; Oct. 24, 1983, U.S. President, *Public Papers: Reagan, 1983*, part 2, 1500–1; Cannon, *President Reagan*, 389, 444, 449; and Reagan, *An American Life*, 463.

46. For the quotations, see Cannon, *President Reagan*, 441; and McFarlane, *Special Trust*, 264.

47. Oct. 25, 1983, U.S. President, *Public Papers: Reagan, 1983*, part 2, 1506; and Reagan, *An American Life*, 457, 451.

48. Fisher, *Presidential War Power*, 141–42; and Cannon, *President Reagan*, 447.

49. See address to the nation, Oct. 27, 1983, U.S. President, *Public Papers: Reagan, 1983*, part 2, 1521; unsigned editorial, "Grenada, by O'Neill, by Orwell," New York *Times*, Nov. 10, 1983, A26; Denise M. Bostdorff, "The Presidency and Promoted Crisis: Reagan, Grenada, and Issue Management," *Presidential Studies Quarterly* 21 (fall 1991): 737; and Wormuth and Firmage, *To Chain the Dog of War*, 256.

50. Apr. 14, 1986, U.S. President, *Public Papers: Reagan, 1986*, part 1, 468, 469.

51. Quoted from Orman, *Presidential Accountability*, 53.

52. Goldwater to William Casey, Apr. 14, 1984, quoted in Marc E. Smyrl, *Conflict or Codetermination?* (Cambridge, Mass., 1988), 122.

53. Television address, May 9, 1984, U.S. President, *Public Papers: Reagan, 1984*, part 1, 661, 664.

54. See Roy Gutman, *Banana Diplomacy* (New York, 1988), 209–12; and Shultz, *Turmoil and Triumph*, 423.

55. See I. M. Destler, "Reagan and the World. An 'Awesome Stubbornness,'" in *The Reagan Legacy*, ed. Charles O. Jones (Chatham, N.J., 1988), 255. In all, Congress passed five Boland Amendments constraining Contra aid. See Terry Eastland, *Energy in the Executive* (New York, 1992), 96–105.

56. Quoted from Reagan, *An American Life*, 484; and Pastor, *Condemned to Repetition*, 250.

57. See U.S. President, *Public Papers: Reagan, 1985*, part 1, (Feb. 21, 1985), 200; (Mar. 1), 229; (Mar. 30), 371; and Reagan, *An American Life*, 477.

58. Message to Congress, May 1, 1985, U.S. President, *Public Papers: Reagan, 1985*, part 1, 548; and news conf., Feb. 18, 1986, ibid., 1986, part 1, 216.

59. March 8 and 16, 1986, ibid., part 1, 308, 352, 353.

60. Quoted in Sung Ho Kim, "The Issues of International Law, Morality, and Prudence," in T. W. Walker, ed., *Reagan versus the Sandinistas* (Boulder, Colo., 1987), 286.

61. Covert Action Finding Regarding Iran, Jan. 17, 1986, photocopy in Kornbluh and Byrne, eds., *Iran-Contra Scandal*, 235. See also xv; and Gregory F. Treverton, "Constraints on 'Covert' Paramilitary Action," in Stern and Halperin, eds., *The U.S. Constitution and the Power to Go to War* (Westport, Conn., 1994), 137.

62. News conf., Nov. 13, 1986, U.S. President, *Public Papers: Reagan, 1986*, part 2, 1546, 1548.

63. News conf., Nov. 19, 1986, and remarks, Nov. 25, ibid., 1568, 1587.

64. The quotations come from Shultz, *Turmoil and Triumph*, 828, 830, 840; and John Tower, chairman, *The Tower Commission Report* (Washington, D.C., 1987), 26–27, 152.

65. Address to the nation, Mar. 4, 1987, U.S. President, *Public Papers: Reagan, 1987*, part 1, 209.

66. For the quotation, the grant of executive clemency by George Bush, Dec. 24, 1992, and the Walsh statement, same date, photocopies, see Kornbluh and Byrne, eds., *Iran-Contra Scandal*, 408, 374–78.

67. Philip S. Khoury, "The Reagan Administration and the Middle East," in Kyvig, ed., *Reagan and the World* (New York, 1990), 77.

68. Quoted from Shultz, *Turmoil and Triumph*, 935.

69. Handwritten to Gorbachev, Feb. 6, 1986, cited in Reagan, *An American Life*, 655.

70. Quoted from Cannon, *President Reagan*, 403.

71. For the quotations, see Robert K. Murray and Tim H. Blessing, *Greatness in the White House*, 2d ed. (University Park, Pa., 1994), 85; Barrett, *Gambling with History*, 41; and Orman, *Comparing Presidential Behavior*, 18.

72. Quoted from Reagan, *An American Life*, 386–87.

NOTES TO CHAPTER 9

1. Quoted in David Mervin, *George Bush and the Guardianship Presidency* (New York, 1996), 26.

2. Margaret G. Warner, "Bush Battles the 'Wimp Factor,'" *Newsweek*, Oct. 19, 1987, 29.

3. Jan. 20, 1989, U.S. President, *Public Papers: George Bush, 1989* (Washington, D.C., 1990), part 1, 3.

4. For the quotations, May 11 and 13, 1989, press conf., see ibid., 537, 538, 547; and

Congressman Henry Hyde of Illionis in James A. Baker III, *The Politics of Diplomacy* (New York, 1995), 187.

5. Quoted from Mary E. Stuckey and Frederick J. Antczak, "Governance as Political Theater: George Bush and the MTV Presidency," in *Leadership and the Bush Presidency*, ed. Ryan J. Barilleaux and Mary E. Stuckey (Westport, Conn., 1992), 27; news conf., Oct. 13, 1989, U.S. President, *Public Papers: Bush, 1989*, part 2, 1336; Margaret E. Scranton, *The Noriega Years* (Boulder, Colo., 1991); and Colin L. Powell, *My American Journey* (New York, 1995), 420.

6. Scranton, *Noriega Years*, 199; and J. A. Baker, *Politics of Diplomacy*, 188–89.

7. Quoted from report to Congress, Dec. 21, 1989, U.S. President, *Public Papers: Bush, 1989*, part 2, 1734; and Christina J. Johns and P. Ward Johnson, *State Crime, the Media, and the Invasion of Panama* (Westport, Conn., 1994), 51.

8. Quoted from Fisher, *Presidential War Power*, 189; and Steve Garber and Phil Williams, "Defense Policy," in Hill and Williams, eds., *Bush Presidency* (New York, 1994), 203.

9. See Johns and Johnson, *State Crime and Panama*, 83, 90.

10. The quotations and data come from Congressman Robert Kastenmeier (D-Wisconsin) in Fisher, *Presidential War Power*, 146; Scranton, *Noriega Years*, 207–8; John Quigley, "The Legality of the United States Invasion of Panama," *Yale Journal of International Law* 15 (1990), 314–15; and Association of the Bar of the City of New York, *The Use of Armed Force in International Affairs: The Case of Panama* (New York, 1992), 2, 63.

11. Exchange with reporters, Aug. 2, 1990, U.S. President, *Public Papers: Bush, 1990*, part 2, 1083, 1084.

12. The first quotation comes from Jean Edward Smith, *George Bush's War* (New York, 1992), 68. For more reliable accounts of Thatcher's caution see Mervin, *Bush and Guardianship Presidency*, 180–82; and Herbert S. Parmet, *George Bush* (New York, 1997), 453–54. The second quotation comes from press conf., Aug. 5, 1990, U.S. President, *Public Papers: Bush, 1990*, part 2, 1120. See also George Bush and Brent Scowcroft, *A World Transformed* (New York, 1998), 333.

13. News conf., Aug. 22, 1990. U.S. President, *Public Papers: Bush, 1990*, part 2, 1160.

14. For the quotations, see Margaret Thatcher, *The Downing Street Years* (New York, 1993), 824; and Bush to the people of Iraq, Sept. 16, 1990, U.S. President, *Public Papers: Bush, 1990*, part 2, 1239–40.

15. Quoted in Powell, *American Journey*, 480.

16. Press conf., Nov. 8, 1990, ibid., 1581.

17. For the quotations, see J. E. Smith, *Bush's War* (Nov. 12, 1990), 206; and Robert J. Spitzer, "The Conflict between Congress and the President over War," in Whicker and others, eds., *Presidency and the Gulf War*, 29.

18. Nov. 15, 1990, quoted in J. E. Smith, *Bush's War*, 208.

19. Nov. 20, 1990, quoted in ibid., 213.

20. Judge Harold H. Green, in *Ronald V. Dellums et al. v. George Bush*, quoted in ibid., 230; and George Bush, "Why We Are in the Gulf," *Newsweek*, Nov. 26, 1990, 28–29.

21. Resolution 678 in Micah L. Sifry and Christopher Cerf, eds., *The Gulf War Reader* (New York, 1991), 156; and news conf., Nov. 30, 1990, U.S. President, *Public Papers: Bush, 1990*, part 2, 1719.

22. Quoted from Larry Berman and Bruce W. Jentleson, "Bush and the Post-Cold-War World: New Challenges for American Leadership," in Campbell and Rockman, eds., *Bush Presidency* (Chatham, N.J., 1991), 107.

23. For a listing of the justifications, see ibid., 117–18.

24. Quoted in Richard Rose, *The Postmodern President* 2d ed. (Chatham, N.J., 1991), 325–26; and Dec. 28, 1990, interview with David Frost in Sifry and Cerf, eds., *Gulf War Reader*, 286.

25. Quoted in Tom Matthews, "The Road to War," *Newsweek*, Jan. 28, 1991, 65.

26. Quoted from J. A. Baker, *Politics of Diplomacy*, 331; and Simpson, ed., *National Security Directives*, 947.

27. Public Law 102–1, Jan. 14, 1991, printed in *U.S. National Security Policy and Strategy, 1987–1994*, ed. Robert A. Vitas and John A. Williams (Westport, Conn., 1996), 224.

28. Quoted from Keynes, *Undeclared War*, 2.

29. See news conf., Jan. 12, 1991, U.S. President, *Public Papers: Bush, 1991*, part 1, 31; and Donald L. Westerfield, *War Powers* (Westport, Conn., 1996), 158.

30. The quotations come from Rose, *Postmodern President*, 315; Charles Tiefer, *The Semi-Sovereign Presidency* (Boulder, Colo., 1994), 12–13; and diary entry, Feb. 26, 1991, in Parmet, *George Bush*, 480.

31. Address to the nation, Feb. 27, 1991, U.S. President, *Public Papers: Bush, 1991*, part 1, 187.

32. For the quotations and statistics, see J. Lehman, *Making War*, 1; and Rose, *Postmodern President*, 317.

33. For the quotations, see Vitali Churkin, spokesman for the Soviet foreign ministry, quoted in Michael R. Beschloss and Strobe Talbott, *At the Highest Levels* (Boston, 1993), 340; John W. Dower, "Japan and the U.S. Samurai Spirit," in *The Persian Gulf War*, ed. Herbert H. Blumberg and Christopher C. French (Lanham, Md., 1994), 533; and Stephen R. Graubard, *Mr. Bush's War* (New York, 1992), xv.

34. Address, Princeton University, May 10, 1991, U.S. President, *Public Papers: Bush, 1991*, part 1, 497–99.

35. For the quotations, see John T. Rourke, *Presidential Wars and American Democracy* (New York, 1993), 11; and Martin Kasindorf, "Divining the George Bush Ex-Presidency," *Los Angeles Times Magazine*, July 23, 1995, 8.

36. J. A. Baker, *Politics of Diplomacy*, 636.

37. Quoted from Beschloss and Talbott, *At the Highest Levels*, 464; Richard J. Stoll, "The Guns of November: Presidential Reelections and the Use of Force, 1947–1982," *Journal of Conflict Resolution* 28 (June 1984): 233, 244; and Tiefer, *Semi-Sovereign Presidency*, 141.

38. Address to the nation, Dec. 4, 1992, U.S. President, *Public Papers: Bush, 1992–93*, part 2, 2175–76; and Sidney Blumenthal, "All the President's Wars," *New Yorker*, Dec. 28, 1992/Jan. 4, 1993, 62.

39. Los Angeles *Times*, Nov. 19, 1993, A2.

40. Quoted from his diary, Jan. 20, 1997, in Parmet, *George Bush*, 510.

41. For the quotations, see George Bush, "I've Had a Wonderful Life," *Parade*, Dec. 1, 1996, 4; Mervin, *Bush and Guardianship Presidency*, 196; and Andrew M. Greeley, *Star-Free Press* (Ventura, Calif.), July 30, 1994, C5.

42. Quoted in David Maraniss, *First in His Class* (New York, 1995), 390.

43. Jan. 20, 1993, U.S. President, *Public Papers: William J. Clinton, 1993* (Washington, D.C., 1994), book 1, 2.

44. Quoted in Stanley A. Renshon, *High Hopes* (New York, 1996), 58; and Bob Woodward, *The Agenda* (New York, 1994), 329.

45. Quoted from John Brummet, *Highwire* (New York, 1994), 210; and Elizabeth Drew, *On the Edge* (New York, 1994), 89.

46. Interview, "Blending Force with Diplomacy," *Time*, Oct. 31, 1994, 35.

47. For the quotations, see radio address, June 12, 1993, U.S. President, *Public Pa-*

pers: Clinton, 1993, book 1, 840; and George Stephanopoulos, *All Too Human* (Boston, 1999), 214.

48. Address to the nation, June 26, 1993, ibid., 938–39; and Michael Ratner and Jules Lobel, "Bombing Baghdad Illegal Reprisal or Self-Defense?" *Legal Times,* July 5, 1993, 24, quoted in Fisher, *Presidential War Power,* 152. See also Warren Christopher, *In the Stream of History* (Stanford, Calif., 1988), 193.

49. Address to the nation, Oct. 7, 1993, U.S. President, *Public Papers: Clinton, 1993,* book 2, 1704.

50. The statements are in message to Congress, Oct. 13, 1993, ibid., 1739–40 and Los Angeles *Times,* Mar. 25, 1994, A10.

51. The statement on sanctions, June 4, 1993, comes from U.S. President, *Public Papers: Clinton, 1993,* book 1, 811; and the other quotation from Larry Berman and Emily O. Goldman, "Clinton's Foreign Policy at Midterm" in Campbell and Rockman, eds., *Clinton Presidency* (Chatham, N.J., 1996), 309–10.

52. News conf., Oct. 15, 1993, U.S. President, *Public Papers: Clinton, 1993,* book 2, 1755.

53. Interview with radio reporters, Oct. 18, 1993, ibid., 1763–64.

54. For Buchwald, see Los Angeles *Times,* Apr. 27, 1994, E2; and for Clinton, see exchange with reporters, Atlanta, May 3, 1994, U.S. President, *Public Papers: Clinton, 1994,* part 1, 819–20.

55. Quoted in Fisher, *Presidential War Power,* 156. See also Thomas Carothers, "Democracy Promotion under Clinton," *Washington Quarterly* 18 (autumn 1995), 15–16.

56. For the quotations, see Drew, *On the Edge,* 428; Georges A. Fauriol and Andrew S. Faiola, "Prelude to Intervention," in Fauriol, ed., *Haitian Frustrations* (Washington, D.C., 1995), 114; and news conf., Aug. 3, 1994, U.S. President, *Public Papers: Clinton, 1994,* book 2, 1419.

57. For the quotations, see address to the nation on Haiti, Sept. 15, 1994, U.S. President, *Public Papers: Clinton, 1994,* book 2, 1558, 1559; and Richard N. Lebow, "Psychological Dimensions of Post-Cold War Foreign Policy" (Oct. 17, 1993), in Renshon, ed., *Clinton Presidency,* 240–41.

58. For the quotations, see statement on airdrops to Bosnia, Feb. 25, 1993; letter of Apr. 13 to congressional leaders, ibid., 430; news conf., Apr. 16, U.S. President, *Public Papers: Clinton, 1993,* book 1, 206, 430, 441; Drew, *On the Edge,* 151; and Martin Walker, *The President We Deserve* (New York, 1996), 263.

59. Letter to congressional leaders on the conflict in Bosnia, Oct. 20, 1993, U.S. President, *Public Papers: Clinton, 1993,* book 2, 1781.

60. For the quotations see Clinton radio address, June 3, 1995, U.S. President, *Weekly Compilation of Presidential Documents,* vol. 31, no. 23, p. 967; and Drew, *On The Edge,* 424.

61. Quoted in the Los Angeles *Times,* Sept. 4, 1995, A12.

62. Quoted from the Santa Barbara *News-Press,* Sept. 12, 1995, A16.

63. Quoted in the Los Angeles *Times,* Sept. 13, 1995, A8.

64. See James Risen, "Building a Better CIA," *Los Angeles Times Magazine,* Oct. 8, 1995, 12–15, 34–38; and Los Angeles *Times,* Oct. 11, 1995, A1, A7.

65. The budget estimate comes from Christopher Andrew, *For the President's Eyes Only* (New York, 1995), 540.

66. Quoted from Alan Tonelson, "Put U.S. Intervention to a Popular Vote," Los Angeles *Times,* Oct. 17, 1995, B9.

67. Announcing Bosnia-Herzegovina Peace Agreement, Nov. 21, 1995, U.S. President, *Weekly Compilation,* vol. 31, no. 47, p. 2050.

68. Quoted by Doyle McManus, Los Angeles *Times,* Nov. 22, 1995, A17.

69. Helen Chenoweth (R-Idaho) quoted in ibid., Dec. 14, 1995, A12; and Clinton, Jan. 23, 1996, in U.S. President, *Weekly Compilation*, vol. 32, no. 3, p. 67.
70. Mike O'Connor, Santa Barbara *News-Press*, May 25, 1998, A14.
71. Quoted in Los Angeles *Times*, Mar. 12, 1996, A7.
72. Ibid., Sept. 4, 1996, A1.
73. Ibid., Sept. 6, 1996, A6.
74. State of the Union message, Feb. 4, 1997, U.S. President, *Weekly Compilation*, vol. 33, no. 6, pp. 143–44.
75. Los Angeles *Times*, Apr. 6, 1997, A6.
76. Ibid., Jan. 29, 1998, A1.
77. Ibid., Feb. 17, 1998, A10 and B7.
78. Ibid., Feb. 19, 1998, A8.
79. Robert L. Borsage quoted in ibid., Feb. 22, 1998, M5.
80. Quoted in ibid.
81. Ibid., Feb. 26, 1998, A8.
82. Santa Barbara *News-Press*, Aug. 21, 1998, A10.
83. Los Angeles *Times*, Aug. 23, 1998, A1.
84. The data and quotations come from ibid., Dec. 18, 1998, A17 and Dec. 20, 1998, A31.
85. Ibid., Jan. 19, 1999, A18.
86. News conf., Feb. 19, 1999, *Weekly Compilation of Presidential Documents*, Feb. 20, 1999, vol. 35, 255.
87. Ibid., Mar. 26, 1999, 471.
88. Los Angeles *Times*, Mar. 24, 1999, A17.
89. Ibid., Mar. 26, 1999, A21.
90. For a portrayal that exaggerates the importance of the Secretary's influence, see Walter Isaacson, "Madeleine's War," *Time*, 153 (May 17, 1999), 24–35.
91. Los Angeles *Times*, May 23, 1999, M1, M6.

NOTES TO CHAPTER 10

1. To Roger Sherman, Richmond Hill, N.Y., July 17, 1789, J. Adams, *Works*, vol. 6, 431.
2. 1921, quoted in Harriet H. Alonso, *Peace as a Women's Issue* (Syracuse, N.Y., 1993), 86.
3. Reardon, *Sexism and the War System*, 38, 42; and Cynthia Enloe, *The Morning After* (Berkeley, Calif., 1993), 20.
4. Quoted in Ambrose, *Nixon*, vol. 3, *Ruin*, 452.
5. Henry S. Commager, "Can We Limit Presidential Power?" in Commager, *The Defeat of America: Presidential Power and the* National Character (New York, 1974), 50–51.
6. Leslie H. Gelb with Richard K. Betts, *The Irony of Vietnam* (Washington, D.C., 1979), 362.
7. Dean Rusk, "The President," *Foreign Affairs* 38 (Apr. 1960), 355, 357, 359; and Thomas A. Bailey, *The Man in the* Street (New York, 1948), 13.
8. The quotations come from Quincy Wright, "The Power of the Executive to Use Military Forces Abroad," *Virginia Journal of International Law* 10 (Dec. 1969), 47, 54; and Lawrence R. Velvel, "Commentary," ibid., 65.
9. Remarks to personnel returning from Somalia, May 5, 1993, U.S. President, *Public Papers: Clinton, 1993*, book 1, 566.

10. John T. Rourke and Russell Farnen, "War, Presidents, and the Constitution," *Presidential Studies Quarterly* 18 (1988): 513.

11. The quotations come from Nixon, *In the Arena,* 207; and Lash, *Roosevelt and Churchill,* 10.

12. James Bryce, *The American Commonwealth,* rev. ed., 2 vols. (New York, 1914), vol. 1, 77, 80.

13. Quoted in Leonard D. White, *The Jacksonians* (New York, 1954), 84; and L. D. White, *The Republican Era,* 105.

14. Counselor to Nixon, quoted in the Los Angeles *Times,* Feb. 8, 1997, A15.

15. Quoted from Graber, *Public Opinion, the President,* 347; and Sherwood, *Roosevelt and Hopkins,* 932.

16. Quoted from Barbara W. Tuchman, *The March of Folly* (New York, 1984), 382.

17. U.S. Senate, "National Commitments," *Miscellaneous Reports on Public Bills* (Washington, D.C., 1967), 26–27.

18. Interview, Mar. 23, 1992, Kathryn S. Olmstead, *Challenging the Secret Government* (Chapel Hill, N.C., 1996), 188.

SELECTED BIBLIOGRAPHY

The literature and primary sources on the presidency and related foreign and military policy are voluminous. No other office or actions and thoughts of its holders are as well documented in print and in archives. This is, therefore, a select listing of the books, articles, newspapers, opinion polls, government documents, letters, memoirs, diaries, and other sources I have consulted that may prove useful to interested readers.

Abbot, Philip. *Strong Presidents: A Theory of Leadership.* Knoxville, Tenn., 1996.

Abel, Elie. *The Missiles of October: The Story of the Cuban Missile Crisis.* Philadelphia, 1966.

Abernathy, M. Glenn, Dilys M. Hill, and Phil Williams, eds. *The Carter Years: The President and Policy Making.* London, 1984.

Abrahamsen, David. *Nixon vs. Nixon: An Emotional Tragedy.* New York, 1977.

Acheson, Dean G. *Present at the Creation: My Years in the State Department.* New York, 1969.

Adair, Douglass. *Fame and the Founding Fathers.* Ed. Trevor Colbourn. New York, 1974.

Adams, Henry. *The Education of Henry Adams.* 1918. Reprint, Boston, 1974.

———. *History of the United States of America during the Administrations of Jefferson and Madison.* Reprint, New York, 1962. First published 1889–91.

———. *The Life of Albert Gallatin.* 1869. Reprint, Philadelphia, 1943.

Adams, John. *A Defence of the Constitutions of the Government of the United States of America.* 3 vols. 1787–88. Reprint, New York, 1971.

———. *The Works of John Adams.* Ed. Charles Francis Adams. 10 vols. Boston, 1850–56.

Adams, John, and John Quincy Adams. *The Selected Writings of John and John Quincy Adams.* Ed. Adrienne Koch and William Peden. New York, 1946.

Adams, John Quincy. *An Eulogy on the Life and Character of James Madison.* Boston, 1836.

———. *Writings of John Quincy Adams.* Ed. Worthington C. Ford. 7 vols. New York, 1912–17.

Adams, Mary P. "Jefferson's Military Policy with Special Reference to the Frontier, 1805–1809." Ph.D. diss., University of Virginia, 1958.

Adams, Sherman. *First-Hand Report: The Inside Story of the Eisenhower Administration.* London, 1962.

Adler, David Gray. "The Constitution and Presidential Warmaking: The Enduring Debate." *Political Science Quarterly* 103 (spring 1988): 1–36.

———. "The President's War-Making Power." In *Inventing the American Presidency,* ed. Thomas E. Cronin, 119–53. Lawrence, Kans., 1989.

Adler, David Gray, and Larry N. George, eds. *The Constitution and the Conduct of American Foreign Policy.* Lawrence, Kans., 1996.

Adler, Emanuel. "Executive Command and Control in Foreign Policy: The CIA's Covert Activities." *Orbis* 23 (fall 1979): 671–96.

Adler, Selig. *The Isolationist Impulse: Its Twentieth Century Reaction.* New York, 1957.

———. *The Uncertain Giant, 1921–1942: American Foreign Policy between the Wars.* New York, 1965.

Aitken, Jonathan. *Nixon: A Life.* Washington, D.C., 1993.

Albertson, Dean, ed. *Eisenhower as President.* New York, 1963.

Alexander, Charles C. *Holding the Line: The Eisenhower Era, 1952–1961.* Bloomington, Ind., 1975.

Alfonso, Oscar M. *Theodore Roosevelt and the Philippines, 1897–1909.* Quezon City, Philippines, 1974.

Allen, Charles F., and Jonathan Portis. *The Comeback Kid: The Life and Career of Bill Clinton.* New York, 1992.

Allison, Graham T. *Essence of Decision: Explaining the Cuban Missile Crisis.* Boston, 1971.

———. "Making War: The President and Congress." *Law and Contemporary Problems* 40 (summer 1976): 86–105.

Allison, Robert J. *The Crescent Obscured: The United States and the Muslim World, 1776–1815.* New York, 1995.

Alonso, Harriet H. *Peace as a Women's Issue: A History of the U.S. Movement for World Peace and Women's Rights.* Syracuse, N.Y., 1993.

Alperovitz, Gar. *The Decision to Use the Atomic Bomb and the Architecture of an American Myth.* New York, 1995.

Ambrose, Stephen E. *Eisenhower: The President.* New York, 1984.

———. *Eisenhower: Soldier, General of the Army, President Elect, 1890–1952.* New York, 1983.

———. *Eisenhower: Soldier and President.* New York, 1990.

———. *Ike's Spies: Eisenhower and the Espionage Establishment.* Garden City, 1981.

———. *Nixon.* 3 vols. New York, 1987–91.

———. "The Presidency and Foreign Policy." *Foreign Affairs* 70 (winter 1992): 120–37.

Ambrosius, Lloyd E. *Wilsonian Statecraft: Theory and Practice of Liberal Internationalism during World War I.* Wilmington, Del., 1991.

American Academy of Political and Social Science. "The Office of the American Executive." *Annals* 307 (Sept. 1956): 1–155.

Ammon, Harry. *James Monroe: The Quest for National* Identity. New York, 1971.

Anderson, David L. "Gerald R. Ford and the President's War in Vietnam." In Anderson, ed. *Shadow on White House,* 184–207.

———. *Trapped by Success: The Eisenhower Administration and Vietnam, 1953–1961.* New York, 1991.

———. ed. *Shadow on the White House: Presidents and the Vietnam War, 1945–1975*. Lawrence, Kans., 1993.

Anderson, Donald F. *William Howard Taft: A Conservative's Conception of the Presidency*. Ithaca, N.Y., 1973.

Anderson, Judith I. *William Howard Taft: An Intimate Biography*. New York, 1981.

Anderson, Martin. *Revolution*. New York, 1988.

Anderson, Patrick. *Electing Jimmy Carter: The Campaign of 1976*. Baton Rouge, La., 1994.

Andrew, Christopher. *For the President's Eyes Only: Secret Intelligence and the American Presidency from Washington to Bush*. New York, 1995

Anhart, Larry. "'The God-Like Prince': John Locke, Executive Prerogative, and the American Presidency." *Presidential Studies Quarterly*, 9 (spring 1979): 121–30.

Arendt, Hannah. "Imperialism, Nationalism, Chauvinism." *Review of Politics*, 7 (Oct. 1945): 441–63.

Asada, Sadao. "The Shock of the Atomic Bombs and Japan's Decision to Surrender—A Reconsideration." *Pacific Historical Review* 67 (Nov. 1998): 377–512.

Association of the Bar of the City of New York. *The Use of Armed Force in International Affairs: The Case of Panama*. New York, 1992.

Austin, Anthony. *The President's War: The Story of the Tonkin Gulf Resolution and How the Nation Was Trapped in Vietnam*. Philadelphia, 1971.

Ayers, Eben A. *Truman in the White House: The Diary of Eben A. Ayers*. Ed. Robert H. Ferrell. Columbia, Mo., 1991.

Bailey, Harry A., Jr., and Jay M. Shafritz, eds. *The American Presidency: Historical and Contemporary Perspectives*. Pacific Grove, Calif., 1988.

Bailey, Thomas A. *Essays Diplomatic and Undiplomatic*. Ed. Alexander DeConde and Armin Rappaport. New York, 1969.

———. *Presidential Greatness: The Image and the Man from George Washington to the Present*. New York, 1966.

———. *Presidential Saints and Sinners*. New York, 1981.

———. *The Pugnacious Presidents: White House Warriors on Parade*. New York, 1980.

———. *Theodore Roosevelt and the Japanese-American Crises*. Stanford, Calif., 1934.

———. *Wilson and the Peacemakers*. 2 vols. New York, 1947.

Bailey, Thomas A., and Paul B. Ryan. *Hitler vs. Roosevelt: The Undeclared Naval War*. New York, 1979.

Baker, George W., Jr. "Benjamin Harrison and Hawaiian Annexation: A Reinterpretation." *Pacific Historical Review* 33 (Aug. 1964): 295–309.

Baker, James A., III. *The Politics of Diplomacy: Revolution, War, and Peace*. New York, 1995.

Ball, George W. *The Past Has Another Pattern: Memoirs*. New York, 1982.

Bamford, Paul W. *The Barbary Pirates. Victims and the Scourge of Christendom*. Minneapolis, 1972.

Bancroft, George. *History of the Formation of the Constitution of the United States of America*. 2 vols. New York, 1882.

Barber, James D. *The Presidential Character: Predicting Performance in the White House.* 4th ed. Englewood Cliffs, N.J., 1992.

Barilleaux, Ryan J. "Post-Modern American Presidency." *Presidency Research* 10 (fall 1987): 15–18.

Barilleaux, Ryan J., and Mary E. Stuckey, eds. *Leadership and the Bush Presidency: Prudence or Drift in an Era of Change.* Westport, Conn., 1992.

Barnard, Harry. *Rutherford B. Hayes and His America.* Indianapolis, 1954.

Barnby, H. G. *The Prisoners of Algiers: An Account of the Forgotten American-Algerian War, 1785–1797.* London, 1966.

Barnes, Trevor. "The Secret Cold War: The C.I.A. and American Foreign Policy in Europe, 1946–1956." Parts 1 and 2. *Historical Journal* 24 (June 1981): 399–415; 25 (Sept. 1982): 649–70.

Barnet, Richard J. *The Rockets' Red Glare: When America Goes to War: The Presidents and the People.* New York, 1990.

———. *Roots of War: The Men and Institutions Behind U.S. Foreign Policy.* New York, 1972.

Barret, David M. "The Mythology Surrounding Lyndon Johnson, His Advisers, and the 1965 Decision to Escalate the Vietnam War." *Political Science Quarterly* 103 (winter 1988–89): 637–63.

———. *Uncertain Warriors: Lyndon Johnson and His Vietnam Advisers.* Lawrence, Kans., 1993.

Barrett, Laurence I. *Gambling with History: Reagan in the White House.* Harmondsworth, England, 1984.

Bauer, K. Jack. *Zachary Taylor: Soldier, Planter, Statesman of the Old Southwest.* Baton Rouge, La., 1985.

Beale, Howard K. *Theodore Roosevelt and the Rise of America to World Power.* Baltimore, 1956.

Beard, Charles A. *American Foreign Policy in the Making, 1932–1940: A Study in Responsibilities.* New Haven, 1946.

———. *The Devil Theory of War.* New York, 1936.

———. *President Roosevelt and the Coming of the War, 1941: A Study in Appearances and Reality.* New Haven, Conn., 1948.

Beck, Kent M. "Necessary Lies, Hidden Truths: Cuba in the 1960 Campaign." *Diplomatic History* 8 (winter 1984): 37–59.

Beck, Robert J. "International Law and the Decision to Invade Grenada: A Ten-Year Retrospective." *Virginia Journal of International Law* 33 (summer 1993): 765–817.

Beeman, Richard, Stephen Botein, and Edward C. Carter II, eds. *Beyond Confederation: Origins of the Constitution and American National Identity.* Chapel Hill, N.C., 1987.

Beisner, Robert L. *Twelve against Empire: The Anti-Imperialists, 1898–1900.* Reprint, New York, 1971.

Belohlavek, John M. *"Let the Eagle Soar!" The Foreign Policy of Andrew Jackson.* Lincoln, Nebr., 1985.

Belz, Herman. "Lincoln and the Constitution: The Dictatorship Question Reconsidered." *Congress and the Presidency* 15 (autumn 1988): 147–64.

Bemis, Samuel F. *John Quincy Adams and the Foundations of American Foreign Policy.* New York, 1956.

———. *John Quincy Adams and the Union.* New York, 1965.

Benjamin, James. "Rhetoric and the Performative Act of Declaring War." *Presidential Studies Quarterly* 21 (winter 1991): 73–84.

Benjamin, Jules R. *The United States and the Origins of the Cuban Revolution: An Empire in an Age of National Liberation.* Princeton, N.J., 1990.

Berdahl, Clarence A. *War Powers of the Executive in the United States.* Urbana, Ill., 1921.

Berdal, Mats R. "Fateful Encounter: The United States and UN Peacekeeping." *Survival* 36 (spring 1994): 30–50.

Berger, Raoul. "Executive Privilege v. Congressional Inquiry." Parts 1 and 2. *UCLA Law Review* 12 (May/Aug. 1965): 1044–1120, 1287–1364.

———. *Executive Privilege: A Constitutional Myth.* Cambridge, Mass., 1974.

———. "The Presidential Monopoly of Foreign Affairs." *Michigan Law Review* 71 (Nov. 1972): 1–58.

———. "War-Making by the President." *University of Pennsylvania Law Review* 129 (Nov. 1972): 29–86.

Bergeron, Paul H. *The Presidency of James K. Polk.* Lawrence, Kans., 1987.

Berle, Adolf. "The President and Foreign Policy." *New Leader* 35 (July 28, 1952): 11–15.

Berman, Larry. "From Intervention to Disengagement: The United States in Vietnam." In Levite, Jentleson, and Berman, eds. *Foreign Military Intervention,* 23–64.

———. *Lyndon Johnson's War: The Road to Stalemate in Vietnam.* New York, 1989.

———. *Planning a Tragedy: The Americanization of the War in Vietnam.* New York, 1982.

———, ed. *Looking Back on the Reagan Presidency.* Baltimore, 1990.

Berman, Larry, and Bruce W. Jentleson. "Bush and the Post-Cold-War World: New Challenges for American Leadership." In Campbell and Rockman, eds. *Bush Presidency,* 93–128.

Berman, Larry, and Emily O. Goldman. "Clinton's Foreign Policy at Midterm." In Campbell and Rockman, eds. *Clinton Presidency,* 290–324.

Bernstein, Barton J. "New Light on the Korean War." *International History Review* 3 (Apr. 1981): 256–77.

———. "Seizing the Contested Terrain of Early Nuclear History: Stimson, Conant, and Their Allies Explain the Decision to Use the Atomic Bomb." *Diplomatic History* 17 (winter 1993): 35–72.

———. "The Truman Administration and the Korean War." In Lacey, ed. *Truman Presidency,* 410–44.

———. "The Truman Administration and the Steel Strike of 1946." *Journal of American History* 52 (March 1966): 791–803.

———, ed. *Politics and Policies of the Truman Administration.* Chicago, 1970.

Bernstein, Carl, and Bob Woodward. *All the President's Men.* New York, 1974.

Bernstein, Irving. *Guns or Butter: The Presidency of Lyndon Johnson.* New York, 1996.

———. *Promises Kept: John F. Kennedy's New Frontier.* New York, 1991.

Bernstein, Richard B. *Amending America: If We Love the Constitution So Much, Why Do We Keep Trying to Change It?* New York, 1993.

Bert, Wayne. *The Reluctant Superpower: United States Policy in Bosnia, 1991–95.* New York, 1997.

Beschloss, Michael R. *The Crisis Years: Kennedy and Khrushchev, 1960–1963.* New York, 1991.

———, ed. *Taking Charge: The Johnson White House Tapes,* 1963–1964. New York, 1997.

Beschloss, Michael R., and Strobe Talbott. *At the Highest Levels: The Inside Story of the End of the Cold War.* Boston, 1993.

Bessette, Joseph M., and Jeffrey Tulis, eds. *The Presidency in the Constitutional Order.* Baton Rouge, La., 1981.

Betts, Richard K. *Soldiers, Statesmen, and Cold War Crises.* Cambridge, Mass., 1977.

Billings-Yun, Melanie. *Decision against War: Eisenhower and Dien Bien Phu, 1954.* New York, 1988.

———. *The Man in the White House: His Powers and Duties.* Rev. ed. New York, 1964.

Bischof, Günter, and Stephen E. Ambrose, eds. *Eisenhower: A Centenary Assessment.* Baton Rouge, La., 1995.

Blair, Clay. *The Forgotten War: America in Korea, 1950–53.* New York, 1987.

Blake, Nelson M. "Background of Cleveland's Venezuelan Policy." *American Historical Review* 47 (Jan. 1942): 259–77.

Blanchard, William H. *Aggression American Style.* Santa Monica, Calif., 1978.

Blechman, Barry M. "The Congressional Role in U.S. Military Policy." *Political Science Quarterly* 106 (spring 1991): 17–32.

Blechman, Barry M., and others. *Force without War: U.S. Armed Forces as a Political Instrument.* Washington, D.C., 1978.

Bledsoe, W. Craig, and others. *Powers of the Presidency.* 2d ed. Washington, D.C., 1997.

Blight, James G., and Peter Kornbluh, eds. *Politics of Illusion: The Bay of Pigs Invasion Reconsidered.* Boulder, Colo., 1998.

Blodgett, Geoffrey. "The Political Leadership of Grover Cleveland." *South Atlantic Quarterly* 82 (Sept. 1983): 288–99.

Blum, John M. *The Republican Roosevelt.* Cambridge, Mass., 1967.

Blum, William. *Killing Hope: U.S. Military Interventions since World War II.* Monroe, Maine, 1995.

Blumberg, Herbert H., and Christopher C. French, eds. *The Persian Gulf War: Views from the Social and Behavioral* Sciences. Lanham, Md., 1994.

Blumenthal, Sidney. "All the President's Wars." *New Yorker,* Dec. 28, 1992/Jan. 4, 1993, 62–72.

Blumenthal, Sidney, and Thomas Byrne Edsall, eds. *The Reagan Legacy.* New York, 1988.

Bogus, Carl T. "The Invasion of Panama and the Rule of Law." *International Lawyer* 26 (fall 1992): 781–87.

Bok, Sissela. *Lying: Moral Choice in Public and Private Life*. New York, 1978.

Bolt, Ernest C., Jr. *Ballots before Bullets: The War Referendum Approach to Peace in America, 1914–1941*. Charlottesville, Va., 1977.

Bolton, John R. "Wrong Turn in Somalia." *Foreign Affairs* 73 (Jan./Feb. 1994): 56–66.

Boose, Lynda. "Techno-Muscularity and the 'Boy Eternal.'" In Kaplan and Pease, eds. *Cultures of United States Imperialism*, 581–616.

Borchard, Edwin. "The Attorney General's Opinion on the Exchange of Destroyers for Naval Bases." *American Journal of International Law* 34 (Oct. 1940): 690–97.

Borden, Morton, ed. *America's Ten Greatest Presidents*. Chicago, 1961.

Borg, Dorothy. *American Policy and the Chinese Revolution, 1925–1928*. New York, 1947.

———. "Notes on Roosevelt's 'Quarantine' Speech." *Political Science Quarterly* 72 (Sept. 1957): 405–53.

Bornet, Vaughn D. *The Presidency of Lyndon B. Johnson*. Lawrence, Kans., 1983.

Bosso, Christopher J. "Congressional and Presidential Scholars: Some Basic Traits." *PS: Political Science and Politics* 22 (Dec. 1989): 839–48.

Bostdorff, Denise M. "The Presidency and Promoted Crisis: Reagan, Grenada, and Issue Management." *Presidential Studies Quarterly* 21 (fall 1991): 737–50.

Bourne, Peter G. *Jimmy Carter: A Comprehensive Biography from Plains to Post-presidency*. New York, 1997.

Bowen, Catherine D. *Miracle at Philadelphia: The Story of the Constitutional Convention, May to September 1787*. Boston, 1966.

Bowie, Robert, and Richard H. Immerman. *Waging Peace: Eisenhower's Strategy for National Security*. New York, 1997.

———. *Waging Peace: How Eisenhower Shaped an Enduring Cold War Strategy*. New York, 1998.

Boyer, Peter J. "Scott Ritter's Private War." *New Yorker*, Nov. 9, 1998, 56–73.

Brandes, Joseph. *Herbert Hoover and Economic Diplomacy: Department of Commerce Policy, 1921–1928*. Pittsburgh, 1962.

Brandon, Henry. *Anatomy of Error: The Inside Story of the Asian War on the Potomac, 1954–1969*. Boston, 1969.

———. *The Retreat of American Power*. Garden City, N.Y., 1973.

Brands, Henry W., Jr. "The Age of Vulnerability: Eisenhower and the National Insecurity State." *American Historical Review* 94 (Oct. 1989): 963–89.

———. *Cold Warriors: Eisenhower's Generation and American Foreign Policy*. New York, 1988.

———. "Decisions on American Armed Interventions: Lebanon, Dominican Republic, and Grenada." *Political Science Quarterly* 102 (winter 1987). 607–24.

———. "Testing Massive Retaliation: Credibility and Crisis Management in the Taiwan Strait." *International Security* 12 (spring 1988): 124–51.

———. *TR: The Last Romantic*. New York, 1997.

———. *The Wages of Globalism: Lyndon Johnson and the Limits of American Power.* New York, 1995.

Brant, Irving. *Impeachment: Trials and Errors.* New York, 1972.

———. *James Madison.* 6 vols. Indianapolis and New York, 1941–61.

Brendon, Piers. *Ike: His Life and Times.* New York, 1986.

Breuer, William B. *Vendetta! Fidel Castro and the Kennedy Brothers.* New York, 1998.

Briggs, Herbert W. "Neglected Aspects of the Destroyer Deal." *American Journal of International Law* 34 (Oct. 1940): 569–87.

Brinkley, Douglas. "The Rising Stock of Jimmy Carter: The 'Hands on' Legacy of Our Thirty-ninth President." *Diplomatic History* 20 (fall 1996): 505–29.

Brodie, Bernard. *War and Politics.* New York, 1973.

Brodie, Fawn. *Richard Nixon: The Shaping of His Character.* New York, 1981.

Brody, Richard. *Assessing the President: The Media, Elite Opinion, and Public Support.* Stanford, Calif., 1991.

Brown, Ralph Adams. *The Presidency of John Adams.* Lawrence, Kans., 1975.

Brown, Roger H. *The Republic in Peril: 1812.* New York, 1964.

Brown, Thomas. *JFK: History of an Image.* Bloomington, Ind., 1988.

Brownlow, Louis W. *The President and the Presidency.* Chicago, 1949.

Bruce, J. Allyn, and David A. Welch. *Cuba on the Brink: Castro, the Missile Crisis, and the Soviet Collapse.* New York, 1993.

Brummet, John. *Highwire: From the Back Roads to the Beltway—The Education of Bill Clinton.* New York, 1994.

Brune, Lester H. "Considerations of Force in Cordell Hull's Diplomacy, July 26 to November 26, 1941." *Diplomatic History* 2 (fall 1978): 389–405.

Bryce, James. *The American Commonwealth.* Rev. ed. 2 vols. New York, 1914.

Brzezinski, Zbigniew. *Power and Principle: Memoirs of the National Security Adviser, 1977–1981.* New York, 1983.

Buchanan, A. Russell. *The United States and World War II.* 2 vols. New York, 1964.

Buhite, Russell D. *Lives at Risk: Hostages and Victims in American Foreign Policy.* Wilmington, Del., 1995.

Bundy, McGeorge. *Danger and Survival: Choices about the Bomb in the First Fifty Years.* New York, 1988.

Bundy, William. *Tangled Web: The Making of Foreign Policy in the Nixon Presidency.* New York, 1998.

Burke, John P. *The Institutional Presidency.* Baltimore, 1992.

Burke, John P., and Fred I. Greenstein. *How Presidents Test Reality: Decisions on Vietnam, 1954 and 1965.* New York, 1989.

Burner, David. *Herbert Hoover: A Public Life.* New York, 1979.

———. *John F. Kennedy and a New Generation.* Boston, 1988.

Burns, James MacGregor. *John Kennedy: A Profile.* New York, 1961.

———. *The Power to Lead: The Crisis of the American Presidency.* New York, 1984.

———. *Presidential Government: The Crucible of Leadership.* Boston, 1966.

———. *Roosevelt: The Lion and the Fox.* New York, 1956.

———. *Roosevelt: The Soldier of Freedom, 1940–1945.* New York, 1970.

Burns, Richard D., and William A. Dixon. "Foreign Policy and the 'Democratic Myth': The Debate on the Ludlow Amendment." *Mid-America* 47 (Oct. 1965): 288–306.

Burton, David H. *Theodore Roosevelt: Confident Imperialist.* Philadelphia, 1968.

Bush, George. *Looking Forward.* New York, 1987.

———. "Why We Are in the Gulf." *Newsweek,* Nov. 26, 1990, 28–29.

Bush, George, and Brent Scowcroft. *A World Transformed.* New York, 1998.

Buzzanco, Robert. *Masters of War: Military Dissent and Politics in the Vietnam Era.* Cambridge, England, 1996.

Calder, Bruce J. *The Impact of Intervention: The Dominican Republic during the U.S. Occupation of 1916–1924.* Austin, Tex., 1984.

Caldwell, Robert G. *James A. Garfield: Party Chieftain.* New York, 1931.

Calhoun, Frederick S. *Power and Principle: Armed Intervention in Wilsonian Foreign Policy.* Kent, Ohio, 1986.

Calhoun, John C. *The Papers of John C. Calhoun.* Ed. Robert L. Meriwether and others. 23 vols. Columbia, S.C., 1959–96.

Califano, Joseph A., Jr. *A Presidential Nation.* New York, 1975.

———. *The Triumph and Tragedy of Lyndon Johnson: The White House Years.* New York, 1991.

Callahan, David. *Unwinnable Wars: American Power and Ethnic Conflict.* New York, 1997.

Campbell, Colin. *The U.S. Presidency in Crisis: A Comparative Perspective.* New York, 1998.

Campbell, Colin, and Bert A. Rockman, eds. *The Bush Presidency: First Appraisals.* Chatham, N.J., 1991.

———. *The Clinton Presidency: First Appraisals.* Chatham, N.J., 1996.

Canfield, Leon H. *The Presidency of Woodrow Wilson: Prelude to a World in Crisis.* Rutherford, N.J., 1966.

Cannon, Lou. *President Reagan: The Role of a Lifetime.* New York, 1991.

———. *Reagan.* New York, 1982.

Cantril, Hadley. *Public Opinion, 1935–1946.* Princeton, N.J., 1951.

Capitanchik, David B. *The Eisenhower Presidency and American Foreign Policy.* London, 1969.

Caraley, Demetrios, ed. *The President's War Powers from the Federalists to Reagan.* New York, 1984.

Caridi, Ronald, Jr. *The Korean War and American Politics: The Republican Party as a Case Study.* Philadelphia, 1968.

Carleton, David, and Michael Stohl. "The Foreign Policy of Human Rights: Rhetoric and Reality from Jimmy Carter to Ronald Reagan." *Human Rights Quarterly* 7 (May 1985): 205–29.

Caro, Robert A. *The Years of Lyndon Johnson: The Path to Power.* New York, 1983.

Carothers, Thomas. "Democracy Promotion under Clinton." *Washington Quarterly* 18 (autumn 1995): 13–25.

Carp, E. Wayne. *To Starve the Army at Pleasure: Continental Army Administration and American Political Culture, 1775–1783.* Chapel Hill, N.C., 1984.

Carpenter, John A. *Ulysses S. Grant.* New York, 1970.

Carroll, John A., and Mary W. Ashworth. *George Washington: First in Peace.* New York, 1957.

Carter, Jimmy. *Keeping Faith: Memoirs of a President.* New York, 1982.

Castel, Albert. *The Presidency of Andrew Johnson.* Lawrence, Kans., 1979.

Catton, Bruce. *Reflections on the Civil War.* New York, 1982.

Chafe, William H. *The Unfinished Journey: America since World War II.* 3d ed. New York, 1995.

Chang, Gordon H. "To the Nuclear Brink: Eisenhower, Dulles, and the Quemoy-Matsu Crisis." *International Security* 12 (spring 1988): 96–123.

Chang, Laurence, and Peter Kornbluh, eds. *The Cuban Missile Crisis, 1962: A National Security Archive Documents Reader.* New York, 1992.

Chayes, Abram. *The Cuban Missile Crisis: International Crises and the Rule of Law.* New York, 1974.

Chen Jian. *China's Road to the Korean War: The Making of the Sino-American Confrontation.* New York, 1994.

Childs, Marquis. *Eisenhower: Captive Hero. A Critical Study of the General and the President.* New York, 1958.

Chitwood, Oliver P. *John Tyler: Champion of the Old South.* 1939 Reprint, New York, 1964.

Chomsky, Noam. *Rethinking Camelot: JFK, the Vietnam War, and U.S. Political Culture.* Boston, 1993.

Christol, Carl Q. "Herbert Hoover: The League of Nations and the World Court." In Hatfield, ed. *Hoover Reassessed,* 335–79.

Christopher, Warren. *In the Stream of History: Shaping Foreign Policy for a New Era.* Stanford, Calif., 1998.

Cigar, Norman. *Genocide in Bosnia: The Policy of "Ethnic Cleansing."* College Station, Tex., 1995.

Clayton, Cornell W., ed. *Government Lawyers: The Federal Legal Bureaucracy and Presidential Politics.* Lawrence, Kans., 1995.

Clements, Kendrick A. *The Presidency of Woodrow Wilson.* Lawrence, Kans., 1992.

———. *Woodrow Wilson: World Statesman.* Boston, 1987.

Clifford, Clark M. *Counsel to the President: A Memoir.* New York, 1991.

Cole, Donald B. *The Presidency of Andrew Jackson.* Lawrence, Kans., 1993.

Coletta, Paolo E. *The Presidency of William Howard Taft.* Lawrence, Kans., 1973.

Conkin, Paul R. *Big Daddy from the Pedernales: Lyndon Baines Johnson.* Boston, 1986.

Connally, Thomas T., and Alfred Steinberg, *My Name Is Tom Connally.* New York, 1954.

Cook, Blanche W. *The Declassified Eisenhower: A Divided Legacy.* New York, 1981.

Cooke, Jacob E. "Country Above Party: John Adams and the 1799 Mission to France." In *Fame and the Founding Fathers.* Ed. Edmund P. Willis, 53–79. Bethlehem, Pa., 1966.

———, ed. *The Federalist.* Middletown, Conn., 1961.

Cooke, Miriam, and Angela Woollacott, eds. *Gendering War Talk.* Princeton, N.J., 1993.

Coolidge, Calvin. *The Autobiography of Calvin Coolidge.* New York, 1931.

———. *The Talkative President: The Off-the-Record Press Conferences of Calvin Coolidge.* Ed. Howard H. Quint and Robert H. Ferrell. Amherst, Mass., 1964.

Cooper, John M. *The Warrior and the Priest: Woodrow Wilson and Theodore Roosevelt.* Cambridge, Mass., 1983.

Corwin, Edward S. *Presidential Power and the Constitution: Essays.* Ithaca, N.Y., 1976.

———. *The President's Control of Foreign Relations.* Princeton, N.J., 1917.

———. *Total War and the Constitution.* New York, 1947.

Corwin, Edward S., Randall W. Bland, Theodore T. Himson, and Jack W. Peltason. *The President: Office and Powers, 1787–1984.* 5th ed. New York, 1984.

Cox, Arthur M. *The Myths of National Security: The Perils of Secret Government.* Boston, 1975.

Cox, Henry B. *War, Foreign Affairs, and Constitutional Power, 1829–1901.* Cambridge, Mass., 1984.

Cox, Richard H. *Locke on War and Peace.* London, 1960.

Crabb, Cecil V., Jr. *The Doctrines of American Foreign Policy: Their Meaning, Role, and Future.* Baton Rouge, La., 1982.

Crabb, Cecil V., Jr., and Kevin V. Mulcahy, *Presidents and Foreign Policy Making: From FDR to Reagan.* Baton Rouge, La., 1986.

Crabb, Cecil V., Jr., and Pat M. Holt. *Invitation to Struggle: Congress, the President, and Foreign Policy.* 4th ed. Washington, D.C., 1992.

Craig, Gordon A., and Alexander L. George. *Force and Statecraft: Diplomatic Problems of Our Time.* 3d ed. New York, 1995.

Cronin, Thomas E. "John F. Kennedy: President and Politician." In Harper and Krieg, eds. *Kennedy: Promise Revisited,* 1–21.

———. "A Resurgent Congress and the Imperial Presidency," *Political Science Quarterly* 95 (summer 1980): 209–37.

———, ed. *Inventing the American Presidency.* Lawrence, Kans., 1989.

———, ed. *The State of the Presidency.* 2d ed. Boston, 1980.

Cronin, Thomas E., and Michael A. Genovese. *The Paradoxes of the American Presidency.* New York, 1998.

Cronon, E. David. "Interpreting the Good Neighbor Policy: The Cuban Crisis of 1933." *Hispanic American Historical Review* 39 (Nov. 1959): 538–67.

Crovitz, L. Gordon, and Jeremy A. Rabkin, eds. *The Fettered Presidency: Legal Constraints on the Executive Branch.* Washington, D.C., 1989.

Cruz, Arturo J., Jr., and Mark Falcoff. "Who Won Nicaragua?" *Commentary* 79 (May 1990): 31–38.

Cumings, Bruce. *The Origins of the Korean War.* 2 vols. Princeton, N.J., 1981–90.

———, ed. *Child of Conflict: The Korea–American Relationship, 1943–1953.* Seattle, 1983.

Cunliffe, Marcus. *American Presidents and the Presidency.* New York, 1968.

———. "Madison (1812–1815)." In May, ed. *Ultimate Decision*, 21–53.

Cunningham, Noble E., Jr. *In Pursuit of Reason: The Life of Thomas Jefferson.* Baton Rouge, La., 1987.

———. *Jeffersonian Republicans in Power: Party Operations, 1801–1809.* Chapel Hill, N.C., 1963.

———. *The Presidency of James Monroe.* Lawrence, Kans., 1996.

Current, Richard N. *The Lincoln Nobody Knows.* New York, 1958.

———. *Secretary Stimson: A Study in Statecraft.* New Brunswick, N.J., 1954.

———. "The Stimson Doctrine and the Hoover Doctrine." *American Historical Review* 59 (April 1954): 513–42.

Curtis, James C. *The Fox at Bay: Martin Van Buren and the Presidency, 1837–1844.* Lexington, Ky., 1970.

Dahl, Robert A. *Congress and Foreign Policy.* New York, 1964.

Dallek, Robert. *Flawed Giant: Lyndon Johnson and His Times*, 1961–1975. New York, 1998.

———. *Franklin D. Roosevelt and American Foreign Policy, 1932–1945.* New York, 1979.

———. *Hail to the Chief: The Making and Unmaking of American Presidents.* New York, 1996.

———. *Lone Star Rising: Lyndon Johnson and His Times, 1908–1960.* New York, 1991.

———. "Lyndon Johnson and Vietnam: The Making of a Tragedy." *Diplomatic History* 20 (spring 1996): 147–62.

———. *Ronald Reagan: The Politics of Symbolism.* Cambridge, Mass., 1984.

D'Amato, Anthony. "The Invasion of Panama Was a Lawful Response to Tyranny." *American Journal of International Law* 84 (Apr. 1990): 516–24.

D'Angelo, John R. "Resort to Force by States to Protect Nationals: The U.S. Rescue Mission to Iran and Its Legality under International Law." *Virginia Journal of International Law* 21 (spring 1981): 485–519.

Dangerfield, George. *The Awakening of American Nationalism, 1815–1828.* New York, 1964.

———. *The Era of Good Feelings.* London, 1953.

Daniels, Josephus. *The Cabinet Diaries of Josephus Daniels, 1913–1921.* Ed. E. David Cronon. Lincoln, Nebr., 1963.

Dauer, Manning J. *The Adams Federalists.* Baltimore, 1953.

Davis, Burke. *Old Hickory: A Life of Andrew Jackson.* New York, 1977.

Davis, Kenneth S. *FDR: A History.* 3 vols. New York, 1972–93.

Davis, Vincent, ed. *The Post-Imperial Presidency.* New Brunswick, N.J. 1980.

Davison, Kenneth E. *The Presidency of Rutherford B. Hayes.* Westport, Conn., 1972.

Davison, W. Phillips. *The Berlin Blockade: A Study in Cold War Politics.* Princeton, N.J., 1958.

Dawson, Joseph G., III, ed. *Commanders in Chief: Presidential Leadership in Modern Wars.* Lawrence, Kans., 1993.

Dean, Robert D. "Masculinity as Ideology: John F. Kennedy and the Domestic Politics of Foreign Policy." *Diplomatic History* 22 (winter 1998): 29–62.

DeBenedetti, Charles, and Charles Chatsworth. *An American Ordeal: The Antiwar Movement of the Vietnam Era.* Syracuse, N.Y., 1990.

DeConde, Alexander. "Dwight D. Eisenhower: Reluctant Use of Power." In Robinson and others. *Powers of the President*, 77–132.

———. *Entangling Alliance: Politics and Diplomacy under George Washington.* Durham, N.C., 1958.

———. "Herbert Hoover and Foreign Policy: A Retrospective Assessment." In Hatfield, ed. *Hoover Reassessed*, 313–34.

———. *Herbert Hoover's Latin-American Policy.* Stanford, Calif., 1951.

———. *The Quasi-War: The Politics and Diplomacy of the Undeclared War with France, 1797–1801.* New York, 1966.

———. *This Affair of Louisiana.* New York, 1976.

De Grazia, Alfred. *Republic in Crisis: Congress against the Executive Force.* New York, 1965.

Denitch, Bogdan. *Ethnic Nationalism: The Tragic Death of Yugoslavia.* Minneapolis, 1994.

Dennett, Tyler. *Roosevelt and the Russo-Japanese War.* New York, 1925.

Denson, John V., ed. *The Costs of War: America's Pyrrhic Victories.* New Brunswick, N.J., 1997.

Destler, Ivan V. "Reagan and the World: An 'Awesome Stubbornness.'" In Jones, ed. *Reagan Legacy*, 241–61.

Detzer, David. *The Brink: Cuban Missile Crisis, 1962.* New York, 1979.

DeWeerd, Harvey A. *President Wilson Fights His War: World War I and the American Intervention.* New York, 1968.

Dickinson, Matthew J. *Bitter Harvest: FDR, Presidential Power and the Growth of the Presidential Branch.* New York, 1997.

Dingman, Roger. "Atomic Diplomacy during the Korean War." *International Security* 13 (winter 1988–89): 50–91.

Dinnerstein, Herbert. *The Making of a Missile Crisis: October 1962.* Baltimore, 1976.

Divine, Robert A. *Eisenhower and the Cold War.* New York, 1981.

———. *The Illusion of Neutrality.* Chicago, 1962.

———. *Second Chance: The Triumph of Internationalism in America during World War II.* New York, 1967.

———. *The Reluctant Belligerent: American Entry into World War II.* New York, 1965.

———. *Roosevelt and World War II.* Baltimore, 1969.

———, ed. *Exploring the Johnson Years.* Austin, Tex., 1981.

Dodge, Mark M., ed. *Herbert Hoover and the Historians.* West Branch, Iowa, 1989.

Doenecke, Justus D. "The Anti-Interventionism of Herbert Hoover." *Journal of Libertarian Studies* 8 (summer 1987): 311–40.

———. *Not to the Swift: The Old Isolationists in the Cold War Era.* Lewisburg, Pa., 1979.

———. *The Presidencies of James A. Garfield and Chester A. Arthur.* Lawrence, Kans., 1981.

Donald, David H. *Charles Sumner and the Rights of Man.* New York, 1970.

———. *Lincoln.* New York, 1995.

Donovan, Robert J. *Conflict and Crisis: The Presidency of Harry S. Truman, 1945–1948.* New York, 1977.

———. *Eisenhower: The Inside Story.* New York, 1956.

———. *Tumultuous Years: The Presidency of Harry S. Truman, 1949–1953.* New York, 1982.

Dozer, Donald M. "Benjamin Harrison and the Presidential Campaign of 1892." *American Historical Review* 54 (Oct. 1948): 49–77.

Draper, Theodore. *The Dominican Revolt: A Case Study in American Policy.* New York, 1968.

———. "Presidential Wars." *New York Review of Books,* Sept. 1991, 64–74.

———. *A Very Thin Line: The Iran-Contra Affair.* New York, 1991.

Drew, Elizabeth. *On the Edge: The Clinton Presidency.* New York, 1994.

D'Souza, Dinesh. *Ronald Reagan: How an Ordinary Man Became an Extraordinary Leader.* New York, 1997.

Duffy, Michael, and Dan Goodgame. *Marching in Place: The Status Quo Presidency of George Bush.* New York, 1992.

Dugger, Ronnie. *On Reagan: The Man and His Presidency.* New York, 1983.

Dulebohn, George R. *Principles of Foreign Policy under the Cleveland Administrations.* Philadelphia, 1941.

Dumbrell, John. *The Carter Presidency: A Re-evaluation.* Rev. ed. Manchester, England, 1995.

Dupuy, R. Ernest, and William H. Baumer. *The Little Wars of the United States.* New York, 1968.

Dyer, Brainerd. *Zachary Taylor.* Baton Rouge, La., 1946.

Eagleton, Thomas F. *War and Presidential Power: A Chronicle of Congressional Surrender.* New York, 1974.

Eastland, Terry. *Energy in the Executive: The Case for the Strong Presidency.* New York, 1992.

Edwards, George C., III. *At The Margins: Presidential Leadership of Congress.* New Haven, Conn., 1989.

Edwards, George C., III, and Stephen J. Wayne. *Studying the Presidency.* Knoxville, Tenn., 1983.

Edwards, George C., III, John H. Kessel, and Bert A. Rockman, eds. *Researching the Presidency: Vital Questions, New Approaches.* Pittsburgh, 1993.

Egan, Clifford L. *Neither Peace nor War: Franco-American Relations, 1803–1812.* Baton Rouge, La., 1983.

Ehrenreich, Barbara. *Blood Rites: Origins and History of the Passions of War.* New York, 1997.

Eisenhower, Dwight D. *The Eisenhower Diaries.* Ed. Robert H. Ferrell. New York, 1981.

———. *Ike's Letters to a Friend, 1941–1958*. Ed. Robert Griffith. Lawrence, Kans., 1984.
———. Letters to the author, July 14 and Aug. 1, 1967.
———. *The Papers of Dwight David Eisenhower*. Ed. Alfred D. Chandler and Louis Galambos. 17 vols. Baltimore, 1970-.
———. *Public Papers of the Presidents of the United States*. 8 vols. Washington, D.C., 1958–61.
———. "Some Thoughts on the Presidency." *Reader's Digest*, Nov. 1968, 49–55.
———. *The White House Years: Mandate for Change, 1953–1956*. Garden City, N.Y., 1963.
———. *The White House Years: Waging Peace, 1956–1961*. Garden City, N.Y., 1965.
Elkins, Stanley, and Eric McKitrick. *The Age of Federalism*. New York, 1993.
Ellis, Joseph J. *American Sphinx: The Character of Thomas Jefferson*. New York, 1997.
———. *Passionate Sage: The Character and Legacy of John Adams*. New York, 1993.
Ellis, L. Ethan. *Frank B. Kellogg and American Foreign Relations, 1925–1929*. New Brunswick, N.J., 1961.
———. *Republican Foreign Policy, 1921–1933*. New Brunswick, N.J., 1968.
Ellis, Richard, and Aaron Wildavsky. *Dilemmas of Presidential Leadership: From Washington through Lincoln*. New Brunswick, N.J., 1989.
Ely, John H. *War and Responsibility: Constitutional Lessons of Vietnam and Its Aftermath*. Princeton, N.J., 1993.
Emerson, J. Terry. "Making War Without a Declaration." *Journal of Legislation* 23 (1990): 23–63.
Enloe, Cynthia. *The Morning After: Sexual Politics at the End of the Cold War*. Berkeley, Calif., 1993.
Erickson, Paul D. *Reagan Speaks: The Making of an American Myth*. New York, 1985.
Esthus, Raymond A. "President Roosevelt's Commitment to Britain to Intervene in a Pacific War." *Mississippi Valley Historical Review* 50 (June 1963), 28–38.
———. *Theodore Roosevelt and the International Rivalries*. Waltham, Mass., 1970.
———. *Theodore Roosevelt and Japan*. Seattle, 1966.
Evans, Rowland, Jr., and Robert Novak. *Lyndon B. Johnson: The Exercise of Power: A Political Biography*. London, 1967.
Fallows, James. "The Passionless Presidency." Part 1 and 2. *Atlantic*, May 1979, 33–48; June 1979, 75–81.
Farrand, Max. *The Framing of the Constitution of the United States*. New Haven, Conn., 1913.
———, ed. *The Records of the Federal Convention of 1787*. Rev. ed. 4 vols. New Haven, 1966.
Fauriol, Georges A., ed. *Haitian Frustrations: Dilemmas for U.S. Policy*. Washington, D.C., 1995.

Fauriol, Georges A., and Andrew S. Faiola. "Prelude to Intervention." In Fauriol, ed. *Haitian Frustrations*, 103–16.

Fausold, Martin L. *The Presidency of Herbert C. Hoover.* Lawrence, Kans., 1985.

Fausold, Martin L., and George T. Mazuzan, eds. *The Hoover Presidency: A Reappraisal.* Albany, N.Y., 1974.

Fehrenbacher, Don E. *Lincoln in Text and Context.* Stanford, Calif., 1987.

Feis, Herbert. *The Atomic Bomb and the End of World War II.* Rev. ed. Princeton, N.J., 1966.

———. *From Trust to Terror: The Onset of the Cold War, 1945–1950.* New York, 1970.

———. *The Road to Pearl Harbor: The Coming of the War between the United States and Japan.* New York, 1950.

Ferling, John E. *The First of Men: A Life of George Washington.* Knoxville, Tenn., 1988.

———. *John Adams: A Life.* Knoxville, Tenn., 1992.

Ferrell, Robert H. *American Diplomacy in the Great Depression: Hoover-Stimson Foreign Policy, 1929–1933.* New Haven, Conn., 1957.

———. *Harry S. Truman: A Life.* Columbia, Mo., 1995.

———. *Harry S. Truman and the Modern American Presidency.* Boston, 1983.

———. *The Presidency of Calvin Coolidge.* Lawrence, Kans., 1998.

———. "Repudiation of a Repudiation." *Journal of American History* 51 (Mar. 1965): 669–73.

———. *Woodrow Wilson and World War I, 1917–1921.* New York, 1985.

Fic, Victor M. *The Collapse of American Policy in Russia and Siberia: Wilson's Decision Not to Intervene, March–October 1918.* New York, 1995.

Fick, Paul M. *The Dysfunctional President: Inside the Mind of Bill Clinton.* New York, 1995.

Field, James A., Jr. *America and the Mediterranean World, 1776–1882.* Princeton, N.J., 1969.

———. "American Imperialism: The Worst Chapter in Almost Any Book." *American Historical Review* 83 (June 1978): 644–68.

Filene, Peter G. *Him/Her/Self: Sex Roles in Modern America.* New York, 1974.

Firestone, Bernard J., and Alexej Ugrinsky. *Gerald R. Ford and the Politics of Post-Watergate America.* 2 vols. Westport, Conn., 1993.

Firestone, Bernard J., and Robert C. Vogt, eds. *Lyndon Baines Johnson and the Uses of Power.* New York, 1988.

Fisher, Louis. *Constitutional Conflicts between Congress and the President.* 3rd ed. Lawrence, Kans., 1991.

———. *The Politics of Shared Power: Congress and the Executive.* 4th ed. College Station, Tex., 1998.

———. *Presidential War Power.* Lawrence, Kans., 1995.

Fleishman, Joel L., and Arthur H. Aufses, eds. "Presidential Power." Parts 1 and 2. *Law and Contemporary Problems* 40 (spring/summer 1976).

Flexner, James T. *George Washington.* 4 vols. Boston, 1965–72.

Foglesong, David S. *America's Secret War against Bolshevism: U.S. Intervention in the Russian Civil War, 1917–1920.* Chapel Hill, N.C., 1995.

Foot, Rosemary. "Making Known the Unknown War: Policy Analysis of the Korean Conflict in the Last Decade." *Diplomatic History* 15 (summer 1991): 411–31.

———. "Nuclear Coercion and the Ending of the Korean Conflict." *International Security* 13 (winter 1988–89): 92–112.

———. *A Substitute for Victory: The Politics of Peacemaking at the Korean Armistice Talks.* Ithaca, N.Y., 1990.

———. *The Wrong War: American Policy and the Dimensions of the Korean Conflict, 1950–1953.* Ithaca, N.Y., 1985.

Ford, Gerald R. "Congress, the Presidency, and National Security Policy." *Presidential Studies Quarterly* 16 (spring 1988), 200–205.

———. *Public Papers of the Presidents of the United States: Gerald R. Ford, 1974–1976.* 6 vols. Washington, D.C., 1975–79.

———. *A Time to Heal: The Autobiography of Gerald R. Ford.* New York, 1979.

Forrestal, James. *The Forrestal Diaries.* Ed. Walter Millis. New York, 1951.

Forsythe, David P., and Ryan C. Hendrickson. "U.S. Use of Force Abroad: What Law for the President?" *Presidential Studies Quarterly* 26 (fall 1996): 950–61.

Franck, Thomas M. "Courts and Foreign Policy." *Foreign Policy* 83 (summer 1991): 66–86.

———, ed. *The Tethered Presidency: Congressional Restraints on Executive Power.* New York, 1981.

Franck, Thomas M., and Edward Weisband, eds. *Secrecy and Foreign Policy.* New York, 1974.

Frankfurter, Felix. *Felix Frankfurter Reminisces.* Ed. Harlan B. Phillips. New York, 1960.

Freidel, Frank B. *Franklin D. Roosevelt.* 4 vols. Boston, 1952–73.

———. *Franklin D. Roosevelt: A Rendezvous with Destiny.* Boston, 1990.

———. "Roosevelt to Reagan: The Birth and Growth of Presidential Libraries." *Prologue 21* (summer 1989): 103–113.

Friedman, David S. "Waging War against Checks and Balances—The Claim of an Unlimited Presidential War Power." *St. John's Law Review* 57 (winter 1983): 213–73.

Friedman, Leon, and Burt Neuborne. *Unquestioning Obedience to the President: The ACLU Case against the Illegal War in Vietnam.* New York, 1972.

Friedman, Leon, and William F. Levantrosser, eds. *Cold War Patriot and Statesman: Richard M. Nixon.* Westport, Conn., 1993.

Frost, David. *"I Gave Them a Sword": Behind the Scenes of the Nixon Interviews.* New York, 1978.

Fry, Joseph A. "William McKinley and the Coming of the Spanish-American War: A Study of the Besmirching and Redemption of an Historical Image." *Diplomatic History* 3 (winter 1979): 77–97.

Fulbright, J. William. *The Arrogance of Power.* New York, 1966.

Fursenko, Aleksandr, and Timothy Naftali. *"One Hell of a Gamble": Khrushchev, Castro, and Kennedy, 1958–1964.* New York, 1997.

Gaddis, John L. "The Emerging Post-Revisionist Synthesis on the Origins of the Cold War." *Diplomatic History* 7 (summer 1983): 171–90.

———. "Intelligence, Espionage, and Cold War Origins." *Diplomatic History* 13 (spring 1989): 191–212.

———. *The Long Peace: Inquiries into the History of the Cold War.* New York, 1987.

———. *Russia, the Soviet Union, and the United States: An Interpretive History.* New York, 1978.

———. "The Tragedy of Cold War History." *Diplomatic History* 17 (winter 1993): 1–16.

———. *The United States and the End of the Cold War: Implications, Reconsiderations, Provocations.* New York, 1992.

———. *The United States and the Origins of the Cold War, 1941–1947.* New York, 1972.

Gallagher, Hugh G. *FDR's Splendid Deception.* New York, 1985.

Gallup, George H. *The Gallup Poll: Public Opinion 1935–1971.* 3 vols. New York, 1972.

Gambino, Richard. *Vendetta: The Story of the Worst Lynching in America.* Garden City, N.Y., 1977.

Gara, Larry. *The Presidency of Franklin Pierce.* Lawrence, Kans., 1991.

Garber, Steve, and Phil Williams. "Defense Policy." In Hill and Williams, eds. *The Bush Presidency*, 184–213.

García, Carlos Bosch. "The Mexican War, Prelude and Peace." In *Diplomatic Claims: Latin American Historians View the United States*, ed. Warren Dean, 37–70. Lanham, Md., 1985.

Gardner, Lloyd C. *Approaching Vietnam: From World War II through Dienbienphu.* New York, 1988.

———. *A Covenant with Power: America and World Order from Wilson to Reagan.* New York, 1984.

———. *Pay Any Price: Lyndon Johnson and the Wars for Vietnam.* Chicago, 1995.

———. *Safe for Democracy: The Anglo-American Response to Revolution, 1913–1923.* New York, 1987.

Garfield, James A. *The Works of James Abram Garfield.* Ed. Burke A. Hinsdale. 2 vols. Boston, 1883.

Garthoff, Raymond. *Détente and Confrontation: American-Soviet Relations from Nixon to Reagan.* Rev. ed. Washington, D.C., 1994.

Gasiorowski, Mark J. *U.S. Foreign Policy and the Shah: Building a Client State in Iran.* Ithaca, N.Y., 1991.

Gelb, Leslie H., with Richard K. Betts. *The Irony of Vietnam: The System Worked.* Washington, D.C., 1979.

Gellman, Irwin F. *Good Neighbor Diplomacy: United States Policies in Latin America, 1933–1945.* Baltimore, 1979.

———. *Roosevelt and Batista: Good Neighbor Diplomacy in Cuba, 1933–1945.* Albuquerque, N.M., 1973.

Genovese, Michael A. *The Nixon Presidency: Power and Politics in Turbulent Times.* New York, 1990.

———. *The Presidency in an Age of Limits.* Westport, Conn., 1993.

George, Alexander L. "The Case for Multiple Advocacy in Making Foreign Policy." *American Political Science Review* 66 (Sept. 1972): 751–95.

George, Alexander L., and Juliette L. George. *Woodrow Wilson and Colonel House: A Personality Study.* New York, 1956.

Geselbracht, Raymond. "The Four Eras in the History of the Presidential Papers." *Prologue* 15 (spring 1983): 37–42.

Geyelin, Philip. *Lyndon B. Johnson and the World.* New York, 1966.

Gibbons, William C. *The U.S. Government and the Vietnam War: Executive and Legislative Roles and Relationships.* 3 vols. Princeton, N.J., 1986.

Giglio, James N. *The Presidency of John F. Kennedy.* Lawrence, Kans., 1991.

Gilbert, Felix. *To the Farewell Address.* Princeton, N.J., 1961.

Gilderhus, Mark T. *Diplomacy and Revolution: U.S.–Mexican Relations under Wilson.* Tucson, Ariz., 1977.

Gilmore, David D. *Manhood in the Making: Cultural Concepts of Masculinity.* New Haven, Conn., 1990.

Giunta, Mary A., ed. *The Emerging Nation: A Documentary History of the Foreign Relations of the United States under the Articles of Confederation, 1780–1789.* 3 vols. Washington, D.C., 1996.

Glad, Betty. *Charles Evans Hughes and the Illusions of Innocence: A Study in American Diplomacy.* Urbana, Ill., 1966.

———. *Jimmy Carter: In Search of the Great White House.* New York, 1980.

Gleijeses, Piero. *The Dominican Crisis: The 1965 Constitutionalist Revolution and American Intervention.* Trans. Lawrence Lipson. Baltimore, 1978.

———. *Shattered Hope: The Guatemalan Revolution and the United States, 1944–1954.* Princeton, N.J., 1991.

Glennon, Michael J. "Can the President Do No Wrong?" *American Journal of International Law* 80 (Oct. 1986): 923–30.

———. *Constitutional Diplomacy.* Princeton, N.J., 1990.

Goebel, Julius. *The Struggle for the Falkland Islands: A Study in Legal and Diplomatic History.* 1927. Reprint, New Haven, 1982.

Goldberg, Joyce S. *The Baltimore Affair.* Notre Dame, Ind., 1986.

Goldman, Eric F. *The Tragedy of Lyndon Johnson.* New York, 1969.

Goldman, Milton F. "President Carter, Western Europe, and Afghanistan in 1980: Inter-Allied Differences over Policy toward the Soviet Invasion." In Rosenbaum and Ugrinsky, eds. *Jimmy Carter,* 19–34.

Goldsmith, William M. *The Growth of Presidential Power: A Documented History.* 3 vols. New York, 1983.

Goldwin, Robert A., and Robert Licht, eds. *Foreign Policy and the Constitution.* Washington, D.C., 1990.

Goodhart, Philip. *Fifty Ships That Saved the World: The Foundation of the Anglo-American Alliance.* New York, 1965.

Goodman, Allan E. *The Lost Peace: America's Search for a Negotiated Settlement of the Vietnam War.* Stanford, Calif., 1978.

Goodwin, Doris K. *No Ordinary Time: Franklin and Eleanor Roosevelt: The Home Front in World War II.* New York, 1994.

Gould, Lewis L. *The Presidency of Theodore Roosevelt.* Lawrence, Kans., 1991.

———. *The Presidency of William McKinley.* Lawrence, Kans., 1980.

———. *The Spanish-American War and President McKinley.* Lawrence, Kans., 1982.

Goulden, Joseph C. *Truth Is the First Casualty: The Gulf of Tonkin Affair—Illusion and Reality.* Chicago, 1969.

Graber, Doris A. *Public Opinion, the President, and Foreign Policy: Four Case Studies from the Formative Years.* New York, 1968.

Graebner, Norman A. *Empire on the Pacific: A Study in American Continental Expansion.* New York, 1955.

———. "The Mexican War: A Study in Causation," *Pacific Historical Review* 49 (Aug. 1980): 495–526.

———. *The New Isolationism: A Study in Politics and Foreign Policy since 1950.* New York, 1956.

Graff, Henry F. *The Tuesday Cabinet: Deliberation and Decision on Peace and War under Lyndon B. Johnson.* Englewood Cliffs, N.J., 1970.

Grant, Ulysses S. *The Papers of Ulysses S. Grant.* Ed. John Y. Simon. 22 vols. Carbondale, Ill., 1967–98.

Graubard, Stephen R. *Mr. Bush's War: Adventures in the Politics of Illusion.* New York, 1992.

Grayson, Benson L. *The Unknown President: The Administration of President Millard Fillmore.* Washington, D.C., 1981.

Green, Fitzhugh. *George Bush: An Intimate Portrait.* New York, 1989.

Greene, John R. *The Presidency of Gerald R. Ford.* Lawrence, Kans., 1995.

Greenstein, Fred I. *The Hidden-Hand Presidency: Eisenhower as Leader.* New York, 1982.

———, ed. *Leadership in the Modern Presidency.* Cambridge, Mass., 1988.

———, ed. *The Reagan Presidency: An Early Assessment.* Baltimore, 1983.

Greenstein, Fred I., Larry Berman, and Alvin S. Felzenberg. *Evolution of the Modern Presidency: A Bibliographical Survey.* Washington, D.C., 1977.

Greenstein, Fred I., and Richard I. Immerman. "What Did Eisenhower Tell Kennedy about Indochina? The Politics of Misperceptions." *Journal of American History* 79 (Sept. 1992): 568–87.

Greer, Thomas H. *What Roosevelt Thought: The Social and Political Ideas of Franklin D. Roosevelt.* East Lansing, Mich., 1958.

Grieb, Kenneth J. *The Latin American Policy of Warren G. Harding.* Fort Worth, Tex., 1976.

Griffeth, Robert. "Old Progressives and the Cold War." *Journal of American History* 71 (Sept. 1979): 334–47.

Guerrero, Manuel de Jesús. *El Machismo Latinoamericano.* New York, 1977.

Guhin, Michael A. *John Foster Dulles: A Statesman and His Times.* New York, 1972.

Gulley, Bill. *Breaking Cover.* New York, 1980.

Gutman, Roy. *Banana Diplomacy: The Making of American Policy in Nicaragua, 1981–1987*. New York, 1988.

Haas, Garland A. *Jimmy Carter and the Politics of Frustration*. Jefferson, N.C., 1992.

Hagan, Kenneth J. *American Gunboat Diplomacy and the Old Navy, 1877–1889*. Westport, Conn., 1973.

Hagerty, James C. *The Diary of James C. Hagerty: Eisenhower in Mid-Course, 1954–1955*. Ed. Robert H. Ferrell. Bloomington, Ind., 1983.

Haig, Alexander M., Jr. *Caveat: Realism, Reagan, and Foreign Policy*. New York, 1984.

Halberstam, David. *The Best and the Brightest*. New York, 1972.

Haldeman, Harry R. *The Haldeman Diaries: Inside the Nixon White House*. New York, 1995.

Haldeman, Harry R., with Joseph DiMona. *The Ends of Power*. New York, 1978.

Haley, P. Edward. *Revolution and Intervention: The Diplomacy of Taft and Wilson with Mexico, 1910–1917*. Cambridge, Mass., 1970.

Hall, David K. "The Laotian War of 1962 and the Indo-Pakistani War of 1971." In Blechman and others. *Force Without War*, 135–221.

Hall, David L. *The Reagan Wars: A Constitutional Perspective on War Powers and the Presidency*. Boulder, Colo., 1991.

Halliday, Jon, and Bruce Cumings. *Korea: The Unknown War*. New York, 1988.

Halperin, Morton H. "Lawful Wars." *Foreign Policy* 72 (fall 1988): 173–95.

Halperin, Morton H., and others. *The Lawless State: Crimes of the U.S. Intelligence Agencies*. Harmondsworth, England, 1977.

Hamby, Alonzo L. "An American Democrat: A Reevaluation of the Personality of Harry S. Truman." *American Political Science Review* 106 (spring 1991): 33–53.

———. *Beyond the New Deal: Harry S. Truman and American Liberalism*. New York, 1973.

———. *Man of the People: A Life of Harry S. Truman*. New York, 1995.

———. "The Mind and Character of Harry S. Truman." In Lacey, ed. *Truman Presidency*, 19–53.

Hamilton, Alexander, John Jay, and James Madison. *The Federalist*. Ed. Jacob E. Cooke. Middletown, Conn., 1961.

Hamilton, Holman. *Zachary Taylor: Soldier in the White House*. Indianapolis, 1951.

Hammond, Paul Y. *LBJ and the Presidential Management of Foreign Relations*. Austin, Tex., 1992.

Hanna, Alfred J., and Kathryn A. Hanna. *Napoleon III and Mexico*. Chapel Hill, N.C., 1971.

Harbaugh, William H. *Power and Responsibility: The Life and Times of Theodore Roosevelt*. New York, 1961.

Hargreaves, Mary W. M. *The Presidency of John Quincy Adams*. Lawrence, Kans., 1985.

Hargrove, Erwin G. *Jimmy Carter as President: Leadership and the Politics of the Public Good*. Baton Rouge, La, 1988.

———. *The Power of the Modern Presidency.* Philadelphia, 1974.

———. *The President as Leader: Appealing to the Better Angels of Our Nature.* Lawrence, Kans., 1998.

Hargrove, Erwin G., and Michael Nelson. *Presidents, Politics, and Policy.* Baltimore, 1984.

Harlow, Neal. *California Conquered: War and Peace on the Pacific, 1846–1850.* Berkeley, Calif., 1982.

Harper, Paul, and Joann P. Krieg, eds. *John F. Kennedy: The Promise Revisited.* New York, 1988.

Harris, Adrienne, and Ynestra King, eds. *Rocking the Ship of State: Toward a Feminist Peace Politics.* Boulder, Colo., 1989.

Hart, John. "President Clinton and the Politics of Symbolism." *Political Science Quarterly* 110 (1995): 385–403.

Hartmann, Robert T. *Palace Politics: An Insider's Account of the Ford Years.* New York, 1980.

Hartsock, Nancy C. M. "Masculinity, Heroism, and the Making of War." In Harris and King, eds. *Rocking the Ship of State,* 133–52.

Hass, Richard N. "Fatal Distraction: Bill Clinton's Foreign Policy." *Foreign Policy* 108 (fall 1997): 112–23.

Hassler, Warren W., Jr. *The President as Commander in Chief.* Menlo Park, Calif., 1971.

Hatfield, Mark O., ed. *Herbert Hoover Reassessed: Essays Commemorating the Fiftieth Anniversary of the Inauguration of Our Thirty-First President.* Washington, D.C., 1981.

Hatzenbuehler, Ronald L., and Robert L. Ivie. *Congress Declares War: Rhetoric, Leadership, and Partisanship in the Early Republic.* Kent, Ohio, 1983.

Haynes, Richard F. *The Awesome Power: Harry S. Truman as Commander in Chief.* Baton Rouge, La., 1973.

Head, Richard G., Frisco W. Short, and Robert C. McFarlane. *Crisis Resolution: Presidential Decision Making in the* Mayaguez *and Korean Confrontations.* Boulder, Colo., 1978.

Healy, David. *Drive to Hegemony: The United States in the Caribbean, 1898–1917.* Madison, Wis., 1988.

———. *US Expansionism: The Imperialist Urge in the 1890s.* Madison, Wis., 1970.

Heckscher, August. *Woodrow Wilson.* New York, 1991.

Heclo, Hugh. *Studying the Presidency: A Report to the Ford Foundation.* New York, 1977.

Heinrichs, Waldo. "President Franklin D. Roosevelt's Intervention in the Battle of the Atlantic, 1941." *Dipomatic History* 10 (fall 1986): 311–32.

———. *Threshold of War: Franklin D. Roosevelt and American Entry into World War II.* New York, 1988.

Henderson, Phillip G. *Managing the Presidency: The Eisenhower Legacy—From Kennedy to Reagan.* Boulder, Colo., 1988.

Henkin, Louis. *Constitutionalism, Democracy, and Foreign Affairs.* New York, 1990.

———. *Foreign Affairs and the United States Constitution.* 2d ed. New York, 1996.

———. "The Invasion of Panama under International Law: A Gross Violation." *Columbia Journal of Transnational Law* 29, no. 2 (1991): 293–317.

Henkin, Louis, Michael J. Glennon, and William D. Rogers, eds. "The United States Constitution in Its Third Century: Foreign Affairs." *The American Journal of International Law* 68 (Oct. 1989): special issue.

Henkin, Louis, and others. *Right v. Might: International Law and the Use of Force.* 2nd ed. New York, 1991.

Herken, Gregg. *Counsels of War.* Expanded ed. New York, 1987.

Hero, Dilip. *Desert Shield to Desert Storm: The Second Gulf War.* London, 1992.

———. *The Winning Weapon: The Atomic Bomb in the Cold War.* New York, 1980.

Herring, George C. *America's Longest War: The United States and Vietnam, 1950–1975.* 2d ed. New York, 1986.

———. *LBJ and Vietnam: A Different Kind of War.* Austin, Tex., 1994.

———. "'Peoples Quite Apart': Americans, South Vietnamese, and the War in Vietnam." *Diplomatic History* 14 (winter 1990): 1–23.

Herring, George C., and Richard H. Immerman. "Eisenhower, Dulles, and Dienbienphu: 'The Day We Didn't Go to War' Revisited." *Journal of American History* 71 (Sept. 1979): 343–63.

Hersey, John. *The Price of Power: Kissinger in the Nixon White House.* New York, 1983.

Hersh, Seymour M. *The Dark Side of Camelot.* New York, 1997.

———. "May-Zelikow Confidential." *Diplomatic History* 22 (fall 1998): 654–61.

Hershberg, James G. "Before 'The Missiles of October': Did Kennedy Plan a Military Strike against Cuba?" *Diplomatic History* 14 (spring 1990): 163–98.

Hesseltine, William B. *Ulysses S. Grant: Politician.* New York, 1935.

Hickey, Donald R. *The War of 1812: A Forgotten Conflict.* Urbana, Ill., 1989.

Hietala, Thomas R. *Manifest Design: Anxious Aggrandizement in Late Jacksonian America.* Ithaca, N.Y., 1985.

Higgins, Trumbull. *The Perfect Failure: Kennedy, Eisenhower, and the CIA at the Bay of Pigs.* New York, 1987.

Hilderbrand, Robert C. *Power and the People: Executive Management of Public Opinion in Foreign Affairs, 1897–1921.* Chapel Hill, N.C., 1981.

Hill, Dilys M., and Phil Williams, eds. *The Bush Presidency: Triumphs and Adversities.* New York, 1994.

Hilsman, Roger. *George Bush Versus Saddam Hussein.* Novato, Calif., 1992.

———. *To Move a Nation: The Politics of Foreign Policy in the Administration of John F. Kennedy.* Garden City, N.Y., 1967.

Hinckley, Barbara. *Less Than Meets the Eye: Foreign Policy Making and the Myth of the Assertive Congress.* Chicago, 1994.

Hirschfield, Robert S., ed. *The Power of the Presidency: Concepts and Controversy.* 2d ed. Chicago, 1973.

Hoff, Joan. *Nixon Reconsidered.* New York, 1994.

———. "A Revisionist View of Nixon's Foreign Policy." *Presidential Studies Quarterly* 26 (winter 1996): 107–29.

Hoff-Wilson, Joan. *Herbert Hoover: Forgotten Progressive.* Boston, 1975.

———. "Richard M. Nixon: The Corporate Presidency." In Greenstein, ed. *Leadership in Modern Presidency*, 164–98.

Hofstadter, Richard. *The American Political Tradition and the Men Who Made It.* New York, 1960.

Hogan, Michael J. *A Cross of Iron: Harry S. Truman and the Origins of the National Security State.* New York, 1998.

———. *The Marshall Plan: America, Britain, and the Reconstruction of Western Europe, 1947–1952.* Cambridge, England, 1987.

———. ed. *America in the World: The Historiography of American Foreign Relations since 1941.* Cambridge, England, 1995.

Hogan, Michael J., and Thomas J. Paterson, eds. *Explaining the History of American Foreign Relations.* New York, 1991.

Hoganson, Kristen L. *Fighting for American Manhood: How Gender Politics Provoked the Spanish-American and Philippine-American Wars.* New Haven, 1998.

Hohenberg, John. *The Bill Clinton Story: Winning the Presidency.* Syracuse, N.Y., 1994.

Holbo, Paul S. "Presidential Leadership in Foreign Affairs: William McKinley and the Turpie-Foraker Amendment." *American Historical Review* 72 (July 1967): 1321–35.

Holbrooke, Richard. *To End a War.* New York, 1998.

Holden, Robert H. "The Real Diplomacy of Violence: United States Military Power in Central America." *International History Review* 15 (May 1993): 283–322.

Holloway, David. *Stalin and the Bomb: The Soviet Union and Atomic Energy, 1939–1956.* New Haven, Conn., 1994.

Holt, Pat M. *The War Powers Resolution: The Role of Congress in U.S. Armed Intervention.* Washington, D.C., 1978.

Hoogenboom, Ari. *The Presidency of Rutherford B. Hayes.* Lawrence, Kans., 1988.

———. *Rutherford B. Hayes: Warrior and President.* Lawrence, Kans., 1995.

Hook, Sidney, *The Hero in History: A Study in Limitation and Possibility.* New York, 1943.

Hoover, Herbert. Interview by author. Aug. 5, 1947. Hoover Library, Stanford University.

———. *The Memoirs of Herbert Hoover.* 3 vols. New York, 1952.

———. *The State Papers and Other Public Writings of Herbert Hoover.* Ed. William S. Myers. 2 vols. Garden City, N.Y., 1934.

Horsman, Reginald. *The Causes of the War of 1812.* Philadelphia., 1962.

———. *The War of 1812.* New York, 1969.

Hoxie, Gordon R. *Command Decision and the Presidency: A Study in National Security Policy and Organization.* New York, 1977.

Hughes, Emmet J. *The Ordeal of Power: A Political Memoir of the Eisenhower Years.* New York, 1963.

Hull, Cordell. *The Memoirs of Cordell Hull.* 2 vols. New York, 1948.

Hunt, Michael H. *Crises in U.S. Foreign Policy: An International History Reader.* New Haven, Conn., 1996.

———. *Lyndon Johnson's War: America's Cold War Crusade in Vietnam, 1945–1968.* New York, 1996.

Hyland, Pat. *Presidential Libraries and Museums.* Washington, D.C., 1995.

Immerman, Richard H. "Between the Unattainable and the Unacceptable: Eisenhower and Dienbienphu." In Melanson and Mayers, eds. *Reevaluating Eisenhower,* 120–54.

———. *The CIA in Guatemala: The Foreign Policy of Intervention.* Austin, Tex., 1982.

———. "The United States and the Geneva Conference of 1954: A New Look." *Diplomatic History* 14 (winter 1990): 43–66.

Irwin, Ray W. *The Diplomatic Relations of the United States with the Barbary Powers, 1776–1818.* Chapel Hill, N.C., 1931.

Isaacson, Walter. "Madeleine's War." *Time* 153 (May 17, 1999), 24–35.

Israel, Fred L., ed. *The State of the Union Messages of the Presidents, 1790–1966.* 3 vols. New York, 1966.

Jackson, Andrew. *Correspondence of Andrew Jackson.* Ed. John S. Bassett. 7 vols. Washington, D.C., 1926–33.

Jackson, Robert H. *South Asian Crisis: India, Pakistan, and Bangla Desh.* New York, 1975.

———. *The Supreme Court in the American System of Government.* Cambridge, Mass., 1955.

Janis, Irving L. *Victims of Groupthink: A Psychological Study of Foreign-Policy Decisions and Fiascoes.* Boston, 1967.

Javits, Jacob K. *Who Makes War: The President Versus Congress.* New York, 1973.

Jefferson, Thomas. *The Papers of Thomas Jefferson.* Ed. Julian P. Boyd and others. 25 vols. Princeton, N.J., 1950–97.

———. *The Republic of Letters: The Correspondence between Thomas Jefferson and James Madison.* Ed. James Morton Smith. 3 vols. New York, 1995.

———. *The Works of Thomas Jefferson.* Ed. Paul L. Ford. 12 vols. New York, 1893–99.

Jeffords, Susan. "Commentary: Culture and National Identity in U.S. Foreign Policy." *Diplomatic History* 18 (winter 1994): 91–96.

Jeffreys-Jones, Rhodri. *The CIA and American Democracy.* New Haven, 1989.

Jensen, Merrill. *The Articles of Confederation: An Interpretation of the Social-Constitutional History of the American Revolution, 1774–1781.* Madison, Wis., 1940.

———. *The New Nation: A History of the United States during the Confederation, 1781–1789.* New York, 1967.

Jentleson, Bruce W. "The Domestic Politics of Desert Shield: Should We Go to War? Who Should Decide?" *Brookings Review* 9 (winter 1990–91): 22–28.

———. *With Friends Like These: Reagan, Bush, and Saddam, 1982–1990.* New York, 1994.

Jervis, Robert. *Perception and Misperception in International Politics.* Princeton, N.J., 1976.

Johns, Christina J., and P. Ward Johnson. *State Crime, the Media, and the Invasion of Panama.* Westport, Conn., 1994.

Johnson, Andrew. *The Papers of Andrew Johnson.* Ed. Leroy P. Graf and Ralph W. Haskins. 13 vols. Knoxville, Tenn., 1967–95.

Johnson, Haynes. *In the Absence of Power: Governing America.* New York, 1980.

———. *Sleepwalking Through History: America in the Reagan Years.* New York, 1991.

Johnson, Lyndon B. *The Vantage Point: Perspectives of the Presidency, 1963–1969.* New York, 1971.

Johnson, Robert H. "Misguided Morality: Ethics and the Reagan Doctrine." *Political Science Quarterly* 103 (fall 1988): 509–29.

Johnson, Walter. *1600 Pennsylvania Avenue: Presidents and the People, 1929–1959.* Boston, 1960.

Johnstone, Robert M., Jr. *Jefferson and the Presidency: Leadership in the Young Republic.* Ithaca, N.Y., 1978.

Jones, Charles O. *The Trusteeship Presidency: Jimmy Carter and the United States Congress.* Baton Rouge, La., 1988.

———, ed. *The Reagan Legacy: Promise and Performance.* Chatham, N.J., 1988.

Jones, Howard. *"A New Kind of War": America's Global Strategy and the Truman Doctrine in Greece.* New York, 1989.

Jones, Howard, and Randall B. Woods. "The Origins of the Cold War: A Symposium." *Diplomatic History 17* (spring 1993): 251–95.

Jones, Joseph M. *The Fifteen Weeks (February 21-June 5, 1947).* New York, 1955.

Jordan, Hamilton. *Crisis: The Last Year of the Carter Presidency.* New York, 1982.

Kaplan, Amy, and Donald Pease, eds. *Cultures of United States Imperialism.* Durham, N.C., 1993.

Kaplan, Lawrence S. *Entangling Alliances with None: American Foreign Policy in the Age of Jefferson.* Kent, Ohio, 1987.

———. *Thomas Jefferson: Westward the Course of Empire.* Wilmington, Del., 1999.

Kasindorf, Martin. "Divining the George Bush Ex-Presidency." *Los Angeles Times Magazine,* July 23, 1995.

Katzenbach, Nicholas deB. "Comparative Roles of the President and the Congress in Foreign Affairs." *Department of State Bulletin* 58 (Sept. 11, 1967): 333–36.

———. "Johnson and Foreign Policy." In Thompson, ed. *Johnson Presidency,* 209–17.

Kaufman, Burton I. "John F. Kennedy as World Leader." *Diplomatic History* 17 (summer 1993): 447–69.

———. *The Korean War: Challenges in Crisis, Credibility, and Command.* Philadelphia, 1986.

———. *The Presidency of James Earl Carter, Jr.* Lawrence, Kans., 1993.

Kearns, Doris. *Lyndon Johnson and the American Dream.* New York, 1976.

Keefer, Edward C. "President Dwight D. Eisenhower and the End of the Korean War." *Diplomatic History* 10 (summer 1986): 267–89.

Kennan, George F. *Soviet-American Relations, 1917–1920.* 2 vols. Princeton, N.J., 1956–1958.

Kennedy, Paul. *The Rise and Fall of the Great Powers: Economic Change and Military Conflict from 1500 to 2000.* New York, 1987.

Kennedy, Robert F. *Thirteen Days: A Memoir of the Cuban Missile Crisis.* New York, 1969.

Kern, Montague, Patricia W. Levering, and Ralph B. Levering. *The Kennedy Crises: The Press, the Presidency, and Foreign Policy.* Chapel Hill, N.C., 1983.

Ketcham, Ralph. "James Madison and the Presidency." In Cronin, ed. *Inventing the American Presidency,* 347–62.

———. *Presidents Above Party: The First American Presidency, 1789–1829.* Chapel Hill, N.C., 1984.

Keynes, Edward. *Undeclared War: Twilight Zone of Constitutional Power.* University Park, Pa., 1982.

Khoury, Philip S. "The Reagan Administration and the Middle East." In Kyvig, ed. *Reagan and the World,* 67–96.

Kimball, Warren F. *The Juggler: Franklin Roosevelt as Wartime Statesman.* Princeton, N.J., 1991.

Kingseed, Cole C. *Eisenhower and the Suez Crisis of 1956.* Baton Rouge, La., 1995.

Kirkpatrick, Jeanne J. *The Reagan Phenomenon and Other Speeches on Foreign Policy.* Washington, D.C., 1983.

Kissinger, Henry A. *White House Years.* Boston, 1979.

———. *Years of Upheaval.* Boston, 1982.

Klafter, Craig E. "United States Involvement in the Falkland Islands Crisis of 1831–1833." *Journal of the Early Republic* 4 (winter 1984): 395–420.

Klare, Michael T. *Beyond the 'Vietnam Syndrome': US Interventionism in the 1980s.* Washington, D.C., 1981.

Klein, Philip S. *President James Buchanan: A Biography.* University Park, Penn., 1962.

Knott, Stephen F. *Secret and Sanctioned: Covert Operations and the American Presidency.* New York, 1996.

Knox, Dudley W., ed. *Naval Documents Related to the United States Wars with the Barbary Powers.* 6 vols. Washington, D.C., 1939–44.

Koch, Adrienne, ed. *Notes of Debates in the Federal Convention of 1787 Reported by James Madison.* Columbus, Ohio, 1966.

Koenig, Louis W. *The Chief Executive.* 3d ed. New York, 1975.

Koh, Harold Hongju. *The National Security Constitution: Sharing Power after the Iran-Contra Affair.* New Haven, Conn., 1990.

Kolko, Gabriel. *Century of War: Politics, Conflict, and Society.* New York, 1994.

Kolko, Gabriel, and Joyce Kolko. *The Limits of Power: The World and United States Foreign Policy, 1945–54.* New York, 1972.

Kornbluh, Peter. "The Covert War." In Walker, ed. *Reagan versus the Sandinistas,* 21–38.

———. *Nicaragua: The Price of Intervention: Reagan's Wars against the Sandinistas.* Washington, D.C., 1987.

Kornbluh, Peter, and Malcolm Byrne, eds. *The Iran-Contra Scandal: The Declassified History.* New York, 1993.

Kuklick, Bruce. *The Good Ruler: From Herbert Hoover to Richard Nixon.* New Brunswick, N.J., 1988.

Kunz, Diane B. *The Economic Diplomacy of the Suez Crisis.* Chapel Hill, N.C., 1991.

Kupchan, Charles A. "Getting In: The Initial Stage of Military Intervention." In Levite, Jentleson, and Berman, eds. *Foreign Military Intervention,* 241–60.

Kutler, Stanley I. *The Wars of Watergate: The Last Crisis of Richard Nixon.* New York, 1990.

———, ed. *Abuse of Power: The New Nixon Tapes.* New York, 1997.

Kyvig, David E., ed. *Reagan and the World.* New York, 1990.

Lacey, Michael J., ed. *The Truman Presidency.* New York, 1989.

Lael, Richard L. *Arrogant Diplomacy: U.S. Policy toward Colombia, 1903–1922.* Wilmington, Del., 1987.

LaFeber, Walter. "The Background of Cleveland's Venezuelan Policy: A Reinterpretation." *American Historical Review* 66 (July 1961): 947–67.

———. *The New Empire: An Interpretation of American Expansion, 1860–1898.* Ithaca, N.Y., 1963.

———. *The Panama Canal: The Crisis in Historical Perspective.* New York, 1979.

Lagon, Mark P. *The Reagan Doctrine: Sources of American Conduct in the Cold War's Last Chapter.* Westport, Conn., 1994.

Lamb, Christopher J. *Belief Systems and Decision Making in the* Mayaguez *Crisis.* Gainesville, Fla., 1988.

Langer, William L., and S. Everett Gleason. *The Challenge to Isolation, 1937–1940.* New York, 1952.

———. *The Undeclared War, 1940–1941.* New York, 1953.

Langley, Lester D. *The Banana Wars: An Inner History of the American Empire, 1900–1934.* Lexington, Ken., 1983.

Langston, Thomas S. *Ideologues and Presidents: From the New Deal to the Reagan Revolution.* Baltimore, 1992.

Lasch, Christopher. *The American Liberals and the Russian Revolution.* New York, 1962.

Lash, Joseph P. *Roosevelt and Churchill, 1939–1941: The Partnership That Saved the West.* New York, 1976.

Latner, Richard B. *The Presidency of Andrew Jackson: White House Politics, 1829–1837.* Athens, Ga., 1979.

Layne, Christopher and Benjamin Schwarz. "American Hegemony—Without an Enemy." *Foreign Policy* 92 (1993): 5–23.

Lebow, Richard N. *Between War and Peace: The Nature of International Crisis.* Baltimore, 1981.

———. "Psychological Dimensions of Post–Cold War Foreign Policy." In Renshon, ed. *Clinton Presidency,* 235–45.

Lee, Jong R. "Rally around the Flag: Foreign Policy Events and Presidential Popularity." *Presidential Studies Quarterly* 7 (1977): 252–55.

Leech, Margaret. *In the Days of McKinley.* New York, 1959.

Leffler, Melvyn P. *A Preponderance of Power: National Security, the Truman Administration, and the Cold War.* Stanford, Calif., 1992.

Lehman, John. *Making War: The 200-Year-Old Battle between the President and Congress over How America Goes to War.* New York, 1992.

Lehman, Kenneth. "Revolutions and Attributions: Making Sense of Eisenhower Administration Policies in Bolivia and Guatemala." *Diplomatic History* 21 (spring 1997): 185–213.

Lens, Sidney. *Permanent War: The Militarization of America.* New York, 1987.

Leuchtenburg, William E. *The FDR Years: On Roosevelt and His Legacy.* New York, 1995.

———. *Franklin D. Roosevelt and the New Deal.* New York, 1963.

Levin, N. Gordon, Jr. *Woodrow Wilson and World Politics: America's Response to War and Revolution.* New York, 1968.

Levitan, David M. "The Foreign Relations Power: An Analysis of Mr. Justice Sutherland's Theory." *Yale Law Journal* 45 (Apr. 1946): 467–97.

Levite, Ariel E., Bruce W. Jentleson, and Larry Berman, eds. *Foreign Military Intervention: The Dynamics of Protracted Conflict.* New York, 1992.

Levy, Leonard W. *Jefferson and Civil Liberties: The Darker Side.* Cambridge, Mass., 1963.

———. *Original Intent and the Framers' Constitution.* New York, 1988.

Levy, Leonard W., and Louis Fisher, eds. *Encyclopedia of the American Presidency.* 4 vols. New York, 1994.

Lifton, Robert J., and Greg Mitchell. *Hiroshima in America: Fifty Years of Denial.* New York, 1995.

Liggio, Leonard P., and James J. Martin, eds. *Watershed of Empire: Essays on New Deal Foreign Policy.* Colorado Springs, 1976.

Lincoln, Abraham. *The Collected Works of Abraham Lincoln.* Ed. Roy P. Basler. 9 vols. New Brunswick, N.J., 1953–55.

Linderman, Gerald F. *The Mirror of War: American Society and the Spanish-American War.* Ann Arbor, Mich., 1974.

Link, Arthur S. *Wilson: Campaigns for Progressivism and Peace, 1916–1917.* Princeton, N.J., 1965.

———. *Wilson: The Struggle for Neutrality, 1914–1915.* Princeton, N.J., 1960.

———. *Woodrow Wilson and the Progressive Era, 1910–1917.* New York, 1954.

———. *Woodrow Wilson: Revolution, War, and Peace.* Arlington Heights, Ill., 1979.

Little, Douglas. "His Finest Hour? Eisenhower, Lebanon, and the 1958 Middle East Crisis." *Diplomatic History* 20 (winter 1996): 27–54.

Lobel, Jules. "Covert War and Congressional Authority: Hidden War and Forgotten Power." *University of Pennsylvania Law Review* 134 (June 1986): 1035–1110.

Locke, John. *Two Treatises of Government.* Ed. Peter Laslett. Cambridge, England, 1988.

Lofgren, Charles A. "Mr. Truman's War: A Debate and Its Aftermath." *Review of Politics* 31 (Apr. 1969): 223–41.

———. "United States v. Curtiss-Wright Export Corporation: An Historical Reassessment." *Yale Law Journal* 83 (Nov. 1973): 1–32.

———. "War-Making under the Constitution: The Original Understanding." *Yale Law Journal* 81 (March 1972): 672–702.

Logevall, Fredrik. *Choosing War: The Lost Chance for Peace and the Escalation of War in Vietnam.* Berkeley, 1999.

———. "Vietnam and the Question of What Might Have Been." Paper presented to the Cold War History Group, University of California, Santa Barbara, May 20, 1997.

Long, David F. "'Martial Thunder': The First Official American Armed Intervention in Asia." *Pacific Historical Review* 42 (May 1973): 143–62.

Long, John W. "American Intervention in Russia: The Northern Expedition, 1918–19." *Diplomatic History* 6 (winter 1982): 45–67.

Los Angeles *Times.* Selected issues, 1980–1999.

Lott, Davis N., ed. *The Presidents Speak: The Inaugural Addresses of the American Presidents from Washington to Lincoln.* New York, 1994.

Lowenthal, Abraham F. *The Dominican Intervention.* Cambridge, Mass., 1972.

Lowi, Theodore J. *The Personal President: Power Invested, Promise Unfulfilled.* Ithaca, N.Y., 1985.

———. "Presidential Power: Restoring the Balance." *Political Science Quarterly* 100 (summer 1985): 185–213.

Lukas, J. Anthony. *Nightmare: The Underside of the Nixon Years.* New York, 1976.

Lyon, Peter. *Eisenhower: Portrait of the Hero.* Boston, 1974.

Maass, Peter. *Love Thy Neighbor: Story of War.* New York, 1996.

McAuliffe, Mary S. "Commentary: Eisenhower the President." *Journal of American History* 68 (Dec. 1981): 625–32.

McClellan, David S. *Dean G. Acheson: The State Department Years.* New York, 1976.

McClintock, Michael. *Instruments of Statecraft: U.S. Guerrilla Warfare, Counterinsurgency, and Counterterrorism, 1940–1990.* New York, 1992.

McClure, Wallace. *International Executive Agreements: Democratic Procedure under the Constitution of the United States.* New York, 1941.

McCormick, Richard P. *The Presidential Game: The Origins of American Presidential Politics.* New York, 1982.

McCoy, Charles A. *Polk and the Presidency.* Austin, Texas, 1960.

McCoy, Donald R. *Calvin Coolidge: The Quiet President.* New York, 1967.

———. *The National Archives: America's Ministry of Documents, 1934–1968.* Chapel Hill, N.C., 1978.

———. *The Presidency of Harry S. Truman.* Lawrence, Kans., 1984.

McCoy, Drew R. *The Last of the Founding Fathers: James Madison and the Republican Legacy.* Cambridge, Mass., 1989.

McCullough, David. *Truman.* New York, 1992.

McDonald, Forrest. *Alexander Hamilton: A Biography.* New York, 1979.

———. *E Pluribus Unum: The Formation of the American Republic, 1776–1790.* Boston, 1965.

———. *The Presidency of George Washington.* Lawrence, Kans., 1974.

———. *The Presidency of Thomas Jefferson.* Lawrence, Kans., 1978.

McDougall, Walter A. *Promised Land, Crusader State: The American Encounter with the World since 1776*. Boston, 1997.

McElroy, Robert. *Grover Cleveland: The Man and the Statesman*. 2 vols. New York, 1923.

McFadden, David W. *Alternative Paths: Soviets and Americans, 1917–1920*. New York, 1993.

McFarlane, Robert C. *Special Trust*. New York, 1994.

McFeely, William S. *Grant: A Biography*. New York, 1981.

"Machismo Diplomacy" (unsigned editorial). *The Nation*, May 31, 1975, 642–3.

McKay, Ernest A. *Against Wilson and War, 1914–1917*. Malabar, Fla., 1996.

McLaughlin, Andrew C. *The Confederation and the Constitution, 1783–1789*. New York, 1962.

McLean, David. "American Nationalism, the China Myth, and the Truman Doctrine: The Question of Accommodation with Peking, 1949–50." *Diplomatic History* 10 (winter 1986): 25–42.

McMahan, Jeff. *Reagan and the World: Imperial Policy in the New Cold War*. London, 1984.

McMahon, Robert J. "Credibility and World Power: Exploring the Psychological Dimension in Postwar American Diplomacy." *Diplomatic History* 15 (fall 1991): 455–71.

McNamara, Robert S. *In Retrospect: The Tragedy and Lessons of Vietnam*. New York, 1995.

McPherson, James M. *Abraham Lincoln and the Second American Revolution*. New York, 1990.

———. *Battle Cry of Freedom: The Civil War Era*. New York, 1988.

———. *Ordeal by Fire: The Civil War and Reconstruction*. New York, 1982.

Madison, James. *Letters and Other Writings of James Madison, Fourth President of the United States*. 4 vols. Philadelphia., 1865.

———. *The Mind of the Founder: James Madison*. Ed. Marvin Meyers. Indianapolis, 1973.

———. *The Republic of Letters: The Correspondence between Thomas Jefferson and James Madison*. Ed. James Morton Smith. 3 vols. New York, 1995.

———. *The Writings of James Madison*. Ed. Gaillard Hunt. 9 vols. New York, 1900–1910.

Maechling, Charles, Jr. "Washington's Illegal Invasion (Panama)." *Foreign Policy* 79 (summer 1990): 113–31.

Mahon, John K. *The War of 1812*. Gainesville, Fla., 1972.

Main, Jackson Turner. *The Anti-Federalists: Critics of the Constitution, 1781–1788*. Chapel Hill, N.C., 1961.

Malone, Dumas. *Jefferson and His Time*. 6 vols. Boston, 1948–81.

Mann, Thomas E., ed. *A Question of Balance: The President, the Congress, and Foreign Policy*. Washington, 1990.

Maraniss, David. *First in His Class: A Biography of Bill Clinton*. New York, 1995.

Marcus, Maeva. *Truman and the Steel Seizure Case: The Limits of Presidential Power*. New York, 1977.

Margolis, Lawrence. *Executive Agreements and Presidential Power in Foreign Policy.* New York, 1986.

Marks, Frederick W., III. *Independence on Trial: Foreign Affairs and the Making of the Constitution.* Baton Rouge, La., 1973.

———. "Morality as a Drive Wheel in the Diplomacy of Theodore Roosvelt." *Diplomatic History* 2 (winter 1978): 43–62.

———. "Parochialism in American Foreign Relations: An Historical Overview." *SHAFR Newsletter* 26 (Mar. 1995): 1–19.

———. *Velvet on Iron: The Diplomacy of Theodore Roosevelt.* Lincoln, Nebr., 1979.

———. *Wind over Sand: The Diplomacy of Franklin Roosevelt.* Athens, Ga., 1988.

Marshall, Jonathan, and others, *The Iran-Contra Connection: Secret Teams and Covert Operations in the Reagan Era.* Boston, 1987.

Matray, James I. *The Reluctant Crusade: American Foreign Policy in Korea, 1941–1950.* Honolulu, 1985.

Matthews, Joseph J. "Informal Diplomacy in the Venezuelan Crisis of 1896." *Mississippi Valley Historical Review* 50 (Sept. 1963): 195–212.

Matthews, Richard K. *If Men Were Angels: James Madison and the Heartless Empire of Reason.* Lawrence, Kans., 1998.

Matthews, Tom. "The Road to War." *Newsweek*, Jan. 28, 1991, 54–65.

Matthewson, Tim. "Jefferson and Haiti." *Journal of Southern History* 61 (May 1995): 209–48.

May, Christopher N. *In the Name of War: Judicial Review and the War Powers since 1918.* Cambridge, Mass., 1989.

May, Ernest R. *Imperial Democracy: The Emergence of America as a Great Power.* New York, 1961.

———. *Lessons of the Past: The Use and Misuse of History in American Foreign Policy.* New York, 1973.

———. *The Making of the Monroe Doctrine.* Cambridge, Mass., 1975.

———, ed. *Knowing One's Enemies: Intelligence Assessment before the Two World Wars.* Princeton, N.J., 1984.

———, ed. *The Ultimate Decision: The President as Commander in Chief.* New York, 1960.

May, Ernest R., and Philip D. Zelikow. "Camelot Confidential." *Diplomatic History* 22 (fall 1998): 642–53.

———, eds. *The Kennedy Tapes: Inside the White House during the Cuban Missile Crisis.* Cambridge, Mass., 1997.

Mayer, David N. *The Constitutional Thought of Thomas Jefferson.* Charlottesville, Va., 1994.

Maynes, Charles W. "A Workable Clinton Doctrine." *Foreign Policy* 93 (winter 1993–94), 3–20.

Mayo, Bernard. *Henry Clay: Spokesman of the New West.* Boston, 1937.

Medland, William J. *The Cuban Missile Crisis of 1962: Needless or Necessary.* New York, 1988.

Meeker, Leonard C. "The Legality of United States Participation in the Defense of Viet-Nam." *Department of State Bulletin* 54 (Mar. 28, 1966): 474–89.

Melanson, Richard A., and David Mayers, eds. *Reevaluating Eisenhower: American Foreign Policy in the 1950s.* Urbana, Ill., 1987.

Merk, Frederick. *Fruits of Propaganda in the Tyler Administration.* Cambridge, Mass., 1971.

———. *Manifest Destiny and Mission in American History: A Reinterpretation.* New York, 1963.

———. *The Monroe Doctrine and American Expansionism, 1843–1849.* New York, 1966.

Merli, Frank J., and Theodore A. Wilson, eds. *Makers of American Diplomacy.* 2 vols. New York, 1974.

Merrill, Horace S. *Bourbon Leader: Grover Cleveland and the Democratic Party.* Boston, 1957.

Mervin, David. *George Bush and the Guardianship Presidency.* New York, 1996.

———. *Ronald Reagan and the American Presidency.* London, 1990.

Milkis, Sidney M., and Michael Nelson. *The American Presidency: Origins and Development, 1776–1990.* 2d ed. Washington, D.C., 1994.

Miller, Merle. *Plain Speaking: An Oral Biography of Harry S. Truman.* New York, 1974.

Miller, Stuart C. *"Benevolent Assimilation": The American Conquest of the Philippines, 1899–1903.* New Haven, Conn., 1982.

Millis, Walter. *The Martial Spirit: A Study of Our War with Spain.* 1931. Reprint, New York, 1965.

Miroff, Bruce. "John Adams and the Presidency." In Cronin, ed., *Inventing the American Presidency,* 304–23.

———. *Pragmatic Illusions: The Presidential Politics of John F. Kennedy.* New York, 1976.

Monroe, James. *The Writings of James Monroe.* Ed. Stanislaus M. Hamilton. 7 vols. New York, 1898–1903.

Moore, John Bassett. *The Collected Papers of John Bassett Moore.* 7 vols. New Haven, Conn., 1944.

Morgan, Edmund S. *Inventing the People: The Rise of Popular Sovereignty in England and America.* New York, 1988.

Morgan, H. Wayne. *America's Road to Empire: The War with Spain and Overseas Expansion.* New York, 1965.

———. *William McKinley and His America.* Syracuse, N.Y., 1963.

Morison, Samuel E., Frederick Merk, and Frank Freidel. *Dissent in Three American Wars.* Cambridge, Mass., 1970.

Morley, Morris H., ed. *Crisis and Confrontation: Ronald Reagan's Foreign Policy.* Totowa, N.J., 1988.

Morris, Eric. *Blockade: Berlin and the Cold War.* London, 1973.

Morris, Kenneth E. *Jimmy Carter: American Moralist.* Athens, Ga., 1996.

Morris, Roger. *Partners in Power: The Clintons and Their America.* New York, 1996.

———. *Richard Milhous Nixon: The Rise of an American Politician.* New York, 1990.

Moses, Russell L. *Freeing the Hostages: Reexamining U.S.–Iranian Negotiations and Soviet Policy, 1979–1981.* Pittsburgh, 1996.

Mowry, George E. *The Era of Theodore Roosevelt, 1900–1912.* New York, 1958.

Mueller, John E. "Trends in Popular Support for the Wars in Korea and Vietnam." *American Political Science Review* 65 (June 1971): 358–75.

———. *War, Presidents, and Public Opinion.* New York, 1973.

Mugridge, Ian. *The View from Xanadu: William Randolph Hearst and United States Foreign Policy.* Montréal, 1995.

Mullen, William F. *Presidential Power and Politics.* New York, 1976.

Munro, Dana G. *Intervention and Dollar Diplomacy in the Caribbean, 1900–1921.* Princeton, N.J., 1964.

Muravchik, Joshua. *Exporting Democracy: Fulfilling America's Destiny.* Washington, D.C., 1991.

———. *The Uncertain Crusade: Jimmy Carter and the Dilemmas of Human Rights Policy.* Lanham, Md., 1986.

Murphy, Robert, *Diplomat among Warriors.* Garden City, 1964.

Murray, Robert K. *The Harding Era: Warren G. Harding and His Administration.* Minneapolis, 1969.

Murray, Robert K., and Tim H. Blessing. *Greatness in the White House: Rating the Presidents.* 2nd ed. University Park, Pa., 1994.

Murray, Williamson, MacGregor Knox, and Alvin Bernstein, eds. *The Making of Strategy: Rulers, States, and War.* New York, 1996.

Musicant, Ivan. *The Banana Wars: A History of United States Military Intervention in Latin America from the Spanish-American War to the Invasion of Panama.* New York, 1990.

Muslin, Hyman L., and Thomas H. Jobe. *Lyndon Johnson, the Tragic Self: A Psychohistorical Portrait.* New York, 1991.

Myers, William S. *The Foreign Policies of Herbert Hoover.* New York, 1940.

Nacos, Brigitte L. *The Press, Presidents, and Crises.* New York, 1990.

Nanda, Ved P. "The Validity of United States Intervention in Panama under International Law." *American Journal of International Law* 84 (Apr. 1990): 494–503.

Nash, Philip. *The Other Missiles of October: Eisenhower, Kennedy, and the Jupiters, 1957–1963.* Chapel Hill, N.C., 1997.

Neff, Donald. *Warriors at Suez: Eisenhower Takes America into the Middle East.* New York, 1981.

Nelson, Anna K. "The 'Top of Policy Hill': President Eisenhower and the National Security Council." *Diplomatic History* 7 (fall 1983): 307–26.

Nelson, Michael, ed. *Guide to the Presidency.* 2 vols. Washington, D.C., 1996.

Neu, Charles E. *An Uncertain Friendship: Theodore Roosevelt and Japan, 1906–1909.* Cambridge, Mass., 1967.

Neumann, William L. *America Encounters Japan: From Perry to MacArthur.* Baltimore, 1963.

Neustadt, Richard E. *Presidential Power and the Modern Presidents: The Politics of Leadership from Roosevelt to Reagan.* Rev. ed. New York, 1990.

Neustadt, Richard E., and Ernest R. May. *Thinking in Time: The Uses of History for Decision Makers.* New York, 1986.

Nevins, Allan. *Grover Cleveland: A Study in Courage.* New York, 1932.

———. *Hamilton Fish: The Inner History of the Grant Administration.* Rev. ed. 2 vols. New York, 1957.

Newman, John M. *JFK and Vietnam: Deception, Intrigue, and the Struggle for Power.* New York, 1992.

New York *Times.* Selected issues.

Nichols, Roy F. *Franklin Pierce: Young Hickory of the Granite Hills.* 2d ed. Philadelphia, 1958.

Niven, John. *Martin Van Buren: The Romantic Age of American Politics.* New York, 1983.

Nixon, Richard M. *In the Arena: A Memoir of Victory, Defeat, and Renewal.* New York, 1990.

———. *Public Papers of the Presidents of the United States: Richard Nixon, 1969–1974.* 6 vols. Washington, D.C., 1975.

———. *The Real War.* New York, 1980.

———. *RN: The Memoirs of Richard Nixon.* New York, 1978.

———. *Six Crises.* Garden City, N.Y., 1962.

Nolan, Cathal J. "The Last Hurrah of Conservative Isolationism: Eisenhower, Congress, and the Bricker Amendment." *Presidential Studies Quarterly* 22 (spring 1992): 337–49.

Notter, Harley. *The Origins of the Foreign Policy of Woodrow Wilson.* Baltimore, 1937.

Oakley, Meredith L. *On the Make: The Rise of Bill Clinton.* Washington, D.C., 1994.

Oates, Stephen B. *With Malice toward None: The Life of Abraham Lincoln.* New York, 1977.

O'Brien, Connor Cruise. *The Long Affair: Thomas Jefferson and the French Revolution, 1785–1800.* Chicago, 1996.

O'Connor, Raymond G. "Harry S. Truman: New Dimensions of Power." In Robinson and others. *Powers of the President,* 15–76.

Offner, Arnold A. "'Another Such Victory': President Truman, American Foreign Policy, and the Cold War." *Diplomatic History* 23 (spring 1999), 127–55.

Offner, John L. *An Unwanted War: The Diplomacy of the United States and Spain over Cuba, 1895–1898.* Chapel Hill, N.C., 1992.

Olmstead, Kathryn S. *Challenging the Secret Government: The Post-Watergate Investigations of the CIA and FBI.* Chapel Hill, N.C., 1996.

———. "Reclaiming Executive Power: The Ford Administration's Response to the Intelligence Investigations." *Presidential Studies Quarterly* 26 (summer 1996): 723–37.

Orban, Edmond. *La présidence moderne aux États-Unis: Personnalité et institutionnalisation.* Montréal, 1974.

Orman, John. *Comparing Presidential Behavior: Carter, Reagan, and the Macho Presidential Style.* Westport, Conn., 1987.

———. "The Macho Presidential Style." *Indiana Social Studies Quarterly* 29 (Feb. 1977): 51–60.

———. *Presidential Accountability: New and Recurring Problems.* New York, 1990.

———. *Presidential Secrecy and Deception: Beyond the Power to Persuade.* Westport, Conn., 1980.

Osborne, John. *White House Watch: The Ford Years.* Washington, D.C., 1977.

Osgood, Robert E., and others. *Retreat from Empire? The First Nixon Administration.* Baltimore, 1973.

Owsley. Frank L., Jr., and Gene A. Smith. *Filibusters and Expansionists: Jeffersonian Manifest Destiny, 1800–1821.* Tuscaloosa, Ala., 1997.

Oye, Kenneth A., and others. *Eagle Resurgent? The Reagan Era in American Foreign Policy.* Boston, 1987.

Pach, Charles J., Jr., and Elmo Richardson. *The Presidency of Dwight D. Eisenhower.* Rev. ed. Lawrence, Kans., 1991.

Paige, Glenn D. *The Korean Decision, June 24–30, 1950.* New York, 1968.

Palmer, Bruce, Jr. *Intervention in the Caribbean: The Dominican Crisis of 1965.* Louisville, Ky., 1989.

Paludan, Phillip S. *The Presidency of Abraham Lincoln.* Lawrence, Kans., 1994.

Parmet, Herbert S. *Eisenhower and the American Crusades.* New York, 1972.

———. *George Bush: The Life of a Lone Star Yankee.* New York, 1997.

———. *JFK: The Presidency of John F. Kennedy.* New York, 1983.

——— *Richard Nixon and His America.* Boston, 1990.

Paschal, Joel F. *Mr. Justice Sutherland: A Man against the State.* Princeton, N.J., 1951.

Pastor, Robert A. *Condemned to Repetition: The United States and Nicaragua.* Princeton, N.J., 1987.

Paterson, Thomas G. *Contesting Castro: The United States and the Triumph of the Cuban Revolution.* New York, 1994.

———. "John F. Kennedy's Quest for Victory and Global Crisis." In Paterson, ed. *Kennedy's Quest for Victory,* 3–23.

———. "The Limits of Hegemony: The United States and the Cuban Revolution." *Occasional Paper,* no. 5. Latin American Consortium of New England. Storrs, Conn., 1996.

———. *Meeting the Communist Threat: Truman to Reagan.* New York, 1988.

———. *On Every Front: The Making and the Unmaking of the Cold War.* Rev. ed. New York, 1992.

———. "Presidential Foreign Policy, Public Opinion, and Congress: The Truman Years." *Diplomatic History* 3 (winter 1979): 1–18.

———, ed. *Kennedy's Quest for Victory: American Foreign Policy, 1961–1963.* New York, 1989.

Paterson, Thomas G., and William J. Brophy. "October Missiles and November Elections: The Cuban Missile Crisis and American Politics, 1962." *Journal of American History* 73 (June 1986): 87–119.

Patrick, Rombert W. *Florida Fiasco: Rampant Rebels on the Georgia-Florida Border, 1810–1815*. Athens, Ga., 1954.

Pérez, Louis A., Jr. *The War of 1898: The United States and Cuba in History and Historiography*. Chapel Hill, N.C., 1998.

Perkins, Bradford. *Castlereagh and Adams: England and the United States, 1812–1823*. Berkeley, Calif., 1964.

———. *Prologue to War: England and the United States, 1805–1812*. Berkeley, Calif., 1963.

Perkins, Dexter. *A History of the Monroe Doctrine*. Rev. ed. Boston, 1955.

Perusse, Roland I. *Haitian Democracy Restored, 1991–1995*. Lanham, Md., 1995.

Pessen, Edward. *The Log Cabin Myth: The Social Backgrounds of the Presidents*. New Haven, 1984.

Peterson, Merrill D. *Thomas Jefferson and the New Nation: A Biography*. New York, 1970.

Peterson, Norma L. *The Presidencies of William Henry Harrison and John Tyler*. Lawrence, Kans., 1989.

Pfiffner, James P. "Presidential Policy-Making and the Gulf War." In Whicker and others, eds. *Presidency and Gulf War*, 3–23.

———. *The Strategic Presidency: Hitting the Ground Running*. 2nd ed. Lawrence, Kans., 1996.

Phelps, Glenn A. *George Washington and American Constitutionalism*. Lawrence, Kans., 1993.

Pious, Richard M. *The American Presidency*. New York, 1986.

Plesur, Milton. *America's Outward Thrust: Approaches to Foreign Affairs, 1895–1890*. DeKalb, Ill., 1971.

Pletcher, David M. *The Awkward Years: American Foreign Relations under Garfield and Arthur*. Columbia, Mo., 1962.

———. *The Diplomacy of Annexation: Texas, Oregon, and the Mexican War*. Columbia, Mo., 1973.

Polenberg, Richard. *Reorganizing Roosevelt's Government: The Controversy over Executive Reorganization, 1936–1939*. Cambridge, Mass., 1966.

Polk, James K. *The Diary of James K. Polk during His Presidency, 1845 to 1849*. Ed. Milo M. Quaife. 4 vols. Chicago, 1910.

———. "Letters of James K. Polk to Cave Johnson, 1833–1848." Ed. St. George L. Sioussat. *Tennessee Historical Magazine* 1 (Sept. 1915): 209–56.

Porter, Gareth. *A Peace Denied: The United States, Vietnam, and the Paris Agreement*. Bloomington, Ind., 1975.

Powell, Colin L. *My American Journey*. New York, 1995.

Prados, John. *The Hidden History of the Vietnam War*. Chicago, 1995.

———. *Presidents' Secret Wars: CIA and Pentagon Covert Operations since World War II*. New York, 1986.

Prange, Gordon W. *At Dawn We Slept: The Untold Story of Pearl Harbor*. New York, 1981.

Price, Raymond. *With Nixon*. New York, 1977.

Pringle, Henry F. *The Life and Times of William Howard Taft.* 2 vols. New York, 1939.

———. *Theodore Roosevelt: A Biography.* New York, 1931.

Purifoy, Lewis M. *Harry Truman's China Policy: McCarthyism and the Diplomacy of Hysteria, 1947–1951.* New York, 1976.

Pusey, Merlo J. *Eisenhower the President.* New York, 1956.

———. *The Way We Go to War.* Boston, 1969.

Quigley, John. "The Legality of the United States Invasion of Panama," *Yale Journal of International Law* 15 (summer 1990): 276–315.

Quirk, Robert E. *An Affair of Honor: Woodrow Wilson and the Occupation of Veracruz.* Lexington, Ky., 1962.

Rabe, Stephen G. "The Caribbean Triangle: Betancourt, Castro, and Trujillo and U.S. Foreign Policy, 1958–1963." *Diplomatic History* 20 (winter 1996): 55–78.

———. *Eisenhower and Latin America: The Foreign Policy of Anticommunism.* Chapel Hill, N.C., 1988.

———. "Eisenhower Revisionism: A Decade of Scholarship." *Diplomatic History* 17 (winter 1993): 97–115.

Rader, Doston. "'I've Had a Wonderful Life': An Interview With Former President George Bush." *Parade,* Dec. 1, 1996, 4–6.

Rakove, Jack N. *Original Meanings: Politics and Ideas in the Making of the Constitution.* New York, 1996.

Randall, James G. *Constitutional Problems under Lincoln.* Rev. ed. Urbana, Ill., 1951.

———. "Lincoln in the Rôle of Dictator," *South Atlantic Quarterly,* 28, 236–52.

Randall, James G., and Richard N. Current. *Lincoln the President.* 4 vols. New York, 1945–55.

Range, Willard. *Franklin D. Roosevelt's World Order.* Athens, Ga., 1959.

Rappaport, Armin. *Henry L. Stimson and Japan, 1931–33.* Chicago, 1963.

Rayback, Robert J. *Millard Fillmore: Biography of a President.* Buffalo, N.Y., 1959.

Reagan, Ronald. *An American Life.* New York, 1990.

Reardon, Betty. *Sexism and the War System.* New York, 1985.

Record, Jeffrey. *Hollow Victory: A Contrary View of the Gulf War.* Washington, 1993.

Reedy, George E. *Lyndon B. Johnson: A Memoir.* New York, 1982.

———. *The Twilight of the Presidency.* New York, 1970.

Reeves, Richard. "Jerry Ford and His Flying Circus: A Presidential Diary." *New York,* Nov. 25, 1974, 42–46.

———. *President Kennedy: Profile of Power.* New York, 1993.

Reeves, Thomas C. *Gentleman Boss: Chester Alan Arthur.* New York, 1975.

———. *A Question of Character: A Life of John F. Kennedy.* New York, 1991.

Reichard, Garry W. "Early Returns: Assessing Jimmy Carter." *Presidential Studies Quarterly* 20 (summer 1990): 603–20.

Reichley, A. James. *Conservatives in an Age of Change: The Nixon and Ford Administrations.* Washington, D.C., 1981.

Remini, Robert V. *Andrew Jackson and the Course of American Democracy, 1833–1845*. New York, 1984.

Renshon, Stanley A. *High Hopes: The Clinton Presidency and the Politics of Ambition*. New York, 1996.

———, ed. *The Clinton Presidency: Campaigning, Governing, and the Psychology of Leadership*. Boulder, Colo., 1995.

Rhodes, Benjamin D. *The Anglo-American Winter War with Russia, 1918–1919: A Diplomatic and Military Tragicomedy*. New York, 1988.

Ricard, Serge. *Théodore Roosevelt et la justification de l'impérialisme*. Aix-en-Provence, France, 1986.

———, ed. *An American Empire: Expansionist Cultures and Policies, 1881–1917*. Aix-en-Provence, France, 1990.

Riccards, Michael P. *The Ferocious Engine of Democracy: A History of the American Presidency*. 2 vols. Lanham, Md., 1995.

———. *A Republic, If You Can Keep It: The Foundations of the American Presidency, 1700–1800*. New York, 1987.

Richardson, James D., ed. *A Compilation of the Messages and Papers of the Presidents, 1789–1897*. 10 vols. Washington, D.C., 1896–97, with additional volumes.

Risen, James. "Building a Better CIA." *Los Angeles Times Magazine*, Oct. 8, 1995, 12–15, 34–38.

Robinson, Edgar E. *The Roosevelt Leadership, 1933–1945*. Philadelphia, 1955.

Robinson, Edgar E., and Vaughn D. Bornet. *Herbert Hoover: President of the United States*. Stanford, Calif., 1975.

Robinson, Edgar E., and others. *Powers of the President in Foreign Affairs, 1945–1965*. San Francisco, 1966.

Roche, John P. "Executive Power and Domestic Emergency: The Quest for Prerogative." *Western Political Quarterly* 5 (Dec. 1952): 592–618.

Rockman, Bert. "The Modern Presidency and Theories of Accountability: Old Wine *and* Old Bottles." *Congress and the Presidency* 15 (autumn 1986): 135–56.

Rogers, James Grafton. *World Policing and the Constitution*. Boston, 1945.

Rogin, Michael P. *Ronald Reagan, the Movie, and Other Episodes in Political Demonology*. Berkeley, Calif., 1987.

Rolle, Andrew. *John Charles Frémont: Character as Destiny*. Norman, Okla., 1991.

Roosevelt, Franklin D. *Franklin D. Roosevelt and Foreign Affairs*. Ed. Edgar B. Nixon. 3 vols. Cambridge, Mass., 1969.

———. *The Public Papers and Addresses of Franklin D. Roosevelt*. Ed. Samuel I. Rosenman. 13 vols. New York, 1938–50.

———. *The Roosevelt Letters: Being the Personal Correspondence of Franklin Delano Roosevelt*. Ed. Elliott Roosevelt. 3 vols. London, 1949–1952.

Roosevelt, Theodore. *The Letters of Theodore Roosevelt*. Ed. Elting E. Morison. 8 vols. Cambridge, Mass., 1951–54.

———. *Presidential Addresses and State Papers*. 2 vols. New York, 1904.

———. *The Works of Theodore Roosevelt*. Ed. Herman Hagedorn. 20 vols. New York, 1926.

Root, Elihu. *The Military and Colonial Policy of the United States: Addresses and Reports*. Cambridge, Mass., 1916.

Rosati, Jerel A. *The Carter Administration's Quest for Global Community: Beliefs and Their Impact on Behavior.* Columbia, S.C., 1987.

———. "Jimmy Carter, a Man Before His Time? The Emergence and Collapse of the First Pre–Cold War Presidency." *Political Science Quarterly* 23 (summer 1993): 459–76.

Rose, Gary L. *The American Presidency under Siege.* Albany, N.Y., 1997.

Rose, Richard. *The Postmodern President: George Bush Meets the World.* 2d ed. Chatham, N.J., 1991.

Rosenbaum, Herbert D., and Alexej Ugrinsky, eds. *Jimmy Carter: Foreign Policy and Post-Presidential Years.* Westport, Conn., 1994.

Rosenberg, David A. "American Atomic Strategy and the Hydrogen Bomb Decision." *Journal of American History* 66 (June 1979): 62–87.

Rosenman, Samuel I. *Working with Roosevelt.* New York, 1952.

Rossiter, Clinton. *The American Presidency.* New York, 1956.

Rossiter, Clinton, and Richard P. Longaker. *The Supreme Court and the Commander in Chief.* Expanded ed. Ithaca, N.Y., 1976.

Rotter, Andrew J. "Gender Relations, Foreign Relations: The United States and South Asia, 1947–1964." *Journal of American History* 81 (Sept. 1994): 518–42.

Rotundo, E. Anthony. *American Manhood: Transformations in Masculinity from the Revolution to the Modern Era.* New York, 1993.

Rourke, John T. *Congress and the Presidency in U.S. Foreign Policymaking: A Study of Interaction and Influence, 1945–1982.* Boulder, Colo., 1983.

———. *Presidential Wars and American Democracy: Rally 'round the Chief.* New York, 1993.

Rourke, John T., and Russell Farnen. "War, Presidents, and the Constitution." *Presidential Studies Quarterly* 18 (1988): 513–22.

Rubin, Barry. *Paved with Good Intentions: The American Experience and Iran.* New York, 1980.

Rubner, Michael. "The Reagan Administration, the 1973 War Powers Resolution, and the Invasion of Grenada." *Political Science Quarterly* 100 (winter 1985–86): 627–47.

Rugger, Ronnie. *On Reagan: The Man and His Presidency.* New York, 1983.

Runkel, David R. *Campaign for President: The Managers Look at '88.* Dover, Mass., 1989.

Rusk, Dean. "The President." *Foreign Affairs* 38 (Apr. 1960): 353–69.

Rusk, Dean, as told to Richard Rusk. *As I Saw It.* New York, 1990.

Russell, Francis. *The Shadow of Blooming Grove: Warren G. Harding in His Times.* New York, 1968.

Russett, Bruce M. *Controlling the Sword: The Democratic Governance of National Security.* Cambridge, Mass., 1990.

———. *No Clear and Present Danger: A Skeptical View of the United States Entry into World War II.* New York, 1972.

Rutland, Robert A. *James Madison: The Founding Father.* New York, 1987.

———. *The Presidency of James Madison.* Lawrence, Kans., 1990.

Ryan, Paul B. *The Iranian Rescue Mission: Why It Failed.* Annapolis, Md., 1985.

Santa Barbara *News-Press.* Selected issues, 1980–1999.

Schandler, Herbert Y. *The Unmaking of a President: Lyndon Johnson and Vietnam.* Princeton, N.J., 1977.

Schapsmeier, Edward L., and Frederick H. *Gerald R. Ford's Date with Destiny: A Political Biography.* New York, 1989.

Schell, Jonathan. *The Time of Illusion.* New York, 1976.

Schelling, Thomas C. *Arms and Influence.* New Haven, Conn., 1966.

Schick, Frank L., and others. *Records of the Presidency: Presidential Papers and Libraries from Washington to Reagan.* Phoenix, Ariz., 1989.

Schild, Georg. *Between Ideology and Realpolitik: Woodrow Wilson and the Russian Revolution, 1917–1921.* Westport, Conn., 1995.

Schlesinger, Arthur M., Jr. "After the Imperial Presidency." In Schlesinger, *Cycles of American History,* 277–336.

———. *The Age of Roosevelt.* 3 vols. Boston, 1957–1960.

———. *The Cycles of American History.* Boston, 1986.

———. *The Imperial Presidency.* Boston, 1973.

———. *The Politics of Hope.* Boston, 1962.

———. *A Thousand Days: John F. Kennedy in the White House.* New York, 1967.

Schmitt, Gary J. "Thomas Jefferson and the Presidency." In Cronin, ed. *Inventing the American Presidency,* 326–46.

Schmitt, Karl M. *Mexico and the United States, 1821–1973: Conflict and Coexistence.* New York, 1974.

Scholes, Walter V., and Marie V. Scholes. *The Foreign Policies of the Taft Administration.* Columbia, Mo., 1970.

Schoonover, Thomas D. *The United States in Central America, 1860–1911: Episodes of Social Imperialism and Imperial Rivalry in the World System.* Durham, N.C., 1991.

Schramm, Martin. *Running for President: The Carter Campaign.* New York, 1977.

Schroeder, John H. *Mr. Polk's War: American Opposition and Dissent, 1846–1848.* Madison, Wis., 1973.

Schroeder, Paul W. *The Axis Alliance and Japanese-American Relations, 1941.* Ithaca, N.Y., 1958.

Schulzinger, Robert D. *Henry Kissinger: Doctor of Diplomacy.* New York, 1989.

———. *A Time for War: The United States and Vietnam, 1941–1975.* New York, 1997.

Scigliano, Robert. "The President's 'Prerogative Power.'" In Cronin, ed. *Inventing the American Presidency,* 236–56.

———. *The Supreme Court and the Presidency.* New York, 1971.

Scowcroft, Brent. "Ford as President and His Foreign Policy." In Thompson, ed. *Ford Presidency,* 309–18.

Scranton, Margaret E. *The Noriega Years: U.S.-Panamanian Relations, 1981–1990.* Boulder, Colo., 1991.

Sefton, James E. *Andrew Johnson and the Uses of Constitutional Power.* Boston, 1980.

Sellers, Charles G. *James K. Polk: Continentalist, 1843–1846.* Princeton, N.J., 1966.

———. James K. Polk: Jacksonian, 1795–1843. Princeton, N.J., 1957.

Shafer, Byron E., ed. *Is America Different? A New Look at American Exceptionalism.* Oxford, England, 1991.

Shawcross, William. *Sideshow: Kissinger, Nixon, and the Destruction of Cambodia.* New York, 1979.

Sherry, Michael S. *In the Shadow of War: The United States since the 1930s.* New Haven, Conn., 1995.

Sherwin, Martin J. *A World Destroyed: The Atomic Bomb and the Grand Alliance.* New York, 1975.

Sherwood, Robert E. *Roosevelt and Hopkins: An Intimate History.* Rev. ed. New York, 1950.

Shogan, Robert. *Hard Bargain: How FDR Twisted Churchill's Arm, Evaded the Law, and Changed the Role of the American Presidency.* New York, 1995.

———. *None of the Above: Why Presidents Fail—And What Can Be Done about It.* New York, 1982.

Shoup, Lawrence H. *The Carter Presidency and Beyond: Power and Politics in the 1980s.* Palo Alto, Calif., 1980.

Schultz, George P. *Turmoil and Triumph: My Years as Secretary of State.* New York, 1993.

Sick, Gary. *All Fall Down: America's Tragic Encounter with Iran.* New York, 1985.

———. *October Surprise: America's Hostages in Iran and the Election of Ronald Reagan.* New York, 1991.

Sidak, J. Gregory. "To Declare War." *Duke Law Journal* 41 (Sept. 1991): 36–121.

Sidey, Hugh. *John F. Kennedy, President.* New York, 1963.

———. *A Very Personal Presidency: Lyndon Johnson in the White House.* New York, 1968.

Siegel, Katherine A. S. *Loans and Legitimacy: The Evolution of Soviet-American Relations, 1919–1933,* Lexington, Ken., 1996.

Sievers, Harry J. *Benjamin Harrison.* 3 vols. Chicago, 1952–68.

Sifry, Micah L., and Christopher Cerf, eds. *The Gulf War Reader: History, Documents, Opinions.* New York, 1991.

Sigmund, Paul E. *The Overthrow of Allende and the Politics of Chile, 1964–1976.* Pittsburgh, 1977.

Silverberg, Marshall. "The Separation of Powers and Control of the CIA's Covert Operations." *Texas Law Review* 68 (Feb. 1990): 575–622.

Simonton, Dean K. "Putting the Best Leaders in the White House: Personality, Politics, Performance." *Political Psychology* 14 (Sept. 1993): 537–48.

Simpson, Brooks D. *The Reconstruction Presidents.* Lawrence, Kans., 1998.

Simpson, Christopher, ed. *National Security Directives of the Reagan and Bush Administrations: The Declassified History of U.S. Political and Military Policy, 1981–1991.* Boulder Colo., 1995.

Skowronek, Stephen. *The Politics Presidents Make: Leadership from John Adams to George Bush.* Cambridge, Mass., 1993.

Slater, Jerome. *Intervention and Negotiation: The United States and the Dominican Revolution.* New York, 1970.

Small, Melvin. "Containing Domestic Enemies: Richard M. Nixon and the War at Home." In Anderson, ed. *Shadow on White House*, 130–51.

———. "Influencing the Decision Makers: The Vietnam Experience." *Journal of Peace Research* 24 (June 1987): 185–98.

———. *Johnson, Nixon, and the Doves.* New Brunswick, N.J., 1988.

Small, Norman J. *Some Presidential Interpretations of the Presidency.* Baltimore, 1932.

Smist, Frank J., Jr. *Congress Oversees the United States Intelligence Community, 1947–1989.* Knoxville, Tenn., 1990.

Smith, A. Merriman. *Meet Mr. Eisenhower.* New York, 1955.

Smith, Elbert B. *The Presidencies of Zachary Taylor and Millard Fillmore.* Lawrence, Kans., 1988.

———. *The Presidency of James Buchanan.* Lawrence, Kans., 1975.

Smith, Gaddis. *The Last Years of the Monroe Doctrine, 1945–1993.* New York, 1994.

———. *Morality, Reason, and Power: American Diplomacy in the Carter Years.* New York, 1986.

Smith, Geoffrey S. "Commentary: Security, Gender, and the Historical Process." *Diplomatic History* 18 (winter 1994): 79–90.

———. "National Security and Personal Isolation: Sex, Gender, and Disease in the Cold War United States." *International History Review* 14 (May 1992): 307–37.

Smith, Jean Edward. *George Bush's War.* New York, 1992.

Smith, J. Malcolm, and Cornelius Cotter. *Powers of the President During Crises.* 1960. Reprint, Washington, D.C., 1972.

Smith, Joseph B. *The Plot to Steal Florida: James Madison's Phony War.* New York, 1983.

Smith, Page. *John Adams.* 2 vols. Garden City, N.Y., 1962.

Smith, Tony. *The United States and the Worldwide Struggle for Democracy in the Twentieth Century.* Princeton, N.J., 1994.

Smyrl, Marc E. *Conflict or Codetermination? Congress, the President, and the Power to Make War.* Cambridge, Mass., 1988.

Socolofsky, Homer E., and Allan B. Spetter. *The Presidency of Benjamin Harrison.* Lawrence, Kans., 1987.

Sofaer, Abraham D. *War, Foreign Affairs and Constitutional Power: The Origins.* Cambridge, Mass., 1976.

Sofka, James R. "The Jeffersonian Idea of National Security: Commerce, the Atlantic Balance of Power, and the Barbary War, 1786–1805." *Diplomatic History* 21 (fall 1997): 519–44.

Sorenson, Leonard R. "The Federalist Papers on the Constitutionality of Executive Prerogative." *Presidential Studies Quarterly* 19 (winter 1989): 267–83.

Sorenson, Theodore C. *Kennedy.* New York, 1965.

Spencer, Donald S. *The Carter Implosion: Jimmy Carter and the Amateur Style of Diplomacy.* New York, 1988.

Spetter, Allan B. "Harrison and Blaine: Foreign Policy, 1889–1893." *Indiana Magazine of History* 65 (Sept. 1969): 215–27.

Spitzer, Robert J. *The Presidency and Public Policy: The Four Arenas of Presidential Power.* University, Ala., 1983.

———. *President and Congress: Executive Hegemony at the Crossroads of American Government.* Philadelphia, 1993.

Sprague, Dean. *Freedom under Lincoln.* Boston, 1965.

Stagg, John C. A. *Mr. Madison's War: Politics, Diplomacy, and Warfare in the Early American Republic, 1783–1830.* Princeton, N.J., 1983.

Stans, Maurice. "A Balance Sheet." In Thompson, ed. *Nixon Presidency,* 29–50.

Steel, Ronald. *Walter Lippmann and the American Century.* Boston, 1980.

Steinberg, Alfred. *Sam Johnson's Boy: A Close-up of the President from Texas.* New York, 1968.

Stenberg, Richard R. "Polk and Frémont, 1845–1846." *Pacific Historical Review.* 7, no. 3 (1938): 211–27.

Stephanopolous, George. *All Too Human: A Political Education.* Boston, 1999.

Stephanson, Anders. *Manifest Destiny: American Expansionism and the Empire of Right.* New York, 1995.

Stern, Gary M., and Morton H. Halperin, eds. *The U.S. Constitution and the Power to Go to War: Historical and Current Perspectives.* Westport, Conn., 1994.

Stid, Daniel D. *The President as Statesman: Woodrow Wilson and the Constitution.* Lawrence, Kans., 1998.

Stimson, Henry L., and McGeorge Bundy. *On Active Service in Peace and War.* New York, 1948.

Stoessinger, John G. *Why Nations Go To War.* 4th ed. New York, 1985.

Stoll, Richard J. "The Guns of November: Presidential Reelections and the Use of Force, 1947–1982." *Journal of Conflict Resolution* 28 (June 1984): 231–46.

Story, Joseph. *Commentaries on the Constitution of the United States.* 3 vols. 1833. Reprint, Boston, 1970.

Strober, Gerald S., and Deborah H. Strober. *Nixon: An Oral History of His Presidency.* New York, 1994.

———. *Reagan: The Man and His Presidency.* Boston, 1998.

Stuart, Reginald G. *The Half-way Pacifist: Thomas Jefferson's View of War.* Toronto, 1978.

Stueck, William. "The Korean War as International History," *Diplomatic History* 10 (fall 1986): 291–309.

———. *The Korean War: An International History of the Korean War.* Princeton, N.J., 1995.

Sulzberger, Cyrus L. *The World and Richard Nixon.* New York, 1987.

Sung Ho Kim. "The Issues of International Law, Morality, and Prudence." In Walker, ed. *Reagan versus the Sandinistas,* 265–84.

Szulc, Tad. *The Illusion of Peace: Foreign Policy in the Nixon Years.* New York, 1978.

Taft, William Howard. *Our Chief Magistrate and His Powers.* New York, 1925.

Tananbaum, Duane A. "The Bricker Amendment Controversy: Its Origins and Eisenhower's Role." *Diplomatic History* 9 (winter 1985): 73–93.

———. *The Bricker Amendment Controversy: A Test of Eisenhower's Political Leadership.* Ithaca, N.Y., 1988.

Tansill, Charles C. *Back Door to War: The Roosevelt Foreign Policy, 1933–1941.* Chicago, 1952.

Taylor, Sandra C. "Lyndon Johnson and the Vietnamese." In Anderson, ed. *Shadow on White House,* 113–29.

Thach, Charles C. *The Creation of the Presidency, 1775–1789: A Study in Constitutional History.* Baltimore, 1969.

Thatcher, Margaret. *The Downing Street Years.* New York, 1993.

Theoharis, Athan G., ed. *The Truman Presidency: The Origins of the Imperial Presidency and the National Security State.* Stanfordville, N.Y., 1979.

Thomas, Ann Van Wynen, and A. J. Thomas Jr. *The War-Making Powers of the President: Constitutional and International Law Aspects.* Dallas, Tex., 1982.

Thomas, Norman C., Joseph A. Pitka, and Richard A. Watson. *The Politics of the Presidency.* Washington, D.C., 1993.

Thompson, Kenneth W., ed. *The Carter Presidency: Fourteen Intimate Perspectives.* Lanham, Md., 1990.

———. *The Eisenhower Presidency: Eleven Intimate Perspectives of Dwight D. Eisenhower.* Lanham, Md., 1984.

———. *The Ford Presidency: Twenty-Two Intimate Perspectives of Gerald R. Ford.* Lanham, Md., 1988.

———. *Foreign Policy in the Reagan Presidency: Nine Intimate Perspectives.* Lanham, Md., 1993.

———. *The Johnson Presidency: Twenty Intimate Perspectives of Lyndon B. Johnson.* Lanham, Md., 1986.

———. *The Kennedy Presidency: Seventeen Intimate Perspectives of John F. Kennedy.* Lanham, Md., 1985.

———. *The Nixon Presidency: Twenty-Two Intimate Perspectives of Richard M. Nixon.* Lanham, Md., 1987.

———. *The Truman Presidency: Intimate Perspectives.* Frederick, Md., 1984.

Thompson, Robert Smith. *The Missiles of October: The Declassified Story of John F. Kennedy and the Cuban Missile Crisis.* New York, 1992.

Thornton, Richard C. *The Carter Years: Toward a New Global Order.* New York, 1991.

———. *The Nixon-Kissinger Years: Reshaping America's Foreign Policy.* New York, 1989.

Tiefer, Charles. *The Semi-Sovereign Presidency: The Bush Administration's Strategy for Governing without Congress.* Boulder, Colo., 1994.

Tigar, M. E. "Judicial Power, the 'Political Question Doctrine,' and Foreign Relations." *UCLA Law Review* 17 (June 1970): 1135–79.

Tocqueville, Alexis de. *Democracy in America.* Eds. J. P. Mayer and Max Lerner. Trans. George Lawrence. 2 vols. in one. New York, 1966.

Tourtellot, Arthur B. *The Presidents on the Presidency.* Garden City, N.Y., 1964.

Tower, John, chairman. *The Tower Commission Report.* Washington, D.C., 1987.

T. R. B., *New Republic,* Feb. 18, 1957, 2.

Trani, Eugene P. "Woodrow Wilson and the Decision to Intervene in Russia: A Reconsideration." *Journal of Modern History* 48 (1976): 440–61.

Trani, Eugene P., and David L. Wilson. *The Presidency of Warren G. Harding.* Lawrence, Kans., 1977.

Trask, David F. *The War with Spain in 1898.* New York, 1981.

Trefousse, Hans L. *Andrew Johnson: A Biography.* New York, 1989.

Treverton, Gregory F. "Constraints on 'Covert' Paramilitary Action." In Stern and Halperin, eds. *U.S. Constitution,* 133–48.

———. *Covert Action: The Limits of Intervention in the Postwar World.* New York, 1987.

Truman, Harry S. *The Autobiography of Harry S. Truman.* Ed. Robert H. Ferrell. Boulder, Colo., 1980.

———. *Memoirs.* 2 vols. Garden City, N.Y., 1955–56.

———. "My View of the Presidency." *Look,* Nov. 11, 1958, 25–30.

———. *Off the Record: The Private Papers of Harry S. Truman.* Ed. Robert H. Ferrell. New York, 1980.

Truman, Margaret. *Harry S. Truman.* New York, 1973.

Tuchman, Barbara W. *The March of Folly: From Troy to Vietnam.* New York, 1984.

Tucker, Glenn. *Dawn Like Thunder: The Barbary Wars and the Birth of the U.S. Navy.* Indianapolis, 1963.

Tucker, Robert W., and David C. Hendrickson. *Empire of Liberty: The Statecraft of Thomas Jefferson.* New York, 1990.

Tugwell, Rexford G. *The Democratic Roosevelt: A Biography of Franklin D. Roosevelt.* 1957. Reprint, Garden City, N.Y., 1969.

———. *The Enlargement of the Presidency.* Garden City, N.Y., 1960.

Tugwell, Rexford G., and Thomas E. Cronin, eds. *The Presidency Reappraised.* New York, 1974.

Tulis, Jeffrey K. *The Rhetorical Presidency.* Princeton, N.J., 1987.

Tumulty, Joseph P. *Woodrow Wilson as I Knew Him.* Garden City, N.Y., 1921.

Turner, Stansfield. *Secrecy and Democracy: The CIA in Transition.* Boston, 1985.

Tuveson, Ernest Lee. *Redeemer Nation: The Idea of America's Millenial Role.* Chicago, 1968.

United States, Department of State. "Authority of the President to Repel the Attack in Korea." *Department of State Bulletin* 23 (July 31, 1950): 173–78.

———. *Foreign Relations of the United States, 1952–1954.* 16 vols. Washington, D.C., 1983–86.

United States, President. *Public Papers of the Presidents of the United States.* Washington, D.C., 1963–98.

———. *Weekly Compilation of Presidential Documents.* Vols. 31–35. Washington, D.C., 1995–98.

United States, President's Special Review Board. *See* Tower, John, chairman.

United States, Senate. "National Commitments." *Miscellaneous Reports on Public Bills.* Vol. 5, no. 797. 90th Cong., 1st session, Nov. 20, 1967.

Unterberger, Betty Miller. *America's Siberian Expedition, 1918–1920: A Study of National Policy.* Durham, N.C., 1956.

———. "Wilson vs. the Bolsheviks." *Diplomatic History* 21 (winter 1997): 127–31.

———, ed. *American Intervention in the Russian Civil War.* Lexington, Mass., 1969.

Valenti, Jack. *A Very Human President.* New York, 1975.

Van Alstyne, William. "Congress, the President, and the Power to Declare War: A Requiem for Vietnam." *University of Pennsylvania Law Review* 121 (Nov. 1972): 1–2.

Vance, Cyrus R. *Hard Choices: Critical Years in America's Foreign Policy.* New York, 1983.

VanDeMark, Brian. *Into the Quagmire: Lyndon Johnson and the Escalation of the Vietnam War.* New York, 1991.

Vandenberg, Arthur H. *The Private Papers of Senator Vandenberg.* Ed. Arthur H. Vandenberg Jr. and Joe Alex Morris. Boston, 1952.

Veit, Fritz. *Presidential Libraries and Collections.* New York, 1987.

Vertzberger, Yaacov Y. I. *Risk Taking and Decisionmaking: Foreign Military Intervention Decisions.* Stanford, Calif., 1998.

Vinson, J. Chalmers. "Military Force and American Foreign Policy, 1919–1939." In *Isolation and Security: Ideas and Interests in Twentieth-Century American Foreign Policy,* ed. Alexander DeConde, 56–81. Durham, N.C., 1957.

Vitas, Robert A., and John A. Williams, eds. *U.S. National Security Policy and Strategy, 1987–1994: Documents and Policy Proposals.* Westport, Conn., 1996.

Vivian, James F. "The 'Taking' of the Panama Canal Zone: Myth and Reality." *Diplomatic History* 4 (winter 1980): 95–100.

Volwiler, Albert T. "Harrison, Blaine, and American Foreign Policy, 1889–1893." *Proceedings of the American Philosophical Society* 79 (Nov. 15, 1938): 637–48.

Von Hoffman, Nicholas. *Make-Believe Presidents: Illusions of Power from McKinley to Carter.* New York, 1978.

Walker, J. Samuel. "The Decision to Use the Bomb: A Historiographical Update." *Diplomatic History* 14 (winter 1990): 97–114.

———. *Prompt and Utter Destruction: Truman and the Use of Atomic Bombs Against Japan.* Chapel Hill, N.C., 1997.

Walker, Martin. *The President We Deserve: Bill Clinton: His Rise, Falls, and Comebacks.* New York, 1996.

Walker, Thomas W., ed. *Reagan versus the Sandinistas: The Undeclared War on Nicaragua.* Boulder, Colo., 1987.

Walters, Raymond, Jr. *Albert Gallatin: Jeffersonian Financier and Diplomat.* New York, 1957.

Walton, Richard J. *Cold War and Counterrevolution: The Foreign Policy of John F. Kennedy.* Baltimore, 1973.

Walworth, Arthur. *Woodrow Wilson.* 3d ed. 2 vols. New York, 1978.

Warburg, Gerald F. *Conflict and Consensus: The Struggle between Congress and the President over Foreign Policymaking.* New York, 1989.

Warner, Margaret G. "Bush Battles the 'Wimp Factor.'" *Newsweek,* Oct. 19, 1987, 28–36.

Warshaw, Shirley, ed. *Reexamining the Eisenhower Presidency.* Westport, Conn., 1993.

Washington, George. *The Papers of George Washington.* Presidential Series, ed. W. W. Abbot and Dorothy Twohig, vol. 4. Charlottesville, Va., 1993.

———. *The Writings of George Washington.* Ed. John C. Fitzpatrick. 39 vols. Washington, D.C., 1931–44.

Washington Post. Selected issues, 1970–1998.

Watson, Bruce W., and Peter G. Tsouras, eds. *Operation Just Cause: The U.S. Intervention in Panama.* Boulder, Colo., 1991.

Watts, Steven. *The Republic Reborn: War and the Making of Liberal America, 1790–1820.* Baltimore, 1987.

Webster, Daniel. *The Papers of Daniel Webster.* 5 vols. Correspondence. Vol. 1. Ed. Charles M. Wiltse. Hanover, N.H., 1974–89.

Wecter, Dixon. *The Hero in America.* Ann Arbor, Mich., 1963.

Weeks, William E. *John Quincy Adams and American Global Empire.* Lexington, Ky., 1992.

———. "John Quincy Adams's 'Great Gun' and the Rhetoric of American Empire." *Diplomatic History* 14 (winter 1990): 25–42.

Weems, John E. *To Conquer a Peace: The War between the United States and Mexico.* New York, 1974.

Weisburd, A. Mark. *Use of Force: The Practice of States since World War II.* University Park, Pa., 1997.

Weissmann, Stephen R. *A Culture of Deference: Congress's Failure of Leadership in Foreign Policy.* New York, 1995.

Welch, Richard E., Jr. *The Presidencies of Grover Cleveland.* Lawrence, Kans., 1988.

———. *Response to Revolution: The United States and the Cuban Revolution, 1959–1961.* Chapel Hill, N.C., 1985.

Welles, Sumner. *Naboth's Vineyard: The Dominican Republic, 1844–1925.* 2 vols. New York, 1928.

Westerfield, Donald L. *War Powers: The President, the Congress, and the Question of War.* Westport, Conn., 1996.

Whicker, Marcia Lynn, and Raymond A. Moore. *When Presidents Are Great.* Englewood Cliffs, N.J., 1988.

Whicker, Marcia Lynn, James P. Pfiffner, and Raymond A. Moore, eds. *The Presidency and the Persian Gulf War.* Westport, Conn., 1993.

White, Howard. *Executive Influence in Determining Military Policy in the United States.* Urbana, Ill., 1925.

White, Leonard D. *The Federalists: A Study in Administrative History.* New York, 1948.

———. *The Jacksonians.* New York, 1954.

———. *The Jeffersonians.* New York, 1951.

———. *The Republican Era: 1869–1901.* New York, 1958.

White, Mark J. *Missiles in Cuba: Kennedy, Khrushchev, Castro, and the 1962 Crisis.* Chicago, 1997.

White, Theodore H. *Breach of Faith: The Fall of Richard Nixon.* New York, 1975.

———. *The Making of the President, 1964.* New York, 1965.

White, William Allen. *The Autobiography of William Allen White.* New York, 1946.

———. *A Puritan in Babylon: The Story of Calvin Coolidge.* New York, 1938.

Wicker, Tom. *JFK and LBJ: The Influence of Personality upon Politics.* New York, 1968.

———. *One of Us: Richard Nixon and the American Dream.* 2d ed. New York, 1995.

Wicks, Daniel H. "Dress Rehearsal: United States Intervention in the Isthmus of Panama, 1885." *Pacific Historical Review* 49 (Nov. 1980): 581–605.

Wildavsky, Aaron. *The Beleaguered Presidency.* New Brunswick, N.J., 1991.

———, ed. *The Presidency.* Boston, 1969.

Wilkinson, Rupert. *American Tough: The Tough-Guy Tradition and American Character.* Westport, Conn., 1984.

Williams, T. Harry. *Americans at War: The Development of the American Military System.* Baton Rouge, La., 1966.

———. *Lincoln the Commander in Chief.* Historical Bulletin no. 15, Lincoln Fellowship of Wisconsin. Madison, 1956.

Williams, Walter. *Mismanaging America: The Rise of the Anti-Analytical Presidency.* Lawrence, Kans., 1990.

Williams, William A. "American Intervention In Russia, 1917–1920." Parts 1 and 2. *Studies on the Left* 3 (fall 1963): 24–48; 4 (winter 1964); 39–57.

———. *Empire As a Way of Life.* New York, 1980.

———. "The Legend of Isolationism in the 1920s." *Science and Society* 18 (winter 1954): 1–20.

———. *The Tragedy of American Diplomacy.* New York, 1962.

Wills, Garry. *John Wayne's America: The Politics of Celebrity.* New York, 1997.

———. *Nixon Agonistes: The Crisis of the Self-Made Man.* Boston, 1970.

Wilmerding, Lucius, Jr. "The President and the Law." *Political Science Quarterly* 67 (Sept. 1952): 321–38.

Wilson, Don W. "Presidential Libraries: Developing to Maturity." *Presidential Studies Quarterly* 21 (fall 1991): 771–79.

Wilson, Major L. *The Presidency of Martin Van Buren.* Lawrence, Kans., 1984.

Wilson, Robert A., ed. *Character Above All: Ten Presidents from FDR to George Bush.* New York, 1995.

Wilson, Woodrow. *Congressional Government: A Study in American Politics.* 1885. Reprint, Cleveland, 1956.

———. *Constitutional Government in the United States.* New York, 1908.

———. *The Papers of Woodrow Wilson.* Ed. Arthur S. Link. 69 vols. Princeton, N.J., 1966–94.

Wise, David. *The American Police State: The Government against the People.* New York, 1976.

Wise, David, and Thomas B. Ross. *The Invisible Government.* New York, 1964.

Wofford, Harris. *Of Kennedys and Kings: Making Sense of the Sixties.* New York, 1980.

Wolfers, Arnold. "'National Security' as an Ambiguous Symbol." *Political Science Quarterly* 67 (Dec. 1952): 481–502.

Wood, Bryce. *The Making of the Good Neighbor Policy.* New York, 1961.

Wood, Gordon S. *The Creation of the American Republic, 1776–1787.* Chapel Hill, N.C., 1969.

Woodward, Bob. *The Agenda: Inside the Clinton White House.* New York, 1994.

———. *The Commanders.* New York, 1991.

———. *Veil: The Secret Wars of the CIA, 1981–1987.* New York, 1987.

Woodward, Bob, and Carl Bernstein. *All the President's Men.* New York, 1975.

Woodward, C. Vann, ed. *Responses of the Presidents to Charges of Misconduct.* New York, 1974.

Wormuth, Francis D. "The Nixon Theory of the War Power: A Critique." *California Law Review* 60 (May 1972): 623–703.

Wormuth, Francis D., and Edwin B. Firmage. *To Chain the Dog of War: The War Power of Congress in History and Law.* 2d ed. Urbana, Ill., 1989.

Wright, Jim. "The Power of the Executive to Use Military Forces Abroad." *Virginia Journal of International Law* 10 (Dec. 1969): 43–57, and "Commentary," 56–64.

Yanaga, Chitoshi. *Japan Since Perry.* New York, 1949.

Yergin, Daniel. *Shattered Peace: The Origins of the Cold War.* Rev. ed. New York, 1990.

Zeifman, Jerry. *Without Honor: Crimes of Camelot and the Impeachment of Richard Nixon.* New York, 1995.

Zoellick, Robert B. "The Reluctant Wilsonian: President Clinton and Foreign Policy." *SAIS Review* 14 (1994): 1–14.

INDEX

ALEXANDER DECONDE is Professor of History, Emeritus, at the University of California, Santa Barbara. He is the author of a number of books and essays on foreign policy and the presidency, including *History of American Foreign Policy*, a two-volume work, and *Ethnicity, Race, and American Foreign Policy: A History*, also published by Northeastern University Press.